# The World of Dylan Thomas

UNIVERSITY OF MIAMI PUBLICATIONS
IN
ENGLISH AND AMERICAN LITERATURE

*Number VI*                    *November, 1962*

CLARK EMERY

# THE WORLD OF
## Dylan Thomas

**UNIVERSITY OF MIAMI PRESS**

*Coral Gables • Florida*

Third Printing, 1968

Copyright © 1962 by
University of Miami Press
Library of Congress Catalog Card No.: 62-21742
Manufactured in the United States of America

*All that shapes from the caul and suckle,*

*Stroke of mechanical flesh on mine,*

*Square in these worlds the mortal circle.*

## ACKNOWLEDGEMENTS

I am indebted to J. M. Dent and Sons and to New Directions for permission to quote from *The Collected Poems of Dylan Thomas* (copyright 1952 by J. M. Dent and Sons, Ltd.; copyright 1957 by New Directions); and to New Directions for permission to quote from *Adventures in the Skin Trade and Other Stories, Portrait of the Artist as a Young Dog*, and *Quite Early One Morning* (copyrights respectively by New Directions 1955, 1940, and 1954.)

# CONTENTS

3. THE WORK OF WORDS

4. THE WRONG RAIN

## 5. FABULOUS, DEAR GOD

## 6. THE INTRICATE IMAGE

# INTRODUCTION

## I

How many Thomases had Dylan? There were several, but all were linked by acquired impiety. First was the child who was father of the man: the child of *The Peaches* with the demon-haunted imagination, cribbed in the domesticated fussiness of the Victorian parlor, reveling in the slops of the pig-sty, frightened by drunken Uncle Jim, solaced by Annie, impressed by evangelistic Gwilym, forsaken by his rich friend Jack.*

The child's sense of aloneness in an alien world of adults pervades the story. He sits in a cart in a dangerous street while his uncle drinks in company inside the tavern; he dreams in the "warm, safe island" of his bed while all Swansea flows and rolls outside the house; he thinks that he "had been walking long, damp passages all [his] life, and climbing stairs in the dark, alone"; because of his Uncle's temper, he loses the companionship of a friend; he turns away even from the entrancing Gwilym when the latter in his religiosity pries. Only Annie's loving warmth welcomes him into a community of souls:

> One minute I was small and cold, skulking dead-scared down a black passage in my stiff, best suit, with my hollow belly thumping and my heart like a time bomb, clutching my grammar school cap, unfamiliar to myself, a snub-nosed story-teller lost in his own adventures and longing to be home; the next I was a royal nephew in smart town clothes, embraced and welcomed, standing in the snug centre of my stories and listening to the clock announcing me.

The tyranny of the Uncle; of a religion whose basic commandment is "Prepare to Meet thy God"; of a God who can "see and spy and watch us all the time . . . in the terrible shadows, pitch black, pitch black . . ."; of a preacher who insists on public confession "of the worst thing you've done"; of the respectability which shamed Annie, who wore her best black dress (smelling of mothballs) but had forgotten to change out of her gym shoes: such tyranny Thomas fought or mocked the rest of his life. And he needed and sought for the rest of his life the warmth and light of Annie's arms and Annie's kitchen.

The story is built on a series of contrasts: the obvious ones of light and dark, warm and cold, big and small, inside and outside, rich and poor; and more subtle ones — the child's grasp of fact and his escape in imagination from it; the declension of the abstract to the concrete (God's

---

*I realize that this is fiction rather than autobiography. However, Thomas is regularly the real toad in his imaginary gardens.

omnipresence expressed thus: "God, mun, you're like a bloody cat"); and the fitting of domestic and gory into one context (". . . she told me, as she cut bread and butter . . . how Aunt Rach Morgan . . . had fallen on her belly on a scythe"). Such appraisal, if not reconciliation, of opposites characterizes Thomas's poems from the first to the last.

Thomas's often-remarked distaste for cleanliness and neatness is anticipated here: "I wanted to wear my old suit, to look like a proper farm boy and have manure in my shoes and hear it squelch as I walked"; and his preoccupation with sex — he wanted to "see a cow have calves and a bull on top of a cow." Both are the normal desires of any boy in the country. In this instance, they are not affecting a normal boy and they accordingly assume an out-of-the-ordinary significance.

So with Mrs. Williams ("with a jutting bosom and thick legs, her ankles swollen over her pointed shoes") descending upon the farm-house in her Daimler to remove her son to more respectable surroundings. There can be small doubt that her image came to represent a whole class, in Britain and in the United States, which needed to be opposed and which he did oppose by putting on consciously, or by almost unconsciously lapsing into, the truculence and uncouthness so at odds with his natural warmth and friendliness. The phony, telephony world undid him.

*The Peaches* shows the observant but unawakened rebel; *The Fight,* the dedicated poet, walking the avenues like a prince, reciting his poems aloud, his veiled and passioned thoughts issuing from his mind's "well of furtive lust."

In this story Thomas is wry about his own early pretensions, but he is not acerb, as, in *How to Make a Poet,* he is about others', for behind his own pretentiousness he knew there existed an integrity of purpose: he intended to be a poet, not a First just down from Oxford and slated for the diplomatic, with a volume of verses on the remainder shelves.

This meant resistance, an avoidance of being sucked into compromise. But it was a resistance that went forward and back; against, on the one hand, the forces that had tried to mold him into a workaday Welshman, and, on the other, those that would try to shape him into a London litterateur.

In *Adventures in the Skin Trade,* he signalizes his departure from Wales by shredding photographs of his mother and sister, defacing his schoolmaster-father's already-graded history papers, and destroying the tea-service. It is a purposeful rite: ". . . come and see me break the china without any noise so that I can never come back."

Having disposed of these, he turns his attention to society at large. On the train to London, he monopolizes the lavatory for hours, redeeming the time by ripping and flushing away names and addresses of people in

London who could be of use to him. "Home and help were over . . . . Many people have begun worse, he said aloud. I am ignorant, lazy, dishonest, and sentimental, I have the pull over nobody."

Thomas in his lavatory is country-cousin to the Byronic hero, rootless and alone, self-pitying, self-loathing, and given to theatrical gesture. His vanity is too great for his self-depreciation to be authentic, and of this he is aware. (A letter written to Vernon Watkins in 1938 shows that he was never at evens with himself: "A sense of humour is, I hope, about to be lost: but not quite yet: the self-drama continues: bluff after bluff until I see myself as one: then again the deadly humour.")

In a society he despises for taking stances, he is himself a stance-taker. His doubt must be whether an element of hypocrisy taints his own stand against hypocrisy. The doubt is not resolved in this prose piece. He knows pretty well what he is against: "I have always been brought up to believe that Mortimer Street is what is right, and I would not wish that on anybody." But he is uncertain of what he is for and too conscious of his own inadequacy to dare even to plan a positive program. He is left with only a snook to cock.

His start in London is not auspicious: he is rebellious but uncertain; fearful, but so determined to defeat fear as to act with rashness; obsessed with the idea of breaking all ties, but guilt-ridden. It is quite in the order of things that his first experience of "Life" should devolve into a series of anticlimaxes.

But it is experience. He participates in "the life of that mythical man-in-the-street," and finds it other than degraded. "The ceaseless toil for bread and butter, the ogres of unemployment, the pettifogging gods of gentility, the hollow lies of the marriage-bed" may have made the man-in-the-street "a mere bundle of repressions and useless habits," and Thomas may have fought against himself being infected. Nevertheless, coming to understand that his own fears, guilts, excessive responses, and anticlimaxes were, as Gertrude remarked to Hamlet, common, he is moved to a compassion that does not dull his rebelliousness but illuminates it:

The light of the one weak lamp in a rusty circle fell across the brick-heaps and the broken wood and the dust that had been houses once, where the small and hardly known and never-to-be-forgotten people of the dirty town had lived and loved and died and, always, lost.

But his sympathy for the losers did not imply an active campaign for their restitution. Thomas seems never to have been doctrinaire in any way. He does not discuss the Depression as such; he does not seriously join organizations with colored shirts to combat it; he is not moved by the class-guilt which anguished his immediate predecessors in literary circles —his guilt is, like Joyce's, his own. His business, as he saw it, was to observe, to experience, to understand, and to utter the life, love, death of the individual, in his common-placeness and his uniqueness, not to construct Tables of Organization.

He did not, of course, advocate poverty as a seed-bed for nurturing the toughly alive and quaintly idiosyncratic. But he was also not unaware of the homogenized creamlessness that could result from universal middle-class liberalism. ("The reason I haven't written for such a time is . . . because I have been in London, in penury, and in doubt: In London because money lives and breeds there; in penury, because it doesn't; and in doubt as to whether I should continue as an outlaw or take my fate for a walk in the straight and bowler-treed paths.") The tyranny of re-spectability bulked larger in his mind than that of poverty; and the tryanny of time does not reveal itself, as it does in Yeats, as an impoverishment of the physical body, but as a closing of the shades of the prison-house upon the growing boy. Children, drunkards, and lovers (that is, outlaws) rather than soberly-married adults are the heroes of Thomas's stories and poems. Thomas inveterately allies himself with those who do not think that the law is instinct with perfect virtue and that its enforcers take that virtue upon themselves. He sees the law (moral, ecclesiastical, or other-wise) not as an end but as a means the infringement of which need not impugn the true end.

If he did not have a program to advocate, he did have a vocation to pursue — learning the craft of poetry. However boisterously he socialized in these early days and later, apparently dissipating his time and powers, a dedicated part of him was always monastically secluded, quietly sifting the worldly experience to salvage whatever could be put to poetical use. His dissipating was not a dissipating of his powers but a defense against their being dissipated by the demands of Mortimer Street. Believing with Blake that the road of excess leads to the palace of wisdom, he swore the vows of poverty, disobedience, and unchastity, damning braces, bless-ing relaxes.

He understood his responsibility. As he remarked:

. . . a poet is a poet for such a very tiny bit of his life; for the rest, he is a human being, one of whose responsibilities is to know and feel, as much as he can, all that is moving around and within him, so that his poetry, when he comes to write it, can be his attempt at an expression of the summit of man's experience on this very peculiar and, in 1946, this apparently hell-bent earth.

The paradox of the poet is that the more intently he honors his responsibility to himself the more effectively he can discharge his duty to society. It may be for his own satisfaction, but it is in society's interest that he learn his craft: the turning to his own account of the successes in manner and matter of his forerunners; the discriminating among values; the stabilizing of a point of view; the teaming of sense and sensibility; the meshing of inner and outer worlds.

It was not easy for Thomas, for these are labors of ordering and organizing undertaken by one whom Dostoievski might have been describing: "... I feel as though I were split in two. ... It's just as though one's second self were standing beside one; one is sensible and rational oneself; but the other self is impelled to do something perfectly senseless." A divided self in a splintering world for whom traditional or dogmatic systematizations were repugnant. How difficult he found the process of sorting out and fitting together is revealed in a letter to Watkins:

... I'm almost afraid of all the once-necessary artifices and obscurities, and can't, for the life or death of me, get any real liberation, any diffusion or dilution or anything, into the churning bulk of the words; I seem, more than ever, to be tightly packing away everything I have and know into a mad-doctor's bag, and then locking it up: all you can see is the bag, all you can know is that it's full to the clasp, all you have to trust is that the invisible and intangible things packed away are — if they *could* only be seen and touched — worth quite a lot.

He would have liked to be as he imagined Watkins to be: "... the one happy person I know, the one who, contrary to facts and, in a certain way, to circumstances, seems to be almost entirely uncomplicated; not, either, the uncomplication of a beginning person, but that of a person who has worked through all the beginnings and finds himself a new beginning in the middle. . . ."

It is perhaps not irrelevant that at the time (1936) when he wrote this, Thomas was reviewing for the *Morning Post* almost exclusively mystery stories. Mysteries appeal to intellectuals essentially because in them reason, order, and certitude triumph. The story itself has a volitional definiteness of narrative line; the hero is unambiguously the controlling agent; the rational dispels the irrational, the god-like objective (with wisdom, temperance, justice, and fortitude) quells conflicting subjectivities; the aberrational is reduced to the normal; in the final chapter, the hot soul gets refreshing answers. It may be that Thomas found refreshment here. And support for an opinion. In answer to the question asked in 1934, "Do you think there can now be use for narrative poetry?" he answered:

Yes. Narrative is essential. Much of the flat, abstract poetry of the present has no narrative movement, no movement at all, and is consequently dead. There must be a progressive line, or theme, of movement in every poem. The more subjective a poem, the clearer the narrative line. Narrative, in its widest sense, satisfies what Eliot, talking of "meaning," calls "one habit of the reader." Let the narrative take that one logical habit of the reader along with its movement, and the essence of the poem will do its work on him.

When, much later, he commented on his early poems, he did not visualize them as Poirots or Peter Wimseys, but as bobbies:

> . . . I like to think that the poems most narrowly odd are among those I wrote earliest, and that the later poems are wider and deeper. . . .
> I do not remember—that is the point—the first impulse that pumped and shoved most of the earlier poems along, and they are still too near to me, with their vehement beat-pounding black and green rhythms like those of a very young policeman exploding, for me to see the written evidence of it.

Nevertheless, in spite of facts and circumstances, and devotedly, if vehemently, pounding his beat, he realized the potential of his precocity. He was only twenty when his first book of poems was published. And his second appeared only two years later.

Neither was gladly received by what Durrell's Pursewarden calls the "muffin-eating moralists." For them, Georgian poetry, with its good-mannered pastoralism, was still the norm. And among the elect there were two groups who viewed the newcomer with no particular enthusiasm: the aged eagles appraising the Western shards for their potential of despair; and the young airmen, also surveying the terrain and noting the areas of decay but more constructively, in the context of the New Plan, mapping locations for industrial parks and workers' communities.

Thomas's volumes did not encourage the Left, justify the Right, or satiate the Middle with formulas. But there was a new note here, and a new world, which, brave or not, demanded attention. For every million who rejected, there were a baker's dozen to accept, and now, these few years after his death, only a stubborn few would deny him his place in the Establishment—not among the Giants and Titans, but somewhere not too remote from the Marvells and Landors who without ever achieving the big thing are still indispensable to the anthologists.

## II

Thomas has said that his poetry is "the record of my individual struggle from darkness towards some measure of light." And, having been asked whether he had been influenced by Freud, he replied:

Yes, whatever is hidden should be made naked. To be stripped of darkness is to be clean, to strip of darkness is to make clean. Poetry, recording the stripping of the individual darkness, must, inevitably, cast light on what has been hidden for too long, and, by so doing, make clean the naked exposure.

A movement from darkness to light may mean one of several things: physically, the emergence from the womb to the light of day; intellectually, the progress from information through knowledge to wisdom; emotionally, a dissipating of the murkiness surrounding ends and confusing will; socially, a displacement of tabu and euphemism by honesty; religiously, an illumination of obsessive guilt by grace; cosmologically, the creation, by fortuitous concourse or by fiat; biologically, the working out of evolutionary process; aesthetically, the inception and growth of a poem; weatherwise, the progress of the seasons.

A problem in interpreting some of Thomas's poems will consist in determining which movement from which darkness to which light is being described. Suppose, for example, that he seems to be following, with obstetrical manual at hand, the progress of an organism through its ovular, embryonic, and fetal stages to birth. Is his subject no more than this? No, he may be exploring the relation between phylogeny and ontogeny, or microcosm and macrocosm. Or the progress of the organism may offer a narrative structure for the working out of social, psychological, or moral judgments. And if the organism happens to be Christ, an entirely new dimension is added, and the additional question of whether Christ is a member of the Trinity, a facsimile of Lawrence's Man Who Died, an epitome of all the fertility-deities in *The Golden Bough,* or Thomas raised to the nth degree.

Since, like the modern psychologists, Thomas does devote so much attention to the unborn child, the problem of his debt to them arises immediately. Thomas applauded Freud for having done what he himself proposed to do: "Freud cast light on a little of the darkness he had exposed." But he seems to feel that poetry has capacities beyond those of psychology.

Benefiting by the sight of the light and the knowledge of the hidden nakedness, poetry must drag further into the clean nakedness of light more even of the hidden causes than Freud could realize.

The inference is that Thomas was not a close student of Freud and did not feel a need to be. He merely recognized a similarity of interest and of purpose and perhaps found a reservoir of images as useful as those in Christianity.

And here another problem arises, not a specifically Thomas problem but one relating to the Freudian or Jungian interpretation of poetry in general. A kind of sentence not uncommonly encountered in doctoral dissertations in this psycho-analyzing era might run something like this: "Apart from the obvious sexual meaning, the branching trees in 'Where'er you walk, trees crowd into a shade,' signify, in their shade-casting function, surrogates of death; this antipodal phallus-malice complex (analogous to the more common womb-tomb cluster) provides the ironic paradox without which wit is deprived of the tension necessary to its success and becomes mere Romantic irony."

It would seem plausible that in this species of sentence the jargon conceals an over-simplification, one consisting in an arbitrary choice among a number of alternatives. The critic interpreting a symbol needs to consider whether the poet has made a conscious, reason-determined choice; has been impelled by sub-rational forces to make a choice that he mistakenly thinks he has willed; has willed away will so that choice would be imposed upon him; has volitionally adopted his symbol because of his knowledge of Freud; has, in the light of his knowledge of Freud, willed to reverse the meaning of the Freudian symbol; or has been compelled to will the reversal of the Freudian symbol. Unless one accepts an iron-clad cause-and-effect determinism (and, as is likely, an ascription of all effects to a single cause), there would seem to be reason to differentiate among consciously-, unconsciously-, and self-consciously-used symbols. That still-life involving two radishes and a spear of asparagus: was the painter compelled by color, or form, or texture, or possibilities of arrangement? Or by his libido? Or by his sense of humor (and a low estimation of Freudian critics)? Or by the fact that his kitchen afforded no other vegetables? And there remains always the broader question: How much more nearly than "Robert Burton says" does "Freud says" equate with what "God says."

Some tentativeness in ascribing Freudian or Jungian meanings to Thomas's symbols is valid because, though Thomas affirmed Freud's ends, he had read only desultorily in and about the modern schools of psychology and was neither a scholar nor an enthusiast. Some hint of his attitude is exhibited in this anecdote of Brinnin's:

Approaching Manhattan, we shot into a long dimly lighted tunnel. "I can never help shuddering a little when I have to go through one of these passages," I said. "Do you suppose it has something to do with memories of birth trauma?" Dylan snorted, and as we came from darkness into icy light made a high cooing sound: "Ee-ee-EE—it *does* remind me of Mummy," he said.

Elder Olson, warning that "the reader who seeks to interpret the symbols of Thomas in terms of Freud is not likely to find the poetry very clear," cites a few danger spots:

> Whereas, for Freud, fruit symbolizes the female breast and definitely does not symbolize offspring, it is generally a child-symbol for Thomas. . . . Whereas, for Freud, caves, churches, and chapels refer to the female genitalia, Thomas uses caves to signify the innermost recesses of the self, and churches and chapels—particularly sunken ones—to signify lost pristine faiths. Thomas associates ladders and climbing, not with sexual intercourse, but with man's spiritual ascent.

Thomas was influenced by modern psychology (as who is not), affirmed its ends insofar as they coincided with his own, and made use of some of its findings. But he remains at most a lay writer and it remains for the reader to extract a meaning from each symbol in its context, not to impose upon it the meaning traditionally ascribed.

His connection with Surrealism seems to have been similarly disengaged. As belated Romantics, the Surrealists observed that children live at an intersection of the world of fact and the world of imagination, these two worlds blending to form one. But education, devised by Gradgrinds to perpetuate Gradgrinds, separates the two and derogates the world of imagination so that adult life conforms to a practical and rational conventionalism. However, imaginistic and mystical tendencies are not destroyed but pressed down into the subconscious. The purpose of the Surrealist is to liberate these tendencies, re-integrate those bifurcated worlds, so that the individual, once more at one with himself, can achieve a communion with the basic forces of nature impossible to the intellectual-izing, imagination-depressing, emotion-aborting half-man. If, as is premised, this submerged world has its order, and this an order more nearly in harmony with universal order than that artifacted by intellect, dreams have a logic which can be apprehended. Derangement of our normalized faculties, cultivation of the dream-like state of mind, the evocation of images by psychic automatism facilitate understanding of that logic.

The close affinity between Surrealism and the tenets of psycho-analysis is immediately evident. David Gascoyne (whose *Man's Life is this Meat* was, like Thomas's *Eighteen Poems,* issued by the Parton Bookshop) emphasizes it:

> Surrealism, profiting from the discoveries of Freud and a few other

scientific explorers of the unconscious, has conceived poetry as being, on the one hand, a perpetual functioning of the psyche, a perpetual flow of irrational thought in the form of images taking place in every human mind and needing only a certain predisposition and discipline in order to be brought to light in the form of written words (or plastic images), and on the other hand, a universally valid attitude to experience, a possible mode of living.

Since the Surrealists were undermining the logic and the values of Mortimer Street, since their concern was "the stripping of the individual darkness," and since they felt, as Thomas did, Love to be a "tremendous cosmic experience in which man participates anonymously through the sublime act of eternal creation," Thomas could not but sympathize with what in general the movement stood for. But he did not join their party. He could learn from them, derive from them a sense of support in an unpopular cause, as Yeats sought support in theosophy and Rosicrucianism. Unlike Yeats—or, in another sense, Eliot, the bank cleric—he felt no need to become a joiner, as also, unlike Yeats, he did not feel required to systematize his insights outside his poems. Throughout his life, he praised God without benefit of clergy.

Thomas, then, avoided the cults. So far as his relations with individual poets of his time are concerned, affinities bulk larger than borrowings or even influences. An alert young writer in the '20's and early '30's, learning his craft, forming his sensibility, and organizing his ideas, enjoyed a number of alternatives. He could carry on the tradition of escapist Georgian sweet-song; he could hew out crabbed Metaphysical think-pieces; he could be cryptically precise in the Classical-Imagist vein; he could render ineffable states of being after the fashion of the Symbolists; he could communicate his Yea yea or Nay nay according to the Party line; or he could join a fringe group such as the Dadaists or their successors and defy the alphabet. He could adopt the plain speech of a Hardy or Frost or the aristocratic ornateness of a Sitwell; the Anglo-Saxonisms of Hopkins or the Latinisms of Hart Crane; the iambics and pentameters and sonnets of Rupert Brooke or the cadences of Pound and Eliot; the pylons and aircraft of the Auden group, or Cummings' cathedrals and prostitutes. Express train or chestnut tree, waste land or bridge, Dedalus or Bloom, Malatesta or Lenin, light or primordial ooze, rood tree or golden bough, libido or archetype might preoccupy his thought and dictate his theme.

Thomas made the most of the broad possibilities. It has been said that birth, copulation, and death are his constant theme. This is, at least in its aphoristic statement, a gross over-simplification. True, he goes into the physiology of birth as no poet before him had done, is not unaware of and not averse to state the causal relation between copulation and birth, recognizes that what gets born also dies. He'd be a damn' fool if he didn't. But the Eliot words are too confining. Thomas is not concerned merely with birth—but with every sort of creation. He is not concerned merely with the physical act of sex—but with every form of human relation. He is not concerned merely with mortality—but with the possibility that mortality can be transcended.

To say, as also is commonly said, that for Thomas all is womb-tomb, tomb-womb is again too aphoristic; it has the unfortunate mnemonic quality and about the same relation to truth as a singing commercial. His poems about friendship, tyranny, rebellion against the bourgeoisie, man's inhumanity, faith and reason, science and myth, dogma and free thought, the integration of the personality, tradition and the individual talent, body and soul, the poetic process, the natural scene, and—above all—love belie such a narrowing of his scope. It is true that in these latter some elementary text gives him the physiology of birth and sex, and that Freud, harnessing birth and death, love and hate, joy and guilt, offers dramatic psychological insights. But this is only where he starts, not where he ends. With Donne, Blake, Whitman, and Lawrence he raises sex (not without difficulty, of course; he was not the most integrated of persons) to love without emasculation. He is not out of accord with Whitman and Hardy in their tenderness (it is not too strong a word) for life human and natural. He explores with the Apostles, Donne, Hopkins, Thompson a more exalted love. And in Frazer and Darwin discovers conflicting testimony relative to love in man, God, and nature. He need not have studied them and scarcely even have read them. A poet takes easily what suits him from book or conversation, and is not required to footnote.

There can be no question that in the crafting of his poems he learned from the Metaphysical poets. "Vision and Prayer" is the only obviously shaped poem, but the shaping process is at work in, for example, "Now"; in "Author's Prologue," with its tricky rhyme scheme; in the experiment in caesura, "I Dreamed My Genesis"; in the exercise in 1-endings in "I, in My Intricate Image."

There are other resemblances. Like the anti-Petrarchan Donne, he avoids the sugar-sweet and introduces words, images, and figures which may contribute to a poem's truth but not to its "Beauty": "spentout cancer," "maiden's slime," "blew out the blood gauze," "red, wagged root." He is not perturbed that Love has its consummation in a conjunction of sewer pipes. Like the Donne of "Batter my heart" and "Extasie," and the Hopkins of the Terrible Sonnets, he does not shudder away from agonizing stress or physical pain. Finally, a good many of his poems have

· 11

the dramatic structure and quality which mark such a poem as "The Pulley." It is an illusory, almost entirely verbal drama, for very few of the poems establish conflict between real protagonists and antagonists. But Thomas has a trick of transmuting states of being or abstractions into characters which conflict with or act upon the poem's speaker in a dramatic way. Thomas does not doze off, he fellows sleep; he does not age, time tracks him down; he does not fall in love, love's rub tickles him; dreams whack their limbs, the wind punishes with frosty fingers, grief crawls off, time's mouth sucks. And always there is action: the force drives and blasts; my hero bares and unpacks; dry worlds lever; images stalk; gods thump; hands grumble.

The influence of Joyce coincides with that of the seventeenth-century poets. His denigration of "wine-dark" into "snot-green" sea, his urine-scented kidneys, his general recognition that if man is little lower than the angels he is little higher than the beasts, could not have failed to affect Thomas. Joyce followed Aquinas in organizing hierarchically the various kinds of love that man comprising body, intellect, and soul is capable of, and he did not ignore or tiptoe round its lowest manifestation. He followed Aquinas as well in his effort, after analysis, towards synthesis. If, in *Ulysses,* Bloom and Dedalus and Molly are differentiated, in *Finnegan's Wake,* HCE is united—within himself, with his contemporaries, his forebears, and his posterity. To achieve a simultaneity of spectral colors and their resolution into whiteness, Joyce uses the dynamic pun, as in the title itself with its linkage of Irish hero and workman, romance and comic song, fish and man, birth and death and rebirth. This is not word-play: the word is made to work too hard. And Thomas has a similar seriousness of purpose and a similar end in view in his exploitation of the same device. His search for the light in darkness is no less a search for the unity in variety.

No trace of Bloom reveals itself in the Joyce of *Chamber Music;* he is here the lad with the delicate air and the musical ear. And he and Thomas part company. Though Thomas's poems lend themselves to reading aloud, it cannot be said that many of them have song-like qualities. I do not mean that they cannot be given musical accompaniment (as Stravinski has in fact done) but that they do not have in themselves the mellifluousness which we associate with song. Their vowels do not elope with ease, "Like summer birds o'er summer seas." There is something of the throat-and-mouth-taxing quality of Donne and Hardy in such lines as "Split up the brawned womb's weather," "Her fist of a face died clenched on a round pain," "Pluck, cock, my sea eye, said medusa's scripture." His are poems constructed for declamation rather than singing and offer the pleasures of soliloquy rather than lyric. The sentences crackle with verbs but are heavy with nouns: "Chimes cheat the prison spire, pelter / In time like outlaw rains"; "Fishermen of mermen / Creep and harp on the tide, sinking their charmed, bent pin"; "And the shipyards of Galilee's footprints hide a navy of doves." Declaimed, such words and images have a music, but, both too pictorial and too ideational, they are not singable.

Thomas's poems are really more like chamber music than Joyce's. They state, vary, repeat, sum up their themes; often they have the effect of a competition of voices; they require of the listener cooperation of ear and mind; and most of them have that excitement of forward drive that hearing (and watching) a string quartet usually generates. Listening to Thomas read is to feel like Europa raped.

Thompson in "The Hound of Heaven" achieves this effect, and Swinburne, though the latter does not so much grab and bolt as waft. But the closest resemblance is to Hopkins. The immediacy of attack; the long sentence with its sense of the urgent need to get everything in and doing so with adjective-clusters, catalogs, compounds; the enforced suspension achieved by situating appositives and modifiers between subject and verb, or series of phrases and clauses before the subject; the open-and-aboveboard parallelism defied by syntactical ambiguity: all these devices Hopkins and Thomas use in common.

In "Author's Prologue" for example, the subject and verb of the first sentence are retarded for twenty-three lines; in "After the Funeral," eleven clogged lines precede them; in "A Refusal to Mourn," there are ten; six lines separate subject and verb in "The Conversation of Prayer," and twelve in "To Others than You."

The structural look and character of the stanzas of "Now" give an illusion of lucidity. It is only an illusion:

Now
Say nay,
Man dry man,
Dry lover mine
The deadrock base and blow the flowered anchor,
Should he, for centre sake, hop in the dust,
Forsake, the fool, the hardiness of anger.


Now
Say nay,
Sir no say,
Death to the yes,
The yes to death, the yesman and the answer,
Should he who split his children with a cure
Have brotherless his sister on the handsaw.

After the eye's moment of delight in the poem's design comes the mind's hour of struggle with the meaning. It is an exhausting struggle and made the more so, in many poems, because Thomas also attacks his reader physically. In characteristic first lines, he is called upon to act ("O make me a wall and a mask . . ."), to respond kinesthetically ("The spire cranes"), to feel the impact, thudding or sharp, of dentals ("If my head hurt a hair's foot"), literally to widen and narrow his eyes (in "Vision and Prayer"), to participate in intimate activities ("I dreamed my genesis in sweat of sleep"). His breath taken away by this sudden attack, he is kept breathless by the periodicity of the sentence which follows. The mind wearies under the strain of carrying so much on its shoulders. Or it may have to expend energy in the carpentry of fitting words together, as in "mankind making / Bird beast and flower / Fathering. . . ." And a fatiguing tension results from the reader's resistance, when he wants to pause and observe, to Thomas's pushing him down-hill with image ("torrent salmon sun," "seashaken house," "breakneck of rocks"), with "and"-connected series (as in "A Winter's Tale"), or with enjambement. It is easy to fall and skin a shin in a Thomas poem. And the reader, afflicted with images of pain, becomes sensitive to physical hurt as the hypochondriac reader of medical books becomes sensitive to symptoms: redhaired cancers, cataracted eyes, snipped flesh, raw-edged nerves, whacked limbs, bruised thumbs, rack-twisted sinews, lopped tongues, pin-sharp tear drops, the cramp of love—Thomas seems to have omitted only the bamboo splinter under the finger-nail.

The multiplicity of sensuous detail (so much of it painful), the propulsion, the verbal activity, the run-over line, the emphasis of alliteration, the periodicity: Thomas did not necessarily derive them from Hopkins, but he did not ignore them when he found them there.

As for another of his characteristic devices, the off-rhyme, he could have found examples in Hopkins; but the practice of Wilfrid Owens and of the Auden group was closer to hand. At the time, indeed, full rhyme was very nearly out of fashion.

Briefly, Thomas blends the qualities of several literary lines, each different in one way or another but all related in their essential non-conformism. There is the Blake-Wordsworth-Shelley-Yeats line with its propensity toward adulation of the child or other outsider; the Donne-Blake-Whitman-Lawrence-Joyce-Yeats line with its concept of total love; the Donne-Herbert-Joyce-Eliot-Auden line with its crafting, its wit, its functional word-play; the Keats-Hopkins line with its crowding sensuosity; the Donne-Browning-Hardy-Eliot line with its verbal ruggedness and its sense of poem as drama.

Different in the sound and tone and manner of their work, all these were alike in being at outs with a prevailing dogma—a literary fashion, a moral code, a social situation, a religious creed. And all are linked, too, in that they are seeking God: a lost Christian God, the true Christian God, or a substitute in Nature or Art or History or Man.

And so is Thomas. The body of his poetry is a record of the search, a search never satisfactorily concluded. And here another problem arises: the problem of interpreting a poet whose attitude toward Christianity is never constant but who constantly uses Christian symbols. For his insistent questions, Thomas found answers that satisfied the intellect, and answers that satisfied the heart. Only rarely did the answers satisfy both simultaneously. Because he made the search, he is, as Watkins has said, a religious poet. Because he affirms a crucified Christ and is witness to the test, the fall, the judgment, the agony, and the redemption *in himself*, he may be said to be a kind of Christian. But in his sectlessness and his sexfullness, he is a Christian with a difference, one who may be said by more orthodox Christians not to be one at all. Life, light, love are as Apollonian as Christian, and the sacrifice is just as Dionysian. There is something in Thomas of the Malatesta who built his Tempio celebrating an illicit love for Ixotta over a shrine of Mary.

No new thing appears in Thomas's teachings. That living is a dying, and dying a changed living; that love can conquer all though all things conspire to conquer love, and that to be all-conquering it must be totalitarian but not monolithic (love's pyramid has many mansions); that the country is holy; that to seek Him there or elsewhere — or to flee Him — is to find Him, though uncertainly; that reason is tethered by a short rope to a stout stake; that the world's mavericks are blest; that the things of Mortimer Street will not leave the saddle unless they are vigorously bucked off. The themes are traditional — that is to say, trite. Trite except that what is common to man is novel to a man, for whom the world is born with his birth.

Thomas can sometimes denounce, but he can never wholly renounce Christianity. He is not the one to cry, "Thou hast conquered, O Pale Galilean," but rather to exclaim, "who would have thought the young man to have so much blood in him." It is not the Christ of Mortimer Street or of St. Paul's: Blake, Shelley, Freud, Darwin, Frazer, Yeats, Lawrence, and their like have seen to that. But He is deep as a well, wider than a church-door, and He will be served. Thomas both denied and served Him.

Thomas's great appeal is to the child of the twentieth century moved by the Christian story but not led to become, or remain, an organization-Christian; seeking a faith which does not deny but assimilates Frazer, Freud, Darwin; seeking a solidarity which does not mean conformity

· 15

to the tabus of the elders or the demands of the bureaucratic state; seeking a retreat from the responsibilities of the too-early adulthood compelled by the needs of a world in revolution; seeking escape from suburban monotone to pastoral idiosyncrasy.

It is an appeal heightened because Thomas is young like them (even into middle age), awkward, rash, sloppy in manner and dress, but good-hearted and "with a sense of humor"; not a Prufrock nor a Beckett (they may appreciate Eliot's resonance and wit, but they cannot identify with him, as they cannot with the aloof Yeats, the suspect Pound, the cold Joyce, the public-school Auden, the porcelain-finished Stevens, or even the erratic Cummings and too-queer Crane).

There are color and excitement, and youthfulness and honesty in Thomas's poems. And an affirmation that neither denies nor conceals the facts of existence but accepts them. Thomas offers religion in the sense that it is "the sign of the hard-pressed creature, the heart of a heartless world, the soul of soulless circumstances." The times are such that what he offers has been gratefully received because it is (in the sense of "capable of meeting") equal to even if not True.

### III

Nowhere among the poems, not even in so annunciatory a poem as "Vision and Prayer," is it clear that Thomas ever fully succeeded in integrating sense and sensibility. Told to reason by the heart, he had been unable to quiet an active mind's insistence upon validating the conclusions reached. What "Vision and Prayer" represents is not so much a coupling of the dissidents as a subjugation of one to the other — a silencing of the voice which contended that the point of terminus is suspiciously similar to the point of departure, and the line of reasoning a trip round Robin Hood's Barn.

Examination of Thomas's language reveals that, failing successful integration, it was inevitable that heart would assume hegemony over head.

In the collected poems, Thomas employs a working vocabulary of around thirty-six hundred words. As would be expected in a lyric poet, the first-person pronoun is ubiquitous, appearing between two and three hundred times as subject and over seventy as object. But it is the next forty most-used words that, putting the *I* in its context, are most revealing. These are as follows:

100-200 uses — sea, man, love
90-100 — like
80-90 — sun, eye, as, time
70-80 — lie (in its verbal forms; and as noun)

60-70 — night, wind, water, light
50-60 — sleep, over
40-50 — green, moon, house, sky, turn, ghost, fire, grave, star, tree, white, world
30-40 — stone, tongue, wound, see, sing, tell, still (in both senses), summer
20-30 — walk, word, seed, weather, voice, year, lover.

The characteristics of these words are clear at a glance: most are mono-syllables, none having more than two syllables; Latinisms are at a mini-mum; most words concern the areas of normal experience, especially the normal experience of a child; some are abstract, but most relate to sensory experience, preeminently sight and sound; considered together, they have a pastoral quality somewhere between that of the Twenty-third Psalm and that of "Anyone lived in a pretty how town."

Some generalizations could be made from even so small a selection, but there is interest as well as value in making a more elaborate analysis. Adding to the words already listed those used from ten to twenty times, and roughly classifying them under descriptive heads, does more than put the "I" in context; it creates its world. Thus:

*Persons:* Adam, boy, bride, child, enemy, Eve, father, fellow, gentle-man, girl, I, infant, king, ladies, lovers, man, me, mother, sir, sister, son, strangers, tailor, thief, woman.
*Body:* blood, body, bone, brain, breath, cadaver, cancer, ear, eye, face, finger, fist, flesh, foot, hair, hand, head, heart, heel, jaw, limbs, lips, loin, marrow, mouth, nerves, skin, skull, smile, tears, thigh, throat, womb, wound.
*Home:* bed, candle, clock, cloth, cradle, door, key, lamp, room, sheet, thread.
*Food:* bread, milk, salt.
*Imagination:* dream, ghost, image, spell, tale, word.
*Church:* bell, blessed, chime, christen, cross, devil, dome, faith, glory, God, grace, grave, guilt, heaven, hell, holy, hymn, miracle, praise, pray, priest, saint, sin, soul, spire, spirit.
*Outdoors: (General)* — air, bud, bush, cloud, dew, dust, farm, field, flood, flower, fountain, frost, fruit, garden, grain, grape, grass, ground, hay, hill, ice, lake, leaved, lightning, moon, mountain, rain, river, rock, root, scythe, seed, shade, shadow, sky, snow, star, stick, stone, storm, straw, stream, street, sun, thorn, thunder, wind, wood.
*(Fauna):* beast, bird, claw, cock, feather, fin, fish, fox, gulls, hawk, heron, horse, insect, maggot, owl, wings, worm.

*(Sea):* bay, boat, harbour, sand, sea, shell, ship, shore, tide.

*Condition: (General)* — alone, bare, blind, born, bright, calm, charm, cold, cool, damp, dark, dead, dear, death, deep, dry, dumb, fear, foul, full, fury, gay, good, great, grief, hard, hollow, hooded, hunger, innocent, joy, labour, legged; life, light, living, lost, loud, love, mad, male, mortal, naked, old, pain, proud, quick, rest, ruin, secret, silence, slow, small, still, sweet, tall, think, young.

*(Color):* black, blue, colour, gold, golden, green, red, white.

*(Shape):* circle, crooked, round, shape.

*(Actions):* awake, blow, bow, break, burn, call, carve, cast, climb, cling, coil, come, cry, cut, dance, descend, desire, die, dive, drift, drive, drop, drown, enter, fall, find, flash, fly, flow, fold, fork, give, glide, grow, hammer, hang, hear, hold, hide, jump, keep, kill, kiss, kneel, knock, know, lay, lead, leap, learn, leave, let, lie, lock, look, make, mark, may, move, murder, must, open, pack, print, pull, rage, raise, ride, ring, rise, roar, run, say, sail, see, set, shot, sing, sleep, snap, speak, spin, stand, strike, suck, suffer, swing, take, tap, tell, throw.

*Time:* always, beginning, day, dusk, end, ever, first, forever, genesis, hour, last, midnight, morning, never, night, once, season, second, spring, summer, winter, year.

*Place:* away, back, center, city, country, down, earth, far, high, home, house, island, land, low, near, over, place, side, world.

*Quantity:* all, every, half, double, inch, least, little, long, many, more, nothing, some.

*Miscellaneous: (Element)* — air, earth, fire, flame, water.

*(Number)* — five, four, one, three, two.

*(Dress)* — armour, coat, shroud.

*(Etc.)* — as, drum, globe, horn, how, iron, jack, like, name, oil, only, rod, sake, sound, stroke, than.

It is still the limited world of the seaside-village child. His family surrounds him; his body intrigues him; his home protects him; church bells ring for him; landscape and seascape encircle him; his imagination peoples them; he knows fear and joy, love and pain, bright and dark, damp and dry, quick and slow; he responds to primary instead of pastel colors, knows his numbers to five; awakes, breaks, calls, climbs, clings, cries, cuts, dances, falls, hides, jumps, learns, and so on; finds things to be ever or never or in season, high and low and near and far, and all or nothing at all. It is a world solid with things: with things that blow and dive and drift and flash and fly, that rage and roar and snap and spin. And in the center of it all is himself until, after bread and milk and possibly hearthstone tale, or an hour in the front parlor where are to be found the Bible and the Illustrated Handy-Reference Home Medical Manual, he is sent with candle or lamp to bed and sleep and dream.

Particular, concrete, active, short, Anglo-Saxon — these are the old, familiar, first-learned words, the words of immediate impact, "commoner than water." It is of these words that Thomas makes his exotic poems. One is reminded of Powys's remark about Rabelais:

> In *Gargantua* Rabelais' "terrible-infant" mentality shows itself in the way he uses what might be called the child's *foreground mind* in regard to geography. The garden-fence; the paddock beyond the church; the sloping meadow above the ruins; the orchard beyond the brook; the village green and the village pond — all these things, enlarged, extended, increased, deepened, widened and heightened, as everything is to a little child, become the background of the whole Cosmic Battle.

It is with Thomas's comparisons as with his vocabulary: ordinariness is of their essence. They are not those striven for by the writer calculating originality, but those learned early from parent, servant, aunt, and village post-mistress. Thomas seems to have gone to comparisons as to words to link the present with the traditional past, as Eliot went to Virgil, Dante, Shakespeare, Andrewes, and the like to link with the tradition on another level. Consider the following:

> *thick as thieves, cold as butter, lightly as a feather, cold as stone, dead as nails, meek as milk, straight as a young elm, white as wool, cold as snow, white as the skeleton, quiet as a bone, white as milk, sucked like a sponge, ran like a wind, sing like a bird.*

The list could be extended, but these will suffice to show how careful Thomas was never to divorce himself utterly from his plain-as-an-old-shoe heritage of language and figure.

Nor does he cut himself off from traditional rhythms and stanza forms. This is particularly true of the earlier poems. Where Pound and Eliot had made a fetish of "breaking the pentameter," Thomas writes line after line of five-beat iambics:

I see the boys of summer in their ruin . . . .
A process in the weather of the heart . . . .
The force that drives the water through the rocks . . . .
My hero bares his nerves along my wrist . . . .

Arranged in stanzas running from three to seventeen lines, they are made to work together with trimeters, tetrameters, and hexameters; they are varied ("Drives my green age; that blasts the roots of trees"); they are weakened by free use of feminine endings ("And that's the rub, the only rub that tickles"); they are made, by enjambement, to overflow. Nevertheless, the iambic beat and the pentameter length prevail, allying the poems with all the sonnets, odes, pastorals, epistles, epics, and dramas that have meant home and mother to the English ear.

In the later poems, the beat becomes less insistent: trochees, anapests, and spondees are mixed with the iambs, lines are shortened and lengthened, with the result that rhythm is subtly transmuted to cadence. But nowhere does he exercise an extravagant freedom, nor is he anywhere (so far as metre and structure are concerned) an innovator. Thirty years of experimentation had made what Thomas was to do in these respects quite customary.

So too with his disinclination to use full rhyme. All of his poems use some sort of linking sound-effect: the six-line stanza of "I, in My Intricate Image" is held together by 1-sounds—peril, natural, devil, parallel; "Poem on His Birthday" rhymes vowel-sounds—sun-scud, sea-beak, birds-spurn, grave-age; in "Love in the Asylum," consonants have the duty—birds-clouds-words, possessed-dust-last; he shows a Miltonic fondness for internal rhyme:

Time *by,* their dust was flesh the swineherd rooted *sly,*
Flared in the reek of the wiving *sty* with the rush
Light of his *thighs,* spreadeagle to the dunghill *sky.*

But Owen, Auden, Day Lewis, and others had domesticated these methods of echo-linking long before Thomas made his appearance in the literary world.

In all these respects, then, Thomas's poetry is at a far remove from the eccentric or exotic. And an additional homeliness is impressed upon many of the poems because of Thomas's fondness for parallel structure. "Foster the Light," "The Seed-at-Zero," "Light Breaks Where No Sun Shines," "Now," "In the Beginning," "The Force that Drives the Green Fuse," all derive a similitude of classical lucidity from this classical device.

A reader of these previous paragraphs unacquainted with Thomas's poems might easily get the idea that we are concerned with a kind of Welsh counterpart of Robert Frost. One can imagine how great his shock would be when he confronted a poem in the flesh. For if Thomas never writes a poem with a line like Cummings'

a: crimflitteringish is are floatsis ing fallall! mil, sky, milbrightlions

he writes few that sustain the homely simplicity of, say, Frost's "I'm going out to clean the pasture spring," a tone that Frost can keep going not merely through a poem but through a whole volume.

Perhaps, since I have made a point of Thomas's pastoral language and his refusal of idiosyncratic forms, and both are characteristic of Frost, it will be instructive to learn where and how they part company. The point of departure is not far to seek. Frost is a man who is wise in fact, and a poet whose wisdom comprehends his learning. Thomas is an adolescent only wise in theory (and superficially learned), and a poet whose work is a record of his struggle to turn learning into wisdom. In this, he is rather more like Hart Crane than any other, gaining not dissimilar triumphs and suffering from similar disabilities.

Frost, like Yeats enjoying a security in his powers, feels no need to court ambiguity. He is fully aware of the impingement of the mystery upon daily life and upon the ordinary individual. In his simplest lyrics as well as in his more extended dramatic pieces, though he seems only to describe what meets the eye and ear, he invokes in his reader an awareness of underlying and surrounding potentialities. The language is consistently that of everyday social usage; the characters are real and human; the experiences are normal and seen in their externalities; the reader is guided into their context by a trustworthy, tolerant Virgil who can afford to eschew the use of tricks of language and ingenious "metaphysical" devices. The descent from Frost's first level to that underneathness, the exploration of which is the reason for his poem, is easily made—every step is there, solid and well-lighted. The darkness is not in the means but at the end, and that is, ultimately, not a darkness to be illuminated but to be rendered bearable.

This is as true of Yeats the poet as it is of Frost. Yeats the philosopher-cum-historian-cum-psychologist is a horse of another color ("the tygers of wrath are wiser than the horses of instruction"); his system, though not good, should have been interred with his bones.

It is not true of Thomas. Many of his "characters" bear no resemblance to human beings. They are speaking entities, like "sea-weedy," or "the hollow agent"; or un-named, un-characterized figures, like the fisherman and the girl in "The Ballad of the Long-Legged Bait"; or projections of peculiar aspects of his own peculiar self—"my neophyte," "my animal," "my hero," and the like. As would be expected, there are no Chloes and Strephons here. More to the point, there are few Warrens and Marys or recognizable human beings at all.

Further, as a guide through his poems, Thomas is about as assuring as the Delphic Oracle. Often enough, there are no guide-posts—as in "The Boys of Summer," where it is difficult to determine the number of the speakers. Where the number can be ascertained, their location in time and space is concealed, as in "I Fellowed Sleep." And if we know their number and their location, we will probably not know their character or status—as in "The Seed-at-Zero."

Speaking, acting, but un-humanized personifications, not of abstractions but of biological entities (eggs, spermatozoa, foetuses) which may be abstractions, moving through a fantastic, shifting landscape, ambiguous in themselves and made the more confounding by contrived ambiguities of style—puns, unspecified symbols, elusive syntax; the whole so magnified by melodramatic use of language as to make difficult achieving any sense of proportion or possibility of differentiation; these are the characteristics which run counter to Thomas's fondness for the simple, familiar, immediately-definable word and figure.

Indeed, it is from the familiar village words—grains, wounds, water, journey, fire, heat and cold, light and dark, breaking ground, insect, wind, word, sewing, hatching, green, womb, seaweed, marrow, hair, weather, worm, stone, feather, scissors, scythe, fork, clothes, tallow, and others—that the ambiguities arise that mark his poems as native but unwarbled, since they furnish the symbols.

The ambiguity implicit in giving the concrete noun an abstract meaning is enhanced because Thomas does not maintain through the body of his work a simple A to A relation but varies the relation according to context. Therefore, each time a given word of symbolic potential appears, it must be approached questioningly: Is the word, regardless of earlier or later use, in this instance being used as a symbol? If so, with an identical meaning? Is it being used specifically (quasi allegorically), or in a connotational sort of way? Does it have an ascertainable and limited number of associations? If not, where does the reader stop the association-finding process in order to equate with Thomas's intention rather than to exercise his own ingenuity?

The following paragraph quoted from an elaborate study of Thomas's imagery exhibits the need for such questions. The author has earlier stated that birds are "a universal symbol of resurrection and the spirit," and this without qualification, so that the skeptical reader begins at once to query. All birds—even the vulture and carrion crow? All birds equally—the yellow-bellied sapsucker no less than the dove? All birds in the same way—the Roman eagle, the Thanksgiving turkey, the thievish magpie, the self-deluding ostrich, the hot sparrow? But the author has not stayed for a question, and she goes on:

> . . . The heron, who appears in "Poem in October," "Over Sir John's Hill," "Poem on His Birthday," and "Prologue," is clearly a holy and spiritual bird: "heron-priested shore," "herons, steeple-stemmed, bless," "the fishing holy stalking heron." It may also be significant

that the heron was sacred to the Egyptians, and was associated by them with the phoenix. In Chapter LXXXIV of *The Book of the Dead,* the heron is one of the transformations of Osiris.

Now, in "Prologue" the heron simply takes its place in a long series of things seen, among them gulls, pipers, and geese, and is in no way singled out from the other water-birds, nor even in any way described. Here it is not clearly "holy and spiritual" but clearly a bird among birds. In "Poem in October," Thomas is aware of

. . . the mussel pooled and the heron/Priested shore.

And when he goes out for a walk, the heron dives. If one automatically responds with "spiritual" when the stimulus "heron" is given, one will give the above phrase a deep meaning—though some difficulty may attach to lending the mussels an equivalent significance. But there seems to be no reason to believe that Thomas is saying any more than that the pools are full of mussels and the herons stand around (hungrily?) like priests. That is, Thomas is employing not symbol but metaphor. (How does one interpret the heron's dive symbolically?)

"Over Sir John's Hill" presents a somewhat different case. Here we have the "fishing holy stalking heron," the "elegiac fisherbird," "saint heron hymning," and "the tilting whispering/Heron." And Thomas depicts himself and the heron grieving the death of the small birds. This latter action, if taken seriously, would be an egregious example of pathetic fallacy. But such emphasis is placed upon the heron as a killer (he stalks and stabs and fishes and bows his tilted *headstone*) that it is clear that Thomas's real intention is precisely to compel us to recognize the absurdity of pathetic fallacy—of reading human motives and emotions into natural events. The heron here is a symbol, but not of resurrection or of the spiritual but of natural process, which is in itself holy. Heron, hawk, and small birds are of the company of Wallace Stevens' quail that "Whistle about us their spontaneous cries" in this "old chaos of the sun" where we live "unsponsored, free." The title of another Stevens poem sums up Thomas's bare-bones theme very neatly: "Frogs Eat Butterflies. Snakes Eat Frogs. Hogs Eat Snakes. Men Eat Hogs." But Thomas fleshes out these bare bones. His herons spear *and* spire; they "walk in their shroud," but they are "steeple-stemmed." Merely by being alive and following their natures, they glorify the natural order of which they are a part. Further, in their killing and being killed, blessing is involved (the word *blessing* derives from *bloedsian,* to consecrate with blood). But no tincture of supernaturalism enters in.

Briefly, in none of the poems cited is it necessary or useful to concern oneself with the transformation of Osiris or the resurrective proclivities of the phoenix; such ingenuity leads inevitably to misinterpretation. Again, in none of the poems is the heron exactly the heron of other poems. In "Prologue," he is an unimportant member of a group and to be regarded literally; in "Poem in October," he is still a bird, but important to the seascape and given a metaphorical heightening; in "Over Sir John's Hill" and "Poem on His Birthday," though he is further heightened to become a full-fledged symbol, it is not a "universal symbol" but Thomas's and one whose symbolic reference is confined to these poems.

These warnings—against identifying Thomas's symbols with "universal symbolism," against going too far in the search for allusiveness, against responding to a word with Pavlovian automatism—apply most particularly to the later poems. In the obscurer poems, the reader may need, at first, to go to these excesses, to explore all possibilities. But having done so, he must be prepared, however regretfully, to give up those associational meanings which do not consort with Thomas's general practice and are not contextually relevant.

This, I suppose, is the ultimate test of the explicator's cleverness and learning: when they cloud the issue instead of enriching the poetry, they need to be taken in hand. Thomas asked to be read literally. His statement obviously cannot be taken so. Yet when the temptation is strong to rebuild Thomas's cottage into an edifice, it should be remembered. The heron is not one of Thomas's key symbols. There are others, however, that appear with some regularity, and, though shifting in meaning according to context, maintain a consistent general sense. Most of these are relatively conventional or logically arrived at.

Thomas's Adam is Scripture's natural man, once innocent as a child, then tempted like an adolescent, now in his adulthood guilty and conscious of being subject to Time and Death. His Jesus is also Scripture's, redeeming through sacrificial love that guilt, and vanquishing Death.

But it is Adam and Jesus as they appear in each man, not as they appear in a book, that coerce Thomas's attention. He sees the history of man in scientific terms: as a slow development from primitive, sea-born simplicity to its present land-locked complexity. And he sees this history (as he sees the Adam-Jesus history) recapitulated in each individual. He can therefore use the sea or water as a symbol for the spawning-ground of life either of man or of a man, and the sun as a symbol for the life-maintaining, growth-inducing force which the spawn of sea or of womb comes to experience.

But he can graft upon the information of the scientist the wisdom of Scripture. So this spawn becomes the Adam who was tempted to aspire and lost his acceptant simplicity, and the Jesus who, practicing aspiration of another order, regains it.

It is the wisdom of Scripture. It is also the wisdom of Blake:

Thou art a Man, God is no more;
Thy own humanity learn to adore,
For that is my Spirit of Life.

Man's complexity consists in his having become not a mortal but a mortal ghost. As, with the animals, his cells multiply "like the sand which is upon the seashore," he develops a cadaver which undergoes winds and weathers, the fevers and chills of life, the ripening and decay of time, and at length the feather touch or scissors-snip of death. But here is no cessation, for the cells will continue their process, "Turning [as Beddoes puts it] to daisies gently in the grave." But unlike the animal, within that cadaver (crocodile-skin, suit of armor, or similar hard cover) and unhappy in its confinement, is the spirit, recognizing and defying death, imagining eternity, aspiring to immortality, perhaps crying out (in Beddoes' words):

By heaven and hell and all the fools between them,
I will not die, nor sleep, nor wink my eyes,
But think myself into a God.

Few of Thomas's symbols describing the experience of ascent and descent (assent and dissent) are, as I have said, in any way exotic or eccentric. As a matter of fact I have woven many into the preceding paragraph. They apply to any villager's life and are part of almost any villager's language. Such as do not I shall consider later, as they appear in the poems.

As Thomas breathed in the village vocabulary, he breathed in its stock phrases. These he put to his own use, as he did the single words, sometimes by raising them to symbolic significance, always by varying them to produce that sort of fillip that Wilde's subversion of the sentential evokes. For example:

Shall fall awake, skull of state, jaw for news, tooth and tail, five and country senses, dressed to die, stations of the breath, sins and days, the pyre yet to be lighted, up to his tears, the quick of night, near and fire, garden of wilderness, once below a time, lie down and live, the nick of love, happy as the grass was green, the sparrows hail.

Each of these wittily and fancifully refurbishes a cliché, each enriches the earlier meaning, in part by alerting attention through a greater particularity, but more especially by insinuating an opposing concept which, considered in conjunction with the original, produces a third, that of life's paradoxical ambivalence. The head of state whose hand signs the paper is indeed a death's head; the dandy dressed to kill is a dying animal; there is much sensitive life, and movement is often necessarily rapid, in the dead of night; the wilderness with humans is as much a garden as Eden is a wilderness without; the borning child does wake fallen, and the dying man goes prone to life. An effect of multiplied pastoralism is produced in "five and country senses." The value of "country" is increased merely by supplying the "and" in place of the expected comma. That value is redoubled by the hint of "five and twenty blackbirds."

Some of these are inversions ("quick of night"); some are particularizing interpretations ("sins and days"); some are simple shifts in meaning ("the nick of love"). But all have the effect of the *double-entendre:* two sets of words are heard and seen. Though they are not exactly puns, they have their effect, the two meanings clenched like interlocking gear-teeth and producing, as was said, from opposed movements, a third.

And this brings us to Thomas's exploitation of the pun. "Puns," declared Fowler, "are good, bad, and indifferent, and only those who lack the wit to make them are unaware of the fact." Puns may be classified according to their function as well as their quality. There are puns in Thomas's poems of no particular moment—or, rather, of only momentary effect—products, one might say, of the fancy. But there are also puns which, sometimes by their location in a crucial position, sometimes through being repeated with variations, assist in the enunciation or development of the theme—have, that is, a structural importance.

Cursory reading will turn up a sufficiency of plays on words that have a flickering, temporary value and may be said to attest to the poet's high spirits, or his inability (like Shakespeare's) to leave well enough alone. When he refers to "my prowed dove," "the Welshing rich," Sodom "The bum city," and the like, the response will be at best a wry amusement, at worst a downright disgust. And since such plays may distract attention from the matter at hand and may destroy the continuity of tone, the poet loses more than he gains.

More importantly, the problem is posed of differentiating between these, which might be called Puns Picayune, and those which in their ambivalence attest to the world's ambivalence. Is it, for example, word-play that confuses or word-work that clarifies the issue in the last stanza of "Before I Knocked"?

You who bow down at cross and altar,
Remember me and pity Him
Who took my flesh and bone for armour
And doublecrossed my mother's womb.

Since "double-crossed" may mean twice-traversed, twice-crucified, cheated (in any of several ways), or a combination of these, it is impossible to specify Thomas's understanding of the Incarnation. For the reader seeking definition, the pun is egregious. But it is not so for the reader less interested in fixing Thomas's position than in a realization of the meanings within meanings involved in a mystery. He could scarcely hope to find elsewhere so compressedly rich a statement.

Now, since Thomas is not content with multi-directional words but writes poems which make simultaneous statements of antithetical themes or compress two stories into a simultaneous narration, it is clear that structural punning is basic to Thomas's method and is the element of his work which offers the greatest challenge.

So far as the multi-directional words are concerned, the reader has his choice of puzzling out all the possibilities without fixing on one and ending with a question, or making an arbitrary choice of a single meaning and running the risk of error or an impoverishment. Thus, when Thomas, in "Grief, Thief of Time," exhorts his fathers to

> Bulls-eye the outlaw through a eunuch crack
> And free the twin-boxed grief,

W. Y. Tindall explains as follows:

> Peeping at the intruder through a "eunuch crack" is an occupation for Susanna's impotent elders. Their bullseye is both dark lantern and eye of a bull. By such lights their peeping somehow frees grief from twin boxes, which are twin beds, twin coffins, or testicles—as you please.

But surely this is being too tentative and too generous. If it please me that it be beds, I have one poem, coffins, another, or testicles, still another. And since, to the ingenious mind, "twin-boxed" opens up still other possibilities, we have other possible poems, unless, somehow or other, this variety of twins is brought to a unity. In short, anarchy obtains. (William York Tindall's *Reader's Guide to Dylan Thomas* came to hand too late for my use save in this paragraph. Though in format—a generalizing introduction followed by close studies of the poems—his book and mine agree, they diverge so markedly in other respects that each may be considered a kind of corrective of the other.)

My own effort in such of the poems as I have explicated has been to come to the best possible single meaning. I have not tried to point out every opening among the trees but to find the single trail that leads home. I have no doubt missed some delightful scenery, and it may be that I have spent more than one evening in the wrong house. However, the sights I saw were delightful enough; I was made very comfortable in those homes away from home.

A note upon the organization of this book: the usual procedure in approaching Thomas's poems is to start at the beginning and drive to the end. But consideration of the *Collected Poems* as a whole suggests that a more meaningful method might be to group poems of a similar nature, permitting the specimens within each group to comment upon one another. I have therefore analyzed the poems into the following categories: poems revealing the poet as a human being; as a student of human relationships; as a practicing poet; as a war poet; as a seeker of God; as an amateur philosopher.

These compartments are, of course, not water-tight. And it will certainly turn out that I have made some errors in my classification. These are the risks to be expected in seeking a new angle of vision. Suffice it to say, I am convinced that the gain justifies the risk.

I wish to express my gratitude to Marjorie Buhr, Dr. Barbara Charlesworth, Joan Cronin, and my wife, Professor Adele Emery, who have been, during the writing of this book, hard-to-please but ministering angels.

# 1

Thomas and Friends

# Fern Hill

Nothing of the Wordsworthian mighty prophet, seer blest, best philosopher appears in this description of Thomas as a child, nor does the poem suggest that like Traherne at age four ("sitting in a little obscure room in my father's poor house") Thomas reasoned: "If there be a God, certainly he must be infinite in goodness." The poem makes no effort to articulate the fervors of Christian mysticism, nor to probe behind childhood's simple creed of delight and liberty to ascertain the nature of the "master-light of all our seeing."

Without either religious or philosophic underpinning, and written with no ostensible purpose save to evoke the delight and liberty of childhood, it may perhaps seem a less substantial work than Wordsworth's or Traherne's, a local color piece rather than a landscape of the soul. But it does succeed in that evocation: it is dramatic where Traherne is exclamatory; it is real, putting the child—and the reader—in nature whereas Traherne puts him in his *idea* of nature, a kind of jewel-box; it is objective, the older Thomas and his problems removed from the poem as Wordsworth is not; and it has a delicate rightness of touch that the heavy-handed Wordsworth ("Behold the child among his newborn blisses," *et seq.*) cannot match.

All three poets are concerned with a loss, the forfeiture of something peculiar to childhood. What may make the loss seem inconsequential in Thomas is that it is not a loss within an ideational context which, understood in its relation to that context, is recognized as other than loss. Traherne can praise God for the burning, ardent desire that destroyed his childish innocence. And Wordsworth, having relinquished only one delight, gained more and profounder joys. In each case, the deprivation is philosophically justified, like the *felix culpa* of Christian ideology.

In "Fern Hill," childhood was and childhooded ended—because time passed. God does not figure; there are no intimations of immortality or parallelings of Platonic epistemology; it is not custom or society which eclipses the first light which shined on him in his infancy. The poem has only to do with a natural course of events. There is not even, implicitly or explicitly, a hinting of the necessary complementary relationships of innocence and experience, as in Blake.

Yet, for all that, the poem does not mildly impinge upon or glance off the reader's consciousness. It has the striking-force of drama, not of lyricism. And analysis shows that every stanza, in tiny hints of things to come unrecognized by the sacrificial victim, points to the inevitable reversal of fortune. Time throughout is the omnipotent antagonist; the hero adopts a variety of *personae:* the Prince; the Shepherd; the Runner; and Adam.

The poem opens with a subtle, unemphasized opposition. The boy is playing about the house and under the apple trees as "happy as the grass was green"—that is, as happy as the day was long. And the rest of the stanza describes a daytime scene. But the line immediately succeeding "happy as the grass was green" skips ahead to the time of an end of playing —"The night above the dingle starry." The line is quite out of place: this is not a nocturnal stanza. But the amusing accent of *dingle* and the affirmative connotation of *starry* so take the darkness out of *night* that one scarcely realizes that an incongruity has been perpetrated. It is further concealed by its being narrowly hemmed in by *green* and *golden*. Yet the darkness of that night—under that grass so green—remains.

The antagonist is introduced as a permissive avuncular sort, letting the young dauphin have and go his ways. But only within limits. In revising the old formula to *"once below a time,"* Thomas has stated exactly the relative positions of life and time. But Thomas's pleasant ingenuity here and the phrase's reminder of "happy as the grass was green" distract attention from the serious, literal meaning and keep us in a world of timeless make-believe.

Thomas employs equal finesse and with the same result in the last line: "Down the rivers of the windfall light." The basic metaphor, rivers of light, is strong in its suggestion of an unceasing flow. The contradictory significance of the odd epithet *windfall* almost escapes attention. The temptation is to relate it to "easy under the apple boughs." Light thus is that which comes easily, naturally, and as a kind of largesse. The concept of a decay and end of light has little or no initial impact.

In the second stanza, Thomas is overt enough in the phrase "the sun that is young once only." But in "And the sabbath rang slowly," he is at his tricks again. On the one hand there is the idea that every day is a holiday and a holy day, as long as one of those Victorian Sunday afternoons which never seemed to end. These days were not, however, Sundays but sun's days, and they died with the light of the dying sun.

This idea is made explicit in the third stanza in "All the sun long it was running. . . ." And in this phrase is the next contradiction—between *long* and *running*. It is not only Thomas who is running but also the horses of the day. Only barely hinted at, behind all the lovely activity of the running, there is the quiet looking up from the grave. Runners do not look upward; but Thomas sees high hayfields and smoke from the chimneys. And there is a oneness, an assimilation of himself into the four elements:

> it was air
And playing, lovely and watery
And fire green as grass.

One cannot avoid thinking of Housman's athletes and brook-leapers.

In the second half of the stanza, the child is actually lying down and looking up. His movement does not cease—he *rides* to sleep. But it is a less dramatic movement than that of the farm about him, which flies into space, and of the horses, which transform into *eques nocti*.

This diminishment in the darkness foretokens the change-to-come from child's-eye view of the farm to man's-eye view, a change which amounts to a reversal of a telescope. When Brinnin visited Thomas in 1953, they went to Fern Hill. "It all seemed much smaller and emptier than he remembered, Dylan said . . ." (p. 237). Shriveled and colorless were words he found apt to describe what had once been "Adam and maiden."

For the child, the farm so fabulously wafted away, fabulously returns, like the Prodigal, or Adam restored to the Garden (his exclusion a bad dream), or Peter waking to find himself unforsworn. But merely to name the Prodigal, and Adam, and Peter is to bespeak the inevitable loss of simplicity, of innocence, of faith. Even this fourth stanza, so wondrously "white with the dew," has its hints of mortality. They are not emphatically expressed, to be noted and filed away by the intellect; they are only hints in the atmosphere, causing chills at the spine like those premonitions of winter ineffably evident on even the hottest Indian Summer day.

What Thomas has achieved is to create a child's world from the viewpoint of the child who has never lost it. Wordsworth and Traherne speak from a remove, as adults, the sense of loss (and recognition of compensatory gain) strong upon them; theirs is a re-creation, not a creation; they are not in the child's world but looking back and expounding upon it. Thomas does not, until his final stanza, express his tragic point at all, but such is his skill that it was felt, if not understood, before the completion of his opening sentence.

# Twenty-Four Years

When Milton wrote the sonnet celebrating *his* twenty-fourth birthday, he did not lament his mortality (though Time is a "Suttle thief") but the lesser, or greater, fact that his late spring showed no bud or blossom. The poem opens and closes on a melancholy note, though in the turn of the sestet the melancholy is mitigated by his faith in his "great task Master's" purposes. The mitigation, however, is slight: Milton's acceptance of the possibility of a lot "however mean" more clearly bespeaks resignation than joyful acceptance.

Thomas's poem, more heavily freighted at its beginning with a morbid sorrow, turns more sharply, and with greater unexpectedness than Milton's and rings out in its last line with a faith in which no trace of resignation is to be found. As Shapiro says, it has the Whitman sound.

The poem opens with tears—and a typical conceit, which branches in three directions: that Time has stolen his three and twentieth year brings tears to his eyes; his tears are reminded that the function of eyes is to weep; this day of recollection calls to mind the tears shed in the past. These are not idle tears; he knows very well what they mean: for one thing, better for man never to have been born. But they mean a second thing, too, since to stop with this would be to dwell too despairingly on the 16th and 19th verses of *Genesis*, 3: ". . . in sorrow thou shalt bring forth children"; "In the sweat of thy face shalt thou eat bread, till thou return unto the ground." Even under this dictum, Adam and Eve buried the dead past, and at least to this degree undiscommoded, fared forward.

Thomas now becomes autobiographical and takes us back to *his* Paradise and his expulsion. But where for Adam and Eve God had made "coats of skin, and clothed them," Thomas the poet has to tailor his own. This he does and sets out on his journey quoting tags of Shakespeare—"Let her not walk i' the sun," "god kissing carrion," "Will you walk out of the air?", "Fear no more the heat o' the sun," and the like.

Now "to manhood . . . arriv'd so near," the fated dandy advances (and nothing, not even death, obtrudes a let or halt) to the place of first principles, where the long, alimentary journey through the earth to the sun begins.

In this concluding section of the poem, Thomas has chosen his words with exceeding care. In the first two lines,

Dressed to die, the sensual strut begun,
With my red veins full of money . . .

the learned word *sensual* stands out from its company of popular words. Not much, because the reader is still savoring the aptness of "Dressed to die," but enough to prepare for the Latinate severity (heightened by the contrasting "town") of

In the final direction of the elementary town
I advance . . .

which in turn gives way to the simple certitude of "for as long as forever is." More complicated, it is even more effective than Cummings' structural use of the Latin derivative to bring into context Imperial Rome and Dodge City in "Buffalo Bill's *defunct*." Notable too is the contrast between *advance*, which connotes "hastening a process" and *forever*, which posits an unchanging condition (even though of process), becoming transmuted to being and brought to the final *is*.

34 ·

# Poem in October

Only two poems (in *Collected Poems*) but six years separate "Poem in October" from "Twenty-four Years." And there are other points of separation. The earlier poem was brief (9 lines), conceited, short-sentenced; the later, almost eight times as long, is rhetorical rather than witty, and has several sentences longer in themselves than the entire earlier poem.

As for over-all effect, the contrast is impressive. There, with tears, he looked back to the death-touched beginning of himself on his own in a low-ceilinged, confining place. Here, morning-sounds from a beneficent nature call him outside into an expansive dawning day. There the imagery is of social things—clothes and money. But the town mentioned is the lonely grave. Here, the poem is populated with shells, birds, horses, trees, fruits; and the town, though asleep, is full of living people. There he encounters a carnivorous sun; here a "springful of larks" in a summery October sun on the hill he has climbed to escape an autumnal shower.

In each poem the past is evoked; but only in the later does the glory and the freshness of youth appear. In the former, the mother is reduced to a groin; in the latter, she (is this her only appearance in the poems as a person?) walks with him through the parables of sunlight. There, his tears are the real and despairingly reflective tears of adulthood; here, they are the recollected quick-to-come, quick-to-go tears of childhood. There an incipient adult was too close to his youth and perhaps too sensitively obsessed with the fair guerdon which he hoped to find to turn the facts of youth into solacing myth; here, he is at the right distance in time to assimilate the tears and joys so that we witness the child in the young man in the old-man time of the year. In sum, there he had advanced twenty-four years toward the elementary town—as if in a straight line; here, he spirals toward that town, picking up, as the lines intersect, the heaven of his childhood for his journey's relief.

Stuart Holroyd has commented with respect to this poem ". . . never throughout his life did Dylan Thomas lose the freshness and the immediacy of the child's vision of nature." (*Casebook,* 147.) I think that the above contrasting of the two birthday poems would indicate that he had indeed lost it but had found it again. A faith finds expression in "I advance for as long as forever is," a certitude, one may say, greater than Arnold's in "Dover Beach." But essentially it is faith in an abstraction, a process. He is not (as Holroyd says he is) divining "what Hopkins called 'the freshness deep down things'." There is no freshness (save that of the Teddy-boy) in "Twenty-four Years." But in "Poem in October" there is an acknowledgement that the world has seemed so various, so beautiful, so new, that real reason exists for believing that joy, love, light, certitude, and peace have not yet been wholly alienated from human existence.

It is a "true joy" that he feels, not one arrived at by recording only the sunny hours. The poem starts in "rainy autumn," and Thomas carries his own rainy days with him. He rises above them, but he looks down upon a misty, brown, autumnal scene and is compelled to imagine the life and color of spring and summer. Then the weather changes and he no longer needs to imagine—he can see how beautiful the summer has been. It is a bounty in which he as a child had participated, finding his own plenitude in nature's, learning from the singing birds the mystery of song with the result that his is a flying name.

The weather turns again; the wind blows, and the earth is blooded with leaves. Nevertheless, it is with a certain equanimity that he can witness the evidence of mortality.

Derek Stanford has found a syntactical difficulty in the first stanza of this otherwise quite lucid poem:

> It was my thirtieth year to heaven
> Woke to my hearing from harbour and neighbour wood
> And the mussel pooled and the heron
> Priested shore
> The morning beckon . . . .

The construction is peculiar, but it diagrams, and it can be simplified as follows: My thirtieth year started with my hearing the morning (to) beckon myself to set foot . . . . The oddity is that Thomas *hears* a beckoning; but since the word has the general sense of "entice" or "lure," he cannot be charged with really indecorous verbal gymnastics.

The last word recalls Geoffrey Grigson's "How Much Me Now Your Acrobatics Amaze," in his book of criticism *The Harp of Aeolus.* Of *Deaths and Entrances,* in which this was an early poem, he writes that it "shows, not a theme, not meditation, but simply obsession: — obsession with birth, death, and love, and obsession mainly in a muddle of images with only the frailest ineptitude of structure." Mr. Grigson was a very angry man, and the heads of a number of Thomas's poems rolled in the dust. He did not bring this poem, for better or for worse, under his purview. This is unfortunate. It would take, I think, a very great artist in anger to maintain his passion against this altogether delightful poem. It would be interesting to see Mr. Grigson at the top of his bent.

# Poem on his Birthday

Midway the journey of his life, Thomas wrote, in "Poem on his Birthday," what might be called his Profane Comedy. Contrasting himself, rational and anxious, loving and disillusioned, prescient and afraid, with animals working their ways to death, "doing what they are told," he "sings toward anguish." His way to death will be dark, and terror will rage before he comes to the place of light — a place that never was or will be, inhabited by a fabled, unborn God. Because neither heaven nor God has objective existence, he can only pray "faithlessly unto Him," and because "dark is a long way," he must mourn the "voyage to ruin [he] must run." Yet he has blessings to count: the four elements; his five senses; the exalting power of love (even though it creates now-incredible heavens), the sea his progenitor, the harmonizing of sea-song and sphere-music in the singing flesh, and above all a faith increasing as death comes nearer, a faith in the beneficent purposes of the cosmic scheme enhanced by a recognition of membership in an infinite community of souls. Rather less coldly and not at all as defiantly as Margaret Fuller, yet with his own sort of realism, he accepts the universe.

It is this realism, the realism of the tragic vision, that particularly marks this poem. The comparable poem "Twenty-four Years" is almost altogether materialistic and egocentric; physiological death, not life, is emphasized; the protagonist is not in any way related to society or to nature — save in being born to die; and the poem's statement amounts to this: when my body lies a-mouldering in the grave, my thermo-dynamic energy will go marching on.

The other birthday poem, "Poem in October," discovers the beauty and spirituality of nature and places the poet joyfully in its heart of light; but it is a remembered child's world he emphasizes, the poem merely touching upon present and future. The two contrary views coalesce into a single vision in the present poem: he both sees the beaks and hears the songs of the birds; sees that herons spire *and* spear; sees the *ad infinitum* Swiftian world of lesser and bigger fleas (but not belittlingly); sees, as Aristotle would have it seen, that terror must rage before love (pity) can unbolt the dark.

Here Thomas comes to his maturity, morbid obsessions and sentimental wishes alike sloughed off. He seems to have solved, for himself, the problem posed the Victorians by the higher criticism of science. Unlike Tennyson, Thomas does not kick against the pricks of things as they are. He does not abstract, personify, and capitalize the natural course of events into Nature Red in Tooth and Claw. His outlook is sane; he defers to the sentimentalist's outrageous fortune with a Stoic's good manners.

But he is not passively self-centered in his stoicism: he prays like a Christian, to a God though "fabulous" yet "dear." A reasoned unfaith, seeing clearly, gives way to a felt faith, seeing whole. Seeing, one might say, that a mustard seed sun moves mountains of casuistry, and that a living illusion improves upon a dead reality.

Thomas's is a "more triumphant faith" than Tennyson's. Clearer-sighted than the latter (in whose time the shocking doctrines of Darwin and Zola had not been placed in perspective), perhaps assisted by the meliorism of Hardy, he can "sail out to die" with an unvitiated energy. Tennyson, as he "puts out to sea," seems tired to death. Nor does Thomas carry the chip on the shoulder of Browning, who as a flyweight dancing about and jabbing at a Dempsey-death (Fear Dempsey?) makes himself ridiculous. What Thomas recognizes is that the dying man, though conscious, is helplessly down for the count, though he permits him, if he wishes it (as in "Do not go gentle"), the privilege of beating the canvas in impotent rage, accepting the decision, hating the weakness that caused it. But this is the privilege of a dying man, not a necessary corollary of the process of dying. Men may also "endure their going hence, even as their coming hither" and, however tomorrow weeps, sing "like birds i' the cage."

Ralph Mills is not so convinced as I am that Thomas has triumphed over despair. In his view, Thomas's " knowledge transposes every action into terms of a struggle that dissolves in futility." (*Accent,* 134.) And he finds Thomas in so sorry a state that only mixed metaphors can realize it:

> Thomas himself, strung out on the rack of time that pulls him apart between past and future, clutches at the shards of memory; and from these, and from his anguish, he culls an image of hope which his language makes actual. Belief is not in question here; the case is one of a response by feeling and imagination to the unrelieved potency of fact.

I cannot agree to any part of this. It is true that Thomas observes that snakes eat frogs, hogs eat snakes, and so on, that he has experienced wrecked loves, and that he has anguish to look forward to. But in the same voice that he prays for the privilege of mourning his "voyage to ruin," he prays for the privilege of counting his blessings, among which is this, that the farther he advances the more triumphantly the world "Spins its morning of praise." This does not seem to me "a struggle that dissolves in futility," nor a hope verbalized out of anguish, but the joyous statement of an unblinkered faith. W. S. Merwin (*Casebook,* 64) expresses it almost too strongly:

> . . . the exultation of such marvelous poems as 'Poem in October,' 'Fern Hill,' 'Poem on his Birthday,' and 'Author's Prologue' is not an exultation proper to the liberal humanist: it is the exuberance of

a man drunk with the holiness and wonder of creation, with the reality and terror and ubiquity of death, but with love as God, as more powerful than death.

According to Bill Read (*Casebook,* 269), who visited Thomas while the poem was in progress, the poet planned the second half of the poem as follows:

Now exactly half of this three score and ten years have gone. He looks back at his times: his loves, his hates, all he has seen, and sees the logical process of death in every thing he has been and done. His death lurks for him, and for all, in the next lunatic war. And, still singing, still praising the radiant earth, still loving, though remotely, the animal creation also gladly pursuing their inevitable and grievous ends, he goes towards his. Why should he praise God and the beauty of the world, as he moves to horrible death? He does not like the deep zero dark, and the nearer he gets to it, the louder he sings, the higher the salmon leap, the shriller the birds carol.

Why should he praise God? I think that one answer is in the phrase "the logical process of death" and its pictorial equivalent "the higher the salmon leap." The anguish that Mills finds in the poem, and I do not, is that of one who so hates the inevitability of the syllogism that he can take no pleasure in its perfection; or, if this can be conceived, of the salmon who, refusing to run the river to the spawning grounds, remains at sea a nervous wreck. To see the process of death as logical deprives it of its terror, invests it with an underlying rationale which can be praised.

Where, in stanza 5, Thomas speaks of skull and scar, wrecked loves, falling stars, and blind cage, and in the eighth, he is "alone/With all the living," in the concluding verse he speaks of bouncing hills and singing dew larks, and his "shining men" are "no more alone." To give his expression even greater substance, he has woven in recollections of Dante, Shakespeare, Donne, and Blake in their most exultant or loving moods, those of the *Paradise,* of "Hark, hark, the lark," of "No man is an island," and of "O no, no, I see an innumerable company of the Heavenly host crying, 'Holy, Holy, Holy is the Lord God Almighty.'"

## *Once Below a Time*

The succession of "Ceremony after a Fire Raid" by "Once Below a Time" in *Collected Poems,* approximates Mardi Gras' galling Easter's kibe. This is Thomas self-concerned, mocking, bringing quips and cranks—

though at the end he yearns for a peaceful hermitage. It is the clotted, cloudy, conceited Thomas of "How Shall My Animal," who has apparently decided to work up "Twenty-four Years" into a full-scale operation.

The difficulties begin at once with "Once Below a Time." Olson's explanation is that "if something can exist *in* time, it can also exist *out* of time; if what exists in time exists once *upon* a time, what does not yet exist in time can be said to be once *below* a time." (Olson, p. 59.) The inference to be drawn is that the poem (or at least the early part of it) deals with Thomas unborn.

Thomas did not so use the phrase in "Fern Hill" ("and once below a time I lordly had the trees and leaves"), and I do not think he does here. I have had poor success getting mastiff collars, birds, ships, and the like into the pre-natal state. They seem to work somewhat better in a relation to adolescence. And I take the poem to be Thomas's *Prelude* — an account of the early stages in his development as a poet. It should be read with "The Fight" (in *Portrait*) and "Reminiscences of Childhood," and "How to be a Poet" (*Quite Early*) at hand.

*　　*　　*　　*　　*

I

In my early adolescence, before time really mattered, in a town on the rim of coal-mining Wales, when my body was outgrowing my installment-plan clothes (alas, not soon enough torn in love-play near the ash-pit—behind "the impressive gas works and slaughter house"?) and my spirit was outgrowing my body, in secret I warbled my wood-notes, like Pope lisped in numbers, a young inebriate bird dog of an artist (I am his Highness' dog at Kew) pretending to be a mastiff (". . . like a wolf! Look at his long stride!"), singing my ashpit-elegy: "When I am strewn low/And all my ashes are/Dust in a dumb provoking show . . .," cheaply dressed and provincially reared, rather corny, but a tercel, an adventurer launching out in a frigate.

Then I amazed with my time-upsetting precocity my makers and molders by bursting upon child's-play Swansea as a Triton blowing his wreathéd horn; then, though still a Welsh provincial (for the English, a mountain man "clothed in the skins of animals . . . and always singing," as flamboyant as a Lawrentian primitive hot out of Australia—the weave of the wale being concealed by feathers and leaves), I broke out of Welsh clumsiness, flew up through the lubber's hole ("I flap my arms and slowly leave the ground, only a few inches at first, then gaining air till I fly. . .") to astonish the obelisked opinion-molders in London. ("And Crippe goes to his publishers. A contract is drawn up, Messrs. Stich and Time undertaking to publish his next book of verse on condition that they have the first option on his next nine novels.")

I imagined myself (still without experience) a high flyer (a John Donne), a storied great soul; I wore the vatic garments and thought I deceived the Master Tailor. I flew over fabled seas of thought, breasted the wave, said Sail on, sail on; but the Tailor saw through my disguises, knew my phony exploring for what it was, recognized me as a pretender. It was a relief to subside into my homespun self in an everyday world, to paddle in the duck-pond, no longer the pretended roué, but not ever forgetting the noisy splash I had made. ("On the other hand, too many artists of Wales stay in Wales too long, giants in the dark behind the parish pump. . . .")

Now pretty much stripped of fantasies, I would like to "live, unseen, unknown. . .Steal from the world, and not a stone/Tell where I lie." ("Of the poet who merely writes because he wants to write, who does not deeply mind if he is published or not, and who can put up with poverty and total lack of recognition in his lifetime, nothing of any pertinent value can be said.")

\*     \*     \*     \*     \*

His hope of the last sentence, to "lie down and live/As quiet as a bone," was unfortunately a vain one. He was married, a father, a significant writer—and the war had begun. Whatever the status of his cherry-capped dangler, for him the requisite position was clear: "There is only one position for an artist anywhere: and that is, upright."

# *Lament*

According to Elizabeth Hardwick (*Casebook,* 154), Thomas aroused "the most sacrificial longings" in American women. "He had lost his looks, he was disorganized to a degree beyond belief, he had a wife and children in genuine need, and yet young ladies *felt* they had fallen in love with him." Caitlin puts it more vigorously: ". . . they were candidly, if not prepossessingly, spreadeagled; from the first tomtomed rumor of a famous name. They conducted their courting with the ferocity and tenacity of caged amazons; and nothing less than the evaporation of their prey would make them let go." (*Ibid.,* p. 250.)

It would appear that Thomas made no strenuous gestures of rejection. And one may wonder whether "Lament" was not written consciously as an encore piece, light-heartedly broaching possibilities, in its candid self-deprecation arousing sympathy and diminishing the thought of danger, well-calculated to produce an ambience of permissiveness. It would be particularly effective after "Fern Hill," with its appeal to the yearning, protective mother-instinct, and the poems which elevate sex to a sacramental level.

Planned gambit or not, it is an effective encore. The reiterated stanza pattern, the incrementally varied refrain, the lilting anapests, the alliteration and onomatopoeia, the activity in the verbs and participles, the forward rush of the long sentences, the titillating tactual and clear visual impressions, the opportunities for hamming the rake's progress, for "booming blue thunder into the teen-agers' delighted bras and briefs," the demand it makes for audience-participation—all combine to bring down a curtain in the George M. Cohan manner.

But it is not merely good theatre. The poem is as good on the page as on the stage. The subtleties of depiction and of gradation lost to the listener reveal themselves to the reader. Only the latter has time to consider the variant connotations of the words and images. For example, the quite delicate allusion to the boy's balancing between childhood and adolescence: his new and sniggering appreciation of the Marjorie Daws, the little women (and bigger ones too); his exciting but guilt-provoking experiments with his changed body —

> I tiptoed shy in the gooseberry wood
> The rude owl cried like a telltale tit.

Though, as the next stanza says, he was inexperienced as a calf and had not much wax for his candle, he had a wicked imagination. No wonder he thought himself the spitting image of the town roarers and feared his ejection from the chapel's mouth, he with that spit to plunge into the roast beef of Old England, that flowering rod, that rammer of explosives.

Tom-cat and then bull, he prowls the night and serves the herd. Then, the flesh become weak, the spirit becomes exigent and Thomas unhappily willing. He shoves his spirit, as though it were the rod he had so often rammed, heavenward to find a soul-mate. Which is to say, simply, that the sinner repented; his anchor dived "through the floors of a church." He is repentant, but only through physical necessity, and he still unregenerately contrasts his sleeping in bed with his earlier ramping in clover quilts. Nevertheless, harp-playing virtues have their claws in him; he approaches death, made dainty by the deodorant of sanctity.

But it is impossible to stay with analysis for any length of time. One has got to stand up and roar the poem out or indulge in memory of Thomas doing it, and think again what an alluring invitation to the dance it is. See an old unhappy bull, harmless as mutton, says the poet, and another daisy-chained Europa is carried away.

Is there a serious thing to be said of the poem? A question for which there are as many answers as writers about Thomas concerns his attitude toward sex and love. For example, Stuart Holroyd writes: "Whereas the pantheist normally sees God in all things, Thomas saw sex in all things. In fact, sex, together with the processes analogous to it in the natural world, was Dylan Thomas's god. The sexual act between man and woman was there invested with a grave significance." (*Casebook,* 144.) But Shapiro writes in a quite different tone: "In place of love about which Thomas is almost always profoundly bitter, there is sex, the instrument and physical process of love. The activity of sex, Thomas hopes in his poems, will somehow lead us to love in life and in the cosmos. As he grows older, love recedes and sex becomes a nightmare, a Black Mass." (*Casebook,* 173.)

I am not inclined to think that either of these generalizations applies to the body of Thomas's work. I know that neither applies to "Lament." Is sex in this poem really a nightmare, or really invested with a grave significance? Of course not — the poem is, as any sane teen-ager intuitively and any normal person of middle age experientially knows, true-to-life and neither grave nor nightmarish. It requires a concrete idealist to find otherwise.

But if the generalizations do not apply here, are there other poems to which they fail to apply? If so, how many? And the questions become more searching. Does Holroyd, by magnifying the poet into a Pantheist, unconsciously alter the poems to fit the philosopher? When Shapiro says that he finds in the poems "the satanism, the vomitous horror, the self-elected crucifixion of the artist," does he really find it there or does he project it out of a discontent of his own?

Monks *manqués,* contemporary critics often deal with literary products as though they were the Revealed Word and, forgetting that poets are human beings possessing a luckiness with language, conceptualize them as Prophets or Case Histories. I cannot forget the reaction of an academic friend (for some time exposed to Thomas criticism) to a picture of Thomas with his wife and daughter in a rowboat: "For Christ's sake, how human he looks!"

And he was human. He fits Lawrence's description of a "mortal" to a T:

> a thing of kisses and strife
> a lit-up shaft of rain
> a calling column of blood
> a rose tree bronzey with thorns
> a mixture of yea and nay
> a rainbow of love and hate
> a wind that blows back and forth
> a creature of conflict, like a cataract.

In short, he was a man, not a formula, and a poet who could write "After the Funeral" and "Ballad of the Long-legged Bait"; "Lament" and "Unluckily for a Death"; "The Hunchback in the Park" and "I Make this in a Warring Absence"; "In Country Sleep" and "In my Craft or Sullen Art" — each of which is a poem defining an aspect of love, each of which is quite different from the others. Generalization will not cover them.

Is there (this was the original question) a serious thing to say about "Lament"? Yes: it is an enjoyable poem.

Is there a serious thing to say about Thomas-criticism (including this)? Yes: it is like Life, that bowl of cherries: don't take it serious, it's too mysterious.

## Ears in the Turrets Hear

A significant personal problem for Thomas was simply this: that, as a provincial, small-town Welshman in the big city, he did not know whom to trust. It was for him a particularly pressing problem since the sentimental streak in him was so broad and deep that he could be easily taken advantage of and hurt, and the teeth in him were so sharp that he could return the wound with interest (". . . he would flood me with a contempt of words," writes Caitlin: "there is no fury like the weak, against the weak; and he knew how to use words insultingly, as well as poetically"). So, though he could, and most often did, come to such a philosophic outlook as is expressed in "If I Were Tickled," it was an *official* philosophy, and his real feelings were less certainly engaged. He was never without some fear of the injury that his peers could do to him. Partly, then, because of his animus against middle-class conventionality, partly because of his fear, and partly because of his sentimentalism (which did, often, become exalted into true compassion), his most outspoken affirmations are for the underdogs and outsiders.

But he had his doubts of giving himself too freely even here, since he was perfectly aware of difficulties into which his sentimentalism could lead him. David Holbrook thinks he gave himself to no one and speaks of his "withdrawal of sympathetic tenderness, a lack of capacity to enter into and understand the lives of others, culminating in the expressions of repulsive disdain of humanity. . . ." A repulsive disdain for Thomas and all his works so moves Holbrook that he makes no effort toward any semblance of objectivity. Yet Thomas himself recognized a deficiency, of the sort Holbrook describes, in his poem "Once it was the Colour of Saying," which needs to be read in connection with the present poem.

His problem is both personal and philosophical. On the lower level, the question to be answered is a relatively simple one: Is it to his advantage to live in a house by the side of the road and be a friend to man? or should his be the house that makes no answer to the Traveller? Relatively simple for Thomas as a human being, but not so simple for Thomas as a poet concerned with the necessity of maintaining the integrity of his personal vision. The blandishments of middle-class success, on the one hand, the prestige to be attained by turning out anti-middle-class propaganda, on the other: for this fundamentally outgoing person to withdraw from either camp and go it alone, courting the criticism of both, was a real difficulty. Yet he had learned it from Blake: "You must leave Fathers & Mothers & Houses & Lands if they stand in the way of Art." And like Blake, he did maintain his integrity, at least as a poet. What happened to him as a man, particularly under the insidious influence of the United States, is another matter. However much he permitted himself to be pawed as a person, he permitted no fingering of that part of him which was poet. This is why he regularly greeted his academic inquisitors with rudeness or buffoonery.

But such a retreat, on the social level, stirs questions (in the second stanza) on the philosophical level. If the poet's success is so much dependent upon his being a singular man, what about his success as a creature in the universe? If individuality comes, can solipsism be far behind? No poet, one would think, can afford to lose the wind that passes "like a fire," however dearly he prizes isolated safety. And yet, as Tennyson wrote, who had some difficulty resolving this problem:

O Godlike isolation which art mine,
 I can but count thee perfect gain,
What time I watch the darkening droves of swine
 That range on yonder plain.

Questions of this sort are raised in this poem, explicitly and implicitly, and no answers offered. But the record of the body of his work clearly reveals what the answer was. He never did deny love (though he could deny parochial Christian love); he never believed that the universe was his, but always that he was the universe's; he saw all dualities as aspects of a unity; he recognized all entities as cooperative participators. In brief, all the bells (peltering in time) tolled for him.

# O Make Me a Mask - To Others than You

When Isaac Watts reflected upon "the hazard of loving the creatures," he discovered the hazard to be in this:

Souls unborn [that] the tie of friendship binds
And partners of our blood,
Seize a large portion of our minds
And leave the less for God.

This was not exactly Thomas's difficulty with friends. Yet, in "Ears in the Turrets Hear," his treatment of the subject was generalized and philosophical. He did not there come to a conclusion; he only asked the question of whether engagement or disengagement would conduce to the more satifactory mode of living.

In "O Make Me a Mask," and "To Others than You," the problem has been brought down to the level of personal experience, and it is clear that his experience with engagement has not proved satisfactory. Motivated by an enlightened self-interest, his prayer in the first of these poems is about equally selfish and unselfish. He asks for the ability to conceal under a childishly innocent demeanor his desire to strike out at those who sidle near, ogle, and clutch (their pince-nez glittering) the precocious provincial; the ability to keep a sharp tongue from sallying out (leaving the oratory vacant) to pierce the unarmed, or a trumpet tongue from declaring a truce where there is none; the ability to put on the impenetrable and wooden face of stupidity to turn away foolish questions; and the ability to counterfeit grief and to conceal the dilating means used to appear teary-eyed, so that with sharp dry eyes (a touch of deadly nightshade in their glance) he can pierce the front that others put up, can catch them out in the hypocrisy of their consolation.

A possible immediate cause for the poem would be a knock-down fight with Caitlin producing a "widower grief" and a sensitivity to the curiosity of acquaintances and the comforting or man-to-man sanity of friends. But no immediate cause was necessary. Thomas knew himself to be regarded as a particularly strange animal in the Bohemian zoo, knew that he over-reacted to inquisitive scrutiny, knew that he harmed himself in his reaction. In its humor and apparent good-humor, this prayer for a mask has a mask of its own which conceals the seriousness with which he prays.

Thomas does not write this as an angry young man, though his sensibilities have been exacerbated, since he discovers as great a fault in himself as in those about him. In "To Others Than You," a combination of disillusion and shame has moved him to unsheathe a "bayonet tongue." One hopes that he sent the poem with its ironic title to the friend who failed him, and on subsequent meetings concealed his knowledge and his wrath behind mask and wall.

The poem is composed of two sentences, the first of one line, the second of twenty. The opener, a challenge to the duel, shows Thomas's technique of compression: "Friend by enemy I call you out" has the double meaning — "enemy in the guise of friend, I have identified your nature"; and "presumed friend, as my enemy I call you to accounts." The rest of the poem, developing the metaphor of friend as stage-magician, describes the relation between them, and ends on a cynical generalization.

You with friendly eyes as bright and spurious as a brass coin; you who, concealing the ace of malice with the queen of sympathy, persuading me (a child wooed by fake rock-candy) by the sweet friendliness of your eye to divulge my secret; you whom reflection shows to have been a master of illusion, with attention-diverting smile and patter and hand quicker than the eye, in a position to smash my heart like a watch taken from a gentleman in the audience—and really smashing it; you once were a spiritual companion so frank and understanding that I would never have believed (while the balls of truth you threw up came down lies) that my supposed friends, whose faults I knew and accepted in the context of their virtues, were false as the dummies seen on the stage and made to move by illusionists on concealed stilts. (This last I have seen in vaudeville. I have no way of knowing what music hall turn Thomas had in mind.)

It is an ingenious exercise in diatribe, and an ingenious working out of the prestidigitational metaphor.

# *The Hunchback in the Park*

What could have been a poem as sloppily sentimental as Wordsworth's "Goody Blake" turns out to be perhaps Thomas's tidiest, best-controlled piece of work.

The social misfit, become so through no fault of his own, tormented by cruel boys, living on bread and water because hypocritical Christian neighbors shun him, housed in a kennel, dreaming of the love he can never have: it is a subject made to order for Dickens or Victor Hugo.

Everything itemized in the previous paragraph is in the poem, but nothing offends. The reporter has a sharp, un-teary eye for detail, a matter-of-fact delivery, the good taste to keep his distance from his subject. He neither generalizes nor moralizes (A hunchback's a man, for a' that; Not without hope we suffer or mourn; Alas for the rarity of Christian charity). And yet the poem, rich in implication, is a far cry from a vignette. It is, indeed, a meditation on freedom and its limitations.

The great virtue of a park, of course, consists in its being an oasis of freedom, an eden in the urban wilderness. Those who go there do so as released galley slaves — the sailors in this poem almost literally so. On the long voyage home, they had lived propped between wood and water, and dreamed of women straight as elms. On leave, the pub, the movies, the dance-hall, the park, each offers its form of expansiveness after confinement. A breed outside the law, they enjoy a leeway impossible to, sometimes envied by, the sellers and buyers of things and services. Until their leave is over.

For the children, home, school, and church are the prisons. When they escape, they express their exultation in aggression (like drunken sailors). They dream of slaughtering tigers but in fact annoy a cripple — not out of cruelty, but as a release.

Incapable of doing society's work, they are social misfits, parasites, charity cases. They are resented, and knowing it are in turn resentful. But their shore leave will soon be over, and the routine of ship-work will keep them in line.

The nurses and swans — even the trees and the water — are kept things, palace favorites, and have the freedom suitable to such. The nurses, of course, also have a responsibility like that of the park keeper — tidying up the saplings in their prams. More useful, less decorative than swans, there is a degree of difference between them.

And the hunchback epitomizes them all. In his way, as not being a competitive threat, as being incapable of forcing demands, he is a palace favorite — a being everyone can feel superior to. He has his freedom — nobody chained him up. He is not coerced by responsibilities, nor by the proprieties. He does not have to get ahead, since he has no place to go. He is secure in the solitary anonymity so sought for by Romantic heroes.

But chained to his useless body (a cup filled with gravel), he is unfree; he has what the others want; he wants what the others have. He is always on shore leave; but, so to speak, the CPO of his malformation is always on his back. And so he dreams, but not of tigers.

Whether Thomas intended a little parable of the artist as odd man out is open to question. Intended or not, the poem obviously fits the bill. The artist is of necessity a solitary mister, he is often poor, he is resented by those who do the useful work of the world, he is not respectable, he does seem to waste time propped between trees and water, he does have a monkey on his back. And worst of all (what boots it with uncessant care?) he has no assurance that his name will be holy writ in holy water.

If the poem entertains such an interpretation, a pleasant irony is invoked. For Thomas plays a double role: he is now, as the writer of the poem, the hunchbacked social misfit; he was, when the actual event took place in Cwmdonkin Park, one of the truant, taunting boys.

# The Tombstone Told when She Died

The basic paradox of this "Hardy-like" (as Thomas thought it) "ballad-like" poem is that, though Life did not, Death did consummate the virgin's marriage: that which aborted fulfillment itself fulfilled. If it does not say that the last shall be first, it does at least suggest that sometimes losers are winners.

Many opposites are brought together: past-present, virginity-sexuality, death-birth, naked-clothed, sun-rain, red-white, wept-smiled, stone-flesh, and the like. (The girl herself is at once a virgin, a married woman, and a corpse.) Their being harmonized makes credible the underlying identification of Death and Love. (Thomas changed the last line's "*great* floods of his hair" to "*dear* floods" because he "wanted the girl's *terrible* reaction to orgastic (sic) death to be suddenly altered into a kind of despairing love" — Watkins, p. 44.)

The poem is complicated by a shifting time-scheme which, bringing together Thomas in the womb, the girl in the grave, Thomas as man at the grave, and the girl on her marriage-day death-bed, lends such a sense of simultaneity that again the opposition of Death and Love is concealed and diminished.

The historical time-schedule is as follows:

1. The virgin marries and dies.

2. Thomas, in the womb, learns of death and thus, by projection, of the virgin's pre-decease.

3. Thomas sees her tombstone and imagines her speaking.

4. Thomas hears gossip about her death.

But times—and places—are so collapsed, in part by complexities of sentence-structure, that there is no sense of time's progression or of a retrospective back-glance but of convolution.

The poem opens on Thomas's encountering the tombstone. The three end-stopped lines indicate his pause of curiosity, his being brought to a stand-still by the two names, his remaining before the stone as he figures out the situation and makes some quick chronological calculations. The exposition then begins.

> The virgin now at rest was married in this town which I luckily happened upon one rainy day. Her marriage occurred before I was conceived—that is, before I could conceive that the rain it raineth every day on her or some other's grave, before I could have any precognition of life disappearing, like a set sun, from her face.

This last image, I think, results from Thomas's looking into one of those shell-and-glass ornaments cemented into tombstones, seeing his own very lively face and imagining the life draining out. Since the speaker in "Before I Knocked" felt the fall of rain when his "flesh's armour" was still "in a molten form," it must be inferred that Thomas had not achieved this state when the girl married.

The tombstone, with its names and dates told no more than this. But Thomas leaves the grave-yard and elsewhere adds to his fund of information. This he retails in a sentence made complex by three adverbial constructions, each of which refers to a different time.

The sentence, re-ordered, says a quite simple thing: After having seen the tombstone, I came to hear that this girl, who was married but who died before the marriage was consummated, imagined her death-pangs to be her initiation into sexual experience. In the terror and pain of her illusory deflowering, she wept and cried out, her face contorted, but her eyes smiled. All this happened, as I say, before she came to her husband's bed and arms, and, of course, before I, standing by her grave in the rain, was taken back by memory to an early point of my own existence.

Thomas shifts back now to his stand before the tombstone and closes a circle. He who at the very beginning of life had come to recognize in his own womb-experience that life meets death on a disputed barricade learns from the girl in the grave that, for her, at least, the death-experience was identical with what she had thought the sex-experience would be.

Whether one should generalize on the basis of this poem and how far is a question. I do not myself think that Thomas says anything new. He has already remarked, and more effectively, incipient life's premonition of death. His image of death ripping the girl's life as a phallus the maidenhead is vivid enough. But does it lend itself to generalization? This is, after all, a very special case. Is the poem not more moving as an imaginative reconstruction by a compassionate observer of an extraordinary instance of unfulfillment turned by delusion into fulfillment? Pathos relates to individual experience. To lose this to gain a Freudian banality is sheerest cerebralism.

50 ·

# *After the Funeral*

Annie, "a little, brown-skinned, toothless, hunchbacked woman with a cracked sing-song voice" was like this:

> She hurried me to the seat in the side of the cavernous fire-place and took off my shoes . . . She made a mustard bath and strong tea, and told me to put on a pair of my cousin Gwilym's socks and an old coat of uncle's that smelt of rabbit and tobacco. She fussed and clucked and nodded and told me, as she cut bread and butter, her Gwilym was still studying to be a minister . . . (*The Peaches*).

When Thomas sent his poem to Watkins to be typed, he wrote: "By the way, when you type it, will you spell Anne as Ann: I just remember that's the right way: she was an ancient peasant aunt." (Watkins, p. 57.) Which implies that she was close to him as a person, not as a name; and, as name, not as Anne or Ann, but as Annie.

Beyond question, significant personal loss is expressed in his lament—far more than, for example, in Milton's *Lycidas*. And yet, like Milton, Thomas has incorporated in this elegy some satirical comments only loosely related to the subject at hand. Like Milton's, they have to do with religious observance.

To see clearly that this is the case, one need only delete the first nine lines (the poem was in fact thus published as "Caseg Broadsheet" No. 5—see Rolph, p. 48). The remaining 31 lines read as a poem complete in itself, but it is not the poem that Thomas had written. It is a poem exalting a woman for her love, humility, devoutness, sense of duty—all these in themselves so great that Thomas's efforts to magnify them rhetorically fail to diminish them. Without the first nine lines, the sentence

> I know her scrubbed and sour humble hands
> Lie with religion in their cramp. . . .

has no ambiguity: it must be taken as purely positive.

But given those introductory lines, that powerful word "cramp" cannot fail to apply as much to Ann's religion as to her hands. Not to Ann as a religious person, but to the religion which she embraced and which, more to the point, embraced her.

The boy in Thomas died (slit his throat) with Ann; the man lives on to observe, with anger, the mule-praises, to hear, with contempt, the asinine orthodoxies of grief. There can be no question that he would like to dissociate himself from them. And yet he is not altogether sure of the rightness of his own position; he is aware, as the poem proceeds, that the smutch of hypocrisy is in his own monstrous images—"blindly/Magnified out of praise." Involved in the poem are these three: the conventional, unloving mourners; the conventional but loving Ann; and the unconventional, unloving (compared to Annie) Thomas wishing to be unconventional and loving, but not sure that a love like Annie's is not dependent upon the conventionality. After all, Ann is of the Victorian world in which stuffed foxes and stale ferns represent "gracious living," precisely the world from which Thomas has fled. It is no wonder that the monumental "Argument of the hewn voice, gesture and psalm" storm him forever over her grave. Her life is a critical comment upon his own.

Nevertheless, whatever his failure with respect to the rest of the world (and the first twenty lines suggest failure), he does achieve the condition of love towards Ann. Stanford has spoken of the poem (p. 86) as "a triumph of poetic sympathy, not through identification but through objective perception." And so the last twenty lines are. But in the opening sentence it is Thomas the rebel, subjectively engaged and embattled, who speaks and who, to emphasize the distinction between Annie and the mourners, needs to refer to her, though she would reject it, in terms of hyperbole. Once rid of his animus, he writes the elegy required.

This is, like *Lycidas*, an occasional poem. When the occasion occurred, Thomas looked through his unpublished manuscripts for usable materials. He found there some lines about death to serve as a point of departure. A comparison of them with the lines as they now appear shows Thomas's normal tendency of starting from the loose, explicit general and working toward the tight-packed particular in which the general has become implicit.

> After the funeral mule praises, brays,
> Shaking of mule heads, betoken
> Grief at the going to the earth of man
> Or woman, at yet another long woe broken,
> Another theme to play on and surprise
> Fresh faults and till then hidden flaws
> Faded beyond ears and eyes,
> At he or she, loved or else hated well,
> So far from love in a deep hole.

# Do Not Go Gentle — Elegy

John Malcolm Brinnin met Thomas's parents in 1951, not many months before David Thomas's death. He describes the relationship between father and son in this way:

. . .if he was unquestionably the apple of his mother's eye, in his father's eye he was still an object of curiously dispassionate interest. There was something respectful yet unmistakably distant and wary between the two men, something that made for a mutual lack of ease . . . . I had a rambling chat with Dylan and his father . . . . But no real conversation developed, mainly, I thought, because none of us — especially Dylan — could break through the formal father-and-son relationship to say freely and unguardedly just what he meant. . . . .Not until after Dylan's death did I learn that his father had had an early unrealized ambition as a poet. This revelation. . .explained somewhat my feeling that Dylan's father looked upon him with as much curiosity as with pride. The poet *manqué* had brought forth the poet *reussi*. (Brinnin, p. 112.)

Thomas's father had not been well for some years. As early as 1945, the poet wrote Watkins: "My father is awfully ill these days, with heart disease and unabated pains, and the world that was once the colour of tar is now a darker place." (Watkins, p. 126.)

During his American trip in 1950, he wrote only one letter (Brinnin says) to his parents. In it he expressed his concern about his father's health:

How are you both? How, especially, is Dad? I think a great deal of you both, and very often, though I know you would hardly think so from my not-writing for so very long. But indeed, you are constantly in my mind; I worry very much about Dad's health, or lack of it; and though I hear about you quite often from Catlin, I still do not really get a clear picture of how you are. Is Dad in bed all the time? Oh, I do hope not. And he doesn't still have to have injections, does he? And how is Mother walking now?

But he neglected to mail the letter.

David Thomas was Senior English Master at Swansea Grammar School, an academic, and a man who respected the proprieties that Caitlin has described as of the "pinched penny-pricing gentility," always struggling to "keep up the most trussed-in-belted, camouflaged, and gloved system of appearances" because of the "taxing position of being looked up to by the neighbors . . . ." Daniel Jones, Dylan's early friend, has commented on Dylan's feeling toward anything academic: ". . . at that time, and throughout his life, Dylan hated the academic. But in those early years his antipathy had less discrimination; it was directed not only against the fossils but against much that was significantly alive as well, if he happened

• 53

to find for it an academic association." (Tedlock, 17-18.) Thomas remained at the bottom of his class in all subjects save English.

Perhaps out of these scraps of information an attitude can be defined. The father is an academic; he puts a price upon respectability. He is thus triply an authoritarian: as father, schoolmaster, and conformist. The boy, as a schoolmaster's son, ought to lead his classes. But he does not. The father never betrays his allegiance to Wales. Thomas expatriated himself. (In his film-script of *The Three Weird Sisters* he characterizes the Welshman as having "a lie in his teeth and a hymn on his lips.") The father, for all his rectitude, failed in poetry. The son, independent of all proprieties, succeeded.

A certain reserve could only be expected to exist between the two, so long as each had some semblance of his powers. But Thomas was at all times affected by helplessness. His father's illness, his approaching death leveled the wall between them. The love and respect in the two poems are unquestionably deep and sincere. And yet, years of a kind of aloofness, permitting the opportunity of standing quizzically off and taking stock, ensure that these intensely personal poems retain the measure of impersonality that lends them elegiac strength.

It may be that something of a rebel-son's attitude toward a conforming father (an attitude perforce left unexpressed) breaks out in "Do Not Go Gentle," not, however, directed against the father but by transfer against death. Audacity and pugnacity are of the poem's essence. It is, to begin with, a triumph of audacity to pour such intense feeling on so personal a subject into such a form as the villanelle. Feelings of a certain poignance —a gentle autumnal melancholy, say—are what Austin Dobson and his fellows have led us to expect. To find in a villanelle a dying man *raging, burning, raving* — or being exhorted to it by a wild man — is not a little shocking.

Irrespective of the form, it is indecorous enough that a son should advise his father to eschew the sweet serenity of a hand-folded demise for a bitter, brawling end sure to embarrass bedside attendants.

Theme and form have their thumb-nosing propensities. And the first line adds its contribution: the substitution of adjective for adverb shows its disrespect for the Mosaic law of grammarians, and the punning "good night" has a quota of bitterness.

Strangely, however, the audacity, the pugnacity, are altogether on the surface. What illuminates the poem's inscape is a glowing compassion. All the people in the poem are losers who invoke our sympathy. The philosophers who had thundered but lit no fires; the saints, who at last see abstinence as *contra naturam;* the poets, whose best intentions were reversed; the sober-sides, who realize they have lived half-lives: all hate dying, and with reason. If rage is their privilege, it is even more so for David Thomas, who all his life has behaved with gentleness.

But the testimony of the "Elegy" is that he refused the privilege. He did not rage. He did not even cry. Thus at the last, as he had done for a lifetime, he disappointed his son.

Dylan Thomas was not a man who could contain himself for any length of time. He could not live within himself behind a wall. He had to let his feelings flood out—sometimes brawlingly, as Caitlin's memoirs reveal. And he needed response from those he loved. Here his father failed him. Burning with pride within, he projected no warmth to envelop his son. Coldly kind, proud, just, brave; these were not the attributes, estimable as they may be, to win response from the likes of his son. The day of his death was a cold, dark day (one infers that it was the year's shortest day). But Dylan is not lamenting the day but the many sunless days that had preceded. This darkest day is an image of a life, as the father's blindness is an image of his failure to see the need in his son for outgoing love. "Let him be fathered and found," Thomas prays. His prayer rises from his own need.

But it is pity, not self-pity, that the poem discovers, a pity tempered by justice. Thomas's understanding of his father's emotional disabilities is judicious; his recognition of his own failure balanced and balancing. He does not accuse; he does not recriminate. He is not too proud to cry nor too proud to tell the truth. Fancy can see the poem as the father's counterpart: the confining narrowness of the tercets; the cold calculatedness of the wit and artifice; the burning of the emotion within the shell, epitomized in the eyes hot with unshed tears; the kindness of the sentiment; and so on. Father and son meet in this poem as perhaps they never did in life. Arthur Symons' comment springs to mind: "Pathos which can touch the intellect becomes so transfigured that its tears shine: you can see by their light."

Only the first seventeen lines are Thomas's own. The other twenty-three were taken from manuscript notes and put together by Vernon Watkins to provide a completed poem. "Of the added lines," he says, "sixteen are exactly as Dylan Thomas wrote them, and the remainder are altered only to the extent of an inversion of one or two words. Their order might well have been different."

Their sound, too, I think, had Thomas lived to work them over, might have been different. In his book on Thomas, Henry Treece comments upon the poet's idiosyncrasies in sound and image, and then writes a chapter which he calls "Straight Poet." The difference between the earlier lines of "Elegy" and the later is the difference between "mannered" and "straight."

It is in the first part that one finds the word plays:

The darkest *way,* and did not turn *away*

. . . . .

He lie lightly, at *last,* on the *last,* crossed

. . . . .

Through his un*see*ing eyes to the roots of the *sea.*

There, too, is the structuring of sound, as in the fourth stanza, which, taking off from the third stanza's "breast," runs through "rest," "dust," "darkest," "justice," "unblessed," and "rest"; and the Thomasian epithet-noun combinations: "crossed hill," "crouching room," "blind bed."

What would Thomas have done? Simplified the earlier section? or complicated the latter? Or did he intend the shift in tone as indicating a progression from the complication of dying to the simplicity of death?

No doubt the poem is not what Thomas would have made it. But what Watkins has made of it would surely have pleased him.

# Grief Thief of Time

Thomas wastes no time raising questions in this tantalizing poem. They occur in the first four lines, and being structural, offer the opportunity of constructing at least three poems from the given words.

Grief thief of time crawls off,
The moon-drawn grave, with the seafaring years,
The knave of pain steals off
The sea-halved faith that blew time to his knees . . . .

The questions are these:

1. Does grief crawl off the "moon-drawn grave"?
   If so, why the commas after "off" and "grave"?
2. If "grief" crawls off the "grave," is the latter to be equated with the sea?
3. Is "grave" appositional with "grief"? If so, in what respect is "grief" to be thought "moon-drawn"?
4. Is "grave" an adjective modifying "moon-drawn," which is appositional to "grief"?
5. Does "grief" steal time? Or is it Fagin-time's employee?
6. Does "with the seafaring years" have the sense of "as the years go by"?

7. Or are the "seafaring years" and the "sea-halved faith" the swag which the thief absconds with?

8. Does the comma after "crawls off" have the force of a semi-colon so that the lines read roughly like this: Grief crawls off; pain steals away from the dedicated sailor both the sea and his seafaring—that is, has beached him? Or like this: Grief crawls off; pain, as the years go by, steals from the sea the faith of the seafarers who earlier paid no heed to time?

The syntax and punctuation are such that any of these questions could be answered affirmatively; but no answer would be wholly satisfactory. Some arbitrariness is indicated. But not too much. Suppose that we write two poems—one with a positive, and one with a negative first stanza.

The assumption of the first will be that the seafaring years have ended, the old seamen have kept faith with the sea and are now not unhappily ending their days ashore.

The grief and pain which these now-grave but once-romantic oldsters experienced afloat, which stole their youth and sometimes made them contemplate forswearing the sea (but they never did); that grief, that uselessness which they felt later when beached (how much time they wasted, killed and buried, wishing for what could not be—a berth on a ship going out on the next tide): these have left them. Their faith in themselves, once strong enough to deny any anxiety about age, is now strong enough to keep them content even though it is sea-halved —that is, though they still have only one leg on land. They remember the seafaring years, but they forget the lean times and the storms, remember as living their castaway companions, forget the occupational disease, the crime and punishment. And then, having relived to the full their vigorous youth, they go agedly to bed, eyes still full of the salt sea, to dream of the fabulous ship whose name will never die.

Given this interpretation, the purport of the second stanza is, Good— keep it up—let the bad memories go—redeem the present time; grief poisons the mind, sucks the life's blood, and, turning you introvert, destroys camaraderie. Remember that nothing is lost in your or any death; life takes its meaningful form in relation to all previous deaths.

The negative reading assumes that the old men are in an old-sailors' haven, living in pain and sorrow. The grief and pain of aging have stolen away the vigor and self-reliance necessary for a seafaring life. The old men do temporarily forget their sorrow in selective recollections of the past, but, reminded by their aching bones of the discrepancy between their present and their resilient past, they go to bed in tears to dream of a ship wrecked as they are themselves.

The second stanza, then, must be an admonishment: the nursing of such memories must cease; let grief the thief make his getaway with his useless booty; let go your grief as you must your desire for stallion years; resigned to your unvirile maturity, show him ("bulls-eye the outlaw") for what he is and stop pursuing him through the days and weeks of your remaining life.

There are two possibilities, the one not differing much from the other, except in tone, and both accounting reasonably well for most of the images.

I have, of course, made too much of the business of the old sailors' home. It is a convenient metaphor for the general human condition, the atrophying of the sexual powers. We are all Jack Tars. But in the second stanza the metaphor is all but discarded and attention is focused upon the sneak-thief, who has, like a Disney-character, a clock-face and deft, dagger-pointed hands, and who has stolen the (non-Disneyan) bag of potent sperm, which he takes to bury with those mettlesome years that grief-attended Time has already buried. Thomas urges that the erstwhile stallions and bulls of men not retain any grief for their loss, that they spotlight the plunderer of their testicular vitality (which no doubt caused them some anxiety in their day), that they recognize and accept a fact instead of vainly pursuing an impossibility. Spotlighting the thief, they will have shot him dead-center. In this case, to regain what has been stolen is worse than to lose it. He further urges that they not put under microscopic analysis that mysterious force which, like a covenant, has bound human beings together, but that they accept in faith that all halves are bridged—even that between life and death. For what they mourn as a lost past is not lost and will fit, with time (that does not cease), and death (that does not kill), into the natural universal pattern. Let them with Whitman "mark the outlet and mark the relief and escape," and with him recognize that "All goes onward and outwards, nothing collapses," which is to say that "All shall remain."

It is possible to elevate the poem from the human level and give it a mythic rather than moral significance. Lita Hornick has done so, basing her argument on these two passages:

And salt-eyed stumble bedward where she lies
Who tamed the high tide in a time of stories
And timelessly lies loving with the thief.

．　．　．　．　．

No third eye probe into a rainbow's sex
That bridged the human halves . . .

Of the first she writes:

"She" appears to be the Great Mother, and the thief both time and God (see "In Country Sleep"). In their divine reunion is the promise of perpetual reward.

And of the second:

The "third eye" is the eye of the adept, who can see into the mysterious secrets of the universe. What Thomas appears to be saying in these lines is: let us make no attempt to probe into these secrets with occult mumbo-jumbo. The rainbow appears to be God (Thomas allows an object associated with God to stand for God); and the "rainbow's sex which bridged the human halves" may allude to the Kaballistic conception of a hermaphroditic God, who created the world through intercourse with his feminine emanation (a conception available to Thomas in both Blake and Joyce.) It is "human" halves which are bridged by the divine hermaphrodite, because God is indistinguishable from man.

It is impossible to determine, without knowing how these fragments fit into a total reading of the poem, the validity of her argument. Valid or not, readers of a certain cast of mind will prefer the poem read this way. I myself find more satisfaction in a poem in which a portentous symbolism does not diminish or distract attention from a felt compassion for those that have laboured and are heavy laden.

# When All My Five and Country Senses See

Since all of this poem is written in future tense, that is, of what will occur, given a particular action ("My . . . heart has witnesses" and "The heart is sensual" are in the permanent present tense), it is necessary to assume a present situation which·is to be changed. This assumption can be made in terms of the poem's basic contrast, that between the heart, single and noble, and the senses, many and vulgar. From this contrast can be inferred the controlling metaphor of the poem, to be found in the theory of courtly love, that love's arrows, striking the eye, pierce to the heart, where a terrible beauty is born. Thomas's heart, a courtly lover smitten by love ("sodeynly he wex there-with astoned"), loses contact with his loyal retainers, the common senses. So, as the poem opens, the situation is this: the heart is awake but mad; the eyes dazzle; the four remaining senses are either asleep, or they see as through a glass roseately. What will happen is this:

In due course the senses will awaken to what they conceive as reality. The fingers, forgetful of green genesis, will observe that as the moon nears the end of its zodiacal run, as harvest moon dwindles to half moon, as young stars grow old, as the Prodigal Son descends from Lucullan feasts to husks, love loses its sap, is cut (like a too-long finger-nail), stored, and left unattended. The ears, attuned to dissonances, will see love expelled from the village like a slut to be transported. The sharp-eyed tongue will cry that the wounds inflicted by irrational love mend painfully and the memory leaves a bitter taste. The smoke of the smouldering bush of love will get in the nostril's eyes.

Thus it will be when the heart regains its senses. A certain disillusion will occur. But this is not a poem of the loss of love but of its change. Confessedly, the view is not sanguine from where the senses sit: love is seen as a husk or a nail-paring, as a repudiated illdoer, as a knife-slasher, and as a weed well-burnt. As they see, so they report. But each sees partially, is blind to the bread to be made of the wheat, to the new life in Australia, to the wounds' ultimate mend, to the unusual nature of the burning bush.

The realistic clamor of the peasant-senses will come to the attention, eventually, of their master, and he, no longer doting, will courteously listen and piece their reports together. The responsibility is now his, and the senses may sleep as they wish. The heart, no longer "well neigh wood," and with all available information at its disposal, now knows its love for what it is, one which will endure though the senses fail.

## Unluckily for a Death

For Blake the Fall coincided with the organization of systems of worship, the pronouncement that the Gods had ordered such systems, and the stifling of the truth "that All deities reside in the human breast." In "Incarnate Devil," Thomas expresses much the same idea: Reason, having invented sin, had to invent punishment and hell, pardon and heaven; and the immanent deity was made transcendent, no longer a subjective guardian but an objective warden.

In "Unluckily for a Death," this warden-deity is excluded altogether, and it is Thomas himself who walks in the garden in the cool of the day. The garden he enjoys is his love's body, for the poem as a whole is an argument against continence and for love as "the full assemblage in flower / Of the living flesh . . . ." The language throughout is religious: the girl's body is described as "the endless breviary . . . of your prayed flesh"; in their union, "the ceremony of souls / Is celebrated . . . and communion between suns"; there are "heroic hosts" in her every "inch and glance," and in them "the globe of genesis" is spun. Thomas has simply reversed the process adopted by mystics; where they dramatize the love of God in sexual terms, he has sublimated sexual love by using religious terms. In the process he has made himself God, and Christ ("immortality at my side like Christ the sky") a natural phenomenon.

This is an intense and serious poem and one which Thomas worked and re-re-worked. In the original version, sent to Watkins in 1939, the religious imagery was almost totally absent. Compare its final stanza with that of the poem's final form:

Love, my fate got luckily,
May teach me now with no telling
That every drop of water is both kind and cruel,
With articulate eyes
Tell me the money-coloured sun sees poorly,
Teach that the child who sucks on innocence
Is spinning fast and loose on a fiery wheel,
All that we do, cruelly, kindly,
Will kiss in a huddle:
In the teeth of that black-and-white wedding
I chuck my armed happiness.
Though the puffed phoenix stir in the rocks
And lucklessly fair or sycorax the widow wait,
We abide with our pride, the unalterable light,
On this turning lump of mistakes.

. . . . .

Love, my fate got luckily,
Teaches now with no telling
That the phoenix' bid for heaven and the desire after
Death in the carved nunnery
Both shall fail if I bow not to your blessing
Nor walk in the cool of your mortal garden
With immortality at my side like Christ the sky.
This I know from the native
Tongue of your translating eyes. The young stars told me,
Hurling into beginning like Christ the child.
Lucklessly she must lie patient
And the vaulting bird be still. O my true love, hold me.
In your every inch and glance is the globe of genesis spun,
And the living earth your sons.

In the former, Thomas represents himself as a quite normal young man quite normally extracting joy from love in a muddled, muddy world. Love is as delightful as continence is unnatural, but it is without religious implications. The weaving in of Christian images has turned a tract into an excathedral statement of the idea expressed by Lawrence in his poem "The Body of God":

> any lovely and generous woman
> at her best and her most beautiful, being
> god made manifest.
> any clear and fearless man being
> god very god.

In the poem as it now stands, Thomas postulates three ways of working towards his immortality. The one which he chooses is, of course, Love. The others might be called Hope and Faith: hope for a phoenix-like resurrection after death; and faith in the monastic virtue of continence. Both are "death-biding" and experience-negating; though each has had its proponents as a form of love, neither, Thomas thinks, can properly be so called, since, in each, renunciation supersedes procreation. The irony is that each renounces the flesh to gain an immortality, whereas the only immortality ensues from the action of the flesh.

The poem is organized into four 14-line stanzas. Since the opening sentence runs ten lines into the second stanza, and its subject and verbs are withheld to the fifteenth and sixteenth lines, explication is simplified by starting with the second stanza. The subject-verb set-up is "My holy lucky body is caught and held and kissed." The choice of modifiers for the subject is significant, the two words isolating the body from any purposive external force: the body in itself and in the here and now and in this act of love is sacred; — fortune, providence, grace, or the like have no operational force upon its happiness. To start, then, with the second stanza:

Tabus like clouds envelop lovers — misleading tabus (will o' the wisp) which compass love like a dark Satanic mill (mill of the midst). Nevertheless, my goodly body, loving in this natural world, overcoming the guilt with which indoctrination has stigmatized such loving, is caught, held, kissed. We ignore the dark for the light of Venus, a "star in the east" with the power to minister grace, but a grace of *natural* origin and result ("in the order of the quick"). The dark is illuminated. Your body and your eyes shine round about me, saying peace on earth to men of good will, attesting an incarnation. Souls join; the light of suns is deeply interfused.

My belief in the sanctity of such love, my belief that death is defeated only by physical love, denies two widely-held concepts of immortality: that which extends hope for a resurrection after death; that which makes its joy contingent upon a willed restraint of sexual desire. (Love, in the former, is diverted from the particular and concrete to the general and abstract; in the latter, a future spiritual love is preferred to a present physical love.) The "virtue" of continence may be personified as a woman among ghosts, a grave-yard statue, her natural voluptuousness sheathed in marble, forever faithful to me (like Patience on a monument) though I have not made her my own with a kiss on the fevered forehead or the deathly mouth; nor has the chill nunnery of her lust-inhabited body opened to love under mine, which prefers to her frigid abstinence the summer heat of seduction.

This representation of continence as a devoted woman who would be all the more constant if she were brawlingly loved has nothing of the classic succinctness and simplicity of the personification in, for example, Collins. If there is such a thing as a conceited personification, this is it. Its length, its complexity, its psychological perceptiveness, its careful though dramatic statement indicate that Thomas felt the subject to be so important as to require the most precise definition.

His first stanza and the first ten lines of the second having outlined the general situation, Thomas now makes a plain statement of his choice among the three alternatives and of his reason why.

I shall not cease reading the prayer-book of your body to celebrate "holy" continence, nor shall I pay any heed to death or possible resurrection.

All unnatural monsters are unhappy or fruitless. Continence, astraddle like the Rhodesian Colossus, one foot in heaven and one on earth, is of a kind with the bird-beast, donkey-horse, man-bull, hermaphrodite, and tiger-lion, she being desire-abnegation. So too is the earth-renouncing phoenix (each phoenix is an island unto himself). Love which renounces the flesh — Platonic love, mystical love, ascetic love, a love of an assumed virtue or a love for triangles — produces, if anything, infertile grotesqueries.

This is not to deny the intellectual and spiritual aspects of love but to maintain that only love in its trinitarian physical-intellectual-spiritual unity is true love. This is what, as luck would have it, has been fated for me: that I have learned without being taught that neither hope nor faith (phoenix or nun) has meaning if I do not find my Earthly Paradise in my love for your body and my resurrection therein. Your eyes teach me this; and the light emanating from a material body, as truth issued from a man-child, had taught me. Neither continence nor Platonism now avails. The power of creation is yours; the patterning of life is at your command.

Of all Thomas's poems this most explicitly states his philosophy of love. And most powerfully. Both Treece and Stanford have balked at the third stanza, they being "too humorously struck" by the tigron in tears and so on. I think they have been too analytical, too literal-minded. It is quite true that the tigron does not weep nor the she mule bear minotaurs. Nor, for that matter, is the dark androgynous. But if the passage is not taken part by part but as a surrealistic whole depicting Monstrosity (and Monstrosity, being grotesque, is tragically comic for all but the unsympathetic) it has its strength. All that one needs to get from the passage is an effect of the weeping hotness and congestion of frustration, or an itchy-sweaty tropical effect, from which one is relieved by the refreshing "walk in the cool of your mortal garden." It may be a near thing, but Thomas pulls it off. He does so because, however the images may titillate the risibilities of the intellect, the sounds of the word-combinations still the laugh. If "tigron in tears" provokes a smile, the linkéd sweetness of "androgynous dark" aborts it, and a seriousness is developed by the powerful "striped and noon maned tribe striding to holocaust." The comic asserts itself with the she mule bearing minotaurs (though a sadness underlies); and the mere mention of the duck-billed platypus can raise an unthinking laugh. But this again is cut short by the sound and connotations (reminders of Milton and of Hopkins) of "broody in a milk of birds." Only sound and vague suggestion work — the image is confused —but their work is quite enough. The effect of the whole is pathetic rather than tragic, and perhaps not quite pathetic. It is the effect of the mixed comic and tragic figures on a medieval cathedral. Gothic is the word.

And since it is precisely Thomas's purpose to free love from its Gothic tabus, the stanza co-operates with the others by standing out against them.

# A Grief Ago

This poem will probably never become a popular favorite. It is to be classified among the works that are puzzles before they are poems, and perhaps it is to be further classified as a puzzle that never becomes a poem. Only the explicator who has come to terms with it will feel for it any strong affection, as (according to folk-lore) a mother loves the child whose birth she suffered most.

This is a poem without much charm: it does not sing; it does not read aloud well; it has few if any lines that evoke emotional or imaginative response. Metaphysical wit it has aplenty, but the metaphors are so tangled that one feels a Johnsonian sternness breaking through one's cheerfulness. However, I have achieved an explication of sorts and feel the consequent affection. Possibly a double affection, since (to appeal to folk-lore again) it not only was a hard birth, but the result may not be legitimate.

As I see it, the "she" is Thomas's girl, probably Caitlin. She is a mature woman, ready for love, capable of procreation. Apparently, though all history ought to teach her that sex is the only means of defeating death, she is playing coy mistress (is Thomas's grief). So Thomas writes his very free paraphrase of Marvell's poem. His metaphors are botanical, Biblical, Greek, and possibly zoological.

1. *The girl* I now hold, the girl who is now a fully blossomed flower and (*Numbers* 18, 17) a sweet savour in my nostrils, *was,* a short but distressful time ago, *either* a maidenly rosebud with tomboy vigor who, despite hell and high water, pushing her stem up from the bush, clung to the tower, and achieved full growth; *or* (according to Elder Olson) like a venus's basin (wild teasel) grew in the sun; *or* (two alternative possibilities) like Venus in her scallop or a spiny venus shell (clam) moved from sea to shore;

2. *This girl,* who now causes me anxiety because I violently accelerated the change from chrysalis to butterfly (forced the bud to shoot into flower fast as a gangster's bullet), *this girl was* the bud implicit in Aaron's rod (*Numbers* 17, 8), that is, the stem that the miraculously-budding rose of Erin (and the great mullein, called Aaron's Rod) sent out to be water-lammed (and, perhaps, to be a plaguey nuisance to me with her spines and her "teaseling").

Note: Aaron's rod may also recall the rod that flowered when Tannhauser abandoned the delights of Venusberg. The "horn and ball of water on the frog" elude me. Possibly it is a strengthening of the metamorphosis theme: the horns of the altar or the rams-horn, the water from the rock, the plague of frogs were all implicit in Aaron's rod, the frog and toad are implicit in the tadpole. And, of course, explosion is potential in the powder-horn.

3. *This girl,* who lies (in my arms) just evicted from the innocence of Eden (the marriage-ring a sign of the loss of natural-as-sacramental love) *has hauled* with her, as she grew, the history of her forebears: this is the usual history of man so well exemplified in *Exodus* — the innocence, the sin, the sense of guilt, the promise of pardon, the renewed sin, the punishment, the hope of the promised land — the winds of time and change blowing from all points of the compass rose and deeply impressing the

experience of the departure of the twelve tribes from Egypt, the wandering in the wilderness, the punishments, the eventual achievement.

4. Who, then, is this girl who holds me — as I hold her? The sea of self-identity and procreative urge, like the Red Sea severing the Israelites from the Egyptians, separates her (as though untimely ripped) from her recent enslaving past. The shaping-places prepare her whelping-organs and her instinct for the race's survival, in order that she take a stand against extinction (in order that she coffin-corner and knock out tough-fisted, calloused death).

5. Since that death is always near, not as a life-shaper (water) but a decomposer (acid), I emphasize a point: before the dawn (before Time's fire burn her; before the Assyrians overwhelm Israel — a child being Israel's only hope — *Isaiah,* 8, 9, 10), let her assimilate her ancestry, let her be filled with the procreative urge, and thus connect past and future, thus come out of death's Egyptian captivity to the promised land, thus let, out of the stem of Jesse, come a rod (*Isaiah* 11); let her close her fist and hold tight to this promise of future reward, and with her closed fist strike down the country-handed grave.

# *It is the Sinner's Dust-Tongued Bell*

According to Elder Olson, ". . . the opening stanza of 'It is the sinner's dust-tongued bell' is likely to mean little or nothing unless the reader realizes that the details add up to a Black Mass being celebrated, with Satan officiating as priest, and that Time is being compared to Satan executing this office." (P. 58.)

E. Glyn Lewis says of Thomas that "He and the Christian poets have still more in common in their willingness to enshroud the experience of time with the idea of death and the most objectionable associations." (Tedlock, 176.) To illustrate, he quotes the fifth (and last) stanza and explains that ". . . here time is identified with the sexual act which, holy in itself, is translated by consciousness of time into an abhorrent experience."

Hornick finds in the second, third, and fourth stanzas a "drowning of time . . . followed by the re-awakening of life and the rebirth of man and the vegetable world." (P. 52.)

Putting these together, we have this: Time is officiating at a Black Mass; time is drowned and life is re-awakened; and time becomes the sexual act, which, because of the consciousness of time, is abhorrent.

Obviously the three interpretations differ, although to what degree it is difficult to ascertain since none of the explicators attempts the whole poem. The queer thing here is that though, apparently, the three explicators have different ideas of the poem, each is in part right. There is an element of the Black Mass; there is a regeneration; and time is involved, if not in the sexual act, in a marriage, in which sex is involved. It may therefore be possible to bring the three together in a fourth explication.

The approach to this poem has to be made from its final stanza, in which Thomas makes a show of explaining what he has been talking about:

I mean by time the cast and curfew rascal of our marriage,
At nightbreak born in the fat side, from an animal bed
In a holy room in a wave;
And all love's sinners in sweet cloth kneel to a hyleg image,
Nutmeg, civet, and sea-parsley serve the plagued groom and bride
Who have brought forth the urchin grief.

Mr. Lewis, commenting on this stanza, took the high priori road. And no question about it, Thomas is exploring the deleterious effects of Time. But I think that a couple of facts tying the poem down to a situation involving people need to be considered before moving into abstractions. The facts are these: that this poem was published in January of 1937, and that Thomas married Caitlin Macnamara in 1936. The inference from these facts is that, since each was a maverick unsuited to pull in harness, there was bound to be trouble after mutual passion had begun to diminish.

I take the poem, then, to be a comment upon Thomas's marital status. It appears to me to be a recognition that one manifestation of love has run its course; that there is reason for sorrow and penitence; but that there is also reason to hope for a translation of passionate love into something more durable. The controlling metaphor is that of Holy Week; the poem is a kind of *Miserere*.

What has happened is this: the element of time has had a hardening, fire-damping effect upon a love that began at nightfall as a melting, submerging passion that seemed as holy as profane. Pagan lovers, witness of this untoward event, do what they can to halt the tragedy: they pray to an image of the Life-Giver to halt the movement toward *avareta* the destroyer (these are symbols in astrology) and offer aphrodisiac gifts of musk-nut (nutmeg), musk, and the herb lovage to the couple whose marriage thus far has been blessed only with the spiny hedgehog of grief.

In this time of Love's apparent extinction (curfew does ring tonight)— and now we shift to the first stanza — Thomas is haled by mute-as-death (dust-tongued) bells to repentance for his errors and to prayer for new hope. When does this occur? As the opening stanza says:

It is the sinners' dust-tongued bell claps me to churches
When, with his torch and hourglass, like a sulphur priest,
His beast heel cleft in a sandal,
Time marks a black aisle kindle from the brand of ashes,
Grief with dishevelled hands tear out the altar ghost
And a firewind kill the candle.

Now in this stanza we have muted bells, ashes, a torn-out altar ghost, and an extinguished candle. The derivation of these from the events of Holy Week (and Ash Wednesday) seems certain. No bells may be rung from the *Gloria* of the Mass of Maundy Thursday until the same on Holy Saturday; the faithful are "branded" with ashes on Ash Wednesday; the Blessed Sacrament is removed from the altar and reserved "in a special place from Maundy Thursday till Easter to represent our Lord's body in the tomb"; and at special Matins and Lauds (Tenebrae) on Maundy Thursday, Good Friday, and Holy Saturday fourteen candles are put out and one is hidden behind the altar, the church-aisles thus being darkened. So something like this can be made of the stanza:

When in course of time, the gold-vermilion of our love turns bluebleak, comes to its ashes-to-ashes stage, its butterfly wings burnt (aisle fr. *aile* = wing); when grief sepulchres the holy spirit of love; when its light and joy and grace are extinguished; at this dark hour the necessity is upon me to repent and pray.

It is not so much a Black Mass, as Olson says, as a black time for the lover, though it is true that Time with his torch is imaged as the Satan worshipped by the witch-cults. I think it is clear from Thomas's being clapped "to churches" that he is not undergoing conversion to Christianity or to cultism but finding in church symbolism an objective correlative for his situation.

When, during Tenebrae, the candles are out, a commotion is made in the darkness, symbolizing the convulsion of nature at the death of Christ. Then the lighted candle (hidden behind the altar) is replaced, and the Light of the World is evident again. This is what, using the imagery of the submerged cathedral, Thomas dramatizes in the next stanza and a half:

The asexual drone of Time drowns out the momentary harmonizing of male and female. Mortality expanding like coral calcifies and grief rising like an ocean tide smothers love in its carnal aspect (Love Incarnate); in the emotional turbulence, petitions for reconciliation are ineffectual. The falling of death upon the spirit at the sixth hour affects macrocosm (moon) and microcosm (emperor butterfly) — the whole nature of the lovers. The flame of the candle extinguished (darkness over the earth from the sixth to the ninth hour) there is no joy, no peace (only pyrotechnical displays of temper); only love's spirit is quiet — like a dead thing, an empty cathedral, a plucked hen.

Here, rather confusingly, because there is no sense of transition, no change of voice, occurs the turning point of the poem. A further confusion obtains because Thomas collapses two services — exorcism and baptism — into one. And still a further because Time, earlier a priest, is now a cherub and it is Grief who assumes the priestly office, a shift from hand-wringing to the laying on of hands. Yet it all works out logically:

Old satanic time is dead (as Christ's time on earth has come to its term); the candle is replaced on the altar; the meaning of sacrifice is understood, grief is assuaged, and, after the Lenten period, life resumes its orderly processes; like the phoenix out of red fire, the cock on the steeple rises out of the encroaching coral. If, out of dark-skinned, blue-skied summer the snow and silence of winter develop, out of winter come the color and noise of spring, as from the sepulchre Christ, and from the cocoon the butterfly — and from the grief the maturer understanding of love.

It might be added that in the baptismal service, the child is exorcised and salt is administered as well as water. One might say that for Thomas the salt tears of grief have supplied "the salt of wisdom." His love has undergone baptismal regeneration, may be said to have been infused with grace, though not supernatural. In Thomas has been created a clean heart and a right spirit renewed within him.

## *Not from this Anger*

There are times when it is useful to know what the poet was doing on a given afternoon and how this action related to other earlier or later actions of the same kind. This poem is a case in point.

It appears, from Caitlin's account, that Thomas often felt the urge for intercourse in the afternoon and that she, not similarly urged, refused. A weather of fireworks ensued. Since this connubial contretemps occurred with some regularity, what one wants to know is why Thomas has selected this particular afternoon's refusal as a subject for a poem. Does it stand out from the others as being of greater significance for her or for him? (Assuming, of course, that a third party is not involved.) Is this the time when he came to recognize the uselessness, the folly, the downright immorality of giving way to anger? Is there, that is to say, a behavioral conversion here as there is supposed to be a religious conversion in "Vision and Prayer"?

There can be, I think, no question, that the poems in *Map of Love* reveal a Thomas in process of subduing his egocentricism, of broadening his sympathies. Love's territorial possessions cover more of the map than they would have done in the earlier volumes. For there he posed himself only the easy problem of loving an abstract mankind. Pins on the wall-map sufficed. Now he has a quite concrete Caitlin: the territory has to be governed on the spot in person. Love has its test when the natives are restless.

I do not know that the poem has the significance I have suggested. The external evidence is missing. So what follows is altogether assumption from the imagery. The notable images all have to do with bending, breaking, or muffling — a falling off, or subduing. Anticlimax breaks a mood; the flower's stem is broken; the beast's neck is bent; the hungry belly is concave; the emigrant breaks his home ties; the sky sags; the sun falls; the immersed bell is muffled; the angry grimace is hidden. Various unsuccesses are suggested: of Narcissus, of Phaeton, of Atalanta, of squaring the circle, of the Charites with the apple of discord, etc. But given all this, there is a sense of coming to terms, of subjugating the self to the exigencies of living in tandem.

It is, nevertheless, only a sense and, without information, can be no more. The following is rather more my own poem than an explication of Thomas's.

> She shall not be left to starve or forage (like a character in *Famine*), she shall not be exiled like an Irish emigrant of the white hands (hands like tendrils needing a strong support) because of my anger, which, after her narcissistic refusal (which is suicidal) and her lone-wolfishness (which is starvation-bound) and despite the Ovidian change in my manly tissue, is quite anticlimactic.
> I bear in mind that the light which now shows us desultorily but unbitterly smiling in response to desultory smile will fail as the sun sets. Not from this anger, though her refusal took the clapper out of my bell, shall her smile (irritating me though it does) cause to appear on my mouth or reflect in my eye that snarling (uncircular) grimace that burns my brain.

. . . . .

Here I have assumed that the allusion to sky and sun in the central section (11. 8-10) indicates an understanding that failures can be remedied, that time does not stop here, that this is not the end-all. The sun sets but will rise; the sky, now sagging, will assert its light. Seen in this larger perspective, the personal failure becomes objectified.

The poem that I have written has a psychological soundness; the explication that I have contrived makes a kind of sense of the introductory metaphors. The question is, have I missed the tone and therefore the true purport of the poem? It is not impossible to read the opening and concluding lines like this: She shall not receive from me in my anger, in the disappointment of my roused expectancy, so much as a bellyful of weeds . . . .My anger will not permit that her attempted smile of reconciliation have for me more substance than the mirror-image of her mouth which I see in such hot wrath.

The rest of the poem could be made to fit this pattern. Nor would it need to be done with mirrors. I prefer the first because it shows Thomas as maintaining the maturity of compassionate outlook which he has enunciated in the preceding poem, "Once it was the Colour of Saying." One would think that the poet would prefer to be seen in print at his best. But the possibility that he has no objection to being seen human as opposed to humane cannot be ignored.

A third alternative, which has its amusing aspects, is to assume a maturity of wit rather than of compassion; that is, that Thomas has written a riddling poem capable of either interpretation with the diabolical intention of unsettling the coy mistress who has unsettled him.

# Out of the Sighs

No verse preceding this one in the *Collected Poems* and scarcely one that follows expresses an emotional intensity, comes as close to tragic statement, as does this taut, unexclamatory lyric. Here, if ever, Thomas achieved the felt thought, the thought emotion. Here, as so rarely, the clever inventor of rhetorical devices stands aside to permit the reader to see in person a man of sensibility grappling with an experience.

It is not impossible that the poem is a dramatic monologue rather than personal reflection. The words, especially those of the first and last stanzas are not inappropriate to an agonized Christ. It is a measure of the worth of the poem that, whether or not it is intended to, it meets the challenge of that situation.

As in the poems commonly called "metaphysical," there is no feeling of a *fait accompli* but, rather, a sense of process, of the poem's working itself out; the reader is not permitted to view the jewel but is haled into the tunnel to sweat with the artist as he mines it. So the difficulty of this poem is not that of so many of the others—the play with word-play, the distinguishing of letter from symbol, and the establishment of the symbol's literal meaning, the finding of the one way through the maze of double-entry syntax, and the like — but the following of a tortured mind as it tortuously works towards self-reconciliation. The skills required for this poem are the skills required for "The Extasie."

The subject, however, recalls Emily Dickinson rather than Donne, the Emily Dickinson of "After Great Pain a Formal Feeling Comes," "Success is Counted Sweetest," and "Pain has an Element of Blank." In the first of these particularly, the psychological progression — from grief to formal feeling to a spiritual questioning which lapses into a forgetful stupor which seems a "quartz contentment" — very closely parallels Thomas's first stanza.

The full progression in Thomas is (as I see it): happiness in the sun; fight and bitter words; separation; agony and grief (the latter knocked down); growth of the spirit; its forgetfulness; its cries (and sighs); its minimal comfort in the sighs; regrets; continuation of pain after regret is found useless; the cure of pain (perhaps) by loving generosity.

This is certainly a poem to which prose explication will do an injustice, for here what Thomas's heart feels is more important than what his mind thinks. Prose may illuminate the latter; the former is the province of poetry. The poem is ultimately its own best commentary. Nevertheless, like Mt. Everest, the poem is there.

1. After the tragic event, one sighs and finds some relief, but not of grief because that has disappeared in the formal feeling that follows great pain. The relief is from the deadness of that formal feeling. Though there seems "no reason for going on," the spirit reasserts itself and turns attention to the matter of living; but memory will not be downed, the spirit undergoes anguish, there are tears, which subside into sighs, and reason begins to prevail. Reason finds some comfort — cold, but comfort — in a solid logical conclusion: if one cannot love well, one cannot love well. At least, one knows where one stands — and can even shrug a shoulder and review the situation with some semblance of calm, and, by generalizing, objectify it.

2. (The generalization): For the weakest the outlook is not for death but for prolonged suffering. Though the wound heals and the pain is assuaged, the ache will continue longer than it should, even after his regrets for leaving the woman whose bitter words have cut him have vanished. The ache will continue *because* in feeling no regrets he recognizes a self-centeredness in himself.

3. Were feeling regret for a wasted happiness enough, and were a resumption of relations but without a definition of this new basis enough, with lies to lend assurance that the basis was firm, I could verbalize away my suffering.

4. But this is as much as to say that man is as simple, as merely physical as a dog. The resumed relation, lacking spiritual unanimity, would indeed be merely physical ("bone, blood, and sinew"). But such a relation no more solves the root of the problem than supplying food cures a dog's distemper or, groping under the dog's plate, a man's.

Therefore, as being all I have to give, I offer my home, my table, and a governing hand.

The crux of the poem is in the last two lines, the supposed resolution. "For all there is to give I offer" might mean

> I offer all there is for anyone to give —
> In return for all there is to give, I offer —
> In place of all there is to give, I offer —

And "Crumbs, barn, and halter" might be construed as poverty, vaga-bondage, and a noose at the end. (This would be the choice if the speaker were assumed to be Christ.) At all events, the barn he offers is well-situated on Cold Comfort Farm.

# I Make This in a Warring Absence

This 68-line poem is what Thomas referred to as one of his "long exhausters." He spent nearly a year in its construction, a single line, Watkins says (p. 30), occupying him for several days. No small part of this labor was devoted exclusively to his rhyme-words: as, in "I In My Intricate Image," he experimented with line-endings in *l*, here he has worked with *n*'s. In the first two stanzas, each line ends with the nasal; the third varies to *ence;* the fourth permits one deviant — the end-word *follows;* the fifth is regular; the sixth opens with dentals but closes with *nd*'s; the seventh pursues this combination; the eighth continues with *n*'s and *d*'s, but adds *m*'s; and the ninth offers a surprise ending of sibilants and liquids.

But the harassed reader cannot avoid thinking that Thomas spent his year ensuring that his poem would require an equivalent time of study. Syntax, image, metaphor, and symbol are so manipulated as to produce as obscure a poem as Thomas ever wrote. There are keys for some of his difficult poems: the general understanding of his thesis may assist toward opening up his particular images; the connecting of the poem to an objective situation helps; a recognition of what he has recently been reading will give a clue; analogy with another, less obscure poem or with Thomas's prose is useful; comment by Thomas himself sometimes clarifies. Here, though such keys present themselves, they only unlock doors leading to darker rooms or rooms with further doors.

There are, for example, hints that he has the book of *Jeremiah* in mind as he writes. The most obvious allusion is in the couplet

> Comes love's anatomist with sun-gloved hand
> Who picks the live heart on a diamond

which is based upon 17, 1:

> The sin of Judah is written with a pen of iron,
> and with the point of a diamond: it is graven
> upon the table of their heart, and upon the horns
> of your altars. . . .

And it is not impossible that stanza 1 recalls some words from other verses in the same chapter. Verse 23 refers to the stiff-neckedness of the Jews, and Thomas to a "stone-necked minute"; verse 13's reference to "the fountain of living waters" and verses 7 and 8

> Blessed is the man that trusteth in the Lord, and
> whose hope the Lord is.
> For he shall be as a tree planted by the waters, and
> that spreadeth out her roots by the river

may have served toward the making of Thomas's

> When, praise is blessed, her pride in mast and fountain
> . . . . . . . . . . . . . . . . .
> In that proud sailing tree with branches driven
> Through the last vault and vegetable groyne.

The emphasis in *Jeremiah* upon sin and separation echoes the poem's concern with pride and absence but it does not assist toward determining who or what is absent from what or whom—although 16, 9, makes an oblique comment: "I will cause to cease . . . the voice of mirth, and the voice of gladness, the voice of the bridegroom, and the voice of the bride."

Thomas's own comment upon the poem is tantalizing in its incompleteness. It explains particularly the first half of the last stanza and by extension and in general terms the three preceding stanzas:

> Once upon a time, before my death and resurrection,
> before the 'terrible' world had shown itself to me
> (however lyingly, as lines 6 & 7 of the last verse
> might indicate) as not so terrible after all, a wind had
> blown that had frightened everything & created the first
> ice & the first frost by frightening the falling snow so
> much that the blood of each flake froze. (Watkins, p. 30.)

74 ·

But nothing here nor in the poem explains the cause or the meaning of this frightening wind nor its relation, if there is one, with Thomas's death and resurrection.

Does the poem have an objective situation as its immediate cause? According to Lita Hornick, ". . . the poem appears to revolve around a concrete dramatic situation, the birth of a child, resulting in a father's jealousy and reconciliation." (P. 182.) This seems improbable, unless the poet was looking some distance into the future, since the poem was written in 1937 and Llewellyn was not born until 1939. However, the poem's original title was "Poem to Caitlin," and one may assume some other cause of a divisiveness occurring between the two lovers. So we could arrive, from the hints given, at this as a description of the general format of the poem: Thomas and Caitlin quarrel and are separated (physically and/or spiritually); he quells his pride and ill will and is reborn to love and forgiveness. But it is a very superficial description and is open to the objection that the poem seems to have greater depth and scope than one on the subject of a connubial spat.

The question becomes this: how far does the poem depart from the personal, how far from home does it go in its exploration of the map of love? This question cannot be satisfactorily answered because, of all things, of an ambiguous pronominal reference. The poem's *raison d'etre* is set forth in the opening sentence, which comprises the first two stanzas:

I make this in a warring absence when
Each ancient, stone-necked minute of love's season
Harbours my anchored tongue, slips the quaystone,
When, praise is blessed, her pride in mast and fountain
Sailed and set dazzling by the handshaped ocean,
In that proud sailing tree with branches driven
Through the last vault and vegetable groyne,
And this weak house to marrow-columned heaven,

Is corner-cast, breath's rag, scrawled weed, a vain
And opium head, crow stalk, puffed, cut, and blown,
Or like the tide-looped breast knot reefed again
Or rent ancestrally the roped sea-hymen,
And, pride is last, is like a child alone
By magnet winds to her blind mother drawn,
Bread and milk mansion in a toothless town.

Everything turns on the reference of *her* in "her pride." It could be Caitlin — the poem had her name in the title as a possible antecedent. But it no longer has. Did he drop the title to forestall too narrow an interpretation? It could be "love," in which case the poem becomes the anatomy of an abstraction. It could be, in the first stanza, "love's season"—

that is, spring or youth or the span of virile years—or "anchored tongue" (ships being feminine), but the later stanzas do not support these candidates.

Or, the "her" of the first two stanzas may refer to "tongue," and the "she" of the next three stanzas to Caitlin. This last, I think, makes the most interesting poem and discovers in the metaphors the greatest richness. It is at least worth trying as a working hypothesis.

> During a separation following a quarrel I make this poem. It is a time in which every stubbornness-producing moment of recollection prevents my poetic utterance: My tongue is like a ship neither unloading cargo at the dock nor sailing the ocean but tied to a buoy in the harbor. It is a time when (since the affirmation of life is a holy thing) that tongue's pride in a craft and art moved and illuminated by the great poet-shaped, poetry-shaping tradition, the poet's joy in oneness with organic life ("the great rooted blossomer") and "custom" ("the spreading laurel tree"), his pride that in his creative aliveness he transcends his mortal body, is diminished to a tossed-aside rag of breath, the spreading laurel of it diminished to a weed—cut and puffed away like a dandelion, a poppy, a ranunculus; it is a time when this tongue (as ship) is abandoned (mast and crow's nest down, sails tattered and windless), either its breast-line fouled on the buoy by the ship's unchecked circling or its skin rock-punctured (the line having parted), and (the first in pride shall be last), a derelict helpless as a child, is drawn by the winds to the breast (and ultimately the womb) of the sea.

In brief, Caitlin's absence has sunk him both as man and as poet.

As was said, the initial question of the third stanza is identical with that of the first two: is "she" Caitlin or Thomas's muse (tongue)? Caitlin seems the better choice. If the first two stanzas concentrate on what has happened to Thomas the poet, and from his point of view, the next two reveal what she has done to him as man and give the reason why.

> Her absence produces in me conflicting emotions. Sure of my innocence, I have a nettle's sting when touched; fearful of my guilt, my gift of tongues is that of a cloth pigeon. I see phoniness: virgins that are not virginal; seed-pearls of great price; Prufrock's sea-girls (perhaps I shall not see them anymore). She is always perverse: the reluctant sacrificial maiden and the foretokener of magnificent sexual union; she is as stubborn before me as a rock before the sucking sea; I see worlds in the grains of sand to which she disintegrates.

I need to say that I have given my imagination full rein in this stanza, there being no apparent common denominator among the images, and pretty much written a poem of my own. The best I can say for it is that it accounts for the images in terms of my understanding of Caitlin's character and her relations with Thomas and in terms of the psychological state Thomas may be thought to have been in.

> She is a contrary woman: the avid man who devotedly (but with intent to assault) follows her in her phoenix-flight to the fiery nest of renewal, and who invokes frustrated passion, unexpectedly meets with cold silence, his hope withered, desire unsatisfied; no less unreasonably, her iciest mood will suddenly melt into the heat of a summer noon.

One can easily imagine the battle between this passionately individualistic pair which occasioned this poem. The first rather than the second part of the stanza unquestionably describes the immediate cause. And now, deprived of Caitlin's presence as well as of her body, cooperative or uncooperative, he begins to act "like a child alone."

> Violent and woman-ridden as Samson (and feeling like him, "more blameless than the Philistines"), Thomas walks on the shore near the cemetery, thinking with pleasure of Caitlin's destruction. But shocked by the enormity of this noxious thought, he utterly goes to pieces. Since to kill love is to commit self-slaughter, Thomas lies dead, entombed in his own ruinous thoughts, sunk eight yards (one crucial agony) deep in the sea's primitivism, his mind bereft of all humanizing elements, until reason reasserts itself.
>
> Now, having recognized his sin, he makes his confession and explanation. The whole history of man lies behind his sin against love. The primal curse crawls with aspiring life out of the primal ooze. The lizard that came to walk upright is still implicit in the human seed. Man in his highest (as poet and lover) can be fouled on the line (like the second stanza's ship) and make a circle back to poetryless beast. The man aspiring to "marrow-columned heaven" may find his "weak house" so overcome by one aspect of his heredity that he falls back into the "vegetable groyne."

Thus Thomas sees himself in his vision: alive to sex and violence, dead to humanizing love. But this look at the worst having been exacted, man's animal origin and potential having been exposed, he now has his look at the best and sees, so to speak, Nilus' mud instinct with life.

> Eyes blind in the womb, blinded even in post-natal perception have seen beyond sight—he has seen through them rather than with them;

the magical brew of life bubbling in its cauldron has turned liquid solid, pushed embryonic root into flourishing tree—and to this mortality added immortality, the bird that flies from its nest in the tree to its column of renewal: the hand that can clench and assassinate can caress and create. So, stretching hands of faith (however lame) and trusting the larger hope (however faintly), Thomas sees Nature red in tooth and claw exit, hears the war drum throb no longer, sees "Men, my brothers, men the workers, ever reaping something new"— in short, sees the terrible world "as not so terrible after all."

I have probably made more of Thomas's little hint of Tennyson than he did. Nevertheless, some of what Thomas appears to be saying was said quite clearly in the evolutionary sections of *In Memoriam*.

Now, in the final stanza the pardoned penitent makes his restitution ("Yet this I make in a forgiving presence.") And once more there is a problem of identity.

Delivered seas my love from her proud place
Walks with no wound, nor lightning in her face. . . .

Bearing in mind Thomas's rather portentous description of his birth and death, can "my love" be merely Caitlin? Since further severances are foretokened—

And though my love pulls the pale, nippled air,
Prides of tomorrow suckling in her eyes—

and a forgiveness of her is in progress, it could very well be. But such a narrowing, after the preceding three stanzas, has the quality of anticlimax. The alternative is to read "my love" as that humanizing affirmation of life in Thomas the poet-prophet which had been destroyed four stanzas before and had needed to be resurrected.

And I see no objection (since the words of the stanza will bear either interpretation) to harmonizing the two contrapuntally, thus giving the poem its biographical interest and its "philosophical" significance simultaneously. Man's nervous system is so constituted, after all, that domestic hitches can color philosophical premises.

Thunderhead has been displaced by cumulus; my love walks without peril (hate gone from her eyes), a sea delivered from boisterousness; Zephyrus follows Boreas. And, though my love will suck pride in from the very air about her, I, from a cloud of pride, forgiving and forgiven, make this poem.

Very little critical comment has been devoted to this poem. One reason may be that it is not an easy poem to read with the same spirit that its author writ. Finding it impossible to survey the whole, the honest critic will forgo picking out the slight faults since, in their context, they may not be faults at all. The obtrusive line "His mother had a tongue that lapped up mud," taken alone may seem merely vulgar and melodramatic; at work with its fellows, it might be true and trenchant. Such a critic may hesitate, too, to speak favorably of lines or phrases that strike his fancy, not wishing to have inferred from his approval an understanding that he lacks.

I do not know that I have read the poem that Thomas wrote, but I have read a whole poem, a poem intense, dramatic, ingenious, psychologically searching, carefully organized, a poem intelligently dealing with a significant subject and containing lines as good as his best. There are clevernesses that do not ring true — "limp-treed and uneating silence," "Destruction. . . brays through the jawbone," and the like; repetitions of himself, as in the "pyramid" passage; overly-complicated metaphors, as in the first two stanzas; and melodramatic utterance, as in the seventh. Yet the poem succeeds as an organized whole, and the survey of the whole renders less conspicuous the faults and more satisfying the virtues.

## *Into her Lying Down Head*

Of the first version of these three prosodically intricate 23-line stanzas, Thomas wrote to Watkins: "I've never worked harder on anything, maybe too hard: I made such a difficult shape, too." (Watkins, 92.) He still had work to do, mainly with the concluding ten lines, which underwent total revision, before he was satisfied.

He asks Watkins for a title, himself suggests "Modern Love," (saying, "It is a poem about modern love"), and then gives a brief description of the poem's theme:

> All over the world love is being betrayed as always, and a million years have not calmed the uncalculated ferocity of each betrayal or the terrible loneliness afterwards. Man is denying his partner man or woman and whores with the whole night, begetting a monstrous brood; one day the brood will not die when the day comes but will hang on to the breast and the parts and squeeze his partner out of bed. (Watkins, p. 92.)

Stanford's comments (pp. 119-20) that it "celebrates what the songwriters nicely refer to as one night of love" and that it resembles Lawrence's poem about the mating of whales do not apply.

The curtain of the poem rises upon Thomas and Caitlin in bed, she sleeping, dreaming, sometimes moaning or crying out, he thinking about her, himself, lovers in general—and of a poem to be written on the subject. No man's or woman's love, he thinks, is focused exclusively upon the partner; present conscious promiscuous desire and memory of earlier loves make such focus impossible. If these are hidden in the subconscious, they will appear as dreams. Man, the heaven-headed, who discovered love, is still, simultaneously, the sex-impelled sea-bottom animal who must betray it. Of such thoughts he made this poem:

## I

Into her head through closed eye and pillowed ear came his enemies, her dream-lovers; to the beast-full ark of her mind a fired-up dove brought not peace but a man. From the dark sea of her subconscious (a ripple of the sea of human origin), unbridled sex flooded her mind; her daytime decorum broached, literary and historical figures, strangers noticed in passing, the city slicker taking her like a country girl behind the barn, all possessed her during the night; she was, so to speak, a tramp abroad on the Isle of Man, made pig-blind by Circean charms; like Eve knowing her nakedness, she is parted from her "nuptial bower" to "wander down/Into a lower world, to this obscure/And wild" of un-Edenlike potential.

## II

Her husband, made aware by her moans of her dreams, lies beside her poisoned by jealousy, (perhaps prosily expressing it) his faith shattered, while a bull-like lover resembling her earliest adolescent sex-partner (whether real or imaginary the one above all others to excite a husband's jealousy) lies with her. She cries out (looking like an angelic Desdemona) loud enough to be heard by the sea (which made her an animal), attesting to the loves in which her husband had no part; he lies alone, when she participates in her nightmare black mass, humiliated because he has no part in her uncalculated but ferocious encounters with the masked priest in the communion of the two backed beast.

## III

Human (rational, individual, imaginative), they lie in bed like two sandgrains on the shore—part of the beach, but independent entities —but the tide of night de-humanizes them; every aspiring but sea-held shell utters this truth: there is no love, only sex, in the sea of the unconscious. The she-bird yearns for the hawk; her mate yearns for

80 ·

tomorrow's flight of betrayal. Each grassblade in the meadow is similarly moved, is similarly separated from fellow-blades, similarly thinks the grass on the other side of the fence greener; each stone is similarly earthed away from the lark-song of love. The husband, alone and agonizing, laments in the only true night—that of the soul: "O my love lies as open to the dream-visitor as to the night-air; not seeking him and with none to defend her, innocent though faithless (because in the sea's chains), she is caught between Eros-Claudius and Agapé-Hamlet, since though Love is impossible without sex, it is betrayed by it. And the brood of her whoredom "will not die when the day comes but will hang on to the breast and the parts and squeeze (her) partner out of bed."

Unquestionably there are flaws in this interpretation. I am particularly dissatisfied with the last ten lines. One might have thought that application to the earlier version would assist, but as comparison of the two reveals, they have little in common:

From the madhouses and menageries
Of jealous night uncage the grain and bird:
    The love of women and men
    Scrapes and sings denied in them
The filth and secret of death is sweeter with the sun than these
        inconstancies,
    A loveless man mourns in the sole night.
Betrayed will his love betrayed find an eye or a hair to hate?
Will his lovely hands let run the daughters and sons of the blood?
Will he rest his pulse in the built breast of impossible great God?
Over the world uncoupling the moon rises up to no good.

            .    .    .    .

    O she lies alone and still,
    Innocent between two wars,
With the incestuous secret brother in the seconds to perpetuate
    the stars,
    A man torn up mourns in the sole night.
And the second comers, the severers, the enemies from the deep
Forgotten dark, rest their pulse and bury their dead in her faithless
    sleep.

In the former, Thomas suggests that her death is preferable to her nocturnal faithlessness. And in contemplating his own response, he advances hate and (apparently) murder as alternatives to religion. I do not find (or, rather, sense) this attitude in the revised poem. Perhaps a case could be made for the "incestuous secret brother's" being death, but I make no sense of this.

On the other hand, the poem does recall lines from *Othello*. For example, Othello's

> O curse of marriage,
> That we can call these delicate creatures ours,
> And not their appetites!

And Iago's "If the balance of our lives had not one scale of reason to poise another of sensuality, the blood and baseness of our natures would conduct us to most preposterous conclusions: but we have reason to cool our raging motions, our carnal stings, our unbitted lusts, whereof I take this that you call love to be a sect or scion." Thomas's roomful of snakes is a reminder of Othello's cry:

> Swell, bosom with thy fraught,
> For 'tis of aspics' tongues!

And Thomas's "made her limbs blind by luminous charms" is not unlike Shakespeare's

> practiced on her with foul charms,
> Abused her delicate youth with drugs or minerals
> That weaken motion . . . .

Certainly the theme of lust, inconstancy, jealousy, and betrayal invites consideration of *Othello* and *Hamlet*. But I do not find that such consideration explains the lines in question.

Without Thomas's hints, the most acute reader could go far wrong on this packed poem—the seminal idea (at least its conclusion) is not an ordinary one. He could wish that, to permit going more nearly right, the hint had been expanded.

# A Saint About to Fall

On its first publication entitled "Poem in the Ninth Month," this piece anticipates the January birth of Llewellyn in 1939. Thomas wrote to Watkins about it:

> As to the big poem—only provisionally called "In September," & called that at all only because it was a terrible war month—I'm at the moment very pleased with it, more than with anything I've done this year. Does "Glory cracked like a flea" shock you? I think you'll

see it must come there, or some equally grotesque contrast. The last line of the 2nd verse might appear just a long jumble of my old anatomical cliches, but if, in the past, I've used "burning brains & hair" etc. too loosely, this time I used them—as the only words—in dead earnest. Remember this is a poem written to a child about to be born—you know I'm going to be a father in January—& telling it what a world it will see, what horrors & hells. The last four lines of the poem, especially the last but two, may seem ragged, but I've altered the rhythm purposely; "you so gentle" must be very soft and gentle, & the last line must roar. It's an optimistic, taking-everything, poem. The two most important words are "Cry Joy". Tell me about this, please, very soon. I'm surer of the words of this poem than of the words in any recent one. I want mostly to know what the general effect of the poem is upon you (though of course you can criticize, as you like, any detail).

Of the three 17-line stanzas the most ingeniously complicated is the first. It is a variation on Wordsworth's theme, "trailing clouds of glory do we come/ From God who is our home." Since an odyssey is involved, Thomas has woven in echoes of the Homeric poem: for example, the shawl recalls Ino's scarf; the unwinding of the woven wall, Penelope's ruse; "song by rock," the Sirens; the "shrivelling flock," Polyphemus.

Unlike Thel, the saintly soul of this poem is not averse to making the journey; yet he is not unaware of what a fall is there to be experienced. For this homeward-looking angel it is not so much farewell as fare forward. Thomas's achievement in the first stanza is to have made a single solution of the two chemical constituents—forward-faring and backward-looking—working in simultaneity rather than succession. Contraries are not disassociated but assimilated. The process begins in the first sentence—though here with flesh and spirit.

A saint about to fall,
The stained flats of heaven hit and razed
To the kissed kite hems of his shawl . . . .

We see a flesh and blood person of dignified mien in the usual saintly gown, a prayer shawl about his shoulders, standing upon "a sea of glass like unto crystal." But immediately the flesh vaporizes, the personality disappears, the sea of glass becomes a dome of many-colored clouds into which the soul about to be born dives. Unrecognizable as a human figure (like Odysseus, supported by the scarf, seen in the waves from a distance), it swims through space as though floating on a cloud or gliding on kite-wings or angel wings (very like a trailing prayer-shawl). This diminishing figure swims or is carried out of the harbor (heaven-haven) past the rocks of the breakwater. Its voice is heard expressing its gratitude that it is seeing the last of harbor and house and ship-yard, hearing the last of friendly bells:

> On the last street wave praised
> The unwinding, song by rock,
> Of the woven wall
> Of his father's house in the sands,
> The vanishing of the musical ship-work and the chucked bells.

But Thomas has so organized his allusions and figures that, at the same time that we have a praise and a looking-backward, we have a looking forward and a sense of danger. Sirens connote peril; what Penelope is weaving and unweaving is a winding-sheet for Laertes; "chucked" bells may be delicately tapped—but also discarded. And the scene described is as much the *terminus ad quem* as the *terminus ab quo*—that is, Thomas's house "in the mud/Of the crotch of the squawking shores."

Similar double duty is done by the next image. The saint praises

> The wound-down cough of the blood-counting clock
> Behind a face of hands . . . .

If the clock is run-down, there is no cough, no counting—in sum, no time. There is only eternity with a wall of saintly faces and hands raised in a gesture, perhaps, of farewell. But for the saint, of course, the clock is wound-up—as he winds down the steep path from heaven to earth.

Arrived in the circle of meteors (as far for angels below heaven as Etna's top is above earth for men), he sings a farewell hymn to his now nearly-invisible brethren washed in the blood of the Lamb, ready to enter one-eyed Polyphemus's cave ("the eyes are already murdered") and become not Noman but Aman. At the last juncture, hungry for the bread and wine of the heaven he has left, he accepts the chaff and the vinegar, and becomes that puzzling combination of flesh and spirit, a human being.

Thomas's worry about "Glory cracked like a flea" was well-founded. The simile does not sustain analysis. Glory is not in any respect flea-like (small, wingless, blood-sucking, parasitic, noted for their powers of leaping, itch-producing). And since the cracking of a flea is such a minor matter (compare the cathartic drama of slapping a blood-filled mosquito), the image does not square with what follows:

> The sun-leaved holy candlewoods
> Drivelled down to one singeing tree
> With a stub of black buds . . . .

And yet, even after one has analyzed it and discovered it absurd visually and rationally, the figure comes off. The feeling evoked is so precisely the right one that the consideration of common sense becomes irrelevant. Oddly, where he succeeds in that first image, he fails in the second. The very powerful contrast between the candlewoods and the singeing tree is weakened because he has tried too obviously for effect in his verb "drivelled." His basic composite image—melting candle and pitch-fed burning tree—is altogether at odds with the added picture of a runny nose or slavering idiot's mouth. He has lost rather than gained power. The same may be said, perhaps, of the succeeding image of fleshification— that is, that "lurched" and "scuttled" are too strong, too over-stated; but the image is consistent and not made to do too much, the interplay of vowels and consonants in satisfyingly mellifluous, and the recollection of Masefield's "Cargoes" enriches the texture. "Crocked," in the last line works less well. It is too apparent that he has a series going—*chucked, cracked, crocked.* It should not have been so undisguised. Further, its slangy connotation (British or American) quarrels unfortunately with the serious note struck in the first half of the line.

The soul safely ensconced in its earthen shelter, Thomas has Caitlin speak to it now about the warring life it is about to encounter:

Come to your life in me in my bird-roared, sea-side house; jerked from the womb by disinfected hands, removed from the hospital to the house, look with faint, puzzled recollection up to the heaven's clouds. With sweet milk in your mouth, see that outside your new home the sour milk of human unkindness is steadily rising; see that the earth's skull becomes analogous (under his influence) to a madman's.

The speaker continues in this hortatory strain:

Yourself explode upon this explosive town; learn careful listening; give your fears in this black madhouse no sustenance; but (innocent doomed to slaughter) remain aware that, fleshified, your perceptions are already narrowed, your heart is geared to the blood-counting clock, and that it is time to fill another vessel and sponge with vinegar.

What Thomas means by "wake to see . . . the old mud hatch *again*" is a question. Perhaps like Thel, the saint has looked down from heaven's Being to earth's Becoming, then in the womb lost sight of everything, and now, born, recovers his vision. In any case—

Wake to the experience of mortality, labor and self-sacrifice, feel the bolted door of your lungs smoothly open and hard air bluster in. And cry joy that, as air enters you so roughly, you, so gentle, enter the rough sea of life, and that this magical second of transition, easily employing all the forces of nature, translates you from solitary peace to vital action, defying mortality, among the living.

# If My Head Hurt a Hair's Foot

No one seems to have liked this companion-piece to "A Saint About to Fall" very much, but probably no one so little as Robert Graves. In the course of a lecture, he offered a pound note to anyone who could make sense of the first stanza:

'If my head hurt a hair's foot
Pack back the downed bone. If the unpricked ball of my breath
Bump on a spout let the bubbles jump out.
Sooner drop with the worm of the ropes round my throat
Than bully ill love in the clouted scene.

Mr. Graves' challenge was accepted, but he had almost as little respect for the interpretation as for the stanza and refused to pay Mr. M. J. C. Hodgart of Pembroke, a member of the Cambridge English Faculty:

He suggests that the child about to be born is here addressing his mother. The child cries out that if he is to cause her any pain by his birth, let him not be born at all. 'If I were to hurt so much as a hair of your head in process of birth push my downy, but bony, head back into the womb' . . . Birth is represented here as a violent movement like a bouncing ball; and the child's breath before birth is compared to an unpricked bubble. Therefore: 'If even this soft bubble of breath should hurt you by bouncing on your spouting blood, prick it and let my life run out in bubbles.' And: 'I would sooner be born hanged with my navel-string coiled around my throat than bully you when I appear on a scene made wretched by baby-clouts, or clouts on the head.'

There are flaws in this argument. The hair's foot, misleadingly identical in sound to hare's foot, is not a hair's root. Also, the physical situation is blurred by the apparent contact of the baby's downy head with the mother's hairy one, and by the description of the navel-string as 'the worm of the ropes'—why 'ropes' in the plural? And by the metaphor of an unpunctured ball bouncing on the top of a spout—as in pleasure fountains; how the bubble of breath could bounce on the flow of lochial blood is not easy to see (blood is not mentioned in the poem). And why should the unpricked bubble become 'bubbles'? And is the infant experienced or ignorant? If ignorant, how can it anticipate baby-clouts, and balls bouncing on fountains? If experienced, how can it make so absurd a suggestion as that the mother should push its head back again to relieve her labour pains? And if it is so considerate and saintly as Mr. Hodgart suggests, why should it ever turn bully?

The general sense of the passage is perfectly obvious. The compassionate fetus, anticipating for his mother a difficult labor, says, if my birth is going to injure you in the slightest degree, refuse the birth; if I am asphyxiated before birth, don't give it a second thought; I would rather die than with hard blows injure a sick and loving person (or a love brought by its nature to this unpretty pass) in this place of rags and bandages and physical pain.

About this there can be no question. The questions revolve about Thomas's medical knowledge and his verbal gymnastics. Respecting the former, how can the mother keep the child in her womb? What is meant by the "unpricked ball of breath" passage? And why does Thomas speak of "ropes" when the umbilical is a single cord?

*Williams Obstetrics* answers all three questions:

> In very exceptional instances uterine contractions come on at or near term, and after continuing for a variable time, disappear without leading to the birth of the child. The latter then dies, and may be retained in utero for months, undergoing mummification or putrefaction, according as the membranes have ruptured or not. This is known as missed labor . . . Flatau has recorded an extraordinary case in which the condition persisted for fifteen years, when the fetal bones were removed from the uterus at autopsy.

· · · · · · · · · · · · · · · · · · ·

> Exceptionally, as the result of compression of the prolapsed cord, premature separation of the placenta, or much less commonly of tetanic contraction of the uterus, whether occurring spontaneously or following the administration of pituitrin, the supply of properly aerated blood through the umbilical vessels may be entirely or partially cut off while the child is still within the uterus. Occasionally a similar condition may be brought about by compression against the symphysis of a cord which is wrapped around the neck of the child, while now and again asphyxia and even death may result when the head is on the perineum, owing to excessive retraction of the active segment of the uterus, with a consequent diminution in the area of placental attachment.

As a result of the action of any of these factors the child may take its first breath while still in the uterus or in the lower portion of the birth canal. In the former case it may draw a certain quantity of amniotic fluid into its lungs, and when respiration begins while the head is in the vagina, a certain amount of mucus is liable to be aspirated. In either event the needed oxygen is not obtained, and the resulting air hunger leads to increased respiratory efforts, which are naturally of no avail. Gradually the accumulation of carbon dioxide and other excrementitious materials in the fetal organism leads to such a pronounced decrease in the irritability of the medulla that eventually the attempts at respiration cease, the intervals between the pulsations of the heart become longer and longer, and the child dies from asphyxia.

. . . . . . . . . . . . . . . . .

The umbilical cord, or funis, extends from the navel of the child to the fetal surface of the placenta. Its exterior presents a dull white, moist appearance, and through it shimmer the umbilical vessels—two arteries and a vein . . . .

A cord frequently presents a twisted appearance, the coiling usually being from left to right. As the vessels are usually longer than the cord, they are frequently folded upon themselves, thus giving rise to nodulations upon the surface which are designated as false knots.

. . . . . . . . . . . . . . . . .

Now for the verbal gymnastics. One of Thomas's most characteristic tricks is to modify or reverse a cliché, sometimes merely out of delight in word-play but often to achieve a shock and illumination comparable to that of successful metaphor. The cliché here is, "I wouldn't hurt a hair of your head," which means, of course, "I wouldn't hurt any part of your body, even so inconsiderable a part as a hair." Reversed, the phrase becomes, "I wouldn't hurt a foot of your hair," which extends the original figure from "hair of your head" to "a foot of a hair of your head." We can play further with the phrase. In the next line is the expression "ball of my breath." *Ball* recalls *foot* in the first line, *breath* visually and aurally suggests "breadth." Since *foot* is a measurement as well as a part of the body, the first line can read like this: "If my head injure you to the extent of a hair's breadth . . . ." Beyond this, there is the implicit "rabbit's foot" in "hair's foot," which, signifying good luck, is antithetical to "ill love" in the last line, leads to the "snared woods" of the succeeding stanza, and here offers the reading, "If my birth prove unlucky . . . ." In brief, though the fetus may not be a gentleman, he is at least the kind of good sport that

Eton is supposed to produce who would never hit a woman when she's down.

The imagery of the independent clause is triune. On the literal level, it means what it says: Cram back my downy, down-directed head. But *pack, back,* and *downed* are all terms used in football or rugby. Thus the sense of strenuous physical effort and of physical combat is introduced. But "downed" also suggests boxing and cock-fighting, even bloodier sports, and looks forward to the next stanza's first line: "All game phrases fit your ring of a cockfight."

The second sentence, though less packed with imagery, is somewhat more difficult. Still, it makes sense. One meaning of *to prick,* is to urge on. The bladder-like lung may be referred to as a ball. The air within the expanded lung is ball-shaped. Now under ordinary circumstances, the child's lungs are "urged" into motion after birth by a sharp slap, and the "ball" of breath is set rolling. Lacking that orthodox sharp slap, the lungs may be said to be "unpricked" — unurged. But if, within the mother, the child begins to breathe, its *unpunctured* ball of breath escapes from the mouth. This occasionally occurs, says the obstetrics manual, in "vertex presentation, when the head is arrested on the pelvic floor, the movements of the mouth being felt or seen through the thinned-out perineum." So the ball of breath is ejected from the lungs without benefit of obstetrician, rolls through the mouth, and strikes the perineum. This last, being the "urogenital triangle in front of the anus," is quite plausibly referred to as a "spout," the pouring end of the pitcher. Under these circumstances the child may be asphyxiated, as was noted in the earlier quotation, bubbles leaving the mouth as the child tries to aspirate. (Since I know nothing about cricket I am free to visualize a bump ball striking a very sticky wicket.)

As for the third sentence, Mr. Graves's objection has already been answered: the twisted cord with its blood-vessels does look like several cords wound together. But there is another reason for Thomas's use of the plural "ropes." The child has to be visualized in several ways: (1) As, say, one of the children in the Laokoon group, being strangled by a constricting serpent ("worm"); (2) as a criminal being hanged; and (3) as a boxer "on the ropes." It is this last that justifies the plural form of the noun. I have already explained "bully ill love in the clouted scene," except for the word *scene.* The word is apt, since the conflict is occurring in an operating theatre — which, of course, bears some resemblance to the squared circle.

The troublesome sentence of the next stanza is the second: "I'll comb the snared woods with a glove on a lamp." It sounds as though the fetus-hero plans an evening's poaching. But the content demands something quite different. It must therefore be that he proposes to adopt the secretive methods of the poachers, but removing snares instead of setting them. In the next line this anti-snare-setter becomes a fighting cock with little taste for the fight. In training, a cock has, each morning, ". . . half an hour's dancing, scratching, and shadow sparring, alone in the little pen in front of his hutch — and, once a week, a five-minute bout with another cock with gloves of chamois leather on the spurs." And unbloodied sparring is as much as this cock (who may also be visualized as a boxer or a wrestler) has a taste for.

At this point, Thomas drops his sporting terminology, but not before it has given him his money's worth. He has alluded to boxing (ring, fight, glove, lamp — as eye, duck, rush, crouch, ropes, clouted, strike); football (foot, ball, pack, back, downed); track (sprint, jump, hammer); rowing (bump); tennis (love); bowling (strike); and so on. There are also puns of a different order — such as prick, cock, ball. These latter bridge the gap between the sporting vocabulary and the physiological facts which comprise the matter of the stanzas. These stanzas, it is clear, would have served Addison well in his essay upon False Wit.

The third stanza repeats the adjuration of the first, adding only the further suggestion (in the last line) of an induced miscarriage. The tone becomes more serious as the word-play slacks off. The only notable pun is in the observation, "The bed is a cross place," which prepares for the larger concepts that are to be used in the mother's reply (as "arc," in "Bend . . . direction like an arc," anticipates Noah's flood in the next stanza). In her reply the mother accepts *Genesis* 3, 16:

I would not exchange my sorrow or agony for a labor such as Mary's or a magical begetting in which pain was prevented by talismanic bits of the Host; I would not be the mother of a pearl. There is no more escaping the thrust of birth than there was escape from the flood in the days when "all flesh had corrupted his way upon the earth." (Thought of the amnion, however absurd in the face of Thomas's rhetorical flourish, is inescapable here.)
You have made your gesture of independence and compassion; like a grain of corn you have enjoyed your protection, like Christ in his three-day sleep you have been translated; now you must face the world and take up the destined cross. There is a mansion of life and a mansion of death — both houses appointed for all living; you must keep your appointments. You must fall into the air and live, give over placenta for breast. You are neither to die nor to stay enwombed. The stone bars your entry to the sepulchre, and your life-making life begins.

Watkins' comment to Thomas that the mother gets all the good lines is quite true. The mother exercises ingenuity in the same degree as the child, but hers is intellectual rather than verbal. Her forte is paradoxical reworking of Scripture where his is sports-page punning. This may have been intended as a means of differentiating character. If so, some little of the curse may be thought to have been taken off the opening stanzas. But not enough to salvage them.

It does not seem possible that the initial conception of a dialogue between fetus and mother could under any circumstances have been made to succeed — unless the child were Christ and the poet a medieval believer. It is something like having Donald Duck make love to Carmen Miranda. To have gilded so festered a lily with ingenuities was to ensure not merely failure but absurdity. Only the last stanza can be excepted from the charge of Clevelandism. Removed from its context and taken alone, it might have a usefulness as an epitaph of superior quality.

## *In Country Sleep*

For Dylan Thomas, says Stuart Holroyd, "the greatest imaginable felicity lay in never emerging from the pristine state of unconscious and instinctive participation in the life of nature. He said so much in one of his last poems, *In Country Sleep*, where the phrase 'country sleep' represents the condition of man before the dawn of consciousness." (*Casebook*, 150.)

This is not quite the fact. The country sleep of which Thomas writes is that of a little girl, a "dear babe that sleepest cradled by his side." No more than Coleridge does Thomas suggest that his child is or recommend that she become an animal. What he hopes for her is two emergences: first, from superstitious fears in solitude to a consciousness of "Religious meanings in the forms of Nature," an awareness that "In Nature there is nothing melancholy," in order that "with the night [she] may associate Joy"; and second, an emergence from this relatively elementary awareness to the more sophisticated recognition that Death is not an external enemy but a cooperative part of nature's constituted order.

He therefore undertakes two jobs of exorcism. One is comparatively easy. Fear of the mysterious country dark, a fear heightened by the evocation, in grim fairy tales, of primitive man's precarious days and nights, he can argue to be foundationless. Moonlight is moonlight is moonlight; there are no ravening skulkers in the dell. She need not now fear nature and its creatures (imaged by the wolf) nor later the frightening natural manifestation of sex ("the tusked prince").

This last he only mentions—as is fitting, given the girl's age—in passing. But the matter of nature's innocence is less easy to establish; after all, the girl has no doubt encountered evidences of what seems to be the murderous rapacity of the animal world. Animal behavior will have to be justified.

Thomas's method of justification is his usual one. Adopting as his thesis the comprehensive generalization that "The country is holy," he Christianizes its inhabitants. The facts of country life are given such an aura of divinity that their real (or apparent) gruesomeness disappears. The blood of the rabbit or chicken which smears the earth becomes a liquid of such quality that both fox and tree reverence it. Thomas's daughter is learning the lesson of Thel. Or even (if we consider rightly the nightbird, the rain, and the spilt blood) the lesson of *I John* 5, 7-8:

> For there are three that bear record in heaven, the
> Father, the Word, and the Holy Ghost: and these
> three are one.
> And there are three that bear witness in earth, the
> spirit, and the water, and the blood: and these three
> agree in one.

One gets the impression, as a matter of fact, that when he wrote this poem, Thomas had been reading the late books of the New Testament and that his mind was full of the Last Things. For example, the poem opens with Thomas's advice not to believe or fear fairy tales. In *II Peter,* 1, 16, *I Timothy,* 1, 4, and *I Timothy,* 4, 7 similar advice is given. To quote the last, "But refuse profane and old wives' fables, and exercise thyself rather unto godliness." Since the country is holy, the child is told to "bide in that country kind." The verb "abide" occurs a dozen or so times in the second and third chapters of *I John* and with great point so far as the meaning of the poem is concerned in verse 28 of Chapter II:

> And now, little children, abide in him; that when he
> shall appear, we may have confidence . . . .

It is the Lord who is to appear, and as a thief in the night, as is attested by *Matthew,* 28, 43; *I Thessalonians,* 5, 2; *II Peter,* 3, 10; and *Revelations,* 3, 3, and 16, 15. Of these, the verse in *Peter* is most explicit:

> But the day of the Lord will come as a Thief in the night;
> in which the heavens shall pass away with a great noise,
> and the elements shall melt with fervent heat, the earth
> also and the works that are therein shall be burned up.

Among other witness of the Thief's coming in Thomas's poem are "The saga from mermen/To seraphim" and an "Illumination of music!" In *Revelations*, 5, are these comparable passages:

> 5, 13: And every creature which is in heaven, and on the
>        earth and under the earth, and such as are in the
>        sea, and all that are in them, heard I saying,
>        Blessing and honor, and glory and power be unto
>        him that sitteth upon the throne . . . .

> 5, 8-9: And when he had taken the book, the four beasts and
>         four and twenty elders fell down before the Lamb,
>         having every one of them harps . . . . And they sung a
>         new song . . . .

The poem ends with its declaration of faith:

> Ever and ever by all your vows believe and fear
> My dear this night he comes and night without end my dear
>                          Since you were born:
> And you shall wake from country sleep, this dawn and each
>      first dawn,
> Your faith as deathless as the outcry of the ruled sun.

As might be expected, equivalent passages in the *Epistles* are not hard to come by. Verses 13 and 14 of *I Peter*, 1 are characteristic:

> Wherefore gird up the loins of your mind, be sober, and
> hope to the end for the grace that is to be brought unto
> you at the revelation of Jesus Christ;

> As obedient children, not fashioning yourselves according to
> the former lusts in your ignorance.

But to get back more specifically to the second of those two emergences. If the child can be convinced that nature is not a place of murder and rapine and that the terrifying creatures of fiction are alive only in books and do not go bump in the countryside, however dark or moon-enchanted the night, can she further be convinced that Death itself must hold for her no terror? (I take the thief in Thomas's poem to be either Time or Death —each equally a translator of life into new manifestations of being.) Here, I think, Thomas does not make so good a case. His concept of the Thief in the night, however sanctified by Christian usage, can scarcely be expected to still a child's alarm.

I do not, when it comes to that, think it stills Thomas's alarm— and I have an impression that he is writing the poem to bolster his own faith as much as the girl's. Contemplation of the last things does not necessarily bring joy. As Stanford says: ". . . though the poem appears to assure us that 'Death shall have no dominion,' there is much sadness in the work, as of one dwelling on an imminent farewell." Whether he has forebodings of the world's end (as a Bible-reader undergoing the London bombings must unavoidably have had), or of the girl's death, or merely of the approaching end of the girl's childhood is not material. In any of these cases, however, admonishments in favor of faith, hope, and love, as opposed to fear, despair, and lust, would be in order and acceptance of life or death in innocence and trust required. He does, of course, relate his Thief to snow, rain, hail, mist, dew, falling star, apple seed, floating cloud, and earth's movement ("No death more natural"), but still the image that persists is of a housebreaker, masked and armed, an aberration from the natural course of events.

For the education of his daughter he might have chosen a more innocuous image. For the adult reader of his poem, it suffices. Thomas has given Death (or Time) the paradoxical nature of Christ, who put his yoke upon the heavy-laden to give them rest and who, the prince of peace, came with a sword. Death comes to steal and will continue to come "night without end" until that time when the plunder is rightfully his. (Until that time she and her faith will be literally "deathless.") But this Thief's coming is a carrying-out rather than a violation of the law; death is a closing, not a breaking of the circle.

The primary emphasis throughout the poem is upon unity in variety. The "saga of prayer" ties past with future; the "saga from mermen to seraphim" links the highest with the lowest; the "saga of prayer," the "vein of birds," the "Pastoral beat of blood through the laced leaves," the "Music of elements" image the union of spiritual, animal, vegetable, and mineral; the four elements unite in a music as the seven spectral colors unite in whiteness; the gull and the foal are in harmony with their environments. And, finally, the wound in the girl's side—her sensitive, mortal life—of the sea salty, goes round the sun, while the earth turns in her heart—and the Thief waits for its cessation, who teaches (Great universal Teacher!) "Himself in all, and all things in himself."

This poem, along with "Over Sir John's Hill" and "In the White Giant's Thigh," was intended to form a part of a long poem to be called *In Country Heaven*. In this poem the earth is dead, and its former inhabitants, now "heavenly hedgerowmen," call out to one another to tell

> . . . what they remember, what they sense in the submerged wilderness
> and on the exposed hairsbreadth of the mind, what they feel trembling
> on the nerves of a nerve, what they know in their Edenic hearts, of

that self-called place. They remember places, fears, loves, exultation, misery, animal joy, ignorance and mysteries, all we know and do not know. (P. 179, *Quite Early One Morning.*)

It was to have been a poem of happiness, "an affirmation of the beautiful and terrible worth of the Earth." But the poem was never completed, and these three parts are best taken as separate poems. As Thomas said:

I do not expect that a first hearing of the three separate poems I am going to read can give any idea of how and where they will, eventually, take their places, in that lofty, pretentious, down-to-earth-and-into-the-secrets, optimistic, ludicrous, knock-me-down moony scheme. I do not yet know myself their relevance to the whole, hypothetical structure. But I do know they belong to it.

# 2

## Love's Anatomist

# I See the Boys of Summer

This poem has been interpreted by W. S. Merwin (Tedlock, 237) as a negative view of life, one which "presents doom in the very moments of man's euphoria," and by Elder Olson as a poem of affirmation in which the boys of summer achieve a universal view of space and time. Derek Stanford seconds Merwin: "In all three sections the note of sterility, of self-destruction, and perversity, is struck." Lita Hornick has not summed up the whole poem, but her reading of the line "Man in his maggot's barren" as meaning "sterile man is envisioned as already dead and digested by the worm" suggests an agreement with Stanford. E. Glynn Lewis, somewhat betwixt and between, finds the first section to be concerned with creation and the second with decay, and the third section to be "a synthesis of these dialectically opposed aspects." (Tedlock, p. 176.)

W. Y. Tindall, giving the theme of the poem as "the life cycle from conception to maturity," and finding that the boys "are ruined because conception is the beginning of death," sees the boys successively as cells, embryos, and adults. R. N. Maude places them "in the substratum of matter and energy conducting the natural processes in objects, very close to those mysterious forces within the molecule that produce mutation (is not their father the uncertainty principle?) and govern the metabolism of the universe. In short, the boys symbolize the potentiality for change in all processes of nature." (*Essays in Criticism*, IV, 417.) On their literal level—that is, as boys—they are, he says, gainsayers, cosmic cupids: "being 'of summer', they go against summer, as Cupid had no mercy on his mother."

A reading of Thomas's short story "A Prospect of the Sea" assists toward characterizing the boys of summer on a somewhat more human level. In it, a boy lies on his back in the corn on a summer day, giving his imagination rein. Later he encounters, and somewhat frightened, has sexual relations with a girl. After the experience, the boy has a summer vision in which he comes "out of love through a wind full of turning knives and a cave full of flesh-white birds on to a new summit, standing like a stone that faces the stars blowing and stands no ceremony from the sea wind, a hard boy angry on a mound. . . ." In his vision he sees from ice field to ice field, from sea rims to sea centres, and deep into the history of man. "He stood on a slope no wider than the living room of the world, *and the two poles kissed behind his shoulders. . . .*"

But before the story ends, the boy is forced to leave "Once upon a time," the lure of love and imagination, for "Do not adventure any more," the demand of morality and reason. The story starts in innocence, progresses to experience, and ends with an image of the Flood and the Ark, into which fly a green-leaf-bearing dove and a raven.

The boys of summer may be thought of as hard, angry, deep-and-far-seeing, aware (perhaps only intuitively) of the need to synthesize dialectical opposites. Here Blake and Lawrence, both favorites of Thomas, apply. Blake's "Without contraries is no Progression," could serve as the epigraph for this poem. And Lawrence's insistence upon polarity parallels Thomas's thought. For example:

> There is a great polarity in life itself. Life itself is dual. And the duality is life and death. And death is not just shadow or mystery. It is the negative reality of life. It is just what we call Matter and Force, among other things.
>
> (*Fantasia of the Unconscious,* p. 217.)

. . . . .

> He believed in sex marriage. But beyond this, he wanted a further conjunction, where man had being and woman had being, two pure beings, each constituting the freedom of the other, balancing each other like two poles of one force, like two angels, or two demons. . . .
> He wanted to be with Ursula as free as with himself, single and clear and cool, yet balanced, polarized with her. The merging, the clutching, the mingling of love was become madly abhorrent to him.
>
> (*Women in Love,* Chap. 16.)

Lawrence is always insistent upon the individual's discovering and maintaining his own identity. And not only in the love situation. The child must break with his parents so that he may "Absolutely act according to [his] own true spontaneous feeling." The parents' imposition of any ideal upon the child, especially what Lawrence calls "the love and benevolence ideal," the official ideal of the bourgeoisie, emphasizes the spiritual mode of life—one pole—at the expense of its polar complement, the physical. So "the great lumbar ganglion, which is the clue to our sensual passionate pride and independence, this ganglion is atrophied by suppression." (Quotes from *Fantasia,* pp. 59-60.) In such circumstances, the child to save himself must make his break from parents, teachers, social codes, and official philosophers. He must grow up on his own—each generation must grow up on its own. And this is a destructive as well as a constructive process, involving the overthrow of Blake's Urizen, "Schoolmaster of souls, great opposer of change . . . dread form of Certainty."

It is such an understanding that the boys of Thomas's poem seem to me to be expounding. In the first four stanzas, an Edwardian or Victorian denizen of Mortimer Street, an upholder of the love and benevolence ideal, a sustainer of the status quo, cries Woe, woe, against the perversity of the younger generation, who do not heed their obligation to the church of tradition, nor prepare, like ants, for the future, and who, instead of offering reasonable, sacramental love, inundate their girls in the flash-flood of released frustration. Blotting out the sun of Eve, they, as it were, deny both due tithings and good tidings.

They sour the sweetness and put out the light, perhaps of Swift (in *The Battle of the Books*) but more probably of Victorian Arnold. They have denied the virtú of the sun that never sinks on the Union Jack; the fools have said there is no man in the moon. In their bellicosity they cannot, or they refuse to, enjoy the warmth and light of the sun, the romance of the moon. "Sun and moon," says Lawrence, "are dynamically polarized to our actual tissue, they affect this tissue all the time." (*Fantasia*, 223.) But for these young cynics, it is Sirius the raging Dog Star that has his tooth in the tissue.

Whether the third stanza speculates upon the future progeny of such skeptics (as Olson thinks) or sees them in their pre-natal past is debatable, and not important. In either case, there is a wry humor in envisioning the analytical mind so busily at work in such a locale. For the boys' present error is in their excessive and sophomoric cerebralism, which compels them to denial and debunking—the usual situation of the young seeking to find their own identity.

They thus seem to an older generation the stony ground which offers seed shallow rooting-place; their maturation will prove a spiritless making-do; of them it will not be said that they "grew in wisdom and stature and in favor with God and man." They will avoid the warmth of the good air. In Lawrence's words, the connection between the spiritual centers, in breast and throat, and the centers of sensual comprehension, below the diaphragm, is ice-blocked.

To continue in Lawrence's terms, because of parental and social emphasis upon the "idealism of love and of the spirit," the

> . . . center of upper sympathy is abnormally, inflamedly excited; and the centers of will are so deranged that they operate in jerks and spasms . . . . And we have the strange cold obstinacy of the spiritual will, cold as hell, fixed in a child. (*Fantasia*, pp. 165-6.)

Mortimer Street, unaware of its complicity in producing this effect, continues imposing its will—doing what is best for the growing boys—perplexed and irritated by their dissident response.

The boys, showing a certain precocity (have they read Lawrence?), reply to Mortimer Street's representative that passive acceptance of the conventional pattern lapses into a time-clock-punching deadness in which moon and midnight lose their life in abstraction. That is, if received ideas (the poor we have always with us; there have always been wars) are not challenged, they move agedly into a wintry fixity (the mind as closed and narrow as a bell-tower), and with a monotonous, non-creative sameness, we go through the same old motions. (Cf. Lawrence, *Women in Love:* "The white races, leaving the arctic north behind them, the vast abstraction of ice and snow, fulfill a mystery of ice-destructive knowledge, snow-abstract annihilation." And Blake ("No Natural Religion"): "The bounded is loathed by its possessor. The same dull round, even of a universe, would soon become a mill with complicated wheels.")

These boys of light are dark deniers in three senses: in their opinion, they deny the wintry darkness described above; in Mortimer Street's, they are destitute of moral light; in Thomas's, they are deniers still in the dark but by virtue of their denials showing promise of achieving the light. What they propose is to direct attention to the interaction of opposites, to establish the fact of polar accord. They will reveal the death implicit in the healthy woman, the new life in the "death-spasm" of sexual love. They offer as example the debt-paying drowned who fill and invigorate the sea through the efforts of the worm who undoes the fibres of the animal bones so that other forms of life may sprout up — the worm gnawing at once-alive vitals as Welsh miners (boys of light) dig in the earth's bowels for dead vegetable matter to give warmth and light to human beings. (Cf. *Adventures in the Skin Trade,* p. 117, which I am paralleling.) They will call from the womb's good earth a scarecrow-man — or a hanged-god-to-be.

Themselves bound by the seasons but summery whatever the season, land-creatures vigorous in their sea-origins (their lives sustained by sea-deaths), they turn all things topsy-turvy: make the sea rise, drop its birds, shift water into deserts, seek artificial wreaths in growing gardens. For, as Blake says *(All Religions Are One),* "As none by traveling over known lands can find out the unknown, So, from already acquired knowledge, Man could not acquire more . . . ."

But man does acquire more because "an universal Poetic Genius exists." And Blake continues: "The Religions of all Nations are derived from each Nation's different reception of the Poetic Genius." Experimentally seeking out the unknown, the boys cross-pollinate Christian beliefs, celebrate Merry Crucifixion and Bloody Xmas; now, venereally, they make love without the Xtian kiss; now, platonically, kiss without the Dionysian love-making.

The poles of sympathy and of volition foretoken a possible crossing. The Mortimer Street critic, however, is not moved. He still sees the boys of summer in their ruin. A superficial observer, he is aware only of what Blake called the Natural Man, subject to destruction, and misses the "Permanent in the [boys'] imagination." To this the boys reply that if they remained, as he has done, in the maggot or larval state, their lives would indeed be barren. But they are prepared to alienate themselves from that wingless, pouch-dark past. (Cf. Lawrence, *Fantasia,* p. 164: "Childhood is a chrysalis from which each must extricate himself. And the struggling youth or maid cannot emerge unless by the energy of all his powers; he can never emerge if the whole mass of the world and the tradition of love hold him back.") Their antagonist, emphasizing hereditary continuity, minimizes the possibility of a radical departure from the past. But the boys have the last word: they are not scions of the voiceless, non-inflammable Victorian bush, but, so to speak, "Lions of flaming fire, raging around and melting the metals into living fluids" ("Marriage of Heaven and Hell"): their symbols are not pacific honey and wax but revolutionary flint and pitch.

Their achievement of self-identity is signalized by the fruitful, sacrificial meeting of the contraries. This is to the satisfaction of Thomas, whose rebellion, like Blake's, takes the shape of calling in question what the religious or conservative call Good ("the passive that obeys Reason") and Evil ("the active springing from Energy"). Not that he believes that the boys have achieved the new Good. They are like Ursula in *The Rainbow:*

> In everything she saw she grasped and grabbed to find the creation of the living God, instead of the old, hard barren form of bygone living. Sometimes great terror possessed her. Sometimes she lost touch, she lost her feeling, she could only know the old horror of the husk which bound in her and all mankind. They were all in prison, they were all going mad.

But Ursula saw the rainbow, saw that it was "arched in their blood and would quiver to life in their spirit, that they would cast off their horny covering of disintegration, that new, clean, naked bodies would issue to a new germination . . . ." And Thomas sees the poles of promise kissing as they cross. The war may not be won, but it is at least in progress.

# *When Once the Twilight Locks No Longer*

As with the previous poem, the initial problem is to determine the *dramatis personae.* Olson's conjecture is simple: man's spirit speaks, explaining how the idea of death originates. Derek Stanford finds three speakers — child, mother, and father — which he sums up as a Tiresias-like human trinity. For Lita Hornick, the speaker and his "creature" are one: God and man and father and son are identical. Further, "the 'creature' appears to be at once the speaker's phallus and his son." (P. 103.) So that, in the second stanza, "The speaker is saying that he sent his phallus or his son (this is a timeless act of sex in which father and son are involved at the same time) 'scouting' upon the body of the eternal Eve, that very womb ('that globe itself') in which the speaker (God or the father) was at one time attached when in the foetal state." (*Loc. cit.*) Stanford, too, finds phalluses in the poem: "my ambassador" in stanza six, and the " 'poppied' pickthank" — " 'poppied' suggesting both its colour and its sleepy sated condition . . . ." (P. 46 Stanford.)

Since I have some difficulty visualizing these ambulatory phalluses, I have striven for a simpler, more literal reading. And I have added something to Olson's brief statement.

As I see it, the speaker is a creator; and his identity depends upon the definition of the words "globe" and "galactic." If these are taken as representing the earth and the Milky Way, then it is a creator on the cosmic scale. This creative spirit, not yet creative, rests in a kind of partial anesthesia. It (or he) may be compared to a vessel whose worm-geared screws are kept inoperative till the locks open to let in the sea and raise the water-level, making progress (useful work) possible.

It is (to discard the metaphor) the God who said, "Let there be light" (instead of twilight); who "called the light Day, and the darkness he called Night," thus creating Time; who made a firmament (which was Heaven) to "divide the waters from the waters," and said, "Let the waters under the heaven be gathered unto one place, and let the dry land appear." So heaven, earth, and the seas were created, and day and night with sun, moon and stars; and God said, "let us make man in our image," and "formed man of the dust of the ground, and breathed into his nostrils the breath of life." (One remembers the long worm of a finger, in Michaelangelo's representation, that sparks Adam to life.) Thus earth furnishes the stuff of which man is formed, and both are enlivened by God, the one "to bring forth grass," the other to become "a living soul" — macrocosm, geocosm, and microcosm inextricably united, the heart of God beating in the ribbed earth of man.

And this Creator sent his living creature forth to reconnoiter the new-made earth.

So much for the first two stanzas. Now, if God is the speaker, the following stanzas can be read as an historical survey. Man in due season arrived at the civilized acceptance of light and life which has come to be called Apollonian. But he turned from Apollo, from the grain-rich sunlight of this-worldliness (perhaps, as Yeats said, "vexed to nightmare by a rocking cradle"), from the magic of life, to death's dream-world, the Babylonian starlight having brought "A fabulous, formless darkness in." There is an irony in man's drowning God's grace as God had drowned man's sins.

The dream (stanza four) is a particularly unpleasant one because attention is focused not on death as a sleep, to which even the weariest river winds, but upon a living process of decay: the malignant, spreading growth of tissue, the liquid exudation from the eyes, the growth of hair on the rotting jaw, the pullulation of insects within the cadaver.

The concept of life-in-death, even the concept of the body as a kind of manure, is not in itself repugnant and may, indeed, be made to have a beauty. In the *Rubaiyat,* for example, it is the red rose, not Caesar's bag of blood, that the reader visualizes. And one remembers Whitman:

And as to you Corpse I think you are good manure,
   but that does not offend me,
I smell the white roses sweet-scented and growing,
I reach to the leafy lips, I reach to the polish'd breasts of melons.


Thomas himself in such a line as "Heads of the characters hammer through daisies" avoids morbidity. But not here. And the reason is that man in his comatose, dreaming state, excessively preoccupied with the horror of the Last Things (seeing through the opacity of cataracted eyes) is incapable of putting death and life into their proper complementary relationship. Thomas is describing a death-oriented life, not a death.

In Lawrence's *Fantasia* is a chapter on sleep and dreams which applies almost specifically. "Sleep," Lawrence says, "is the time when we are given over to the automatic process of the inanimate universe." (P. 246.) And dreams, he goes on, are in their nature automatic. "But the living, wakeful psyche is so flexible and sensitive, it has a horror of automatism. While the soul really lives, its deepest dread is perhaps the dread of automatism. For automatism in life is a forestalling of the death process."

It appears to me that Thomas sees medieval man succumbing to the fear of death and judgment, which he has learned by rote, and becoming a kind of automaton in his constant fearful anticipation of a life-in-death even worse than his present death-in-life.

I say medieval man, but *medieval* is too limiting an epithet. Thomas is referring to anyone whose life is impoverished by superstitious dread. In a sixth stanza printed in *The World I Breathe* but deleted from the *Collected Poems,* he assevers that the ghosts of the hanged and other demonic nightwalkers make "moony suckers" of dreaming men and shoot "fools of vision" in the back — that is, delude, render indecisive, parasitic, and volitionless those who might otherwise act.

Thomas's fifth stanza is a general comment upon the horrendous dream of the fourth. Sleep, he says, is like a ship on the active sea of time. The work of the ship's propellers (or the tidal movement of the sea of time) loosens and brings to light the dead bodies caught in the motionless sea of the tomb. The ship logs the fact of death. But it does not take note of (or at least is silent about) the equally significant fact of the ascension of the spirits of the dead in a new form of life.

What the sleeper sees is what Peter's ghost (in "The Visitor," *Adventures in the Skin Trade*, pp. 116-7), standing on a "green globe of soil," sees in the valley: rats and weasels setting their teeth in the cattle's throats, then flies coming up like a fog to nibble at their dead sides; then the worm and death-beetle at the fibres of the bone. But Peter's ghost sees what the sleeper of the poem is blind to: ". . . the blood that had flowed flowed over the ground, strengthening the blades of the grass, fulfilling the wind-planted seeds in its course, into the mouth of the spring."

Thomas's allusion to the spirits "Who periscope through flowers to the sky," sounds very much like Lawrence, who believes (*Fantasia*, p. 222) that "the sun breathes in the effluence of all that fades and dies"; that "It is the peculiar dynamic polarity of the living soul in every weed or bug or beast, each one separately and individually polarized with the great returning pole of the sun, that maintains the sun alive."

Stanza six resumés the first four stanzas. Here Thomas ascribes to "trick or chance" and not to the action of the stars man's falling asleep. And where, in the third stanza, the evil-working stars assume shape, in the sixth, man, through black magic, materializes a "carcass shape." The shaped stars put man to sleep; the carcass shape steals from man's heart the creative spirit's juices. I do not think a distinction is being made. It was man with his superstitious outlook who attributed to the stars their deathly destiny-shaping influence; it was man who wrought the deadening cleavage cf body from spirit. In each instance physical form (a reification) assumes a supremacy over spiritual activity. In the latter particularly, man had so engrossed himself in contemplation of the dying body as to minimize the *virtú* of revivifying blood, the blood which, as Donne says, "labours to beget/Spirits, as like souls as it can." (In "The Visitor," Peter's ghost was "wound invisible about the ghost of the blood . . . .")

The speaker then exhorts sleeping man to awaken, to disengage himself from the spirit-doping fantasy-monger and his falsehoods, and to join the sun in the job of revitalization. The course is clear of obstacles (cf. "The Visitor": "Now under the roots and now on the tops of the wild trees he and his stranger were racing against the cock. Over and under the falling fences of the light they climbed and shouted."); moony suckers and fools of vision have left the chase; the rewards are there for the taking.

The last stanza carries overtones of the *Communist Manifesto*. Augustus Johns has said (Tedlock, p. 27) that Thomas once joined the Communist Party but "finding that, as a Communist, he would be expected to use his gift for propaganda purposes, he wisely detached himself and returned to his favorite bar, a free citizen once again." Finding total engagement to a dedicated group repugnant, he nevertheless maintained socialist predilections. Recognizing this, the reader can easily imagine that creative spirit which made the world and is immanent in man encouraging his creature to throw off his addiction to the opium of the Mass and set about fashioning his City of the Sun. Or in Lawrence's terms, the creature is encouraged to force the powerful dynamic centers of the lower body to act in subservience so that he becomes "One flood of dynamic flow . . . upwards polarized, in [his] tallness and . . . wide-eyed spirit seeking to bring all the universe into the range of [his] conscious individuality, and eager always to make new worlds, out of this old world, to bud new green tips on the tree of life." (*Fantasia*, p. 265.)

This seems a quite satisfactory reading of the poem. No line has been tortured to make its contribution; the grotesquerie of peripatetic genitals has been avoided. It may be thought a flight of fancy to have imported Apollonianism, medievalism, and socialism. But one does not need to be so specific. These words can be discarded; a still-satisfactory though more generalized meaning still remains.

But it does turn on the identification of the speaker as a creative deity. The phrase "mother milk" in the sixth stanza and the line "That globe itself of hair and bone," the word "galactic" reduced to "lactic" suggests that Thomas may not be working (or not working exclusively) on the cosmological level. Given the structure —Beginning, Promising Development, Temporary Setback, Promise of Further Success — other forms of evolutionary change can be seen as deriving from the given imagery. Assume the speaker to be the vital spirit beginning to work freely in the embryo: the first two stanzas then appear to describe the rupture of the amnion, the draining of the amniotic fluid, the progression through the foetal stage, the birth and the weaning of the child. In its persona as Noah, the spirit sends the infant out to get the lay of the land. The world ("globe") is, of course, physical, like the child's mother — each "a bone and a hank of hair" — but each, like the child, is invested with spirit. Earth, mother, and child are doubly related: all share the same physical constituents; all share the same vital spirit. And in the child (as in the mother) it is the physical, the heart attached to the rib-case, which serves as the seat of the vital spirit.

(Or one may choose to think of the relation between spirit and world in these terms: the external physical world is stitched to the vital spirit— resident of the physical heart of the child — by the apprehensory apparatus's sewing machine.)

The adolescent, in love with life, pays his devoirs to the sun, as in "Fern Hill." But then (perhaps through an imposed superstitious terror as unsoundly based as astrology, perhaps by inference from sleep and bad dreams, but certainly as a concomitant of puberty) guilt and morbidity destroy the magic of life.

There is a passage in Blake's "Tiriel" that is strangely parallel. Tiriel's paradise has become "a dreary sandy plain" for the following reason:

> The child springs from the womb: the father ready stands to form
> The infant head: while the mother idle plays with her dog on her
> couch,
> The young bosom is cold for lack of mother's nourishment; & milk
> Is cut off from the weeping mouth with difficulty & pain.
> The little lids are lifted & the little nostrils open'd;
> The father scourges off all youthful fancies from the new-born man.

Since Har, the father of Tiriel, represents the kind of energy-inhibiting, life-denying moral code which induces guilt and fear of death and judgment, this passage and Thomas's poem have both schematic progression and substantial meaning in common.

It should be understood that I am not concerned with a possible literary debt to Blake, nor, despite the earlier citations, to Lawrence. The purpose of the quotations is only to suggest that Thomas is like Blake and Lawrence (and Whitman) in his denial of significant aspects of the status quo, his exhortation to his readers to blaze new trails. He is of the company of the rebel poets to a far greater degree than he has been understood to be.

# Our Eunuch Dreams

The burden of this poem is this: that given the love that casts out fear and the faith that moves mountains, there is hope for a fit future. The necessary action is to come out of the darkness into sunlight, observing that the sun is quite other than a round disk not unlike a guinea. A modified Hegelian triad gives the poem its structure; for it is out of a past reality posing as a present reality, and out of a present unreality passing for a present reality, that the future reality will emerge — not, however, by synthesis but by recognition and denial.

In Section I, our dreams — hopes and aspirations — castrated, deprived of the qualities of light and love, those qualities that give the steel of the heart its toughness and edge, pretend a youth and manliness they do not possess. Full of desire but incapable of action, their only recourse in their frustration is to wed the victims of history — the futureless present coupling with the dead past. The "repining restlessness," that in Herbert's "The Pulley" brought man from nature to the God of nature, here "unhouses the tomb" of men's bones and girls' shades.

What occurs in Section I is a natural phenomenon and can occur to anyone in any time, given the right conditions. Blake described the situation:

. . . . the youth shut up from
The lustful joy shall forget to generate and create an amorous image
In the shadows of his curtains and in the folds of his silent pillow.

*(Vision of the Daughters of Albion)*

Writing to the "fit fellows" of the future, he exclaimed:

Children of the future Age
Reading this indignant page,
Know that in a former time
Love! sweet Love! was thought a crime. *(A Little Girl Lost)*

Blake's page would have been doubly indignant had he lived "in this our age" where the self-created amorous image of frustrated joy is compounded by Hollywood's mass-production methods. Dreamers Blake's characters may have been, but at least their dream-world was their own. We are voyeurs of other people's dreams — and not even real dreams but canned dreams of dreams. But Hollywood is not to be condemned. It gives us what we want and what we deserve. In "We Are Transmitters," Lawrence parallels Thomas's Section I:

As we live, we are transmitters of life.
And when we fail to transmit life, life fails to flow through us.
That is part of the mystery of sex, it is a flow onwards,
Sexless people transmit nothing.

And in "When I went to the Circus," he observes that the people were uneasy, that "There was no gushing response, as there is at the film." He gives the reason:

When modern people see the carnal body dauntless and
     flickering gay
playing among the elements neatly, beyond competition
and displaying no personality,
modern people are depressed.

Modern people feel themselves at a disadvantage.
They know they have no bodies that could play among the elements.
They have only their personalities, that are best seen flat, on the film,
flat personalities in two dimensions, imponderable and touchless.

We live, then, in a double unreality, both as individuals and as a society. As individuals at night, we fold in our arms the shades of girls, not girls; in the day, instead of sunlit carnal bodies, we exercise flickering, arc-lamped personalities. As a society we are held by the past's dead hand, deluded by synthetic representations of the real. We see, not through our own eye, but the camera's; from preoccupation with the past, we lose faith in the future.

But if this tired (red-eyed) earth were to effect a radical (red-eyed) change, which simulacrum of reality would it destroy? The film's depiction of present-day life with, on the left hand, its underworld of bad other guys, and, on the right, its happy, prosperous, shrewd, patriotic capitalistic good guys like us? Or the Victorian Gothic moral codes that anachronistically prevail?

It would destroy both: blow the old dead back into their graves, expunge the films from the plates, "till," as Blake said, "like a dream, Eternity is obliterated and erased" and the present moment for the loving individual becomes real and rich. We will no longer (in Lawrence's words) "tend, through deliberate idealism or deliberate material purpose, to destroy the soul in its first nature of spontaneous, integral being, and to substitute the second nature, the automatic nature of the mechanical universe." (*Fantasia,* p. 254.)

## *All All and All the Dry Worlds Lever*

Against the denial of the flesh and of the primacy of matter expressed in Eliot's *Ash Wednesday* Thomas has presented here what amounts to a case for dialectical materialism. The universe (not unlike that of Lucretius) and all it contains act according to law, as a machine developed to operate in a given way does so. All is under compulsion — the flower is governed, the lover is driven: almost all seems machine-made, machine-driven — the blood is brassy, screws turn the voice, mechanical flesh acts upon mechanical flesh. But the machine's very compulsiveness defeats itself. The mortal, mechanical flesh, compelled by the mortal, mechanical world to couple, miraculously defeats mortality and the mechanical in a spring flowering. A sufficient quantitative change has produced a qualitative change to produce a higher synthesis.

Derek Stanford, analyzing the opening sentence to read *all-lever-worlds,* interprets the poem in these terms: "Sex, or a process analogous to it, a process of dynamic attraction, is . . . the 'lever' of the world without which things would be 'dry' and separated." In line with this emphasis upon sex, he finds that "Everything, then, issues forth from 'the oil, the pound of lava' (an image of the male seed and the womb's ova); so that the world can be said to be 'all of the flesh,' in just the same way as the poet's 'naked fellow' (the male member) is one with the 'Dug of the sea' and the 'Worm in the scalp'." (P. 61.)

I prefer another syntactical analysis: *worlds-lever-all;* I believe the first stanza to be geological and the second biological, with the naked flesh referring to the whole body (I have some difficulty with that male member turning up as a worm in the scalp).

The poem will then read something like this:

Interaction among the physical bodies of the universe, transmitting and modifying force and motion, makes things what they have been and what they are now — as for example the succession of geologic ages, the icing (or draining) of oceans, the combustion and melting of rock. (There's a magma-ficat instead of Magnificat here.) The earth itself, turning on its axis (and bound to the sun's turning wheel of fire), levers spring out of winter, and the flower (turning to the sun) out of the turning earth. (It does not matter whether or not they wish to turn; they turn.)

How is it then with the human body, in the past (in rudimentary form) thrown up out of the sea and still glandularly connected, and with a glandular stake in the future; and how is it with that body with its death implicit in it (thus by nature grubstaked), a field of force, so to speak, biding its crop-time? The physical universe exerts its force on man too, from flesh to bone (the corpse's lover) to marrow.

But no need to fear the force-exerting world, despite its Lucretian aspect: suppose that the blood is chemically constituted and, in Donne's sense, spiritless; that the heart is a metal-encased pump; that the act of love (tread = to copulate) can be reduced to terms of leverage (trigger and scythe) and machinery (the tractor, the seeder, the mill) — that is, the hard, sharp, mechanical, and lethal.

To know and to accept is to conquer the fear: the body compels the man, the earth (in life or death) confines the body; the atmosphere cages the sharp-eyed carrion crow (or, the flesh, cramping its life within it, also holds to its death). Accept the fact that the bone levers and is levered, that physical forces produce the poetry and govern the way of a man and a maid.

For the physical world, in its compelling, couples all things; spirited egg with spirited ovum; seed-sowing man of the present with his future. And generation, however mechanically accomplished, turns physics to metaphysics.

May, then (knowledge having dissipated fear), the peoples coalesce; may they in the double light of the sun and their inner light of love and hope, develop singleness of purpose. And man, flesh, compelled by sea and igneous rock, driven by the tough and impudent blood from sea to land from womb to tomb, though governed, may flower in the city of spring.

Thus the "all, all and all" which had been the object of the worlds' actions has become the subject, capable of producing action of its own.

Those familiar with Donne's prose may be reminded by Thomas's poem of the tenth "Devotion":

This is Natures nest of Boxes: The Heavens containe the Earth, the Earth, Cities, Cities, Men. And all these are Concentrique; the common center to them all, is decay, ruine; only that is Eccentrique, which was never made; only that place, or garment rather, which we can imagine, but not demonstrate, That light, which is the very emanatior of the light of God, in which the Saints shall dwell, with which the Saints shall be appareld, only that bends not to this Center, to Ruine . . . .

# If I Were Tickled

In "In the Beginning" Thomas will make a point of the mystery of the Three-in-One. "One smile of light" he will discover emanating from the "three-pointed star," and one signature evolving from three syllables. In "If I were Tickled," he discusses the mystery of One-Love-in-Three: the love that is neither that of the ape or of the monk but of man.

Elder Olson finds this a gloomy poem, one in which Thomas, a Hamlet finding surcease from unease in neither life nor death, seeks something that will offer diversion from his fears, if only momentarily. It does not seem so gloomy as all that to me.

In the first stanza, Thomas sets up a birth situation as little humanized and sentimentalized as he can. First, the child-to-be is not normally propagated in an access of love. He is stolen by a crow. Second, he is not normally borne by a mother and born, but dropped like a calf — with some emphasis laid upon the afterbirth. Nevertheless, the possibility exists that the product of this animal process will be moved by his pumping blood to laugh; that is, the child is not an animal but a man. So, one differentiation is made explicit. The second is made in this; that this man-child (no more, no less) will not be concerned with the abstract tabus of his tribe — proscriptions of knowledge, punishments for sin, covenants, redemptive sacrifices. His business is to be, not sub-human nor super-human, but human. In this, he is like his cells, which have only one function, and are not deterred from performing it by extraneous considerations.

In the second stanza, the child goes about his own — not his Father's business — of growing up. This is his one and only concern, as it had been the cell's single business to produce a male or a female — not a little liberal or a little conservative. Again he does not concern himself with such abstractions as Law or War, Crusade or Church Militant.

Arrived at adolescence, he is concerned naturally (like the cells) not conceptually, with girls and boys. He will, naturally, feel the urge for comradeship, called by psychologists Latent Homosexuality, the urge to procreate called by moralists Sin, the wages of which is Death. He will pleasure an itch by scratching — which some call Art.

In the understanding of maturity that sex does not stop a bad future and may inflict one, he will maintain his objectivity, reckoning its goods and ills. (The taste is good, but it gives you cold feet; there are crab-lice in the pneumatic crib.) He will not romanticize nor sentimentalize; he will remain aware of consequences.

Man, says the next stanza, is in part an obsessed, dying animal, an animal capable of being driven out of his senses by sex, the opiate of the animal-people. But he is something more, for he has the non-bestial, the exclusively human power of observing and reflecting upon his animal behavior and end. He can look into the future and relate it to the past; he can, in the present, distinguish the real from the ideal and on a realistic basis raise a hierarchy of values.

And this is the single affirmative, humanizing motive for action of our lives. It is certainly not sex, either as sex, or as some Platonized substitute, such as Romantic Love, Filial Piety, Charity, or Religion.

So what is it that should preoccupy man's attention? Death, love, religion? None of these, for each implies some illusory potential of the other-than-human. The man as sensible and realistic as his cells will be content to be a man identified with men.

In Olson's view, the protagonist of this poem is in constant self-conflict, repelled by the sex that compels him. And he finds the language, product of an imagination "foul as Vulcan's stithy," to be dreadfully revelatory of all this. There can be no denying a total absence of sugar-and-spice. But one may question whether Thomas has been forced by a subconscious aversion to the flesh to depict· it in its ugliest aspects, and that he denies it while essaying to affirm it. The likelihood is equally strong that Thomas has carefully, consciously chosen his ugly images precisely because an affirmation of man must comprehend him in his most ape-like manifestation. The dispassionate realist cannot allow himself to be blind to the fact that, as Swift said, "Celia, Celia, Celia sh-ts." The temple is holy in its altar-precincts *and* its privy.

I do not mean by quoting from him to ally Thomas with Swift. In a provocative essay, Aldous Huxley makes an important distinction:

> Swift's prodigious powers were marshalled on the side of death, not life. How instructive, in this context, is the comparison with Rabelais! Both men were scatological writers. Mass for mass, there is probably more dung and offal piled up in Rabelais's work than in Swift's. But how pleasant is the dung through which Gargantua wades, how almost delectable the offal! The muck is transfigured by love; for Rabelais loved the bowels which Swift so malignantly hated. His was the true amor fati! he accepted reality in its entirety, accepted with gratitude and delight this amazingly improbable world, where flowers spring from manure . . . .

It cannot be justly said that Thomas's muck is transfigured by love. His is not Rabelais's "perfect love." On the other hand, he does not hate it. Indeed, his repugnance touches those who admittedly do and accordingly legislate, and those who, not admitting it, reveal their hate by supernalizing the carnal. Thomas would not be a party to demolishing and fig-leafing the erected phallus of a Hermes and labeling the desecrated statue "Spirit of Communication."

Thomas's effort is to steer a line between Swift and Shelley. (Huxley remarks: "Considered, then, merely as comments on reality, *Gulliver* and *Prometheus* are seen, for all their astonishing differences, to have a common origin — the refusal on the part of their authors to accept the physical reality of the world.") If he is not altogether successful, it must be remembered that this earliest volume is a record of an effort, not of an ultimate achievement. And he achieves more in this poem, I think, than Olson gives him credit for: no reader of Rabelais and of Swift can fail to discern Thomas's much closer kinship with the former than with the latter.

# *When, Like a Running Grave*

In "Unluckily for a Death," Thomas made this most emphatic statement of his concept of love:

All love but for the full assemblage in flower
Of the living flesh is monstrous or immortal,
And the grave its daughters.

But Thomas had come to the idea much earlier. The present poem represents a declaration of independence against either the monstrous or the immortal. It is literally such a declaration, for the controlling metaphor represents a revolution shortly to take place. The actors are these: King Head and Queen Heart, dictatorial rulers; Cadaver, the enslaved general population of the country; I, a Spartacus who, when the time is ripe and the forces (blood) are ready, will lead cadaver to the overthrow of the dictators.

In the single sentence of the first five stanzas, the rebel Thomas outlines his plan—much as Hitler did in *Mein Kampf*. In the first line of the sixth stanza, the dictators answer. (Some of their propaganda has been described in the preceding stanza.) Their argument is quashed in stanzas seven through nine. And in the tenth, Thomas broadcasts his general manifesto: Lovers of the world, unite (physically); tomorrow Death, but today, the world.

If this interpretation surprises anyone, it will do so because it assumes Time to be on Thomas's side up to the last two stanzas, and the opening line—"When like a running grave, time tracks you down"—to be spoken in a spirit of hopeful expectancy. Since Thomas is generally thought to be fearful of time at all times, I do not think that my interpretation will have been the common one. But it is worth considering if for no other reason than this, that it makes sense without deviating from Thomas's syntax and without departing from Thomas's page to Freud's or Jung's. However, it ought to be compared with Olson's (pp. 92-4), Hornick's (pp. 160-7), and Tindall's (*American Scholar*, XVII, 439).

My initial assumption is that Thomas speaks as a young man ready for love in the fullest, not as an elderly gentleman whose powers are on the wane, and not as a Freudian theorist for whom sex and death are philosophically united. He is just a vigorous young man rebelling against society's negation of vigorous youth, that negative masquerading as a positive (sentimental idealism, virtuous continence, or what have you). Given this assumption, the poem reads as follows:

King Platonic Head, Queen Sentimental Heart—when the time is ripe
for your abdication; when I, whom you've kept acquiescent, turn,

· 115

Delilah-like, my homely weapons against you (when the confined phallus becomes errant); when the desire for a new order fills me toe to top (the desire is for physical love—its accoutrements are warlike; but it becomes pregnant as slowly as a turtle drawn by a hearse in slow gear); when age comes to cut my coat to the new pattern and to snip off your heads; then liberate me, who (a craven among cravens) am less possessed of love than a dead body is of a tongue (or a trapped body politic of a spokesman) or of the man-measuring penis (the body politic of its potential). When the vulgar blood knows its strength and the time has inexorably arrived to make fruitful use of that strength (the rebellious heart of the oppressed waxes strong in its hunger), liberate me from maiden heart and idealizing head, for, outwardly polite and neatly dressed, but with brass knucks under my glove, thus far chaste but henceforth a chaser, a man with night-must-fall eye (an end-of-Sunday man), I, to ensure that neither age nor frigidity shall straightjacket me in the grave as an unfulfilled nullity (the button of time preempting the buttonhole of virginity), I march through the land collecting volunteers (make the most of my maturity) while you, my rulers, having the brain in your command, transmit propaganda messages against me and my forces, such as Don't trust the blood; your true friend is virginity; join the eunuchs; keep your bodies clean.

Thomas has made his future program clear, a program to start when the time is right. Head and heart now in one line disparage time's effect upon the body. Thomas permits himself four stanzas to answer:

No, Queen Heart, your skull shows: your virgin city is entered; the blood-red banner with hammer and scythe flies over it. King Head (you death's head in the past, now good as dead), your Platonic planes can't fly. Joy's not a country (body) divided against itself: not a cancerous growth upon the healthy tissue; not an inconsequential, fleeting thing to be blown away; not an abnormal state to be eradicated by ascetic practice; not a removal from the sun and good earth of nature (or, perhaps, not a dark and narrow thoroughfare for Man via the Son of Man). In brief, joy is not *contra naturam*.

I put out the light of abstracting intellect; you are conquered. Joy is a simple coming together of people in the flesh in a country way; it is the evergreen growth through the coffin clothes ("boxy shift"); it is pugilist-Adam's straight right to the jaw of Death. You rule a literally cockshut (twilit) nation only—a Platonic cave, a government of, by, and for political abstractions.

As, when the leaning Pisan tower falls, it cannot again be raised, so with the body of man; the earth races around the sun, the wind changes, summer gives way to autumn and to winter; and man, in the midst of and a part of all this change, himself falls like the tower and disintegrates. Therefore, since the consuming wind produces consuming consumption (the asthmatic whistle sibilant through the mouth's o), since time (an enemy, if not used), lapping you in the mile-run, describes an o about you and ends the race, therefore, my fellow-countrymen, let us unite and honor for his time-defeating stratagem the body's instinct for sexual union and defeat with kisses the O NO of the world's lips.

. . . . .

This is a fascinatingly clever poem. Perhaps too clever. The sentiment may be that of cadaver, but the images are those of King Head. (It might be noted in passing, and probably irrelevantly, that Richard Hughes, whom Thomas came to know quite well, makes amusing use of the idea of dialogue between Head and Heart in his story "Lochinvárovic.)

W. S. Merwin states the case very well for those who do not think the poem a call to arms: "The perception of death as the very urge and joy in the act of love, in the poem, 'When like a Running Grave,' makes both sexual love and the love of the world impossible: the poet advocates despair of either and, instead, love of death himself for his devilish iniquity." (*Casebook*, 61.) But the poet who, two poems earlier, was going to be "a shouter like a cock,/ Blowing the old dead back," and who will shortly after exclaim, "Flower, flower, the people's fusion" seems an unlikely advocate of love of death.

# On the Marriage of a Virgin

Thomas maintains the traditional distinction between sacred and profane love, but with a twist; his sacred love denies neither the flesh to exalt the spirit, nor the spirit to fulfill the demands of the flesh; profane love is that which denies one or the other. Lawrence's distinction is not dissimilar: "Sex is a thing that exists in the head, its reactions are cerebral, and its processes mental. Whereas the phallic reality is warm and spontaneous." St. Francis de Sales had in mind another kind of hunger when he observed that "The spirit cannot endure the body when overfed, but if underfed, the body cannot endure the spirit." But the remark applies in the context of love.

Perhaps the best example of Thomas's sacred love is to be found in the excellent lyric, "On the Marriage of a Virgin." Nothing of frigidity or frustration characterizes the girl in this poem. Her at-one-ment with nature, specifically the warming, lighting, life-giving sun, militates against mis-interpreting her state as in any way perverse or unnatural. She does not wake alone in dread and doubt but in "a multitude of loves," ready and warm and welcoming. It is simply that her time is not yet. Because of her rightness of outlook, her willingness to respond in season to the life-force, hers is a "miraculous virginity" natural as food; hers is a humble accept-ance of the sort that can say "be it unto me according to thy word"— neither a timorous holding back nor a frantic casting about. Which is to say that her spirit and her body are also at one. This unity of sense and sensibility, of Venus and Christ (each of whom supplies a squadron to form the "navy of doves"), has the potential of the loaves and fishes broken and multiplied by Christ.

She has not come to a state of love from one of non-love; she has merely discovered a new and specialized aspect (a new at-one-ment) of her original love of life.

> . . . a man sleeps where fire leapt down and she learns through his arm
> That other sun, the jealous coursing of the unrivalled blood.

She is no less innocent, no more erotic, than she was before; she is, as she was, neither animal nor saint; but in a shared human-ness she has achieved fulfillment, a fulfillment impossible had she acted upon the chilling proposition that it is better to marry than to burn.

Undoubtedly a reason for Thomas's popularity among younger readers, a reason why he can move them to tears as no other poet of the past forty years has been able to do, is attributable to the resolution of their doubts and anxieties by his concept of love. There are contingent reasons. He was one of them, an outsider sent early to bed while Peggy kissed Lionel on the porch and "people were downstairs all over the world." He did not address himself obsessively to the downstairs people's social, political, or economic problems, so remote and abstract. He did not lecture or scold, nor demand that they study their Vergil and Dante. He spoke in their language of their most pressing problem, and in a marvelous voice.

He offered them physical love unattended by shame or guilt but not sentimentalized by Shelleyan Platonism nor made embarrasing by Law-rence's absurd mystique, and yet elevated, as they felt by instinct it should be. Elevated but not phony; serious but not sectarian, and yet not divorced from a tradition. His symbols related it to a non-parochial Christianity not subject to the narrowing influences of Puritan or of Irish priest. It invited them, as they wished to be invited, to disobey authority and promised that in that disobedience they would not lose but gain innocence. For the disobedience that Thomas recommends is a disobedi-ence toward those who are afraid because they are naked and make of their fear a virtue. Thomas is quite as much preoccupied with Eden (and loss of Eden) as Milton was.

Pre-fall Eden is clearly evident in the pastoral quality of such poems as "Poem in October," "Fern Hill," "In the White Giant's Thigh"; it is the goal of the voyager in the Altarwise sonnets; it is functional in "Was there a Time," "Incarnate Devil," "Today this Insect." If, in other poems, Genesis does not appear, Exodus "a chapter from the garden" does. Thomas said truly:

> I know the legend
> Of Adam and Eve is never for a second
> Silent in my service . . . .

There is unquestionably in Thomas's poems some element of man's search for the lost youth or child. But more significant is his positive effort to maintain the child or youth in the man. (*Lament* is a jesting example.)

His celebration of radical innocence invites comparison with that of Wordsworth, Coleridge, and Dickens. As Wordsworth has his idiot boy, Thomas has his hunchback; as Wordsworth teaches the salubrious effects upon character of the rural environment, Thomas counsels his child to "Know the green good," since "The country is holy"; as Wordsworth learns from the daft or the unlettered, Thomas learns from wayside bride and Annie. Coleridge, in "Christabel," and Thomas in "In Country Sleep," depict the shocks that innocence is heir to; certainly the sense of Wordsworth's great ode and of Coleridge's "Dejection" pervades everything Thomas wrote: innocence is Time's prey, but an access of understanding compensates for its loss, assuming firm recognition that we receive in proportion as we give. (Curiously, as Thomas gains the philosophic eye, he sounds in his poetry less the crabbed philosopher, and his poems are infused with a passion and a life missing from his earlier work.) As for the Dickens tie, no one has so successfully broken the Victorian monopoly upon the hearthstone at Christmas-tide as Thomas.

But essentially it is the innocence of Thel that Thomas invokes; an innocence beautiful in its unblooded manifestation, but more richly beautiful when it accepts but is not subjugated by the compulsion of the blood. There was more than wry jest or fearful anticipation in his remark to Rayner Heppenstall as they looked down at Thomas's spittle in the roadway: "Blood, boy! That's the stuff!"

# From Love's First Fever

Re-reading Shelley's "Indian Serenade," one dreams of what Sam Johnson would have said of it in blanced periods; sinking in the slush of inferior Lawrence, one desires Tolstoi's opinion.

It is, I think, with this, the twelfth in the first volume of Thomas's poems, that the rationalist hackles of even the sympathetic critic might begin to rise. There have been, in the preceding poems, good things, clever things, interesting things, promising things in more than sufficient quantity to over-ride doubts raised by Thomas's incessant concern with self, not merely from the cradle to the grave but from the sperm to the maggot, and his first-year medical-student preoccupation with physiology. At this point, however, the rationalist may feel like calling it quits, suffering some ennui from reading *One Little Pepper and How He Grew Six Times*. It is *Marrow Revisited* once too often.

Perhaps it is the shock of coming unexpectedly upon a poem of plain statement that is so unsettling. Preceding poems had required such prodigious feats of the puzzle-solving faculty, such close follow-the-leader attention to Thomas's athletic fancy that this poem seems by comparison an enforced hour's play with girls and dolls. The poem's plain statement disappoints in another way as well. One had wondered whether the obscurities had been dictated by the novelty and difficulties of the subjects attacked, they demanding an obliquity of vision and a subtlety of imagery not ordinarily required. Explication did not reveal that he had pioneered new areas of thought; nevertheless the pleasure of tracking him down had counteracted the disappointment of arrival.

There is little to counteract the disappointment here: no phrase to fall in love with, nothing to stir the imagination or to engage the intellect. The developing child is not a human being; the poem is only a case-history. And the poem's thesis is trite: the child develops from unity to variety to a sense of the unity in variety; the adolescent-as-poet progresses from imitation to individuality. Since the child is equally without personality and philosophical significance, and since the poem lacks both the gusto and the feeling of the miracle of childhood, no poignancy of emotion is possible to the reader.

Far from recalling "Frost at Midnight" or Wordsworth's "Ode," it seems to have its closest relation to the didactic poems of the eighteenth century. As, for example:

The mouth, with proper faculties endued,
First entertains, and then divides, the food;
Two adverse rows of teeth the meat prepare,
On which the glands fermenting juice confer;
Nature has various tender muscles plac'd
By which the artful gullet is embrac'd . . . .

(Blackmore's *Creation*)

The difference is in accidentals: this is third-person expository, and the Thomas is first-person narrative. But in essence they are alike: the informational flatness, the outside-looking-in objectivity, the holding of the metaphysical in abeyance to the physical—these are mutual. So Thomas is weaned and his teeth grow—so, as Holden Caulfield might put it, what?

So this. Some of Thomas's poems emphasize the "mortal error of birth and death," and some celebrate the triumph over it. Others, and this is one of them, suggest means to this happy end.

The means is love—love as a single-splendored thing, like Shelley's white radiance, save that it is not cut off by life's dome but is implicit in the quotidian spectrum. "From Love's First Fever" is a record, as Stanford says, "of the way in which the unitive vision of childhood yields to the adult's multiple vision." The issue of one womb, one mind, suckled by one breast, the child knew the world as one windy nothing: "The sun and moon shed one white light." Then he learned the double, a score, a million. "A million minds gave suck . . ."; but only (or mainly) to the mind. Yet underneath all, unifying all the experiences of growth and change, the one remains—"One sun, one manna, warmed and fed." (An apt epigraph here would be Pound's line: "The splendor—it ALL coheres!") This is Shelley upside-down, for the love is not intellectual but maternal, not coldly aloof in the intense inane, but here and human, and having its effect on Thomas. It is simple, homely love, soft as green grass, warm as the golden sun, that sees a world in a grain of sand, that illuminates song and formalizes light.

Thomas was right to stress the normal, the physical, the centric, the undramatic. For here, not in the flashy, witty, speculative, or newsworthy, is where faith, hope, and love flourish. In *Anna Karenina,* the clever, the politic, the up-to-the-minute, the self-willed (in sum, those removed from tradition based on natural process)—these, in this sanest of all great novels, are the ones who fail. Kitty and Levin, developing humanly, naturally, are, without attempting to be, the conquerors. Levin, like Dobbin, is a non-hero about whom only a flat poem could be written. Thomas has paid himself a great compliment in writing of himself in such a vein.

## Find Meat on Bones

This poem links with "I See the Boys of Summer" in that there are three speakers: an elder, a son, and the editorializing Thomas. But the attitude of the elder in this poem varies from that of the speaker in the earlier poem. Nevertheless, younger and elder are here as much at odds as they were there.

In the first stanza, the elder reveals himself as a teacher in the *carpe diem* school. The young man is to regard women as a source of nourishment, is to cannibalize them. Their death is not to be a source of sorrow, although, like the farmer who eats the cow run dry and plants a tree over the indigestible portion which he has rejected, the young man is permitted a sentimental gesture. But this egocentricity is only an aspect of homocentricity. Instead of coming to terms with the laws of levering nature, the young man is to assert himself against them—a romantic hero alone and defiant against the world, the flesh, and the devil of death. He is to be a combination of Byronic hero, Faust, and Dorian Gray, to forget that it is contraries, not negatives, that produce progression.

Since, like the traditional ballad, the poem develops by means of dialogue, the son now has his say. But since, again like the ballad, it foregoes expository transition, what the young man says is not clear. There are two possibilities. Either he has accepted the advice, destroyed a girl who had mistaken him for a man instead of the devil he was, and, like Dorian Gray, come to see the consequent ruin of himself. Or, despite having tried to be as cynical and self-centered as his adviser, he has himself been vanquished by love.

The ambiguous phrase "told her sin" offers two ways of destroying a girl: by introducing a virgin to fornication, or by causing a non-virgin to feel an unfamiliar guilt. But which of these modes of girl-destruction has the young man employed? And did either of them succeed? What happened to the girl is not specified.

I have chosen arbitrarily to interpret thus:

The young man tried to cannibalize, but "grace and girl" transmuted (to use Pope's terms) self-love to social-love. His sentimental gesture does not attend the girl's death but her love and life.

Against his father's Faustian aspiration (characterized by a Gadarene swinishness and compacted to Mephistopheles, that dangerous French poodle) stand fear of death (for the father the maggot was simply death; the son is not so insensitive) and the idea of the unchangeable though often-hanged god. The young man asserts his incapability of playing Faust to Gretchen, Othello to Desdemona. (It is not impossible that where, in "And the maggot no man can slay," the maggot is immortal, in "The maggot that no man can kill," man is. This latter at least parallels "And the man no rope can hang," and strengthens the case for a conversion of the young man.)

Thomas now comments in his own voice. He agrees that the universe is governed, but not as a tyranny but in terms of a blessed rage for order.

The elder, whose rebellion is a rebellion of despair, continues "crying and cutting himself with stones"; he refuses to be un-possessed; he does not accept the universe. Thomas counsels him:

Before death takes you, O take back this.

# Ballad of the Long-Legged Bait

It may be that no other conclusion can be drawn from examination of Thomas's love poems than this: that he affirms life in all its aspects and manifestations, from egg to decomposing particle, and with a special Lawrentian emphasis upon warm-hearted fornication, and castigates anything which diminishes life, such as hate, envy, avarice, asceticism, and with a special Blakean anger towards any guilt-imposing anti-sensualism. Thomas is conscious of what might be called Cosmic Pullulation: "Every inch of this universe even to the air and sea is crowded with people," he once declared.

The concept differs from Shaw's concept of the Life-Force only in that the latter seems so well-bred, cerebral, and hygienic, however irristible. An essential part of Shaw's wit consists in his manifesting the rapacity of the flesh in thoroughly-dressed young women, intelligent and civilized, who talk their victims into submission. He accordingly runs the risk of being misconstrued as a proponent of the marriage of true minds, a marriage in which carnality is kept in the proper state of second-class citizenship.

Thomas runs the contrary risk of so focusing on the flesh that love's intellectual or spiritual aspect appears to have only a minor significance. The "Ballad of the Long-Legged Bait" may be used to make the point. At a party in New York on his first trip to the United States, he was asked the meaning of the poem and replied, "It's a description of a gigantic——," or words to that effect. Brinnin, who was his embarrassed guide, comments: "His one-sentence explanation of the central meaning of his *Ballad of the Long-Legged Bait* was so lewd and searing as to stop conversation altogether." He excuses Thomas on these grounds:

> That may well have been his intention. He had come for a good time; instead, he was being cornered by scholars and critics as if he were their quarry. One of the wives had even gone so far as to sit with a notebook, pencil in hand, to take down whatever might fall from the lips of this bardic clown . . . . It was the sort of well-meaning affront that never failed to touch off his drive to quench any show of a sacred-flame attitude toward him.

But is it Thomas's remark or his audience's reaction that needs excusing? None of the scholar-critics present would have denied that marriage has, as well as its essential function of continuance of the race, the accidental function of (as Shaw puts it) "gratification of the amoristic sentiments of mankind." The queer thing is that, after a generation of plain-speaking, these post-Joyce-Lawrence-Miller-Celine literati should have preferred that Thomas say, "It's a description of the gratification of my amoristic sentiment."

There can be no question that in this circumstance Thomas was with malice aforethought shocking. Given another audience, he could have said the same thing in dead earnest, without desire to shock. In both circumstances he would be telling the truth, though only in the second would he expect or care that it be received as such. But neither time is he telling the whole truth. The poem, two-directional, means more than that.

The narrative element, insofar as there is narrative, is not complicated. A man embarks upon a voyage from a seacoast town. He throws into the water a "girl alive with his hooks through her lips." While a storm brews above, various forms of sea-life violate the girl, and she dies. The fisherman, with "no more desire than a ghost," reels in his line, various miracles occur, notably the disappearance of the sea, and the fisherman returns to his dryland home.

Thomas may have derived his bait's long legs from Yeats' poem "The Long-legged Fly"; in other respects, the two poems are quite dissimilar. (Titles of two other Yeats poems probably provoked Thomas to thought: "The Wild, Old Wicked Man" describes the hero of "Lament," and "Why Should Not Old Men Be Mad" is the question Thomas asks in "Do Not Go Gentle," which he wrote simultaneously with "Lament.")

For the idea of a girl as bait Thomas needed only to recall his Donne:

. . . then thy selfe art thine owne bait;
That fish, that is not catch'd thereby,
Alas, is wiser farre than I.

Donne imagines his mistress swimming:

When thou wilt swimme in that live bath,
Each fish, which every channell hath,
Will amorously to thee swimme,
Gladder to catch thee, than thou him.

But Donne's poem is playful, flattering, amatory, a call to arms of a passing fancy. Thomas's poem deals with a profound experience, a change of life. There is a difference between referring to a girl as bait and describing the puncture of a lower lip with hooks.

124 ·

Fifty-four stanzas long, the poem does not lend itself to line-by-line explication, but brief analysis will suffice. The narrative breaks into six sections.

1. Stanzas 1-6. The fisherman, bade fond farewells by town and coast, sails into the night and is later seen by passing vessels throwing his baited hook overboard. Quotation marks should set off stanza 2; line 3 of stanza 3; and the lines from "Good-bye . . ." to "raged in blood," in stanzas five and six. The flying anchor of stanza two appears in "An Adventure from a Work in Progress," in its comparable opening scene:

> The boat tugged its anchor, and the anchor flew up from the seabed like an iron arrow and hung poised in a new wind and pointed over the corkscrew channels of the sea to the dark holes and caves in the horizon. He saw birds soaring out of the pitted distance blind by his anchor as he swam with a seal at his side to the boat that stamped the water. He gripped on the bows like a mane, the arrowing anchor shot north, and the boat sped beneath it with winds and invisible fire puffing and licking. His animal boat split the water into a thousand boat-sized seas, bit deep into the flying shoals, halved and multiplied the flying fishes, it dived under waves like a wooden dolphin and wagged the fingering wrack off its stern, it swerved past a black and gold buoy with cathedral chimes and kept cold north.

This flying anchor (related to the symbol for Hope) functions in the poem as an antithesis to the hooks. At first removed from things of the earth earthy—or fleshly—it points the way to true north. When at last it plunges, its flukes hold fast to a church floor.

2. Stanzas 7-15. The fisherman is oblivious of all but the activity of his bait. Bell buoys warn him that she is pleasuring herself among small fish, but that whales are nearby. (The last two lines of stanza eight and the first two of nine should be in quotes. As *castrati,* these "rocked buoys" may be likened to the watchful, suspicious eunuchs of the harem; more significantly, they recall and strengthen the theme of renunciation.)

A storm strikes; the whales come to the bait. She eludes them for a time amid great turbulence.

3. Stanzas 16-21. The bait is taken. The boat (quotes are in force from line 3 of stanza 17 to the end of 21) describes and celebrates (its mast is a bell-spire, its decks are drums) the bait's "wedding" with birds, bulls of Biscay, dolphins, an octopus, a polar eagle, and a seal.

4. Stanzas 22-32. Grave-robbing, meat-eating hyena and air-cleaving, sweet-singing nightingale unite in rejoicing over the bait's death, the

deflation of illusion into reality: the desiring flesh cut down to size and seen in its proper perspective. This desire, imaged as bread, the staff of life, is shredded and scattered, turned by feeding birds and scavenger crabs into its elements to be excreted (bird and crab equate with nightingale and hyena). Thus the desire undergoes its fish-hyena-seabird-change. The temptation of the flesh (personified as Tempter, Sussannah, Sheba, Sin, Lucifer, and Venus) disappears. The change in the quality of love is expressed in the star-striking of Venus, by means of which the natural course of events reasserts itself and the domination of black is overcome.

5. Stanzas 33-44. An arctic frigidity attends upon the desire's death. But this, the sexual death producing the death of desire, also produces life, a life which has its roots in the dead past. A long line of ancestors is reborn. They come to prophesy that the new life must round their mortal circle. But "God" also arises to lend that bleak prospect a meaning, a purposiveness, a quality of love and compassion.

6. Stanzas 45-54. The civilizing function of successful love is described: a future prospect is seen (in terms of the historical past). And the fisherman returns, no animal, no angel, but a man, a husband, and a father. But, though his ship anchors in a church, and he stands in the door of his home safe and sound on land, he has returned by the same streets that led him to the sea in the first place, and his heart, still long-legged, is in his hand ready to be offered to the next passer-by. The cycle is renewable.

The archetypal voyage-motif can be made to serve many purposes, description of the sexual act among them. In this poem, the protagonist leaves the safe and familiar for the alien and perilous—the rational for the irrational. He encounters storms of passion, is party to the rending of flesh, witnesses the deep snouting that tumescence is capable of, feels at one with all animal life, arouses vigorous activity which subsides into a kind of death, feels the subsidence of his own desire, recognizes the miracle of being the agent that connects the past with the future and the miracle of tenderness supplanting lust (both analogous to feelings experienced by travelers), and returns from the perilous seas re-individuated but not forlorn.

Thomas's explanation of the poem was not "lewd and searing," but objectively precise, as far as it went. But beyond this meaning, this Henry Miller line of development, and running counter to it, is its Coleridge line. For the poem, after its fashion, is a re-telling of the Ancient Mariner's tale. At the same time that it projects the experience of the pleasures of the flesh, it is advancing the argument that only through subjugation of the flesh is whole-man-ness possible. Derek Stanford's criticism that "unlike the story of Leda and the Swan or Europa and the Bull, the

*Long-legged Bait* cannot plead (as far as I know) a mythological pur-
pose," is in error. As Glauco Cambon says in his provocative "Two Crazy
Boats" (*English Miscellany,* 7, 251), a comparison of Rimbaud's *Bateau
Ivre* and the present poem:

> . . . they are so similar that one would think they came from the
> same shipyard. The astonishing fact is that Thomas was avowedly
> unaware of his French forerunner's creation when he wrote his
> "Ballad," which, I think, makes the affinity only the more interesting,
> because archetypal instead of derivational. Each in his own idiom,
> poets do sometimes strike the same strings, tapping on the universal
> reservoir of mankind's myths.

Myth reveals through narrative the nature of the relation between the
otherworldly and the worldly, and the force of the imperatives that
govern to ensure the rightness of that relation. A defect of love impels
Coleridge's hero to a breach of the laws of hospitality (if the word applies
to animals). The poem is a record of the response of immutable justice.
The Mariner, at the outset of his voyage, seems to have been unaware
of any deficiency. He can, when it occurs, describe the senseless act, but
he can offer no reason for its commission. (One might infer that a
purposeful power compels the act for his completer self-understanding.)
Thomas's hero, on the other hand, is aware of his deviation from right
love; the voyage is made in order to eradicate an understood sinfulness.

The sin is lust; his single-visioned heart's desire is for the flesh of a girl,
and it is this desire he throws into the sea from whose blood-and-sperm-
spattered waves Venus emerged, and to whose primordial ooze rational
life owes its origin. Restored to its element (defined and differentiated),
reduced to its natural proportions, his lust dies and the fisherman is
rewarded. Bird and fish (the natural) praise him (for no longer being
bird, fish, or beast), and the supernatural evidences itself. The world,
the flesh, and the Devil are defeated; time is given another dimension; an
aspiring, compassionating spirit invests the dead desire; an earthly paradise
succeeds the chaotic seascape; a nature methodized asserts itself; the
prodigal fisherman returns to his home of love (once furious, now not,
but again to be), anchors his ship in a spiritual place and takes his place
at the door of his home, heart-whole, lust-free. The whole thing had been
summed up in the two lines

> The sun shipwrecked west on a pearl
> And the moon swam out of its hulk

which, if not credible naturally, are logical symbolically.

In normal allegory, narrative and theme run together as a team; in this poem they collide headlong. It is no wonder that the poem has a violence and a quality of thickness, even discounting the imagery, which makes the *Rime* seem thin and clear as brook-water by comparison.

And thickening the mixture still further is a third element of meaning. Like "In the Beginning" and others, "Bait" is a "creation" poem, and like "Twilight Locks," a description of an evolutionary process. Consider the fisherman as the creative force modifying chaos through the power of love. The spirit implicit in matter suffers its sea-change and matter assumes new form. The waters under heaven are gathered together and the dry land appears; men and women and animals come to inhabit the earth; the desire in them seeks to become like the original, untrammeled creative force, not rapacious animal lust but formalizing love, and land is cultivated, horses are tamed, cities are built, religions arise.

Elder Olson has, I think, somewhat distorted the poem's meaning. It has, he says, "as its bare theme the notion that salvation must be won through mortification of the flesh." And he says again: ". . . the subjugation of sensual desire becomes mysterious and cruel as the sacrifice of the girl, the salvation takes on the beauty and mystery of the resurrection of the dead and of the past from the sea." (Pp. 24-5.) These, and his later comment (p. 51) that "the fisherman comes to his true home at last, Eden, from which like the Prodigal Son he had been absent; and he possesses his heart again . . . now purified of all sensual desire," in their choice of words from the vocabulary of asceticism and their ignoring that sexual experience is being described lend the poem an aura of religiosity which it does not possess.

In a criticism of Olson's interpretation, Richard Condon has produced another sort of distortion. His argument is that the fisherman embarks upon a "Lawrentian quest for innocence through a mystical immersion in sexuality." (*Explicator,* XVI, p. 37.) The townspeople, he says, are "aghast at his audacity" and warn him not to leave on his dangerous journey. This, it seems to me, is a plain misreading of the first three stanzas, in which the town wishes him luck, the sand whispers an affectionate good-bye, and the "looking land" adjures him, "For my sake sail, and never look back." These are the friendliest farewells imaginable.

But a negative beginning is necessary to his argument, because what he wants to prove is that "The fisherman's quest for a supra-human experience through the sexual act . . . ends in the pathetic knowledge that it is the most human of acts, a solace by which earth-bound mortals seek to escape their mortal plight only to entrench themselves more inescapably in it." That is, the fisherman, who has "seemingly found a release from the spiritual travail of guilt and sin" has also had the "unexpected and horrifying revelation" that the end of sex is "the ineluctably physical commonplace of birth."

I do not think that this was so "unexpected" a revelation to Thomas as Condon implies, nor (see "Vision and Prayer") that he found birth an ineluctable commonplace. I do not, indeed, think that Thomas sought a "mystical" immersion in sexuality. The word "mystical," like Olson's words "mortification" and "salvation," has the wrong connotations. It may apply to the experiences in "A Winter's Tale" and "Vision and Prayer," neither of which involves an immersion in sexuality, but not to "Unluckily for a Death," which does.

I should say that Thomas is trying for a position not unlike that of Wallace Stevens when he said, in "Esthétique du Mal,"

> The greatest poverty is not to live
> In a physical world, to feel that one's desire
> Is too difficult to tell from despair.

A physical world, it must be remembered, whose resident can make, out of what he sees, hears, and feels,

> So many selves, so many sensuous worlds,
> As if the air, the mid-day air, was swarming
> With the metaphysical changes that occur,
> Merely in living as and where we live.

These lines are very cool and clean, unruffled and asexual. They are nevertheless an exaltation of the physical, which includes the turbulently sexual. Stevens does not, of course, rest in the physical, but invests it with such gradational possibilities of qualitative change that it passes beyond itself, as water turns to steam.

As Thomas sounds unlike Shaw, he sounds unlike Stevens. As, intellectually, there is a relation between Thomas and Shaw, there is one between him and Stevens. It does not clearly show because his vocabulary, his images, his focus of attention, and, of course, his own personal history are so different. Where Stevens is trying to establish a philosophical basis of belief, Thomas is trying to find a religious faith. Where Stevens in general eschews Christian imagery, Thomas clings to it. But their fundamental points of view are not by any means so widely divergent.

In brief, I do not think that in this poem Thomas tries to raise sex to a mystique and is disappointed, nor that he is bent upon a "mortification of the flesh" in which he succeeds. The poem has its feet firmly planted in reality: the events in the narrative coincide exactly with the emotional changes that occur to the male enjoying his "gigantic ———." Nor does the poem reveal anything similar to Pauline or Augustinian repugnance for sex. His attitude is Aquinian. It is not that he denies the necessity

· 129

and virtue of animal and vegetable love, but that he does not want them to pre-empt the positions or impede the functions of intellectual and spiritual love. He insists upon the difference between rut and the marriage of true minds as Blake does upon the difference between Innocence and Experience; and he insists upon their necessary interpenetration as Blake does upon the indispensability of a marriage of Heaven and Hell. The sweetness and light of honey and wax are not compromised by being located in the lion's carcass.

# In the White Giant's Thigh

The tone of Wordsworth's little elegy to Lucy is of a dead finality unexpected in one whose intimations were of immortality.

No motion has she now, no force;
   She neither hears nor sees;
Rolled round in earth's diurnal course,
   With rocks, and stones, and trees.

Lucy would seem neither to feel nor to be a presence that disturbs.

The case is quite otherwise with the women of Thomas's poem. In life, they outdid all surrounding nature in their coupling, unconfined, as they were, to periods of rut, uninterrupted by the urge for hibernation. They outdid their farmyard and forest friends; but they were not severed from them. This "hedgerow of joys," this "bloom of wayside brides," came to love as naturally, as uninhibitedly as a "torch of foxes." It is only that the nature in them is raised to a higher power. One does not think of Lucy in these terms.

And in death, the life is still in them. They may be rolled with and barren as boulders in the "cudgelling, hacked hill," but impassive, inexpressive, inactive they are not. The thermodynamic desire in them to procreate did not cease at death. If they did not have breasts for mouthing babes, after the dunghill assignation, they fed the "long desirers," and, dung themselves, were of virtue to the grass and to the trees and, to go all the way with Lawrence, to the meridian sun. In short, having given a bright penny for the old guy, they are still a torch of Fawkes fires.

The poem's irony consists in this: that these butter-ball goose-girls, for whom farm-cart ("gambo") or pig-sty was featherbed enough and who ought to have had so many children they didn't know what to do, in reality had cupboards bare as Mother Hubbard's, that while they lived they produced for their simple Jack Horners no plums, however (like Jack and Jill) they tumbled in the hay. Yet, as the earth did not waste a drop of Jill's spilt water, it did not (though it seemed to them to do so) waste its Jills. Like Guy Fawkes (and John Brown) they failed in their immediate efforts, but their memory is phosphorescent still and, like the moon, "conceiving," since it holds Thomas hard and teaches him "that love that is evergreen."

Though there is pathos, there is no doubt or uncertainty in this poem. Thermodynamic thrift is implicit as it is in so many of Thomas's poems. The rusted kettles and clocks are mineral in the earth of the hay-fields, or where the rust-edged bracken has grown, covering the girls' destroyed homes, the rust-red recalling the sap-stained billhooks that cut the bird-inhabited hedges. What seems to destroy, does not; what appears to be destroyed, is not. The hedge flashed low by the billhooks grows the thicker, as, in an ever-green love, does the hedgerow of joys. The individual is swallowed up; sun and rain enforce anonymity. But the person as process never ceases: each penetrates to the sun's bone as the sun had to theirs, which is why that sun is quenchless. The poem thus ends on a note of triumph, and one must go back to the opening lines to be reminded that, for a human being, neither anonymous integration into the process nor celebration by a wandering poet is enough. As parts of the whole, the women flame; as individuals, they are daughters of darkness, alone and yearning and never to be satisfied.

Though there are points of similarity, this is a quite different poem from "The Tombstone Told." There, instead of a graveyard of girls, unnamed, was a single and identifiable girl with a unique history. There, the girl spoke, as if in her own voice; these are heard through the mournful cry of the curlew. In the former, a real-life situation is dramatically heightened and its pathos given a factitious seriousness through paradox. But it is only apparently philosophical and it has no element of myth.

The present poem, in which the girls are qualities of nature—in life as in death—is a true expression of a philosophical point of view; and no element of historicity, no tricky dramatic device, is permitted to adulterate its significance. It is neither history nor fiction, but myth. That their voice is heard in the curlew's cry is credible, as it is not that the girl's should speak through a tombstone's carved bird.

# Author's Prologue

In outlining "Poem on his Birthday" for Bill Read, Thomas raised the question why a man should exult when confronted by the inevitability of a "lunatic" atomic war. He did, in that poem, exult. And there is, if not exultation, at least a note of hope in this prologue written especially for the soon-to-be-published *Collected Poems*. W. S. Merwin describes it as "not an exultation proper to the liberal humanist; it is the exuberance of a man drunk with the holiness and wonder of creation, with the reality and terror and ubiquity of death, but with love as God, as more powerful than death." (*Casebook,* 64.)

This statement is somewhat stronger than the poem warrants, for accompanying the intoxication with the natural world is a sense of desperate fear for the human. Olson has said that the poem "makes a racket quite beyond any demand of its emotion or thought." (Olson, 21-2.) It *is* a noisy poem, but for a very good reason: the voice of love needs to be raised somewhat to capture attention from the mass media of hate. It may be, too, that Thomas needs to shout to relieve his feeling of solitary ineffectuality. For, as was said, the poem is not a mere declaration of love for created things; underlying this is the urgency of his fear for their survival. The early epithets "speeded," "torrent," "seashaken," and "breakneck" evidence his feeling of the immediacy of the danger.

The situation at the time of writing is this:

1. Hate floods the world.
   As the flood begins,
   Out of the fountainhead
   Of fear, rage red, manalive,
   Molten and mountainous to stream
   Over the wound asleep
   Sheep white hollow farms
   To Wales in my arms.

2. War is imminent.
   . . . The haystacked
   Hollow farms in a throng
   Of waters cluck and cling,
   And barnroofs cockcrow war!

There is room for disagreement over the meaning to be attached to these two sets of lines. Ralph Mills, referring to the "Prologue" as "a poem of praise in time's despite," apparently sees Time as the flood, and

Poetry ("the indestructible product of imagination or spirit, and the sacred vessel that houses man's most intimate statements about himself and his existence") as the Ark (*Accent,* p. 131). So, he goes on, "To thwart the flood, Thomas musters from the love, anger and fright within him the words for an ark of poetic speech."

As Mills sees it, it is out of the flood of emotions—love, fear, and rage—that Thomas builds his poem. As I see it, Thomas builds this poem of love to protect himself (and his friends) from the fear and hate rising about them. I see two objections to Mills' reading. First, the metaphor is not precise: Noah did not use water to build his ark; to be consistent, love must equal the material which withstands the molten streams of fear and rage. Second, the flood does not stream *out of* Thomas but across the farms *to* Thomas holding "Wales in my arms."

Now, if the flood is "manalive" and if it is streaming out of the fountainhead of fear and red rage, Thomas cannot be describing Time, bringing winter and death; or the onset of darkness, bringing the fox to the chickenyard; or the urbanization of industrial England, drowning the pastoral sheep (and church) bells; or the ecological indifference of de-natured man. It must be no less than man-made, man-annihilating war. Nothing else so satisfactorily explains the contrast between the catholic shells pacific in their eternal element and the

> . . . cities of nine
> Days' night whose towers will catch
> In the religious wind
> Like stalks of tall, dry straw. . . .

In this passage of extensive implication, it is the phrase "nine/Days' night" which lends significance. Without that mysterious reference, one might take "religious" as meaning no more than *conscientious,* and visualize the cities' towers as ablaze only with the light of the setting sun. But the two phrases taken together hint at more, at, specifically, the fire-wind which accompanies the atomic blast set off by fanatical, conceptualizing crusaders.

The poem is curiously divided. The first half can be paraphrased as follows:

> In unease, I sing to you, my unknown readers, out of these pages that will be dispersed like leaves from a tree and like them will crumble and lose shape and color in the passage of time. I am writing from my house above the bay of Carmarthen with its seascape and figures. I say I am singing although song is a rebirth from self-immolation, a passionate warbling, compared to my ineptly carpentered tunes.

The sun sets as I chop out my poem to tell you how I, a man as little as any other at the still point of the turning wheel, exult in this earth, risen out of the ocean, noisy with birds, ditched and dug and dynamited by men, enriched by the blood of the dead.

Listen: I praise everything from sea-bottom to hill-top. Look: out of my love and to the best of my ability, I compose my loud-with-praise poem as a means of salvaging life from the flood which now begins to flow like lava out of man's fear and hate over the country-side to the home-land I hold dear.

His address has been to human beings, and its tone has not been unfriendly. But then he suddenly turns his back on them and begins to address the birds and beasts of the countryside. He opens on a note of complaint and disillusion:

Owls, dove, clan of seabirds, jack hare—who hears me as I build my ship except animals made in God's image? Listen, sleeping beasts—the farms are frightened by the flood of hate, and the barn-roofs warn of war. Fish, birds, beasts—speed to the safety of my ark: as the dark comes, there is no murmur of peace save from the drowned-out churches and pastures.

We will sail out alone and shout "Multitudes of arks!" And miraculously other arks, havens of love-for-life, will appear every-where.

So, since the flood (a *fleur du mal*) begins to flower now, come aboard my still-sunlit vessel.

It would appear that Thomas sets out to remind the "strangers" that everything that lives is holy. But recognizing the odds against him as being too great (he is Noah against the world), his poems as being incapable of exerting strong and enduring pressure (they are crumbling leaves and puffballs), he gives up the effort and devotes his attention to his own homestead. His love envelops the creatures of the sea and wood. Perhaps his example within the limited area will prove efficacious. His Ark, like Donne's well-wrought urn, will be observed; and there will be those to beg a pattern of his love. But then, of course, he craftily sends the poem to the strangers, thus working both from the centre out and from the periphery in.

With what degree of hope he sends his message is a question. Analysis reveals this:

1. In his *persona* as Noah, Thomas sets himself apart from men.

2. None of the images referring to human beings are particularly affirmative.

a. Men are kneeling, but to dying fish, not God. "Crow black" may describe the sails rather than the men; even so, the connotation of carrion crow is insistent.

b. Boys are "stabbing." So, of course, is the heron mentioned immediately after. But for the same reason?

c. Cities will be destroyed in a "religious" wind.

d. The earth is "man torn."

e. Fear and rage are "manalive."

3. Not men but beasts listen to the poet. This may mean no more than that he is alone. But why make a point of it?

4. Only beasts are addressed in the last fifty lines.

5. Only beasts are invited to come aboard his ark of refuge.

6. Most of the positive descriptive epithets are of animal origin: *salmon* sun, *sheep white* farms, *horseback* hill, *hogsback* wood, *fox* light. The most noticable contradiction is the uncomplimentary fishwife-cross gulls.

7. The most significant reference to God is the exclamatory and blasphemous "Hail to His beasthood!"

It is, to say the least, disconcerting to encounter such denigration (as it appears to be) of the human in the prologue to a collection of poems, and all the more so since it follows immediately the *Note* in which Thomas professes his intention to have been to write "for the love of Man and in praise of God." But the *Note* itself awakens dubieties. Thomas compares his writing for the reasons described to a sheperd's making ritual observances to the moon from within fairy rings in order to protect his flocks. Asked why, the shepherd answers, "I'd be a damn fool if I didn't!" The shepherd is, of course, naive and superstitious, a fearful practitioner of old-wives' knock-wood pragmatism. Is Thomas's love of Man and praise of God to be designated naive, superstitious, and pragmatic? No doubt Thomas was aiming only at a tone of ingratiating grass-roots humanness. What he has achieved, however, compared, for example, to Bach's "of all music the end and final cause, should be for naught but the glory of God, and the recreation of the spirit," was the merely clever. Light utterance need not necessarily exclude deep feeling, but in this instance it at least arouses suspicion of its absence.

Distinguishing the later poems from the earlier, Olson makes this comment: "There is undoubtedly a development from doubt and fear to faith and hope, and the moving cause is love; he comes to love of

God by learning to love man and the world of nature." (Olson, p. 20.) I think that one might very well come to such a formulation from a reading of the late poems in the volume. But the poet of the "Prologue" is not the poet of "Poem on his Birthday." He is that loneliest of men, Noah; he is at day's end, summer's end, peace's end; he himself writes "at poor peace."

It is true that the poem ends on a note of hope.

> We will ride out alone, and then,
> Under the stars of Wales,
> Cry, Multitudes of arks! Across
> The water lidded lands,
> Manned with their loves they'll move,
> Like wooden islands, hill to hill.

But surely this is exclamatory protestation as compared with the felt faith of

> . . . . the closer I move
> To death, one man through his sundered hulks,
> The louder the sun blooms
> And the tusked, ramshackling sea exults;
> And every wave of the way
> And gale I tackle, the whole world then
> With more triumphant faith
> Than ever was since the world was said,
> Spins its morning of praise.

Olson says again: "The flood is a terror in the early work; in the later, there is refuge from it in the Ark." (P. 20.) My conjecture is that Thomas had indeed at one time come to such a belief but that the later course of human events had compelled its diminution to a thought of what might be. In the certainty of his belief, a quiet statement would have sufficed; the unsubstantial hope requires a shout.

# 3

# The Work of Words

# In My Craft or Sullen Art

It is not a fit audience nor are they a few to whom Thomas proclaims his allegiance. Nor, as he conceives them, are they particularly responsive. Small wonder that the epithet *sullen,* with its connotations of loneliness and moroseness and unrewardedness (cf. Skeat — "a portion served out to a religious person"), darkens this poem.

Is the poem, then, a complaint? or a realistic acceptance? or, in some odd way, a manifesto? It is something of each. The self-righteousness of his divorce from fame, money, popularity, approval of the elite is not without its tincture of self-pitying braggadocio. He may not exactly be all alone beweeping his outcast state, yet neither is there a sense in the poem of his arising from sullen earth to sing hymns. A sense of the highness of his calling reverberates far more thrillingly through "Author's Prologue" than through the present poem. And no one, remembering his fire-horse eagerness when an audience offered, can view with other than irony his strictures against "the strut and trade of charms/On the ivory stages." As Caitlin says: "Nobody ever needed encouragement less, and [in America] he was drowned in it. He gave to those wide-open-beaked readings the concentrated artillery of his flesh and blood, and, above all, his breath." (*Casebook,* 248.) His small-boy vanity shows in the false modesty with which he greeted Brinnin's encomium: "When I had finished reading, Dylan said, as if he were quoting a newspaper headline: 'Randy-dandy, Curly-girly Poet Leaps into Sea from Overdose of Praise,' and made as if to throw himself over the sea wall." (*Casebook,* 205.)

Still, with all his vanity, posturing, attention-demanding, when he went to work, he did so with a seriousness and dignity that made him a different person — one willing to suffer the isolation, uncertainty, tension, and self-mutilation required of the precisionist working in imprecisions and willing to do so with or without profit.

It is as a manifesto, however, that the poem is most interesting. D. R. Howard (*Explicator,* XII, no. 4) has suggested that the poem is intended as an answer to Yeats's "Sailing to Byzantium."

> In that poem, Yeats divorces himself from "the young in one another's arms" in order to pursue "monuments of unaging intellect," the possibility of permanence in a world of flux. Thomas, on the other hand, takes the lovers as the central thing to his art, and the phrase "sullen art" may be a reply to Yeats' demand that "soul clap its hands and sing."

The suggestion has merit. Nothing could be more alien to Thomas's spirit than to deny the flesh, love, and lovers for a mechanical singing bird. Nothing more entrances his interest than "those dying generations" which were the object of Yeats's irony. And his sympathy is never with Carlylean heroes past or present, but with "the scorned — the rejected — the men hemmed in with the spears." Keats forlorn, or Sweeney beset, among the nightingales is to his taste as Agamemnon, or — to take a trio of poets of a certain towering aloofness — Milton, Eliot, Yeats could never be, however much he respected their greatness.

The parallel between Keats and Thomas is close. Both were precocious young men; both extraordinarily sensuous; both outsiders — the one Cockney, the other Welsh; both were sensitive about their intellectual deficiencies; neither was, therefore, ever free from an uneasiness — Keats in the company of Wordsworth or Shelley, Thomas with Eliot and his compeers; each felt a falling-off of his powers; each could therefore speak without a false humility of having writ in water. Keats, more burningly ambitions than Thomas, made his effort, with *Hyperion,* to join the immortals. He knew he had failed. Thomas, perhaps more self-aware, certainly the rocked boy of his age, tried neither the epic nor the tragic vein. He did not hope for the intellectual aristocracy in his audience and was distinctly uncomfortable when their representatives appeared. His aim was lower. Yet it was high enough to justify W. S. Merwin's statement:

> . . . he writes his poems 'Not for ambition or bread,' nor for public acclaim nor for the edification of the self-righteous, nor for the dead, but for the lovers . . . . If the act of love is conceived as the central act of creation, where love, in joy and then in pain and then in joy, overcomes death, it is clear why he should have felt that his poems were so directed. (*Casebook,* 246.)

# How Shall My Animal

This poem has occasioned some difference of opinion. Derek Stanford (p. 84) takes the poem as "the utterance of femininity, of woman's apprehension and knowledge of the male in the act of physical union." Elder Olson defines the Animal as a metaphor for Soul and reads the poem as being concerned with the capture and drawing-out of the Soul from the innermost recesses of self.

In my own conjecture, the speaker is Thomas as wishful Poet-Prophet; the Animal represents elemental stuff from which Poetry and Prophecy are created; the problem is whether that vital stuff does not lose its vitality when brought to the surface. In the second "Memorable Fancy" of his *Marriage of Heaven and Hell*, Blake describes how knowledge is transmitted from generation to generation:

I was in a Printing house in Hell & saw the method in which knowledge is transmitted from generation to generation.

In the first chamber was a Dragon-Man, clearing away the rubbish from a cave's mouth; within, a number of Dragons were hollowing the cave.

In the second chamber was a Viper folding round the rock & the cave, and others adorning it with gold, silver and precious stones.

In the third chamber was an Eagle with wings and feathers of air; he caused the inside of the cave to be infinite: around were numbers of Eagle-like men who built palaces in the immense cliffs.

In the fourth chamber were Lions of flaming fire, raging around & melting the metals into living fluids.

In the fifth chamber were Unnam'd forms, which cast the metals into the expanse.

There they were receiv'd by Men who occupied the sixth chamber, and took the forms of books & were arranged in libraries.

After all that hollowing, infinity-achieving, flaming, and melting, how anticlimactic are the words "took the forms of books & were arranged in libraries." I do not mean that Blake thought them so: he had a sublime trust in his powers of prophetic utterance. But Thomas had no such self-confidence, and he must have felt the anti-climax as I have done. He knew that the stuff was molten within him; but as he willed it forth, it became dry rock. Lawrence (in *Psychoanalysis and the Unconscious*) has described the process graphically:

The brain is, if we may use the word, the terminal instrument of the dynamic consciousness. It transmutes what is a creative flux into a certain fixed cipher. It prints off, like a telegraph instrument, the glyphs and graphic representations which we call percepts, concepts, ideas. It produces a new reality—the idea.

And he expands upon the idea:

Once the mind is awake, being in itself a finality, it feels very assured. "The word became flesh, and began to put on airs," says Norman Douglas wittily. It is exactly what happens. Mentality, being automatic in its principle like the machine, begins to assume life. It begins to affect life, to pretend to make and unmake life. "In the beginning was the Word." This is the presumptuous masquerading of the mind. The Word cannot be the beginning of life. It is the *end* of life, that which falls shed. But it has all the mechanical force of the non-vital universe. It is a great dynamo of super-mechanical force. Given the *will* as accomplice it can even arrogate its machine-motions and automatizations over the whole life, till every tree becomes a clipped teapot and every man a useful mechanism. So we see the brain, like a great dynamo and accumulator, accumulating *mechanical* force, and presuming to apply this mechanical force-control to the living unconscious, subjecting everything spontaneous to certain machine-principles called ideals or ideas.

Thomas's difficulty can be succinctly put: In the beginning was the wordless energy; in the end was the enervated word. The explicator's difficulty does not differ. However:

How shall my dynamic unconscious, trace of which I find in sublimated form in the conscious mind (in the brain within the skull—the seat of spiritual joy and physical rot), endure being intellectualized and verbalized: buried, like a Jew, under a wailing wall; put to sleep, like a princess, by a magical spell; segregated from life's activities, like a mourning widow? How shall this octopus armed with flail-like tentacles, this drunken snail of a libido, which should always be furiously its own self, never compromising with the weatherlike superego; how shall this magical, unconfined, unknown being come to terms with the natural, the confined, the scientifically mapped?

How shall it, like the aurora borealis (or midnight sun) exert magnetic force upon a dry, soulless land—that is, bring color, energy, force to the shallow, the provincial, ratiocinative faculties? How shall it (as a mare) couple with the stud in a blaze of rut and share its pasture—that is, how shall the unconscious join its force to the sympathetic force of the heart? (In *Revelations*, 9, 17, "the heads of the horses were like lions' heads"; the problem, then, is to melt a heart hard as the hoof and shoe of a horse.) Putting the two images together in Yeatsian terms—how are the loins, heart, and head to be brought into unison?

How shall this energy as light, shine, heat, and melt till man's softened earth permit growth, his melted Arctic sea teem with life, his bowels overflow with compassion, his veins squeeze from every corpuscle the demanding utterance? (Cf. Kafka's definition of artistic creation as an "axe to the frozen sea within us.")

What Thomas is getting at in this stanza is again very close to a leading idea in Lawrence—that the solar plexus must balance the cardiac plexus. Lawrence goes so far as to interpret history in terms of these plexuses.

In the previous sympathetic era the flower of the universal blossomed in the navel. But since Egypt the sun's creative activity beams from the breast, the heart of the supreme Man. This is to us the source of light—the loving heart, the Sacred Heart. Against this we contrast the devouring darkness of the lower man, the devouring whirlpool beneath the navel. Even the sophists don't realize that the universal lotus really blossoms in the abdomen — that our lower man, our dark, devouring whirlpool was once the creative source, in human estimation.

Thomas, having asked his question of how the unconscious will endure "burial" ("burial" paradoxically meaning to be brought to light out of its dark depths), now fixes upon his figure of unconscious as octopus and describes his catching of it and the result.

There are those (Thomas says), facile amateurs in life and poetry, who play like children at the edge of reality. They have never heard the mermaids singing; and, to avoid the real and sinister denizens of the deep, they fish shallow with bent pins for hooks and cake for bait. Thomas, on the other hand, fishes deep, almost inaccessible cave-pools, using live bait and nerves for lines. (Lawrence: ". . . consciousness is like a web woven finally in the mind from the various silken strands spun forth from the center of the unconscious.") He uses an open eye-hook, which he sinks in the quarry's tentacle. (The open eye is, perhaps, the "third eye" of the clairvoyant.) Having nailed his revelation, he drags it forth to fix it in his consciousness (as stallion is studded to mare).

But, on the beach out of its element, the octopus, in blood and fury clapped down, is dead fish. What is Thomas's score, then, in this fishing tournament? He has, as the fishermen of mermen have not, made a magnificent catch, but to no *great* good end. The dynamism he sought was a momentary thing. The moment of revelation does not provide an "Aquinas-map" (to use a Poundian phrase) for the understanding of space and time.

Yet, though the fishing expedition is a failure, and the last stanza has its elegiac note, it is not a total failure. Thomas addresses his animal:

You, once vital Samson of an octopus of creative energy but now cold clay, beached, stunned, gasping on the shore, die slowly, lying like a shorn sun-god. Cold scissors of the mind cut and prune, turn your thicket into a topiary garden; the fury of your passion is "reified" into a temple for Philistines; the virgin mouth nails living thought to planks of words, cuts flaming flowers from living bushes, makes the lustful lion fall at her feet, utters negatives like Jehovah to cramp the prophet's style—in short, inhibits the intended utterance.

You, dislodged from your sea-cave, accept the change from sea to earth, from wet to dry, from rest in your element to gasping death on the beach and burial in the earth, and, when your dead eye no longer sees the sun, die like a phoenix. You have, like a stallion, kicked your way out of your stall, leaped with a cry to the answering light and died in my heart.

Where, one may assume, though it is not what it was, and cannot do all that Thomas might have desired, it may in some wise melt the horseshoe of the poet's heart.

.　　.　　.　　.　　.

This is a fiercely compressed and concentrated poem. The animal hero takes shape as a Merlin, a Jew, a princess, a widow, a drunk snail, an octopus, a sun or aurora borealis, a horse, a Samson, a thicket, a temple, a burning bush, a lion, a Moses, a phoenix. And not in succession but with confusing simultaneity. Thomas has served scrambled eggs, not fried eggs in series.

This he has done quite arbitrarily, as witness the straight-forwardness of the original first stanza, simple, personal, but abstract, in which the present complex, impersonal, concrete stanza had its inception.

> How shall the animal
> Whose way I trace
> Into the dark recesses,
> Be durable
> Under such weight as bows me down,
> The bitter certainty of waste
> The knowing that I catch a thought
> To see it crushed
> Beneath your foot, my bantering Philistine?

This is indeed a stanza eyeless in Gaza, as different from its ultimate successor as the mill-hand from the temple-destroyer. A miracle has taken place, but—and this is the astounding thing—a miracle of natural process. The poem has grown—or seems to have grown—like hair. It did not, of course. The strict rhythmic pattern, the careful rhyming, the

144 ·

assiduously worked out puns, the echoed images all attest to the clacking of Thomas's sly scissors. But the bush remains plumed with flames.

I suppose that the most cogent criticism of the poem will be directed at the abrupt shifts from image to image in the treatment of the animal. Of the various images, the most significant are those of the octopus, the horse, and the dead or dying Samson (his appearance prepared for by "spelling wall" in the first stanza). It is clear as soon as these are disentangled from the subsidiary images that a progression from loin to heart to head is involved, and that the images work together quite satisfactorily. (The drunken snail, apparently dropped and forgotten — and unaccountably, it being so vivid — is not dropped; snail and octopus are both members of the phylum of Mollusca, and Thomas simply assimilates the one into the other.)

## Especially When the October Wind

It was a November wind and a more clearly understandable situation in an earlier version of this poem:

> Especially when the November wind
> With frosty fingers punishes my hair,
> Or, beaten on by the straight beams of the sun,
> I walk abroad, feeling my youth like fire
> Burning weak blood and body up,
> Does the brain reel, drunk on the raw
> Spirits of words, and the heart sicken
> Of arid syllables grouped and regrouped with ease. . . .

What he here states — that he feels his youth burning away; that the undiluted spirits of words inebriate his mind; that his heart becomes sick of manipulated, juiceless syllables—is only implied in the published version, and only in part.

> Especially when the October wind
> With frosty fingers punishes my hair,
> Caught by the crabbing sun I walk on fire
> And cast a shadow crab upon the land,
> By the sea's side, hearing the noise of birds
> Hearing the raven cough in winter sticks,
> My busy heart who shudders as she talks
> Sheds the syllabic blood and drains her words.

The raven's cough and the winter sticks suggest youth's departure convincingly enough. But the inebriated brain has been omitted. And it takes some doing to find the above sickened heart in

> My busy heart who shudders as she talks
> Sheds the syllabic blood and drains her words.

Thomas has sacrificed immediate comprehension for the sake of dramatic imagery. And one might be glad that the simpler earlier version is available except for the possibility of its proving a false sign-post. Does the re-written poem, like its antecedent, inveigh against the frustrations attendant upon being a poet? Art is long, says the early version, and life short, and never seems more so than when inspiration refuses to team with craftsmanship.

I think that the new poem, though in the same general area of discourse, has shifted terms somewhat. Thomas's problem has become not so much one of keeping alive the words in syntax's despite as of escaping the habit of seeing things in terms of their names and descriptions, in order to name and describe them better in his own verbalizations. What he wants in his poems is the poet walking on fire and not his shadow crab, the reality not the appearance. He would agree with Stevens that "Nothing must stand/Between you and the shapes you take," and that you must

> Throw away the lights, the definitions,
> And say of what you see in the dark
> That it is this or that it is that
> But do not use the rotted names.

> ("The Man with the Blue Guitar")

What is the grass? the child asked. And Whitman answered, the flag of my disposition, the beautiful uncut hair of graves, the journey-work of the stars, and so on. Which is to admit, as he had done before attempting these flights of fancy, that he did not know, he could only offer the reaction of a moment's mood. The relation of poet to thing is a difficult one. He wants like the scientist to know, but individually rather than generically, and to express, but in words that keep the thing alive.

He must see for himself and express as himself. But as a lover of words and images, both his vision and his vocabulary of images are under constant pressure. The habit of immediate verbalization and of metaphoric play diverts the eye. And there is the danger of never seeing the thing itself but a verbal substitute. He may, after Whitman, never see grass at all without a thought of uncut hair.

Thus it is with Thomas in his second stanza. He is in his study, sur-

146 ·

rounded by books and manuscripts, himself intent upon nothing but the words before him and inside him. A tower of words within a tower of words. As he sees, in the distance, flesh-and-blood women, he completely misdefines them. They walk like trees. They are not women but springboards for the metaphoric leap.

But perhaps this interpretation is too negative, too much in terms of the sickened heart. Perhaps the inebriated brain, contemplating from a distance and unaffected by accidentals, is enabled more easily to get to the raw spirit of the women (and the "star-gestured children") and of the words that describe their inscape.

Or perhaps he has intentionally set a heart-sickening figure—that of the women—against the brain-delighting one of the children, dramatizing what he had stated in his first version's first stanza. Since he drops the human figures at once and never returns to them, one can only speculate as to their function in the poem.

Of these three possibilities, the first appeals as being most credible. In "The Orchards," the young poet Marlais, "struggling with his words like a man with the sun," is thus described:

> The word is too much with us. He raised his pencil so that its shadow fell, a tower of wood and lead, on the clean paper; he fingered the pencil tower, the half-moon of his thumb-nail rising and setting behind the leaden spire. The tower fell, down fell the city of words, the walls of a poem, the symmetrical letters. He marked the disintegration of the ciphers as the light failed, the sun drove down into a foreign morning, and the word of the sea rolled over the sun. Image, all image, he cried to the fallen tower as the night came on, whose harp is the sea? whose burning candle is the sun? An image of man, he rose to his feet and drew the curtains open. Peace, like a simile, lay over the roofs of the town. Image, all image, cried Marlais, stepping through the window on to the level roofs.

From the women and children Thomas turns to the landscape. It is this that seems especially the burden of his song, since it is this that is signalized by the reiterated formula, "Some let me make you . . . ." There are seven such incantatory sentences:

> Some let me make you of the vowelled beeches
> Some of the oaken voices . . . .(notes of the roots)
> Some let me make you of the water's speeches
> Some let me make you of the meadow's signs
> Some let me tell you of the raven's sins
> Some let me make you of autumnal spells
> Some let me make you of the heartless words

Of these the first three, bringing to mind the landscape surrounding the women and children, speak only of life, a tough strength, and longevity. But the next two, although equally countryside images, hint at death. The grass whose green strikes the observer's eye is the grass whose blade will physically penetrate when he has become an ex-observer—if the raven doesn't get there first to "pike out his bonny blue een."

The "life is short" theme and the appearance-reality theme are brought together in the opening sentence of this stanza (the third):

> Behind a pot of ferns the wagging clock
> Tells me the hour's word, the neural meaning
> Flies on the shafted disk, declaims the morning
> And tells the windy weather in the cock.

The clock points to an abstract symbol, say the number 5; the cock notifies of sunrise; the poet says, "It's the middle of the night," and then remembering an unfinished poem or feeling an intestinal gripe, "It's later than you think." In terms of the latter thought, the minute hand, that seems so stationary, is a flying, shafted arrow. What with grass-blades, raven's beak, and arrow, this is a pointed stanza.

The last two of the incantatory constructions speak more of the poet than of the landscape. He is not now concerned with the object but with the subject's reaction to the object, which has become something more than natural landscape and exerts a magical spell.

Here, partly because syntax does, interpretation breaks down.

> (Some let me make you of autumnal spells,
> The spider tongued, and the loud hill of Wales)

What "spider tongued" means and which is the "loud" hill I do not know, and whether they are in apposition with "me" or with "spells" is a question. I shall assume that they modify "spells" and that Thomas is saying, Let me give you an impression of the magical influence of autumn, which emanates from all nature, from the small and noiseless to the large and noisy.*

There can be little question, however, of the autumnal spell's effect. The heart spells from its own sybil's leaves the onset of life's evening straining to be "time's vast, womb-of-all, home-of-all, hearse-of-all night." And surely the dark-vowelled birds are less likely to be the temple-haunting martlets, than the ravens that croaked King Duncan's fatal entrance.

Or so I should think. Derek Stanford, according to whom "this poem (outwardly a landscape-piece) records the creative powers of poetry

---

*Thomas may have buried a little joke in "spider-tongued." There is a class of spiders known as Thomisidae but more commonly known as "crab-spiders."

working on the poet in favorable circumstances," (p. 52) paraphrases the last three lines as follows: "the feeling that foretold me a poem was on its way is now exhausted, since the poem has been written." (P. 55.)

It is possible that this is a poem "about the making of a poem" and that its dark tone occurs only because the poet encompasses with the twirl of his tongue not only the beech's vowelled speech but also the raven's fricative cough. But if on the one hand it does not have the sound of success, on the other it has the feel of greater breadth of meaning.

One of the peculiar problems of the poet is that, as commentator upon life, he must give up living for scrivening, things and people for symbols. He can rarely avoid feeling that he is sacrificing Art for Experience, or Experience for Art. It is the latter sacrifice that is stressed in "The Orchards": "who walks by our stone virgins is our virgin Marlais, wind and fire, and the coward on the burning roofs." I think that the Thomas of this poem can be similarly characterized.

In the story Marlais sat down to write, but "the morning was against him":

> He sharpened his pencil and shut the sky out, shook back his untidy hair, arranged the papers of a devilish story on his desk, and broke the pencil-point with a too-hard scribble of "sea" and "fire" on a clean page. Fire would not set the ruled lines alight, adventure, burning, through the heartless characters, nor water close over the bogy heads and the unwritten words. The story was dead from the devil up . . . .

What does a poet think when the words fail to come—especially in October, the poet's birth-month, or November, the harbinger of winter? He is sensitive to the brevity of time, the enormity of the task, the defects of his talent. He has fears that he may cease to be too soon. And to assuage the fear, if not to remedy the ill, he chants a magical formula.


## Today, this Insect

An assumption admittedly unwarranted but quite credible assists toward an interpretation of this difficult poem. It is this: that Thomas has killed an insect, reflected upon the murder, become curious about the life-cycle of insects, consulted a dictionary, and found the stuff for a poem — but not about insects. Perhaps the contrast between the mystery of life-changes and the dead scientific language that describes it suggested the subject. This subject, baldly put, is: Science destroys myth, which is tragic, since myth supports man's faith and hope through the tragedies of life.

Thomas himself is like an *imago* — adult, sexually mature, and winged. His symbols transcend all spatial limitations — he can apprehend and utter microcosm ("this insect") and macrocosm ("the world"), can comprehend and regulate mundane time and (less successfully by half) the mad and maddening moments when imagination leaps and when it falters. In halving the sentient insect (his nail perhaps the guillotine), he has destroyed the instinct to survive ("trust") and stopped the fabulous process of metamorphosis ("tale"), the two halves of the body evidencing this destruction of innocent confidence and hopeful beginning.

There is a parable in this: as a post-French-Revolution man, he has two attitudes toward the reasonable and the mythic (fact and fiction; truth and superstition); case in point, though rationally he agrees to science's subversion of the factual basis of the Eden story, emotionally he affirms that fertilizing myth.

The louse of cerebralism infects with black death the mythic faculty.

In its *larval* state, the now-dead insect was wingless and wormlike (a dragon to become a fairy prince); within the confines of his Edenic egg, he attains his growth, breaks the egg, and enters the quiescent (shell-shocked) *pupal* state, a last beginning before achieving maturity. A crawler, a chrysalis, and, before its murder, a butterfly (symbol of heart's hope). (Or perhaps it represented a hope for, a drive for flight before it left the egg — a fall from love.) This butterfly, this defenseless pawn even for children, unesteemed (like the donkey in Chesterton's poem who "with ears like errant wings," is mistreated though he bore Christ on Palm Sunday), finds Jericho following close on Eden.

Again the application: the metamorphic process in nature suggests a similar process for man. It is such a process that the Biblical myth dramatizes. Reason, recognizing the fact in the insect, hee-haws the myth into a children's story, a pleasant tale like that of Pandora's box.

Thomas, objecting, declares: The butterfly of myth offers the assurance of hope because the history of the butterfly, a series of miracles, is true.

Reason promises as the only certainty only death. Reason, Gradgrindian, deflating (like Newton finding poetry "ingenious fiddle-faddle") cries down the great revelations: those of Shakespeare, Cervantes, Homer, John, Job's author, and the saints and mystics. But the voice of the hero of the greatest, most revelatory myth of them all replies: "My love for man, my love for the visionaries is deathless (and is deathlessly reciprocated by the visionaries). No revealer of life's secret comes to a conclusion more certain than this (no teller of love tales can expect other than this): that the names of all the legendary sweethearts are carved on (or grow as part of) the immortal Eden tree (the tree of earthly knowledge of love); and that behind the theatrical curtain of fable am I, on the tree of spiritual truth, who as *larva* died, lay three days in the *chrysalis* state, and on the third day rose, an *imago* that has outelbowed space."

# Should Lanterns Shine

The first stanza of this lyric is so charming that it is a pity that the poem as a whole remains curiously unjelled. One might think this not a finished poem but a series of starts and jottings for a poem yet to be written. The appearance of the lines on the page—the block of eight and one of seven, followed by two disconnected couplets—would sustain the belief: like the tadpole, it is a toad that is all head.

The opening lines, with their striking image of the mummy's face, at first glance seen as whole and holy, but instantaneously, under the lantern's gleam, disintegrating, are followed by a set of abstractions which might be entitled "Memoirs of a Schoolboy." The effect of drop-off is like that of an energetic narrative poem with a moral tag—"Thanks, thanks, my worthy friend for the lesson thou hast taught." And the pictorial lines that follow the abstractions,

. . . field and roof lie level and the same
So fast I move defying time, the quiet gentleman
Whose beard wags in Egyptian wind,

depicting Thomas in aerial combat with an aged gentleman, are merely ludicrous. The effort to bring the two stanzas into context by allusion to "Egyptian wind" does not succeed; and it is not helped by the archaic omission of the article, nor by the tone-violating verb of mockery, "wags."

The first of the two caudate couplets reverts to plain statement. The second, one which Longfellow might have discarded, is pictorial but paltry and absurdly removed in every respect from the mysterious and dramatic scene with which the poem starts. We have moved from Rembrandt to Tenniel.

There was, originally, still another couplet—

Regard the moon, it hangs above the lawn;
Regard the lawn, it lies beneath the moon.

This, clearly a couplet for still another poem, Thomas deleted on Watkins' advice.

One might justify Thomas's halts and starts here on the grounds that his subject is precisely indecisiveness, the poem representing what it discusses by an intended and controlled incoherence. I do not think that this argument enhances the poem's value: the intention may have prevailed, but the control did not.

But regardless of the poem's value as poem, what it has to say is of interest, since it poses the problem that has harassed European intellectuals since the advent of organized science, the problem that confronts every religious poet and every poet wrestling up the tower to a religious faith and has confronted them at least since Donne. It is the problem of bringing the eye of reason and the eye of faith into single focus.

At the outset of the scientific movement, Bacon, its greatest propagandist, saw the split that was imminent. Sanguine, he did not feel "that a man can search too far in the Book of God's Word, or in the Book of God's Work." But he expressed a warning: "Only let men beware that they apply both to Charity and not to swelling; to use, and not to ostentation, and again, that they do not unwisely mingle or confound these learnings together."

In due course, however, they were mingled: the natural philosophers so focused attention upon Nature instead of the nature of God that the latter became assimilated into the former. The next step was inevitable: to drain God and benevolent purpose out of nature; to subtract Providence from history; to reduce God to a father-image, father to an ambulatory libido, and religion to an obsessive-compulsive neurosis.

Small wonder that Auden, before he regained his Christian faith, could welcome even "The nursery bogey or the winecellar ghost" since "no nightmare/ Of hostile objects could be as terrible as this Void."

Lawrence once defined belief as "a profound emotion that has the mind's connivance." He had his belief: "My great religion is a belief in the blood, the flesh, as being wiser than the intellect. We can go wrong in our minds. But what our blood feels and believes and says is true."

Thomas has not yet, in this poem, come to his. He recognizes the overpowering question, "What shall I do (as man or as artist) to be saved?" and its concomitant, "What have I done to be damned?" He recognizes, too, that the Christian answer has been rendered suspect by a science which supplies no substitute. Finding available no easy answer, he has no recourse but to wrestle with the questions. He started adult life without a dogma or a creed, though his mind had been tinged, as by soot, by the ambient Welsh Nonconformism. Unlike some of his contemporaries, he came to no absolute conclusion: he did not go gentle into Anglo-Catholicism, like Eliot, or into Roman Catholicism, at his wits' end, like Thomas Merton; he did not forswear Christianity for Confucianism-cum-neo-Platonism, like Pound, or contrive a system that never was on land or sea, like Yeats; he did not, with the assurance of a Stevens, take the Santayana way.

Nevertheless, he wrestled with the tenacity of a Jacob. And, as an artist, he learned (in David Daiches' words) "to handle in brilliant counterpoint all the different explanations of human situations given by religion, science, and folklore." As a man, he was eventually to achieve at worst "poor peace," at best a "more triumphant faith." He had not done so at the time of writing this poem, since he had not discovered the means, had not found provided "For erring judgments an unerring guide."

## *The Spire Cranes*

Thomas's images of this long disease our life are so brutally vivid that the misconception has been generated that he had only a horror of the life-process in time. I do not think that it is the life-process as such that he feels revulsion for but the life-process as it has been thwarted and distorted by social restrictions of various kinds. Far more than Thomas, Celine and Henry Miller have an eye and a nose for the ordure and vomit of society. In Celine there is no relief of the horror; but illuminating Miller's vision of Europe as a hospital and a charnel house, there is always a steady glow of Whitmanesque optimism. On the continuum between hope and despair, Thomas takes a position close to Miller's. He agrees that the situation is awful. But the cause is pin-pointed, and remedy is possible.

In "The Spire Cranes," he states the situation (but this time in non-horrifying symbols) and implies the reason for hope. The symbols are, on the one hand, a church spire on which are to be seen carved birds, and, in the spire, iron bells, and, on the other, the music of the bells, and water (rain-water and sea-water with swimmers). The antithesis is between any restrictive force (such as academicism in literature, bourgeois enforcement of a cloistered virtue, religious preoccupation with ideal being instead of natural process) which induces an aesthetic, moral, or philosophical stasis.

So far as aesthetics is concerned, Thomas is merely re-rhyming the Keats of "Sleep and Poetry":

> Is there so small a range
> In the present strength of manhood, that the high
> Imagination cannot freely fly . . . ?

Songs "do not travel down the dumb wind like prodigals" but are "artifacts of eternity," products of the "built voice"—even song is frozen music. The reaction against Yeats in the "Byzantium" poems is unmistakable.

The spire, of course, implies the church, and the church the sin of dogma against nature and against human freedom. Since bourgeois morality tends to coincide with Calvinist (or Irish Catholic—one remembers the Rotarian approach of the priest in *Dubliners*), the criticism of the one strikes the other.

The poem runs something like this:

The church steeple stretches its neck away from earth, water, food; its craning is quite un-cranelike. Its birds, carved stone, not permitted the hazard and joy of flight ("spilt," "weed," and "froth" are a silent comment on the church's careful, utilitarian, no-nonsense attitude), are no less divorced from nature. It would seem that the Establishment was in control; everything in its demesne is safely lifeless, imprisoned, or abstracted. But when the dead iron of the spire-imprisoned bells sounds, its music escapes the priest's control and falls like "not 'strained" rain upon the water (in whose service the outlaw swimmers are participating), setting the rhythm for the crawl, furnishing background music for the swimmers' embrace ("silver lock") and kiss. The music (and apparently some real birds?) falls away from the church, escapes the trap ("hook"), the shepherd's hook, and (perhaps) the pirate-clutch of Captain Hook-cum-Long John Silver.

The syntax of the last three lines is ambiguous. I take it as direct address: Those pie-in-the-sky-seeking birds are choice images for you, you songs that dare not venture from the contrived voice or that avoid reality in the bell-tower's shelter.

But David Aivaz, who finds the theme of the poem to be "art as illusion, faith as illusion," thinks a Hobson's choice is being offered between art and faith, and he concludes sadly: "The poet implies that the choice is none, since both art and faith ('nightingale and psalm' in another poem, the 'voice' and 'bells' here) are illusory when they deny process." (Tedlock, p. 200.)

I do not think that the choice is between art and faith but between a daring, unrestricted experiencing and a safe, paternalized narrowness. One can choose the course of the prodigal son or of his stay-at-home brother. And since the choice is possible, the final note is optimistic.

## Because the Pleasure-Bird Whistles

About five years ago I read Henry Treece's explication of this poem. I have not looked at it since, nor have I attempted an explication of my own. Just out of curiosity I propose to write without referring to Treece's analysis, which may be found on P. 137 of his book.

It is New Year's Eve and snowing. Thomas stands in the snow spitting and thinking—thinking about himself and his craft. He is alone, self-concerned, probably more than a little drunk. As the poem progresses, the external cold of the night contends with the heat of the alcohol within him. The New Year snow falls thickly, stilling the city's nerves like a drug; Thomas observes the way in which (spat down by the New Year) it falls upon and swaddles ("clouts") the breaking-bubbled spittle which has projected from the tip of his tongue. The bursting bubbles remind him of split eye-balls. The snow cuts him off from the familiar world of people; it is as if he were camping out alone in the wilderness, hunched over a small campfire. The only warmth and illumination, of course, is that within himself (rather more a spirit-lamp than a campfire), and the fire seems to break from his eyes. The snow falls upon him literally, and within him metaphorically. He literally tastes the snow that sifts through his hair (it is very like Thomas to have lost his cap) to his tongue; he metaphorically contemplates the coldness, the rough-tongued lick, the lashing of the times and his place, alone, in the forest of error. The inner campfire begins to blaze and the flaming tongue to find utterance. And at first he pays no heed to the source of the blaze.

But the self-enamoured man begins to take a more philosophical view (even though, like Lot's wife, he is beginning to freeze). Because Lot's wife was punished for looking back to her past in the wicked city of Sodomites, should I (illuminated—in two senses) sever my connections with the burnt-out, pocket-worn past? No—this is absurd, because the cases are not analogous. There is not one law for Lot's wife and for me, as there is not for the pleasure-bird and the blind horse. The comparison of the latter two has offered food for thought; keen analysis has arrived at this conclusion.

Now he is prepared to flesh with meaning the bare bones of the Biblical story. Though no one feeds the dead, the dead feed us. What they have done can violently affect a man whether he is on land or sea and whether poles away from their tombs.

Thomas works himself out of his self-pitying mood (in which he was blinded bird, tortured Pegasus, broken bubble, and mauled boy), expresses his gratitude to those of auld lang syne who supplied some wood for his fire, and no doubt re-enters the pub to take a right good willie-waught in their honor.

## My Hero Bares his Nerves

According to Stanford, "the poem describes an act of masturbation; and 'My Hero' refers, with that unhappy Rabelaisian jocularity which Thomas sometimes employs, to the male member." (P. 56-7.)

He is quite wrong. The most cursory reading of the poem shows that the male member cannot by any stretch of the imagination do what the hero of the poem is described as doing.

Thomas's hero is that part of him which compels him to the writing of poetry. That is, there is Dylan, the lazy Welshman, and there is Thomas, the Poet-as-Hero. Like all normal people, Dylan reverences Thomas for his remarkable abilities but hates him for his insistent calls to action. As this poem opens, the Hero is prodding the Welshman into creativity.

Far from being a description of onanism, the poem is an elaboration of the idea that poetry (if it is to escape being rhetorical or sentimental) must result from the united activity of head, heart, and loins.

In the first stanza, the creative impulse out-loads materials from the brain; nerve impulses run from the bent head on the straight spine to the pen-hand. There is clearly some conflict. The Dylan-head is not particularly eager, but the Thomas-spine permits no evasion of duty.

In the second stanza, Dylan reveals himself as a frustrated day-dreamer, a volitionless complainer, full of self-pity. He badly needs, both as poet and as person, a little recollection in tranquility. Here, perhaps, he feels an urge toward onanism.

The poetic impulse hastens to stimulate Dylan's flagging spirits. He opens up their mutual rib-case and reveals the heart within, which looks like a rather bloody Botticelli. Head and heart are now seen to be functioning properly. And promise is made of a better heat than sensual passion—perhaps the divine afflatus plus its product, an imaged love.

But a third step needs to be taken. The Hero, though he has denied the genitals actual physical play, prepares to use the nervous energy stored therein. (The phallus is certainly the emperor of "all love hunger"; the genitalia, whose sole business is birth, copulation, and death, would naturally praise what the poem calls "the mortal error.")

And then comes the poem's most puzzling line:

He pulls the chain, the cistern moves.

What has happened? In the first line of the stanza the Hero "holds the wire from this box of nerves." Are the wire and the chain identical? If not, why does he hold the one and pull the other? The wire, of course, suggests electrical energy held in abeyance. Pulling the chain, regrettably, suggests flushing an old-fashioned toilet.

I would suggest that we are supposed to visualize both and thus keep a tight grasp on the related ideas that poetry is a simultaneously psychical and physiological process, and that the honest poet never forgets that "Love has pitched his mansion/ In the place of excrement." But if the reader feels strongly the need to expunge the toilet image from his mind's eye, I recommend recall of Blake's aphorism—"The cistern contains, the fountain overflows." This may be the happy ending of the poem: Thomas, the Poet-as-Hero, has so bullied the slothful Dylan, that where a cistern stood a fountain leaps. And the erstwhile lovelorn paper lives happily forever after.

## On No Work of Words

These alliterated tercets in sprung rhythm comprise a Coleridgean *Ode: Dejection* in miniature and a rewriting of Milton's Sonnet XVI. The key metaphor is money, carried forward in such words as *rich, purse, poverty, pounds, treasures, currencies, marked, count, pay, expensive,* and *nut.* The metaphor of Death as croupier works within the larger figure. Not set against this but intertwined with it is the figure of organic life, involving in its vocabulary *lean, bloody, belly, body, hungrily, manna, breath, ancient woods of my blood, nut, seas.* In a really amazing feat of compression, all three are brought together in the line "Ancient woods of my blood, dash down to the nut of the seas," which says three things simultaneously: "Oak, return to your acorn state; blood, return to your sea-water origin; and gambler's profits, return to your initial investment (nut)."

Thomas opens with the complaint that his poverty of invention and paucity of output contrast unfavorably with the example of nature and the fact of his own potential. He censures himself both for not working and for craftily finding reason for not (and probably for minimizing his own fault by blaming the nature of the writer's task).

Like Milton ("When I consider . . .") and Keats ("When I have fears . . .") he feels the pressure of time; like them and Coleridge he feels a moral responsibility. To take of the richness in order to use and return it enriched is the whole duty of man. God, hungry for the redemption of the Israelites, made manifest to them ("when the dew that lay was gone up") the manna to assuage their hunger. But, when Moses commanded, "Let no man leave of it till the morning," they disobeyed, "and it bred worms, and stank." (*Exodus,* 46.) Apparently Thomas, like the Israelites, has failed his commission; instead of the given stuff's being used, it remains in the mine unconverted to energy.

To steal from the treasures in order to add makes for a full life; to steal but to leave unused is a pleasing of death (it is death to leave that talent lodged with you useless). In either case, Death the croupier will rake in every breath, each marked according to its having been taken and used or taken and unused—and the latter counted in "a bad dark."

But to give in to despair is to die before death (with weeping and gnashing of teeth). And Thomas, more bent to serve his Master, makes his oath: Let my blood fail, if I take, either to destroy or to return unchanged, the bounty of this world which exacts of each man his day labour.

## Love in the Asylum

To determine what this poem says is not difficult:

A mad girl has come to share my (mad) room in my (mad) house, escaping from and (like Kate, in Rossetti's "The King's Tragedy") bolting the door against the darkness of the night. Though confined in a narrow bed (like one trapped in a maze), she fools the theoretically heaven-proof house by trailing after her Wordsworthian clouds of glory; still in that bed, she fools the room, like a spirit from the other world, by walking, or by sailing into imaginary male wards.

She, owned and maddened by the sky, brings light through the nightmarishly pulsating, permeable wall. She walks in her sleep and raves on the floors which I have tearfully paced. And I, caught to her, illumined by her, will surely be capable of my own *Lux Sit.*

But to determine what the poem means is not so easy. For Stanford it is a "tender and humorous piece . . . rather out of the Freudian-Romantic tradition in which the later Thomas writes about love." (P. 121.)

Possibly so. If so, is it about Caitlin—or Another?

It could, of course, be a joking celebration of Caitlin's return to his bed after one of their inveterate blow-ups. But the tone of the poem and its obvious similarity to "The Mouse and the Woman" in *Adventures in the Skin Trade* suggest that its theme is a heralding of the return, after an absence, of what used to be called "inspiration."

The girl, though she "sleeps in the narrow trough" of such tercets as compose this poem, yet walks and raves at will, like Stevens' poem, which

. . . goes from the poet's gibberish to
The gibberish of the vulgate and back again,

deluding, like a supreme fictionalist, all things confining. Thomas, who had lost "the folly of the moon" (to quote Stevens again) and become "The prince of the proverbs of pure poverty," has regained his folly (that necessary angel) and feels again the Genesis-urge within him. He may soliloquize now, like the hero of his story:

It is not a little thing, he thought, this writing that lies before me.

It is the telling of a creation. It is the story of birth. Out of him had come another. A being had been born, not out of the womb, but out of the soul and the spinning head. He had come to the cottage on the hill that the being within him might ripen and be born away from the eyes of men. He understood what the wind that took up the woman's cry had cried in his last dream. Let me be born, it had cried. He had given a woman being. His flesh would be upon her, and the life that he had given her would make her walk, talk, and sing. And he knew, too, that it was upon the block of paper she was made absolute. There was an oracle in the lead of the pencil.

All this is mere conjecture, of course. The simple fact is that we are faced with an occasional poem lacking the footnote to specify the occasion. As occasional poems go, it has its virtues—if all the rest is verse, the last line is poetry; but the virtues of occasional verse are something less than transcendent.

## Once it Was the Colour of Saying

"In one's youth," declared Ezra Pound, "one discusses style or one should." Just out of Grammar School, Thomas and his friends "drank coffee-dashes in the Kardomah Café and discussed music and poetry and painting and politics. Einstein and Epstein, Stravinsky and Greta Garbo, death and religion, Picasso and girls . . . communism, symbolism, Bradman, Braque, the Watch Committee, free love, free beer, murder, Michelangelo, ping-pong, ambition, Sibelius and girls . . . How Dan Jones was going to compose the most prodigious symphony, Fred Janes paint the most miraculously meticulous picture, Charlie Fisher catch the poshest trout, Vernon Watkins and Young Thomas write the most boiling poems, how they would ring the bells of London and paint it like a tart . . . Oh, the hissing of the butt-ends in the drains of the coffee-dashes and the gibble-gabble of the morning young lounge lizards as they talked about Augustus John, Emil Jannings, Carnera, Dracula, Amy Johnson, trial marriage, pocket money, the Welsh sea, the London stars, King Kong, anarchy, darts, T. S. Eliot and girls . . . ." (Pp. 78-9, *Quite Early One Morning.*)

From these conversations and from his solitudes young Thomas emerged, a poet with a subject-matter and a style which did ring the bells of London, a subject-matter strange because it dealt with unborn life, a style obscure because, though it did not exactly "freight every rift with ore," loaded words and images with a weight of meaning almost beyond their capacity to bear. There had eventually to come a time when he would come out of the mines and give his donkey-Pegasus a canter. The present poem states his recognition of the need.

Such a turning-point occurred in Yeats's career. "My friends and I," he wrote, "loved symbols, popular beliefs, and old scraps of verse that made Ireland romantic to herself; but the new Ireland, overwhelmed by responsibility, begins to long for psychological truth." In giving up the embroiderings of the old mythologies, Yeats not merely broke with his own past but (powerfully assisted by Pound) in effect ushered in 20th-century poetry.

No such widespread effect attended Thomas's similar declaration of independence from his earlier mode of poetizing. It was, indeed, not so much the later as the earlier Thomas who had impact upon the practice of his contemporaries. What this poem signalizes is Thomas's recognition of a deficiency in himself as a human being, and therefore as a poet, a deficiency not unlike that remarked by Keats in his image of the chamber of maiden-thought.

As Keats saw that he needed to sharpen his vision into the "heart and nature of Man" and to convince his nerves that "the world is full of misery and heartbreak, pain, sickness, and oppression," so Thomas sees that he must give up his aesthetic concern for words in their colors for a human concern with the meaning of *the* word (a cloaking word of many colors), which is Love. A truant school-boy, he had given the unhoused lovers, who asked for bed, a stone. A young poet, he had submerged his human subjects in abstraction and conceited imagery. Now, he says, I shall rid myself of my egocentricity, as, simultaneously, I write out of myself and my experience with human beings instead of my reference books.

G. S. Fraser has said that the poem "gives a foretaste of one of Thomas's main later themes, the reminiscent celebration, through the evoking of a landscape that the perspective of time has made legendary, of childish innocence." (*Casebook,* 45.) It does more. Up to the immediately preceding poem ("After the funeral"), there had been an almost complete absence of identifiable human beings. From this time on, people, as well as shadows, ghosts, halves, seeds, neophytes, and the like, populate his poems. He did not altogether give up his earlier style or his fondness for physiological data. But he has become self-conscious about the latter. Late in 1938 he wrote Watkins concerning "A Saint About to Fall":

> The last line of the 2nd verse might appear just a long jumble of my old anatomical clichés, but if, in the past, I've used "burning brains & hair" etc. too loosely, this time I used them — as the only words—in dead earnest (p. 45).

Thomas's marriage, the birth of his child, the war, the experience of real—not abstract—death, the illness of his father, all these contributed to produce a very changed poet. "La nuance, pas le couleur," wrote Verlaine. Thomas denies both for compassion and humanity.

In his bad-boy *Confessions,* George Moore, who esteemed Verlaine's sentiment, exclaimed:

> Humanity be hanged! Self, and after self a friend; the rest may go to the devil; and be sure that when any man is more stupidly vain and outrageously egotistic than his fellows, he will hide his hideousness in humanitarianism.

But he grew out of it, as Thomas, who had similar feelings toward the equilibrist middle class which his father represented, came to do. The present poem testifies to Thomas's maturation.

# 4

# The Wrong Rain

# The Hand that Signed the Paper

When asked, late in 1934, whether he took his stand "with any political or politico-economic party or creed," Thomas answered:

> I take my stand with any revolutionary body that asserts it to be the right of all men to share, equally and impartially, every production of man from man and from the sources of production at man's disposal, for only through such an essentially revolutionary body can there be the possibility of a communal art. (P. 190, *Quite Early One Morning.*)

A year later this, the most directly political of his poems, was published. Two severances give the poem its tone, the first and more obvious that of the hand from the rest of the body, the second that of male from female. The first, as Stanford has noted, produces a cinematic effect: "In a quick series of photo-flashes, as at a film, we see the hand signing the fatal paper which will lead to war erupting across a continent. Film-like too, the activating hand is shown impersonally, without a head attached, so that the inhuman aspect of the action becomes the more evident." (P. 82.)

The inhumanity goes very deep. The hand writes so easily because, disconnected from heart and head, it is dealing not with human beings but with paper-and-ink statistics. The body politic is not a living body at all. And the thing becomes terrifying when one sees, let us say, an ineffectual and clerk-like type (arthritic and stoop-shouldered) wielding the cosmic power of the moving finger that, having writ, moves on.

A headless body politic, and a heartless one, one of which it can no longer be said that the hand that rocks the cradle rules the world. There are no queens here, only kings. The whole element of the feminine, which is a ministering angel "when pain and anguish wring the brow," is ignored. (One thinks of Hitler and his all-male chorus, the women minding their three K's.) We are transported back to a time, before the intermediaryship of Mary, when ". . . indeed the hand of the Lord was against them to destroy them from among the host, until they were consumed." (*Deut.* 2, 15.)

An interesting parallel to Thomas's poem appears in Donne's sermon over the body of King James:

> And when you shall find that hand that has signed to one of you a Patent for Title, to another for Pension, to another for Pardon, to another for Dispensation, Dead: . . . That Hand that ballanced his own three Kingdomes so equally, as that none of them complain of one another, nor of him; and carried the Keyes of all the Christian world, and locked up, and let out Armies in their due season, Dead; how

poore, how faint, how pale, how momentary, how transitory, how empty, how frivolous, how Dead things, must you necessarily thinke Titles, and Possessions, and Favours, and all, when you see that Hand, which was the hand of Destinie, of Christian Destinie, of the Almighty God, lie dead!

Thomas's is a poem on the other hand.

# When I Woke

It is with the seeming-simple poems, like this aubade in k's, that the interpreter can really go wrong. In the difficult poems, Thomas fires at his reader with a shotgun; the puns and symbols have such an area of dispersion that he can scarcely miss, though he may only wound. But here the precise and simple images are like rifle-bullets, and if missile and target do not coincide not even a feather falls.

The characters of this poem are Thomas, a man with a bill-hook, and a voice in the air. What happens? Morning noises waken Thomas from bad dreams. Among the noises is that made by the bill-hook wielder. Then Thomas hears the voice in the air speak of the town's destruction. And he goes back to sleep. These are the bare bones of the poem, and one may justifiably ask, Shall these bones live? Clearly the poem amounts to nothing on the literal level. And it raises more questions than it answers. For example: Why does Thomas devote eight lines to the bill-hooker, if his only function is to awaken Thomas? What, or whose, is the voice of doom? Why, having heard it, does Thomas calmly go back to sleep? And why are the coins on his eyelids singing like shells?

This last question suggests a second line of inquiry. Perhaps Thomas had not been waked from sleep but from death. So what happens is this: Thomas, in his grave, wakes each morning to the sounds of life (the bill-hooker is tidying up his grave); but this morning he hears what he has been waiting for: God's voice declaring the dissolution of the earth. And Thomas goes back to sleep in joyful anticipation of the coming resurrection of his glorified body.

It makes a certain sense. But Thomas has never before revealed himself a resurrectionist of so distinctly a Catholic persuasion. To the contrary. Further, the poem has neither the sound nor the imagery to support such a concept—unless the intention is to show how local, how personal even, the world's end will be to the dead. This afterthought furnishes a rather amusing poem, a good deal more so than Mr. McLeish's "End of the World." Though the latter is recommended by its walloping last line—

"Nothing, nothing, nothing, nothing at all."—the metaphor of the world as a circus is too trite and too impersonal to generate more than a mild amusement. Thomas's, eliciting an agreement that the end might very well occur so and pleasantly uniting the macabre and the commonplace, sets the imagination to work, but within the context of reality rather than make-believe.

But is this the poem Thomas wrote? Perhaps it is not the end of *the* world but the end of a world which is being described. For example:

> The sound of birds, clocks, and bells propelled me out of an inferno of dreams, where devils and slimy creatures and sexy women writhed about me. Still half-asleep and dreaming, I am fully awakened by the everyday sound of a bill-hook outside my bedroom. An ordinary man with living blood in his veins slashes away the last dream-creature as though it were Aaron's rod returned from its reptile to its proper shape. Bearded like God or like Father Time, he has, in destroying that dream-world, assumed a God-like or Time-like function. I myself, in a Berkeleyan sense am God-like, and re-create the earth each morning; my sight moves upon the face of the bay-waters (and if I'm still a little blind after the night before, a short walk to the bathroom clarifies my creative vision). I cannot, of course, say of the earth I make that it is very good; mine is one in which Death lays his icy hands on mammoths. But on this particular morning, as the God-like laborer woke me to perform my God-like function, I was made aware of the supervention of a mightier force than my own. The radio brought news that the life of my sea-town was to be changed, changed utterly, that it was twenty-five o'clock and God was dead, that day was to have its nightmares no less ruinous ("profligate") than night. I returned to my bed in fear and anger and hopeless loathing. The word that the voice has spoken to me and the bill-hooker, so recently so divinely destructive and creative, is Götterdämmerung.

This too makes sense. And the subject (the morning the war broke over the world) must—the poem was published in the autumn of 1939—have weighed heavy upon Thomas's mind. All the questions initially raised are answered: the bill-hooker is described at length to set up the theme of man as God-like (to be developed in the passage devoted to Thomas as creator) and of man as destroyer (to be developed in the concluding section). The voice of doom is identified as news of war. Thomas does not go back "calmly" to sleep but in trepidation. The coins on his eyelids suggest both death and the war's cause (they are, so to speak, Rhine-gold); and the shells suggest both bombs and bombed-out cities.

# Ceremony after a Fire Raid

"What are you going to do in the war?" Thomas wrote Watkins. "I can't kill & so, I suppose, will have to join the dangerous RAMC." (Watkins, p. 71.) He did not kill, but he saw much death.

Of his poems about wartime death, one concerns his own imagined end, one the real death of a small girl, one that of a centenarian, and this poem that of a just-born infant. As no one in our time has captured and rendered the feel of childhood, in prose or poetry, as Thomas has done, no one has more successfully expressed the pathos of the loss of the newly alive. It must be assumed that his sight of the burnt child was one of the most shocking events of his life.

The seed of the poem is, of course, the visual image: ". . . its kneading mouth/Charred on the black breast . . . its arms full of fires." Surely no one has more vividly and with such economy expressed the horrific end-result of the Olympian scribble by the hand that signed the paper.

Powerful emotion recollected in tranquility. I do not think that Thomas could ever have recollected this scene in tranquility. He was forced, therefore, to particularly stringent efforts of objectification, and for the most part has admirably succeeded. In over-all format, the poem is a burial service ("It really is a Ceremony, and the third part of the poem is the music at the end. Would it be called a voluntary, or is that only music at the beginning?" Watkins, p. 114). After the introduction, in the first stanza, follow hymn, prayer and chant. Part II represents a sermon; and Part III, as he says, the postlude.

In no part of the poem describing the ceremony do the varying emotions get out of hand. With something of Eliot's skill in "Ash Wednesday" (and his careful notice of Eliot's method and devices has aided materially in his effort to objectify), he has differentiated his tone in the three sections, thus proving his control.

But in the first stanza he is not so successful. Pertinently, this is the stanza which contains the shudder-producing visual image. It was too much for him, and in his effort to exert control, he went too far. The result is a conceited stanza.

The opening phrase—"Myselves/The grievers"—though the "v" sounds are pleasant, is a contrived and tricky ambiguity. He may be referring to the several aspects of himself, or to himself and others like him. Its meaning is beside the point. The phrase is obtrusive, drawing attention to the poet's cleverness. The ambiguity is not one that counts, as, for example, Eliot's "Let us go then, you and I . . . ." is. "Among the street" nags for attention as, in advertisements, a preposition substituted for a conjunction does. What he means is open to question; perhaps his effort is to invoke the picture of a shattered, debris-littered street. "Tireless" fails of being the inevitable epithet for death; it has the sound of fake Shakespeare. It would logically apply to personified Death; it does not apply to the state of death. And this is no place for a jesting play on "tired to death."

The pun implicit in "kneading" comes off better: the two meanings work as a team; and the wit does not distract from the thing seen or the emotion felt. The play on the "black breast of the grave/The mother dug" is too clever by half, and cleverness at this point is merely grotesque. The strength of the passage is in the thing seen—"its kneading mouth/Charred on the black breast . . . and its arms full of fires." It was, as I said, too strong for Thomas to bear; the expression of emotion ran the risk of bathos. He tried wit instead and suffered the same come-down.

But the ceremony itself works as a whole and has lines and phrases of exceptional beauty. And in the postlude, Thomas lays some claim to being named a second organ voice of England. Perhaps there is a place for this poem somewhere between Tennyson's "Wellington Ode" and Eliot's "Ash Wednesday."

What Thomas says in the poem he has said before and will say again. It is at all times worth saying. It is simply that the individual human life is precious. This is the sun-like fact that gleams through all the smoky clouds of abstractions, generalizations, platitudes, and rhetoric that are belched out to justify war.

It is not the death of the child as such that is the tragedy; it is its death before it makes its contribution to the future history of mankind. A history which has extended back to Adam and Eve, to the formation of this star, a history which has for twenty centuries been illuminated by the Star of Bethlehem, in this child's burned body ends. That sea of seed in the child's loin, that link with the past and spawning ground of the future, has been sucked dry. And if we recall that Christ died childless but has His present life, we must also recall that the Word had a tongue. The child's only possible impingement upon the future depends upon the memory of its death's never being dislodged from the awakened hearts of the ritualists. The child is beyond cockcrow; we can be shouters like the cock.

Adam and Eve held in their loins all mankind. Every child born is an Adam or Eve; its death is the undoing of generations of men and women, the uprooting of a garden of growth. In the death of a child, Creation and history revert to Chaos and blank.

But there are billions of Adams and Eves, and among them those who will have learned from this death that Love is the last (and the first) light spoken. Their influence will spread, as the sea expands its boundaries; as Christianity flooded Europe; as man populated the globe; as organ-music swells. And there will be glory to this child in its lowness. For its end will have been a beginning: the thunder of genesis announcing a lightning of revelation dividing a bad past from a good future.

I do not know that this is exactly what the thunder said. The subject of the sentence — "masses" — may have the specific Christian sense, or the Marxist. I have given it an in-between, un-technical humanist meaning. And the erupting, fountaining, entering to utter may apply to what happens within an individual rather than to a society. But the note of triumph is so powerful that I have chosen the latter. It *is* a powerful note. And it must be. The flames dwarfing the streets and gutting the cathedral are so awful that only the affirmation of a Gloria can overwhelm them. A Gloria with substance, affirming human life and love in the concrete and particular. It is the fires in the arms of the child that extinguish the fires in the street.

# A Refusal to Mourn

An important question in literary criticism can be approached in these terms: Does Keats's "Ode to a Nightingale," despite its gorgeous imagery and its marvelous seventh stanza, collapse like a pricked balloon when it is read "My head aches," or "My back aches"? Can rhetoric compensate for its intense subjectivity, its self pity, its morbidity betokening a failure of nerve, in short, its failure to come to mature terms with reality?

The dispute will never be resolved so long as there are tough as well as tender-minded critics. And no doubt similar dispute will in future concern Thomas's "Refusal to Mourn."

This is a poem with a big sound. It starts with an emphatic *Never* (which is a very long time); impressively piles up hypenated epithets to regain the altitude briefly lost by "until"; and, gaining momentum, arcs across the whole world's history, from Chaos to Judgment Day, with salient elements of the Burkean sublime — darkness, silence, light, and sea — brought into play. All this in a periodic sentence over two stanzas long.

To what effect? To declare that I, Dylan Thomas (I, I, I) refuse to mourn the death of a child, refuse to let my art become propaganda. One might visualize the vehicle here as an ornate and lumbering circus wagon transporting a piping midget tenor. For the tough-minded observer, informed of Thomas's statement, what possible response exists but a curt "So what?"

But the tough-minded one is exposed as tender-minded if this is his initial rejoinder. He has answered out of emotion, not pausing to determine whether under the magniloquence there lies a tough reasonableness. His first question should have been, "Why not?"

Which is to say that the poem succeeds or fails not because the first three stanzas resound but because the fourth gives or does not give them reason to. If not, then the poem's virtue is merely that of "Roll on, thou deep and dark blue ocean."

It has been said (*Explicator*, XVII, no. 3) that Thomas is refusing the conventional outward show of grief — "the Old Testament tradition of 'sackcloth'," the "meaningless elegies of the 'Christian'." And no doubt he is: the "grave truth" that murders "the mankind of her going" and the "mule praises" over Annie's grave have an identity. But an attack upon convention, a criticism of platitudinizing is too partial and too negative to sustain the cosmic scope of the first stanza.

Nothing less than an Everlasting Yea can accomplish this end. And this is precisely the achievement of the last stanza.

> Deep with the first dead lies London's daughter,
> Robed in the long friends,
> The grains beyond age, the dark veins of her mother,
> Secret by the unmourning water
> Of the riding Thames.
> After the first death, there is no other.

Here the girl assumes with sobriety ("Deep with the first dead") her place in the history of all things. That cosmic plan so sonorously described requires her for its resolution. The idea of the interdependence of macrocosm and microcosm has its sublimity. And those elements developing the first stanza's note of the sublime are carefully matched here: the darkness of the earth, the silence of the dead, the roll of the Thames into the sea, the lustrous dignity of enduring comradeship ("Robed in the long friends"). And somewhat more than matched, since "friends," "grains," "veins" add a humanness (without diminishing the magnitude) that is missing from the first stanza. (There is not much humanity in a "fathering darkness.")

The poem ends on an interesting ambiguity: is the "first death" birth or death? It can be defined either way, and it does not really matter. What Thomas is saying, of course, is what he says so often, that "Death shall have no dominion." And, as usual, he is saying it in terms of a scientific humanism rather than in Old Testament (stanza 2) or New Testament (stanza 3) terms. (The three functionally positive images of these stanzas — "Zion of the water bead," "synagogue of the ear of corn," and "mankind of her going"—really anticipate the affirmation of the final stanza; the overriding tone of the first three stanzas is one of dismissal.)

Will the poem seen in this way satisfy the tough-minded critic? I think that it should. Reflection ought to suggest that "So what?" is silenced and "Why not?" sufficiently answered. Such self-centeredness and petulance as might seem initially to appear are seen on more careful reading to be swallowed up by the mankindness of the poet's motives.

It should, but it will not. In *Decadence: A Philosophical Inquiry* (pp. 312-3), C. E. M. Joad comments:

> Many of the poems which appear in *Horizon* appear to fall within this second category ["the poet drops form altogether and produces phrases and rhythms which having no structure to which to attach themselves, may be likened to the flotsam and jetsam which is carried on the waters of a flood"], consisting, as they do, of a mere saying of things which have neither meaning nor form.
>
> Take, for example, the following by Dylan Thomas from the October number of *Horizon,* 1945. The poem is called 'A Refusal to Mourn the Death, by Fire, of a Child in London'.
> [He quotes the first sentence.]
> Some of the expressions used in this poem seem to be meaningless, for example, sowing 'salt seed' in the 'least valley of sackcloth'; some of the allusions baffle the intellect — what, for instance, is the precise significance of the 'round Zion of the water bead?' Conscious of my own obtuseness of the finer shades of the poetical art, I forebear comment which might be irrelevant; though it is perhaps relevant to point out that from the reading of this poem neither I nor anybody else to whom I have shown it has been able to derive any pleasure at all.

I think that Mr. Joad is not so obtuse as perverse, demanding a prosy denotativeness where poetical connotativeness is to be preferred. But there is a certain precision in the poem. In his first sentence Thomas says, in effect, that he will die before he will weep or mourn. Which is to say that he will complete his mortal circle. (As he expresses it, it is all creation which returns to the darkness whence it came, completing *its* mortal circle; but so, to the dying person, death seems.) Thomas, one with the elements, becomes part of another circle — a drop of water — and of the cycle that water undergoes. Water (or any element) is holy and Zion is a holy place (and, as a hill, at least semi-circular). On Zion is the temple, which bridges the gap between earth and heaven. The water bead (and bead suggests the round rosary bead and the Christian prayers which go heaven-ward) drawn by the sun equally bridges that gap. Thus the drop of water is quite precisely a Zion for the dead Thomas's entry.

As for the other image: to sow salt-impregnated seed is to sow seed that will not germinate, the equivalent of weeping fruitless tears. "The least valley of sackcloth" is simply any place, large or small, given over to public mourning. Thomas refuses to do as Mordecai did, who "put on sackcloth with ashes, and went out into the midst of the city, and cried with a loud and bitter cry."

Mr. Joad thinks of Thomas as a poet who "drops form altogether and produces phrases and rhythms which, having no structure to which to attach themselves, may be likened to the flotsam and jetsam which is carried on the waters of a flood." Now *there* are some allusions that really baffle the intellect. Jetsam is defined as "goods thrown overboard to lighten a vessel in distress." Thus "phrases and rhythms" are goods thrown overboard. But the poet who produces them is their manufacturer, not the captain of a distressed vessel. What is the structure to which these goods should be "attached"? They are stored in, not attached to, the vessel. And what, in this metaphor, is the "form" that the manufacturer-poet "drops"? Is it perhaps the form that was jettisoned, and not the phrases and rhythms after all? No, this figure is quite incapable of explication — nor does it strike, pierce, possess the soul.

## Dawn Raid

Elder Olson has chosen this poem to show that "the very principles which exhibit [Thomas's] genius also exhibit his failures when he fails." (Olson, p. 26.) He finds the poem trifling, fanciful rather than imaginative, its emotion unclear. "The poet seems to be trying to be triumphant about this death; he fails so utterly that he is almost derisive."

Olson is right about Thomas's being derisive. He is wrong about the object of the derision. Being wrong, he misses some of the virtues of the poem.

The first mistake one can make in reading "Dawn Raid" is to approach it with the seriousness that one quite properly brings to "Refusal to Mourn" and "Ceremony." True, all three embody the poet's reaction to wartime death. But it will be remembered that in the former two the question uppermost in his mind was not that of death but of fulfillment. Have the girl and the child been of no more significance than squashed cockroaches? And the answer is No: the girl has not died but been re-assimilated into the source of life; the child, its future as a procreator erased, has changed the future by changing men's hearts.

Neither is in any way extraordinary; each is Everyman. Generalizations from their deaths, in accordance with Thomas's philosophical outlook, are possible and are seriously made. We are concerned with the "mankind," the "Adam and Eve" of their expulsion.

But in the present poem we have read forward from Adam and Eve (universal and mythic) to Methuselah (unique and legendary). Generalizations are not based on exceptional cases, though some cases may, as this one does, lend themselves to ironic commentary. Briefly, to read this poem as one reads the others is like reading without a change of emotional set, "Life is a jest and all things show it," and "They are all gone into the world of light."

Thomas has been at some pains to ensure the right approach. He has adopted the conventional sonnet length and has further treated with convention by using (for him) an unusual number of true rhymes. But his rhythm, predominantly anapestic, is all wrong for the form. It lilts.

When the morning was waking over the world.

And it is all wrong for the subject of the poem. Pippa should be skipping down the street.

Why? Because a very good joke is about to be perpetrated, one which reduces the Power Elite to the absurd by showing them busily breaking butterflies on the wheel.

The poem opens on an "In the Time of the Breaking of Nations" note, the permanence of morning contrasted with the transitoriness of war. An ordinary man (save for his age), acting as routinely, as inevitably — as permanently — as the morning, rises to enjoy it. Then occurs the break in the routine: he dies. But it is a departure from the norm only in a particular sense: he has not died before; in the general sense, death is routinely waking over men like morning over the war.

The death, however, would seem out of the ordinary: the old man is killed by a bomb. And yet this is not what Thomas says: he stresses the point that he "stepped out and he died," not that he was killed. Even as he stepped to the door the locks of his life were yawning loose.

And this is the point of the joke, this is where Thomas becomes derisive. One must imagine the millions of dollars, the myriad of workers at the assembly lines, the legions of military devoted to putting a bomb on the doorstep of an inoffensive old man who is about to fall over dead when the bomb explodes.

And who dies precisely where he wants to die. This is the key

174 ·

line of the poem — "He dropped where he loved . . . ." For a hundred years he had lived on this street. He knew, as old familiar friends, every cobble-stone, every lamp-post, every trash-can — and, of course, every neighbor. His character had been formed, his life shaped by the street. And he in turn had conditioned the character, colored the life of that street. Of course it needs to be told this most excellent jest at the expense of the massed enemies of homely streets. They used a sun to kill the gaffer. This, as Olson says, is not imagination but fancy. But it is a pleasant fancy, and the folk-quality of fancy, warm and good-humored but with a wry recognition of reality, is what is called for here, not the elevated peril of imagination.

He dropped where he loved. Let him lie. ("Leave him be," the street might say, taking some pleasure in the infinitive's ambiguity.)

And now comes the poem's difficult passage. Olson does not explain; he reacts: "We cannot be moved by the ambulance and the storks, symbolic or otherwise." Elmer Brooks (*Explicator,* June 1954) takes the ambulance to be that which conveys our immortal part to its imperishable home; Phyllis Bartlett (*Ibid.,* Dec. 1953), as that which conveys the broken body to a proper burial ground, there to be repaired against the day of physical resurrection.

The figure is certainly not clear. In what respect is the ambulance "heavenly"? Is it drawn by a wound, as though by horses — or drawn *to* the wound, like buzzards by the smell and sight of a dead cat? Does the participle "assembling" modify "wound" or "ambulance"?

Since there is no evidence to support answers, only ingenuity will serve. I feel no compunction about bringing the passage into line with my understanding of the octave of the sonnet.

The kind of street the old man lived on looks suspiciously on strangers and particularly on representatives of bureaucracy. Policemen they may have learned to live with. But not tax collectors, settlement workers, building inspectors, socially-conscious clergymen, and the like. And the arrival of an ambulance, like that of a police car, can cause alarm and excitement even in streets more familiar with and amenable to the incursions of outside officialdom.

So, on one level there is the image of the official ambulance, around which stand the vulturine attendants, themselves surrounded by suspicious natives, aware that something significant has left their lives, not willing to part with it to outsiders. Here "heavenly" means "other-worldly" in the sense of "outside the neighborhood"; the ambulance does come as though attracted to the wound (a testimonial to efficiency, but with grisly undertones); and "assembling" modifies "ambulance."

It is, of course, a Red Cross ambulance which has been put into motion by Christian charity, its symbol the wound of Christ (a wound whose edges were fitted together and healed), a symbol which has held the people of Europe together and produced such organizations as the Red Cross.

But this organization is associated by its symbol with the church, a state church which is part and parcel of the Establishment. Officials of Organized Christianity, motivated by that wounded man on the rude, red tree, may be suspected to have come to ensure the old man's final relation of propriety to the organization. Again, if not hostility on the part of the street, certainly on the part of Thomas, for whom an organized church is not dissimilar from the organized government and military.

The man and the morning which for a hundred years he woke to greet are inseparably united. All the Last Things have already been achieved without the intermediaryship of bureaucracy. And as the sun brought the other world to him, he takes his hundred years of domesticated neighborliness to the sun.

So, as he was uncommon in having been for so long a part of the street, let him remain a part; as he was uncommon in having pricked the bubble of organized efficiency, let him remain apart from it.

In 1917, Wilfred Owen wrote Osbert Sitwell:

> Already I have comprehended a light which will never filter into the dogmas of any national church: namely, that one of Christ's essential commands was: passivity at any price . . . . It may be a chimerical and an ignominious principle, but there it is. It can only be ignored, and I think pulpit professionals are ignoring it very skillfully and successfully indeed.

Thomas would have subscribed to these convictions without reservation. I think that they underlie and give reason for the derisive qualities of this poem.

# On a Wedding Anniversary

The earlier published version of this poem (in *Poetry* (London), 1941) eight lines longer, and with two stanzas devoted to the war-time context before the lovers are introduced, has neither the simplicity nor the intensity of the final one, but it is an interesting poem and does not deserve to be forgotten:

At last, in a wrong rain,
The cold, original voices of the air
Cry, burning, into the crowd,
And the hermit, imagined music sings
Unheard through the street of flares;

The told birds fly again
From every true or crater-carrying cloud
Riding the risk of the night,
And every starfall question, with their wings,
Whether it be death or light;

The sky is torn across
This ragged anniversary of two
Who moved for three years in tune
Through the singing words of the marriage house
And the long walks of their vows.

Now their love lies a loss
And Love and his patients roar on a chain;
The sun's brought down with a shout,
Three years dive headlong, and the mice run out
To see the raiding noon.

The expulsion of Love and the usurpation by Chaos of the provinces
of Harmony in the first stanza, with its montage of Nuremburg rallies,
London blitz, and dispossessed Prospero, is so well realized that one
wonders why the usually thrifty Thomas did not find a use for it elsewhere.
The shift, from the calculated whipping of men (presumably free of will)
into unreasoning beasts, to the scientifically-experimental testing of the
presumably compelled birds, has fine ironic implications. A few deletions
or minor changes, the addition of a stanza or two, and Thomas could
have added another devastating comment on the war to his list.

However, the one that we have will serve. The occasion of his poem
is peculiarly apt for his condemnation of the war. In matrimony, the
ends of which are the procreation and rearing of children, mutual support
and affection, and the satisfaction of desire, the needs of the individual
and of society are harmonized, the tradition brought forward and renewed,
order maintained, nature and grace reconciled. Past and future are
unified by present love. The wedding anniversary is a testimony that the
educing of harmony from chaos has not proved a temporary thing.

War is the enemy of all that matrimony and the wedding anniversary
stand for: graceless, it rips nature; defining Love as Hate, Bethlehem
as Bedlam, it chains lovers in the violent wards; on normal death in its season, like matrimony sacramental, it superimposes death explosive, eccentric.

The first two stanzas of the poem present no difficulty. Perhaps the crater-carrying cloud is slightly off-center: Grigson compares it to veins with ears. But in saturation bombing, the sticks of crater-producing bombs very nearly clouded the sky; and craters-full of earth and debris rose in clouds after the explosions.

The last stanza is clear in its suggestion but obscure on its literal level. And it is a shame to bring prose analysis to bear upon what is evocative enough without it. "Too late in the wrong rain" says all that needs to be said. Why love parted the lovers (because one sent the other to the country, or one joined the WRENS, or what have you) is of no moment. Whether they have come together through dying in a rain of bombs, or whether they are alive and together but for only a final moment, is beside the point. Whether they are killed by flying fragments (ironically by fragmented window and door, the means of vision, welcome, and entry) is irrelevant. Whatever the specific situation, the epitaph applies.

## *There Was a Saviour*

The silent irony of this poem consists in its being a poem about death in war written in the metre of Milton's hymn in honor of Christ's birth, a birth attended by "a universal peace through sea and land."

Paradoxes are plentiful as blackberries, perhaps so numerous as to invoke the law of diminishing returns. Most of them are common to Christian thought: the freedom in bondage, the certainty in uncertainty, the joy of sorrow, the life in death. But the great one is the escape from love made possible by a false idea of Christian love. The purpose of Thomas's poem is to make the new commandment's concluding phrase, "thy neighbor as thyself," seem less a voice-dropping afterthought. That is, it is a sermon on the text of *Luke,* 10, 27.

The poem opens on a third-person, once-upon-a-time note:

There was a savior in whose teachings children, kept cold and dark, found the warmth of love, the light of hope. Wholly captivated by his teaching, they freed themselves from the hopelessness of futile wishing. From the early Christians we hear what the new faith offered them: doing his will on earth despite all odds offered hope of heaven; the apathy of the heavy-laden was transmuted into the calm of the spiritually obligated; in Christ's life-demanding love we found the courage to face death-imposing hate; Hosanna silenced war-cry; sorrow, tears, sacrifice were not purposeless nor suffered alone; dying for him had reason.

Thomas's economy with quotation marks and his habit of de-emphasizing transitions makes it impossible to determine where the "voice of children" ends. My assumption is that it ends with "Under his downy arm you sighed as he struck," the "you" being used as the equivalent of "one." Granted this assumption, the "you" of the following line ("O you who could not cry") becomes the pronoun of direct address. Thomas now speaks, in this winter of a war year, to a nominal Christian, but through him to all Christians who have falsified the teachings of Christ by eliminating the obligation of personal sacrifice and by deleting "on earth" from the Lord's prayer.

O you who had no tear for a man (fallen among thieves) but tears enough for a man long dead and eyes for a far-off heaven, there is beside you now in this unheavenly dark not Christ but me.

Thomas now allies himself to his companion in his false pride (are they together in a black-out? or dirty from working among ruined buildings?), and the two exclaim to the unhallowed year:

O we who felt no Christian charity and took no action when avarice undramatically, attritionally damped the fires and depleted the stores of hearthside friends, but took our refuge in the sweet bye and bye, now weep immensely for strangers, for the destruction of their homes, for the unknown dead and missing; we now see (vividly, as if only we were left to see) that, though these strangers alive meant nothing to us, in their deaths they are near neighbors. [Perhaps their ashes blacken these no longer proud brothers.] We, alone in the dark and feeling as if we were islands to which love had been exiled, incite to action the force that opens all sepulchres.

We are in these last lines taken back to the descriptive phrase, "rarer than radium." Love, like radium, burns, shines, heals — and is derived from pitch-black matter. A particularly apt phrase and probably the only one in the poem often recalled. Indeed, only the first stanza really succeeds. The second is too determinedly paradoxical to seem sincere; those that follow have such a wordy density that reading is like wading through knee-deep water. The phrases that stand out — "Near and fire neighbour," "break a giant tear," "churches of his tears" — are too clever, or melodramatic, or (after "A Refusal to Mourn") familiar to breed respect. Except for the surging final sentence,

we arouse the soft,

Unclenched, armless, silk and rough love that breaks all rocks,

nothing in the poem produces anything like the response of the simple introductory lines

                    There was a saviour
                    Rarer than radium
            Commoner than water, crueller than truth

and even these are saved from triteness by the second line.


# Deaths and Entrances

This poem, which takes its title from Donne's sermon *Death's Duell,*
appears to be a meditation upon the old subject of death's being no
respecter of persons, and a comment upon the Hardyan ironies that war
causes to happen. The imagined scene is the invasion then (late in 1940)
thought to be imminent, the characters are a dear friend, a neighboring
stranger, one's self, and a German invader.

I say it *appears* to be such a meditation, because Lita Hornick interprets the second stanza as being concerned with the birth of a Savior.
Her evidence here is the phrase "wind his globe out of your water
thread." Her argument is that "Twining threads, cords, fibres, and tentacles, which are standard paraphernalia in Thomas's uterine depths, are
said by Jung to be archetypal womb symbols." (P. 105.) Since this
interpretation gives the poem a quite unexpected meaning, it will have
to be taken into account.

The opening line, repeated in each stanza, makes double, possibly
triple use of the word *almost*: the events to be described will occur very
close to the time of invasion; the horror of that evening will be so great
as to seem almost like the one "in which the heavens shall pass away
with a great noise, and the elements shall melt with fervent heat." And,
since the poem was written in August, it may be that Thomas hints at
the irony of an invasion on Christmas Eve.

On such a night there will be near hits and near deaths, exact hits
and certain deaths, among them that of at least one of your closest, most
vital friends — one of those "wild men" of "Do not go gentle," "who
caught and sang the sun in flight." Implicit in these lines is a tragic
contrast: on the one hand, the fire of love and song and eulogy breaking
from the dust-formed body; on the other, the incinerated dust of the
dead singer. Donne says of the latter in *Death's Duell*: ". . . in this
death of *incineration,* and dispersion of dust, we see *nothing* that we call
*that mans . . . .* This death of incineration and dispersion, is, to naturall
*reason,* the most *irrecoverable* death of all . . . ." *

---
*The quotations woven into the following paragraphs are all from Donne's prose, Nonesuch
edition.

180 ·

Another contrast follows: this most-loved of immortal friends, in his sudden incineration, will be delivered "from the manifold deaths of this world, the *omni die* and the *tota die,* the *every days death* and *every houres death,"* imaged in Thomas by the attritional aspects of marriage.

If, in the first stanza, a best friend is compelled to leave off praising you, in the second (when even the dead pilots in their crashing planes are attempting to unlock your life and lock your lips), a stranger (apparently an R.A.F. pilot) will give up his life to save yours — a stranger as distant and as much a comfort to the wayworn traveler as Polaris. Shot, his blood will fertilize the sea as the blood and sperm of Uranus did, producing Love. Exemplifying *John* 15, 13, he is a Christ-like figure, and, in losing his life for another's sake, he has both found and magnified his own. (Your "thin-spun life," unslit by the blind Fury because of his sacrifice, becomes his world of life. He has "paid the debt that [you] owe.")

This death is, then, a triumph, not a tragedy. Though his life has been one of lamentations ("we celebrate our owne funeralls with cries, even at our birth"), "many waters quench not love," and "in the *grave* the *wormes* do not kill us, we breed and feed": as the Christian sucks at Christ's wounds, so the sea-shell at the pilot's. (And of course, every shell fired against the invaders will be contingent upon his life and death.)

The image of the locks and keys connecting this and the final stanza undoubtedly comes from Donne's sermon: "But whether the *gate* of *my prison* be *opened* with an *oyld key* (by a gentle and *preparing sickness*), or the gate bee *hewen downe* by a *violent death.* . . ." In this final stanza it is violent death that is pictured.

On that incendiary eve, when friends (like the Marys) have sought the grave that enemies (like crucifiers) have sought to put you in (you, like Christ, *"passing of mankind through* the *sea* of [your] *blood"*), one enemy will find you out, will thrust aside protectors, and will, ironically, as sun's man (i.e., Samson), blot out the real sun.

Briefly, the "hap" of war stills the praises of your best friend, compels a stranger to die for you, and presents as the last thing you see in life the face of an enemy. (Figuratively speaking: the enemy appears to be in a crashing plane.) Donne wrote the epigraph for the poem:

Stil *pray* wee for a *peaceable life* against *violent death* . . . and for *sober* and *modest assurance* against *distempered* and *diffident death,* but never make *ill conclusions* upon persons overtaken with such deaths . . . *he* [God] received *Sampson,* who went out of this world in *such a manner* . . . .

It is tempting to see in the second stanza an ironically juxtaposed birth of a Savior, and the language is highflown enough ("With every cry since light/Flashed first across his thunder-clapping eyes") to seem applicable to a god. But the same sort of rhetoric resounds in the previous poem ("Do not go gentle"), which deals with mere men. Such language is more easily justified here; it takes resounding words to capture the effect of aerial bombardment. And such a birth destroys the poem's coherence. One must ask these questions: If the dying stranger is a Christ-figure, what is the friend of the first stanza? and the enemy of the last? Are these also Christ-figures? If so, why should a Christ-figure be said to "hold his peace"? why should he "sear just riders back"?

Since such questions, raised, will multiply and answers become increasingly untenable, it seems best to leave the hero of the second stanza a Christ-like figure, not a Christ.

If the violence of the rhetoric still seems excessive, one should recall the violence of Thomas's dreams:

Are you frightened these nights? When I wake up out of burning birdman dreams—they were frying aviators one night in a huge frying pan: it sounds whimsical now, it was appalling then—and hear the sounds of bombs & gunfire only a little way away, I'm so relieved I could laugh or cry. What *is* so frightening, I think, is the idea of grey-clothed, grey-faced, blackarmletted troops marching, one morning, without a sound up a village street. Boots on the cobbles, of course, but no Heil-shouting, grenading, goose-stepping. Just silence. That's what Goebbels has done for me. I get nightmares like invasions, all successful.

# Holy Spring

It may be thought that the title of this poem is somewhat too grandiose for its essentially occasional character. Perhaps better would have been something Wordsworthian like "Lines on the occasion of my rising from a bed on a spring morning, having survived the preceding evening's bombing." Still, the poem does make use of the occasion to proclaim once again the virtue of a natural process which, whatever men may do, never ceases. For this the season is worthy of being named holy. Even if it were not, it would seem so to the man who during the raid expected never to experience it again.

The poem extends to two 12-line stanzas, each comprised of one sentence. Each has minor ambiguities. The first stanza's "I am struck as lonely as a holy maker by the sun," offers three or four possibilities. Derek Stanford is bothered by the lack of punctuation after "No" in the second stanza's

> No
> Praise that the spring time is all
> Gabriel and radiant shrubbery as the morning grows joyful
> Out of the woebegone pyre,

feeling that "the sense would seem to require a pause after the negative; since without it, the general affirmative trend of the second stanza (though menace is heard in the last line) is upset." (Stanford, p. 126.) But he misreads the stanza; the sense is clearly "Let there be no praise . . ." to balance the following "But blessed be hail and upheaval."

To paraphrase the poem:

I climb out of a bed of love (where that death-defeating healer tried again to soothe my mortal, fated body while the principle of death in the form of an army crossed the guarded sea to assault our houses and our lives) to greet another day of a war for which I have no enthusiasm but to which I may have to offer the debt of death I owe life; I call for a confessor and a mirror (which shows me my sins more clearly), but none is left alive or unshattered after the night's raid (such a raid that one thinks of Zeus thundering against the Titans) and, alone in the sun, without even a mirror-image, a poet-maker faced by war's debris, I am as lonely as a creator facing the chaos he must organize — or as much at loose ends as a creator whose work has been taken over by a surrogate.

I offer no praise that the spring is angelically bright as the morning quickens over the bombed city and the mourners cease their weeping (the returning god-sun in his plenitude lavish with light — his quiver is as an open sepulchre, he is a mighty man); but I bless the annunciaation, down-pour, and upthrust, that passion for renewal which, now and always, is the one certain thing for a man alone to praise in his expendable body in his shattered house, and I bless the Nativity and the sepulture of the Jesus-spring, though it be the last time.

Beauty, it must be inferred, is rather beside the point under the circumstances; it is the ever-recurring new testament of spring, which, despite and because of hail and high water, offers reason for hope even in the shambles of the stricken city.

# Lie Still, Sleep Becalmed

Treece speaks of this as Thomas's nearest approach to the traditional sonnet. With quotation marks supplied for lines 9 through 11, the syntax is not in any way eccentric. The vocabulary offers no insurmountable difficulty. The poem is neatly organized, the narrative progressing logically. Nevertheless, it is not, I think, a poem which can be finally interpreted. There must always remain questions to which there are several equally satisfactory answers. The questions are these: Who or what is the wounded sufferer being asked to lie still? What is the nature of the wound? What will happen if he, or she, or it refuses to lie still? Who speaks the poem? Unless all these questions are answered, the poem remains mysterious.

Lita Hornick (p. 26) believes that ". . . the sufferer with the wound in the throat is Thomas's omnipresent 'god-in-hero', taking the archetypal night journey by water, a well known death and birth symbol." This is an interesting identification, but, because it does not answer the question why the god-in-hero should lie still, which is the crux of the poem, does not assist much toward interpretation.

For example:

> Sleep, dying god; we have listened all night to your
> labored breathing.
> We were fearful; and, when you burst into song,
> we heard all the dead cry out.
> We heard all Nature speak in your voice: "Spread the
> sails that I may hasten to my resurrection."
> Sleep, dying god, speak no more; or we shall go
> with you among the dead.

The question is: why should the god's followers be so reluctant to hear the alluring song of death and resurrection?

Stanford (p. 126) is uncertain of the sufferer's identity:

> Whether the poem is a lament for one drowned at sea, or—as I incline to think—is to be taken in conjunction with the next poem in the book, *Vision and Prayer,* which describes the birth of one of the poet's children, it is difficult to say. In *Vision and Prayer,* the poet speaks of how he listens to "the moan/Of the mother hidden," and "the sufferer with the wound/In the throat, burning and turning" of the earlier makes, I believe, a like reference.

Since he too fails to answer the crucial question, he does not make the purport of the poem clear. Taking the child as sufferer, the poem can be read as follows:

> Sleep, child, you with the sharp unaccustomed air in your lungs. During the dark night of waiting, we have been conscious of your life in the mother's living body, you in the amnion, she in the tear-wet bed-sheet.
>
> We listened fearfully to your silent motion producing her agonized pain; and when, finally, you were born and made your first cry (after her screams) we had witnessed, in epitome, the history of the race.
>
> What we heard you say, what the tear-wet, bloody sheet implied, was this: Prepare things for my journey through a painful life to my death. Our answer is this: Sleep, be still, or we *will* make things ready, and accompany you on the journey that all men have made.

Again, all goes well up to the concluding couplet. And again the question: why should they not obey? It is precisely the parents' responsibility.

According to the fourteen members of my seminar in modern poetry, the poem takes these fifteen (one student, currying favor, turned in two papers) shapes:

1. Thomas speaks to a dying man in a life-boat.
2. Thomas speaks to a sea threatening to become stormy.
3. Thomas speaks to a sinking ship.
4. Thomas speaks to a Christ-figure.
5. Thomas speaks to a prospective mother.
6. Thomas speaks to his father.
7. Thomas speaks to his wife.
8. Thomas speaks to his children.
9. Thomas speaks to his phallus.
10. Thomas speaks to his poetic daemon.
11. Thomas speaks to the Earth.
12. Thomas speaks to the all-generating life-stuff.
13. Thomas speaks to the sea-born land-animal, Man.
14. A foetus speaks to its mother.
15. The dead speak to the living.

Each has supported his opinion with a certain ingenuity, deftly, as though already a professional critic, skirting or masking the implausibilities. In every instance, it is the concluding exhortation that poses the problem.

I myself waver between two interpretations. For the first, I assume that Thomas has recently seen a motion picture of the sort exemplified by *Life Boat* and *The Cruel Sea* and has been moved to write his own scenario-sonnet, which might be entitled "Death of a Ship." The ship, torpedoed, burns, fills with water, and slowly settles while such officers and men as have escaped wait in their life-boats for their ship's inevitable end. The storm of singing can be understood as the hissing of steam which occurs as the burning decks settle into the sea surface (the "salt sheet") before the final plunge. Under these circumstances, men who have closely identified themselves with the ship and who see no chance for survival might be tempted to row in close to be pulled down by the sinking vessel's suction.

If this is the sonnet that Thomas wrote, he must be credited with great tact. He has not tried to do what the motion picture can do better; he has personalized but not personified the ship; he has not sentimentalized or melodramatized the reactions of the onlookers. But in avoiding the spectacular, he has not diminished what is surely one of the most profound experiences that men can undergo.

In my second interpretation, I assume that Thomas has been immersed in the study of Walt Whitman and that what he has written here might be called "Vigil Strange I Kept in a Boat One Night." There are in his poem what appear to be echoes from such Whitman favorites as "Out of the Cradle," "When Lilacs Last," "Passage to India," and "To the Man-of-War-Bird." For example:

W. - song of the bleeding throat
T. - wound in the throat

W. - all night long
T. - all night afloat

W. - under the full of the moon
T. - under the mile off moon

W. - sound of the sea
T. - sea sound

W. - burst the wild storm
T. - broke in a storm

W. - Victorious song, death's outlet song . . .
    rising and falling, flooding the night
T. - The voices of all the drowned swam on the wind

W. - Away O soul! hoist instantly the anchor!
    Cut the hawsers — haul out — shake out every sail!

T. - Open a pathway through the slow sad sail,
    Throw wide to the wind the gates of the wandering boat.

W. - Lost in the loving, floating ocean of thee,
    Laved in the flood of thy bliss, O death
T. - . . . ride with you through the drowned.

Suppose Thomas to be with Caitlin on St. George's Channel at night in a small boat — "a speck, a point on the world's floating vast." He hears from the sea-cratered earth, "Whispers of heavenly death . . . mystical breezes wafted soft and low . . . tides of a current flowing, forever flowing . . . ." He feels his soul "turning to thee O vast and well-veil'd death,/And the body gratefully nestling close to thee." Under the hypnotic influence of "sibilant chorals," he may very well ask himself:

> Darest thou now O soul,
> Walk out with me toward the unknown region,
> Where neither ground is for the feet nor any path to follow?

He did not dare. But one may wonder whether he was ever again what he had been

> before what there in the night,
> By the sea under the yellow and sagging moon,
> The messenger there arous'd, the fire, the sweet hell within,
> The unknown want, the destiny of me.

I do not offer this as the poem Thomas wrote but as one of several poems which can be constructed from Thomas's blue-print. But I offer it without apologies. For some poems, the interpretation must be as nearly equivalent as prose paraphrase can be. Others are what might be called "buckshee-poems," offering something unexpected, unearned—something to boot. The present poem I take to be one of the latter, presenting, as it does, with a gratifying generosity, several sonnets, each quite valuable, for the price of one.

Geoffrey Grigson, however, feels himself to have been cheated. He neither understands nor likes the poem. His chief attack in this instance is upon Thomas's rhyming. "Near rhymes have their virtue," he writes, "but only if they come as deliberately as true rhyme, and have, against each other, the proper weight, accent and length." (*Casebook,* 119.) He then quotes the first stanza, with its rhyming of *wound-sound, afloat-sheet,* as an example of Thomas's ineptitude. *Afloat-sheet* particularly bothers him.

I think that he would be hard put to it to determine what *proper* weight, accent, and length are. He has previously cited as poetry worth consideration a passage from Coleridge. In it, Coleridge rhymes *allow'd-crowd*. By what standard does one find the weight, accent, and length of this rhyme proper and that of *afloat-sheet* improper? Of course, one is true and the other half rhyme. But in the same passage, Coleridge rhymes *earth* with *forth*. How can it be determined that Coleridge contrived this "as deliberately as true rhyme," whereas Thomas did not deliberate at all but wrote the "poetry of a child, volcanic and unreasoning"?

It would seem to me, to the contrary, that the most cursory reading of the poem would show how carefully Thomas has worked his sound values. The fricative in *sufferer* to suggest the hard breathing of the wounded man; the contrast between *flowing like blood* and the staccato *salt sheet broke* to indicate a dramatic change; the short *a* in *swam*, bringing the voices up to the wind's height; the inner rhymes and vowel-echoes, the alliteration and onomatopoeia and repetitions, holding the stanzas together. Nothing has been left to chance, nothing has erupted volcanically. Sense-impression and symbol collaborate to produce a poem as dramatic and as evocative as any Thomas wrote.

I have placed this sonnet among the war poems for no better reason than that I should like him to have been moved to describe a naval action.

188 ·

# 5

## Fabulous, Dear God

# Shall Gods be Said

Shall Thomas be said to be serious in this rainy-day poem? It is very difficult to tell. After a series of questions implying a relation between gods and noisy wet weather, he makes the flat statement, "It shall be said that gods are stone," and the stern demand that "the stones speak/With tongues that are all tongues."

If the poem is no more than a joke (and the first three stanzas cannot be taken very seriously two millennia after the expulsion of the gods), then it represents no more than an implied Welsh curse against a rain-storm, a rather heavy-handed rewriting of "Rain, rain, go away."

But the last stanza is invested with a seriousness of tone that suggests a greater seriousness of purpose than that.

> It shall be said that gods are stone.
> Shall a dropped stone drum on the ground,
> Flung gravel chime? Let the stones speak
> With tongues that talk all tongues.

Suppose, then, that the first three stanzas are not aimed specifically at pagan myth but at any parochial anthropomorphic tendency. It is to be noted that the stone and gravel are themselves without personality and are not described as appurtenances of any man-like deity. It is further to be noted that, by reducing to the absurd the sky gods and making stone divine, Thomas has abolished the first line of the Lord's Prayer.

I would suggest, still assuming seriousness of intent, that deleting a possessive, Thomas has re-worked the 24th Psalm to read: "The *earth* is the Lord, and the fulness thereof; the world, and they that dwell therein." He has uplifted a stone and started a heresy; the stone which the religion-builders refused is become the head stone. And all the sermons in head-stones (spoken in all tongues) have this burden: all are of the dust and turn to dust again.

Although, of course, there was that other stone found rolled away from the sepulchre.

# I Have Longed to Move Away

Rebel and atheist too, Thomas here strikes out at the Christian formulation of god-produced destiny and that vice-nature, custom. His rebellion is, however, rather more vocal than active: he is not unlike an old soldier fed to the teeth with routine, drills, and useless forms (paper and otherwise), who would like to desert but is deterred by fear of civilian life's lack of organization—to say nothing of the long arm of the military. (The imagery of the first stanza is preponderantly military: "hissing of the spent lie" = fused artillery rounds; "goes over the hill" = going AWOL; "thunder of calls and notes" = bugle calls.)

Thomas's position is ambivalent. He is half-convinced that the Christian interpretation of life and death drilled into him in his youth is as empty and meaningless as raising a hat in greeting, as fleshless as a kiss over the telephone. But it is clear from the strongest phrases ("the old terrors' continual cry"; and "night's ancient fear") that Thomas fears the dark as much as the early religion-inventors did and does not dare leave the defense they erected against it. He has, then, three courses: to renounce the old lies—to die outside the tradition; to accept, making Pascal's Choice; to separate the truth and life from the false and conventional, accepting the one, renouncing the other.

What course he takes is unclear. Stanford (p. 77) sees it as the first: "Yet if there is some truth ('some life') in this religious orthodoxy, the poet would prefer to die outside of it; since it appears of so mixed a nature." And Stanford is probably right. But some uncertainty persists because Thomas neglects the rhetorical device of emphasis in making a transition in the second stanza from his fear, which presumably defeats his longing, and his statement of defiance. A "nevertheless," or "however" at the fifth line would have helped. Further, he has been imprecise in linking "night's ancient fear" and "the parting of hat from hair." The two are not at all of the same order. The latter may be, the former was not and is not, either convention or lie. If latter-day religiosity, form divorced from reality, is, then he should have distinguished between it and its forgotten source in the terror of the unknown.

G. S. Fraser (*Casebook*, 43) sees the poem in a quite different light— as a piece of "poetical self-criticism":

> The poet is pondering whether he ought to make a bonfire—accompanied by small fireworks, perhaps dangerous ones—of childish fears, obsessions, and superstitions; a bonfire, also, in his writing of poetry of 'given' phrases, lines and images—'ghostly echoes on paper' —about whose source and meaning he is not clear. He is wondering whether he ought to become, like so many of his contemporaries of the 1930s, an 'adult' and 'socially conscious' poet. He decides that he cannot afford to make this bonfire for the reason that the poetic life, the undue fearsomeness and rhetoric—the 'ghosts' and the 'repetition of salutes'—are somehow bound up with the possibility of the full, life-giving poetic vision.

The difference between our interpretations results from his being less powerfully affected by the phrase "night's ancient fear" than I am, and by his not regarding seriously the phrase—"fall to death's feather." I take the former as a repetition of the first stanza's

> . . . old terrors' continual cry
> Growing more terrible as the day
> Goes over the hill into the deep sea.

Both, it seems to me, evoke the primitive man's profound fear of the dark, his uncertainty that the sun will rise again, his need therefore to find means of winning the sun-mover's favor. In the first stanza this image is dissociated from army routine and convention but closely related to the deathly danger of army life. It is not a firecracker that is hissing but the fuse of a high explosive; ("hissing" suggests, of course, the Satan story, that particular part of primitive man's effort to understand and control nature which Thomas is most eager to deny). In the second stanza, the distinction is not clearly made:

> Neither by night's ancient fear,
> The parting of hat from hair,
> Pursed lips at the receiver,
> Shall I fall to death's feather.

But I think the lines should be read as a series: I shall not die by primitive man's terror, nor by society's conventions, nor by transmitted imperatives. These equate with the first stanza's series: "the old terrors' continual cry"; "the repetition of salutes"; and "the thunder of calls and notes"—that is, commands issued by the bugler's pursed lips.

Fraser, however, does not make these differentiations. And he does not think that Thomas is speaking literally of his death when he says "I would not care to die":

> But here he manages to evade deep fears by mocking at shallow fears: '. . . night's ancient fear,/The parting of hat from hair' is simply a grotesque image of a man's being so frightened that his hair stands on end and pushes his hat off: as in a comic drawing by such a cartoonist as H. M. Bateman. The 'receiver' is simply a telephone receiver, and the poet's lips are 'pursed', as in a melodrama, because he is receiving a horrifying message. 'Death's feather' has no deep, obscure symbolic meaning but is simply an allusion to the humorous Cockney phrase: 'You could have knocked me down with a feather!'

I agree that "Death's feather" has no deep, obscure, symbolic meaning. (He borrowed it, perhaps, from Donne's seventh Devotion: "There is scarce anything that hath not killed some body; a haire, a feather hath done it.") But I cannot agree that it is humorous. To be knocked down by death's feather is to be killed dead—and that's no cockney joke. He is quite serious in his refusal to die in terms of myth or of convention. He is serious in his refusal, but not certain in it: the *I shall not,* it must be noticed, changes immediately to "I would not care to."

There is still a third possibility. Placing more weight upon the military imagery of the first stanza, one can argue that Thomas is denouncing the possible requirement that, because of nationalistic or racial fears and socio-economic conventions in which he only partly believes, he should be involved in war. But again those key phrases "old terrors' continual cry" and "night's ancient fear" seem to have implications too broad for so restricted an interpretation.

## Why East Wind Chills

This, like "Out of the Sighs," is one of Thomas's least discussed poems, yet one of his better achievements. Totally different from the former work —immediately understandable, impersonal though warmly sympathetic, keyed-down and un-dramatic, written mostly as if from the outside looking on—it shows that Thomas had more range than he is usually credited with, that he could sing both tight and loose.

Its thesis is a simple one: the ultimate questions will only be ultimately answered; therefore rest content. The tone, so different from that of "Was There a Time," is one not of Stoical but of Epicurean acceptance. The embittered farm-boy of the earlier poem would seem to have fired his shot and got the rancor out of his system.

The theme of death is enunciated in the first phrase and is not absent from any part of the poem. But it is not death as a horror, though its chill is not ignored, but as a sleep. It is like the cold sheets a child climbs into, and warms as he drowses off. The death-images, as I say, are introduced at once and are nicely varied through the progress of the poem: the chill of the east wind; the drying of the "windwell"—the Aeolian bag of winds; the drowning of the west; the "many a hundred falls"—autumns and autumnal windfalls; the "breast's blood," which becomes the child's own, and, when "the stone wounds," turns dry-black on the stone. All these in the initial stanza.

In the second stanza, the images are expressed as unwitting ironies in the actual questions of children:

When cometh Jack Frost? the children ask.
Shall they clasp a comet in their fists?

The funeral-service tone of "cometh," the latent sense of "Jack Frost," the rapid extinction implicit in "comet" are supposed to bring to the reader's heart (as the questions would to the parents') that sudden wrench or chill that children's words and actions often innocently do. It may be thought that Thomas has misstepped here; that these do not sound like a child's questions so much as the questions an ingenious adult would ascribe to a child. But his development of the questions' images in this and in the final stanza is beyond reproach. Will they clasp a comet in their fists? The answer (white as a comet's tail, white as an icicle quietly shining to the quiet moon) will not echo till the children's eyes are frosted windows.

In the third stanza Thomas separates himself from the practical (grown up) limited questioners—the askers of How rather than Why. These ask direction of the stars and a push from the winds; for them, "All things are known," because the metaphysical is non-sense in every sense. Thomas, though not so practical and limiting, is equally content. Hearing the hand-bell ring "Be content" and "Know no answer," he takes his place in the class-room, doing, like Mr. Chips, the best he can.

This is reversal with a vengeance, for only one poem separates this from the bitterly pessimistic "Was There a Time." It is quite possible, of course, that the two poems, though placed together, were written at widely divergent times. (Ralph Maude has adduced evidence to indicate that Thomas has violated chronology in the arrangement of his poems.) If, however, they are contemporaries, their disparity is immensely interesting. Has a fundamental shift in viewpoint occurred? Or is each the expression of a momentary mood? Unfortunately there is no evidence; one must be content to know no answer. And answers are beside the point. It is enough to enjoy the skill with which Thomas handles the movement of this poem: the way in which the lilt of the opening tetrameters and trimeters, the ballad bounce, is muted, counteracted but not stifled, by the retarded and assonantal rhyming, the run-ons, the interspersed pentameters, and the spondees; and the way in which he enforces variation of tone and of rhythm, attention to pause, and concern for sound values in the poem's last six lines. One feels a desire to read this with the care one is willing to bestow upon a run of couplets in Dryden or in Pope.

# In the Beginning

This poem, like the first verse of *John* and in the same way, defies rational analysis. This is as it should be since a mystery by definition does not abide our question and both the faith-full John and the faith-seeking Thomas are concerned with the greatest of the mysteries.

But what defies also invites scrutiny because a mystery, also by definition, is fascinating; and one never knows what serendipitical increment will accrue.

The flower in the crannied wall of Thomas's poem is the first line: "In the beginning was the three-pointed star." The immediate question is, in the beginning of what? Is this, as it appears to be, a pseudo-hexaemeric exercise, or is the poet using the Creation theme as a metaphor for the beginning of something on a smaller scale—of a new faith, of a life, of a poem, of a man's regeneration? But there can be no certain answer to this question until a decision is reached as to who or what is doing the creating. In any case, even though the genesis described here may be a metaphor, it has to be explained as a genesis.

The real problem in the line arises from the "three-pointed star." By utilizing the *Genesis-John* formula, Thomas has put his poem in a Christian context. This being the case, one's first thought must be that Thomas is referring to the Three-Personed God. God is a star. But Thomas cannot mean this literally. He must be trying to vivify the old idea that God is Light, that particular kind of light which we associate with stars. But the light which we associate with stars is dim, cold, unfruitful: "Those rolling fires discover but the sky/Not light us here . . . ." Reason does not find the metaphor as happy as the tone of the passage demands.

Perhaps it is not, then, despite the opening words, God of *Genesis,* and perhaps not God at all. Possibly consideration of the epithet "three-pointed" will assist.

Assimilating the future into the present, many artists represent the Star of Bethlehem as a kind of refulgent cross; their star, disputing the dictionary definition that stipulates five or more points, is four-pointed. Thomas has gone the artists one better; and, in doing so, he has neatly halved the Star of David. This he did either in full awareness and with a purpose, or by unwitting coincidence. If the former, why? Here are possible answers: (1) Because he objects to the Hebraic Jehovah-concept and wants his poem read from a Greek New Testament point of view. (2) Because he wants to deny the distinction, symbolized by the double triangle, between God and Nature.

If he had no thought of denigrating the six-pointed star, why did he seize upon the number three? Again there are speculative answers: (1) Because he is a Trinitarian writing a Christian poem; (2) Because he recognizes three elements working together in any creative process; that is, he is writing a non-Christian poem in which the figure three has no

Christian significance; (3) Because the number has a powerful allusive effect which he can make use of, intending no specific meaning at all.

I do not believe that any reader using the words as they are organized on the page can say finally that Thomas has meant to do one of these things and not another—that is, that Thomas is writing as a Christian, as a pagan, as a pantheist, or as a versifier of some such theory as the nebular hypothesis. The words as they appear hint at each and support none.

For example, there is a definite Christian hint in the second stanza:

> The blood that touched the crosstree and the grail
> Touched the first cloud and left a sign.

But it is an unorthodox statement, since it suggests that Christ's sacrifice was inevitable even before life was created. And unorthodoxy (if not heresy) has already appeared in the first stanza:

> The substance forked that marrowed the first sun;
> And, burning ciphers on the round of space,
> Heaven and hell mixed as they spun.

Whether, as Milton argued, the Creation consisted in God's giving form to Chaos, or, as Roman Catholics believe, God created *ex nihilo,* the original substance did not "fork"—that is, become a compound of good and evil elements. It was one, and it was good, and it produced a world "how good, how fair,/Answering his great Idea."

The Thomas passage quoted above has the sound of versified scientific hypothesis. The note is struck again in the third stanza:

> Life rose and spouted from the rolling seas,
> Burst in the roots, pumped from the earth and rock
> The secret oils that drive the grass.

But it is only a sound, and it is drowned out by the *Genesis-John, Zohar,* Swedenborgian chords. The poem is far too general and far too metaphorical to own any kinship with the verse-treatises of Thomson, Brooke, Desaguliers, *et al.*

As for the poem's being pantheist, one has no assurance that God is in this world that is being created, nor that the world is in God, since there is no certainty that the poem is even theist. In Milton, of course, there is no question. The Son, his golden compasses ready, appears

> Girt with Omnipotence, with Radiance crown'd
> Of Majesty Divine, Sapience and Love
> Immense, and all his Father in him shone.

Even in Dante's more Platonistic account, (*Paradiso,* XIII, 50 ff.) the original source is "il nostro sire." In the Thomas we do have, indeed, a brain and blood which may be argued as being identical with the "clear Vision" and the "warm Love" of "the Primal Power" (*ibid.,* 1.79). And this blood is "shot and scattered to the winds of light." But the question remains: is this the warm love of God or the beneficent warmth of the sun?

Hints of Greek philosophy also appear in the poem, but they seem to perform a structural not an ideational function. It may be said of the first four stanzas that each of the four elements is brought into play: earth in the first, water in the second, fire in the third, and air in the fourth. And one might discern distant allusions to the theories concerning original substance advanced by Democritus, Thales, Heraclitus, Anaximines, and the like. But very distant, indeed.

Any effort to pin the poem down to a specific meaning seems to me self-defeating. The poem does certainly say this: blood and brain—that is, feeling and thought; that is, love and intelligence—are the constituents of the creative imagination; and any creation is accompanied by a sacrifice. That is all we know and all we need to know. What the pale signature is, or the fire, or the translating word, is not *knowable* but only *feelable.* The creative process is beyond description more specific than Thomas has given it. Bruckner climbs a hill; tired and sweaty, he sits down by a stream to rest and eat his lunch. Immediately the slow-movement melody for his next symphony begins to run through his mind. Who can account for it? Not Bruckner, and even less a John Livingston Lowes. The thing cannot be described nor explained. But well-chosen objective correlatives may give us the *impression* of an explanation. Thomas's in the present poem, so concentratedly allusive, so apparently definite though so question-defying, lend that impression as in very few poems on the subject they do.

Analysis, then, is beside the point. "In the beginning was the Word, and the Word was with God, and the Word was God." The statement as it stands is so perfect in its certitude and in the satisfactoriness, the finality of its expression, that it compels acceptance as Truth with a capital T. Begin to worry (as a dog a bone) the preposition (Was the Word at the side of God? Or was it pregnant with God?) or any other part of the sentence and one but evermore goes out by the same door wherein he went. Though nothing may be lost, nothing will be gained.

Still the mind, like the dog, must have its bone of contention. The bone of bones for a dog or a mind is that one which retains its identity and its potency however it is treated—gnawed, licked, buried, kicked, or merely savored. The verse in *John* of course stays whole regardless of all analysis. Thomas's poem has its durability too.

# Incarnate Devil

In this poem, originally called "Poem for Sunday," Thomas is seen teaching his Sunday School class about the origin of evil. Effective teacher that he is, he offers two traditional hypotheses and then turns the discussion to the present and the personal.

Thomas's version of the Eden myth is not quite traditional, however. The garden of Eden is not God's but the devil's and it is not properly a garden but the plains of Asia. Adam and Eve, the leading figures of the myth, are conspicuously absent, so there is no temptation of the woman and no Adamic uxoriousness. Though the devil appears in the form made famous by the Christian mythologists, and by Milton, God is a decidedly reduced deity—a potterer, an amateur music-maker, the executive officer of a penitentiary, who can be visualized uninterestedly waving the pardoned prisoners off to freedom as he concentrates on a difficult bit of double-bowing. Who is being pardoned for what is not mentioned.

Assuming the sentence-order to be *devil - stung awake - circle,* not *circle - stung awake - devil,* the active figure is the talking snake, who, in the time of the shaping of galaxies, venomously put into motion the wheel of fire—the seasonal cycle, the life-death cycle—and turned the circular apple into a shape of sin. All is still abstract—why he does this, for whom, and to what end are questions left unconsidered.

The striking image of the stanza is that of the "bearded apple." The immediately following reference to God explains it in part. It is the apple of Thou Shalt Not, and whoever looks at it sees superimposed the stern bearded face of Jehovah. (The contrast between the wrathful negater and the fiddling pardoner is, I think, intentional.) The emphasis on points—the devil's horns, arrow-tipped tail, and pitch fork, and the serpent's tooth—may lead to a hidden pun: *beard* and *barbe.* At any rate, the love-apple is transformed into a sex-apple, and one recognizes at once the necessity of making oneself an apron.

The second stanza offers an alternative and non-Christian myth. In very primitive times, before man had learned to sail the seas, when man imputed semi-divinity to the moon (which was ancillary to the sun), Priapian gods "Twisted good and evil on an Eastern tree." And when the moon, changeable as the wind, rose, it (the reference is loose but no matter; the description fits both tree and moon) was double-natured.

One would guess that Thomas had been reading Frazer or some other anthropologist and had been struck by the fluid nature of moon-goddesses: of how Artemis the virgin goddess became associated with childbirth; how Hecate, a beneficent deity, becomes a goddess of night, the underworld, and magic, and is identified with Artemis; how Diana assimilates the characteristics of Artemis and Hecate, and as Diana of the Grove is involved in the sacrifice that gave Frazer the name for his book. All of this leads to consideration of Mary, the Diana-like handmaiden of her hanged-god Son.

What Thomas seems to be getting at is that the universality of the archetypal myths is to be accounted for by the universality of the human experience. And he illuminates this by using the terms of the ancient stories to describe what he (and his "Sunday School" listeners) have themselves experienced. We in the sacred waters of the womb have known a paradisal existence, and a golden age in the innocent, Fern-Hill morning of childhood. But—and here occurs the poem's major ambiguity. Who was responsible for that "But"? In the first stanza were introduced a serpent and a fiddling God. Now (shades of Artemis-Hecate-Diana-Mary) we encounter a fiddling serpent. Is it God or is it the devil who brought us loss of Eden and all our woe?

I think that Thomas, like Blake, is of the Devil's party. It is sex, of course, that in the shaping-time of adolescence destroys the innocence of childhood. But it is not a devil but a bearded, Thou-Shalt-Notting Jehovah (invented by the tabu-makers) who, speaking with forked tongue, enunciated the false distinction ("cloven myth"): namely, that sexuality is hell and asceticism (an extinguishing of warmth and light) is heaven. And then, himself to blame for destroying the possibility of innocence in sexuality, is given credit for saving the remorseful sinner from the clutches of the Devil. There is in the poem no devil at all. There is only the Jehovah-image which, from Thomas's point of view, is devilish. In short, the poem is to be read in conjunction with *The Marriage of Heaven and Hell*.

This is a poem which gains from analysis. At first glance, it seems only superficially clever, though the line "Black as the beast and paler than the cross" may bring one up short. But analysis reveals the careful articulation of the images, the richness of allusion, and the significance of the theme. The three stanzas, which at first seem so, are not separate units; each needs the other—nothing in any of them is irrelevant to what is in the others. The surprise at the end has been prepared for in the first stanza, by image, vocabulary, and tone, and, though some legerdemain has been employed, the understanding of the trick does not lead to disappointment. It is a better poem than it has been thought to be.

# This Side of the Truth

The ambivalence in the first line of Thomas's poem about a life that appears to be and is said to be ambivalent but is not, is one of Thomas's neatest and most effective.

Until you have arrived at the Truth, he tells his son, you will know only a partial truth. And then, though he himself has not arrived, he professes to explain the missing part as follows:

> You, youth-blind and self-centered, like a king set apart from reality, may not see that, before you attempt any action, thoughtful or passionate, the distinction between innocence and guilt has been annulled, under an indifferent, amoral heaven, by the fact of death.
>
> The concepts of virtue and sin have no absoluteness of coercion upon you, who are the sea's retainer; they exert control only while you have breath, and they exit with your dead dust into the dark of death, where your stuff becomes the dynamic stuff of natural Process. (By implication, it is moralists, fond of pathetic fallacy, finding the sky mindful and the sun a weeper, who rant about "innocent" dark and "guilty" dark, heaven and hell, and the like.) Your "wicked" wish has been naturally determined (which is why quotes are required), and neither it nor any of your wishes and actions will be labeled and judged when you die: they will "Die in unjudging love." As Nietzsche said: "Whatsoever exists is both just and unjust, and equally justified in both."

Among the comments most nearly applicable to this poem, those of Cyril Bailey are particularly eloquent, and I shall quote a few excerpts to show the tenor of his argument:

> [A] refutation of the pretensions of religion, the release from the two great terrors which beset man's mind: the fear of the arbitrary intervention of the gods in life, and the fear of the punishment of an immortal soul after death.

> . . . at death the soul is dissolved just like the body, and it can have nothing to fear for all time to come.

> A fierce hatred of conventional superstitions and a yearning for intellectual liberty coupled with a sense of awe—deeply religious in reality—in the presence of nature, a strong desire for scientific method and accuracy of observation combined with a profound feeling of the beauty of the world and its works, an unswerving consciousness of natural law and the sequence of cause and effect. . . .

Some critics have been disturbed by the introduction in the last line (after 35 lines of cosmic indifference) of the concept of love. It has been explained, but not very convincingly, as Thomas's expression of the

Universalist doctrine that all men will ultimately be saved. The poem, however, is so completely lacking in Christian overtones that there seems no likelihood that he is advancing even so unorthodox a Christian theory as this. Again Bailey would appear to have the right of it when he says that love is "the creative power of nature, the life-giving force . . . reverence for which may fairly be regarded as his true religion."

I do not know whether Mr. Bailey has read Thomas. The excerpts are quoted from the introduction to his translation of Lucretius published in 1910. But I do not think he would find the Thomas of this poem an alien spirit.

# Before I Knocked

Among the interesting aspects of this poem, not as poem but as document, are these: That Thomas should have written about Christ; that he should have placed Christ neither in heaven nor on earth but in the womb; that he should have situated the poem itself between one on a *process* and one on a *force;* that the poem does not conclusively reveal Thomas to be a believer or a non-believer in the divinity of Christ.

Writers about Christ are, broadly speaking, of two kinds. There are the professing Christians, who, believing in the simultaneity of His manhood and Godhead, differentiate Him from all other human beings and from all mythical deities. And there are those who, as humanists, regard Him as a man whom credulity has deified—a successful Appollonius of Tyana, so to speak. And of the humanists, one school will find the ethical teachings of this Jewish Socrates laudable, another will find them repugnant.

Ordinarily those who write about Christ have an axe to grind. Either they want to strengthen their reader's belief in His divine differentness, or they want to subvert such belief; they want to enlist support for His ethic, or they want to attack it.

It is not clear that any of these motives has actuated Thomas. The ethic is not discussed one way or the other; and the last two stanzas make only an ambiguous statement as to the nature of Christ. What the poem says most clearly is that Jesus developed physically after the fashion of every man. But the emphasis is not upon this development but upon a fore-knowledge or a fore-experiencing of the suffering of life to come.

The question that arises, and is not answered, is this: Is such foreknowledge or foresuffering possible only to a divine man? Or is it the lot of every man? That is, did Thomas choose Christ as his poem's protagonist because He is a special case? or did he choose Him as a representative of the norm of human kind—more widely known, more gifted, but still representative? A Caesar in the estimation of a Cassius?

Or has he attempted a trick in emphasis: his point being not that Christ is man but that man is Christ—that every man is divine and a scapegoat?

I think that a case could be made for each of these three possibilities, but it is not my intention to make a case for any, but merely to point out the ambiguities.

In the first stanza, the protagonist speaks of himself either as a fertilized egg which has not yet gained access to the uterus, or as a spirit, prior to incarnation. As yet shapeless, he will give meaning to that which confines him, as water gives a water-course meaning and as the meaning of Christ has aggrandized the meaning of "Jordan." But the particular point he has to make concerns his relationships:

[I] was brother to Mnetha's daughter
And sister to the fathering worm.

Here arises the first difficulty. The brother of Mnetha's daughter, in Blake's *Tiriel,* is Har. Lita Hornick, following S. Foster Damon, takes Mnetha to be a personification of intelligence and Har to personify poetry. She thus discovers here a correspondence between the artist and God. But Sloss and Wallis define Har as a senile dotard, author of a code of restrictive morality; Northrop Frye has referred to him as a "hideous imbecile"; and so he seems to me. But of course the question is, how would he have seemed to Thomas? For this there is no answer; so, what Thomas meant in this line is purely a matter of conjecture.

The "fathering worm" of the next line may be the worm from whom Thel learns the universal love of God, as she has learned from a Cloud that

Then if thou art the food of worms, O virgin of the skies,
How great thy use, how great thy blessing! everything that lives
Lives not alone nor for itself. . . .

Elder Olson thinks that "there is no real particularity in Thomas's allusion; he is merely saying that Jesus, as yet unconceived, was utterly formless, and had every and no relation to everything and everybody, as a consequence." (Olson, p. 99.)

But Thomas *has* particularized. It is quite uncharacteristic of his general practice to make so direct an allusion as he has done here. What I believe has happened is that Thomas has assumed Thel, who is referred to as "the beauty of the vales of Har," to be the daughter of Mnetha. (Yeats conjectured that Blake originally intended her to be so.) And he has brought Thel and worm together in the person of Jesus to show (in Blake's words) that

God is in the lowest effects as well as in the highest causes; for he is become a worm that he may nourish the weak. For let it be remembered that creation is God descending according to the weakness of man, for our Lord is the Word of God, & everything on earth is the Word of God & in its essence is God. (Sloss-Wallis, II, 273.)

If this conjecture is accepted, some earlier questions are answered: Christ is a special case because history has made Him so; but if "everything on earth" in its essence is God, He is representative. And, further, since "creation is God descending," here and now and everywhere, then this poem is well situated between *A Process* and *The Force* because God is force and process.

The second and third stanzas put Christ in a relation to the physical universe and under the influence of the force that drives the flower. Derek Stanford sees stanza 2 as "a vivid description of the child, from the point of view of its own being during the moment of coitus. . . . The image of the unconceived child's flesh as 'molten' (like the warm amorphous seminal fluid) and of the phallus as 'the rainy hammer', with 'the leaden stars' (where the adjective phonetically suggests the state of being laden) as the drops of ejaculated seed are examples of high poetic inventiveness." (Stanford, pp. 47-8.)

Thomas, however, has put *his* emphasis upon transcendent cosmic forces. The point, of course, is the conjunction of finite and infinite, the simultaneity of transcendence and immanence.

The real difficulty in these two stanzas is in the lines

And the wind was my sister suitor;
Wind in me leaped, the hellborn dew;

Each of the images—wind as suitor, and wind as hell-born dew—seems eccentric. At a hazard, the lines could be explained as follows: the external air woos him out of his womb-haven, and it does so by impelling his growth, the needful oxygen reaching him in the blood coursing through the umbilical. Blood as a prime symbol of mortality is justly "hellborn."

The emphasis in these stanzas is upon the unpleasant or uncomfortable, and the emphasis increases in the fourth. Here the bones harden into their rounded shape and the various organs take form. For the unformed, "molten" organism, this structuring is as torturous as a crucifixion. Indeed, the stanza is usually taken as representing Christ's foreknowledge and foresuffering of the crucifixion. It does not have to be so taken. If *dreams* is defined as the aspirational force that produces growth, only a present activity is taking place. And the next stanza suggests that physical changes occur because of psychic compulsions: thirst causes (or, at least, anticipates) the throat; hunger, the belly; love, the heart. That is, the basic instinctual drives precede the organs that satisfy them. And, of course, the organism's termination is implicit in its initial moment.

In the sixth, a very puzzling stanza, the child is born into the world. The puzzle is this: does the speaker clearly distinguish himself from his "mortal creature"? If so, is he, then, not subject to the dictates of time as that mortal creature is? The latter is cast forth, and cast forth only to *drift* or to drown, controlled, not controlling his destiny.

The fundamental puzzle, of course, is not of Thomas's making. The relation of body to spirit, of time to eternity, of becoming to being has engaged every philosopher and theologian. But what is Thomas's response? The mortal creature becomes acquainted with the salt adventure of tides. This seems a satisfactory image for the vicissitudinal ups and downs and ebbs and flows of life, a life spiced with arrivals and departures, with tears and sweat and the rewards they win. But these are tides "that never touch the shores." If the tide represents the life of experience, is it then infinite? If it is infinite, is it infinite for the *mortal creature* as well as for the *I* who is lodged in it?

These questions are not resolved. And the stanza is in a degree confusing in its unprepared-for shift of tone. In its first sentence we pity a helpless castaway. In the second, we rejoice with a debauchee of dew. This difference is justified if Thomas does rigorously distinguish the *mortal creature* from the *I*. But if he does, ought he not equally distinguish living from eternal life—that is, shore-touching tides from those that touch none?

The next stanza does not elucidate, though it has an expository sound.

> I, born of flesh and ghost, was neither
> A ghost nor man, but mortal ghost.

Some questions: Is the ghost he is born of spirit-in-general, or specifically the Holy Ghost? When he says he is neither ghost nor man, does he exclude all spiritual quality from manhood, or is he saying that I was neither total God (all spirit) nor total man (part spirit, part flesh)? Does the phrase "mortal ghost" mean what it says—a killable spirit (in Christian thought, an impossibility); or does it mean a Man-God, with only the Man-element mortal?

The emphasis is certainly upon mortality: *I*—not any *mortal creature*— *I* was struck down. And *I* was a mortal to my last long breath. And here again we arrive at an unanswered question: what occurs to the *I* after that last breath—total annihilation, metamorphosis, or assumption? All that is said is that a message is carried to his father—the message of a dying Christ. Is a father, with a lower-case *f*, a transcendent Christian God? Is a christ, with a lower-case *c* a Christian Messiah?

Lita Hornick thinks not. She sees the poem as having to do with "the treacherous dealing of God the Father" and makes these identifications: "For Jesus is man and the Father is time, death, the repressive forces of society, and the antagonistic forces of the universe." (Hornick, p. 19.) I do not myself believe that Thomas identifies the father with time, death, and repressive forces exclusively. True, the *I* felt thirst, but he was "made the richer/By sipping at the vine of days," and at least for a time words and water made an unfailing mixture. True, he smelt the maggot, but his "heart knew love." True, he was cast upon the seas, but it was a "salt adventure." The poem is not one of unrelieved tragedy. Whether one is to think it tragic at all depends upon how one interprets the pun on *doublecrossed* in the hortatory final stanza. Here the protagonist speaks, and speaks as though he were Christ, to Christians.

> You who bow down to cross and altar,
> Remember me and pity Him
> Who took my flesh and bone for armour
> And doublecrossed my mother's womb.

The question here is whether or not the Christians addressed are being adjured to have two distinct attitudes toward two separate entities, one a "mortal ghost," the other, God. The juxtaposition of lower-case "me" with upper-case "Him" validates such a conclusion. But if this is the case, what distinction exists between this particular mortal ghost and others in Thomas's poems—the *personae,* for example, of "I Fellowed Sleep," "I Dreamed My Genesis," "My World is Pyramid," or "I, in My Intricate Image"? In plain words, is Jesus the Son of God or a son of God? And if the former, why should He be remembered and God pitied rather than vice versa? (A possible answer is that God deserves such pity as Thel evokes in Blake's *Book of Thel.*) The emphasis throughout the poem is upon mortality, not spirituality, upon the period of gestation, not that of the gospel-teaching years, upon implicit death, not the crucifixion. Still, the narrator refers to himself as his father's "dying christ" (though, again, the lower case diminishes the appellation).

That such questions arise in a poem so apparently lucid suggests that for reasons of his own Thomas intended that his fundamental beliefs remain mysterious.

An anonymous *TLS* reviewer has recently written of Auden: "Juggling with incompatible tones is, of course, an old trick with this poet, and the exact proportions of deliberateness, miscalculation and uncertainty are no easier to estimate now than they ever were." The words are apt for the practice of Thomas. It is not easy to fix upon the exact tone, if there is only one, or to determine how many are harmonized, if there are more than one, in the line "And doublecrossed my mother's womb." There is the rather vulgar thought (but Thomas is commonly vulgar) that the mother was cheated in suffering the pain without the antecedent pleasure, denying Joyce's dictum, "No population without copulation." There is the more exalted idea of the womb's being twice crossed or traversed, "first" as Stanford puts it, "in the form of the Holy Spirit by whom she was made pregnant; and secondly, in the form of the Son of God whom she bore. . . ."

In suffering the agony of birth as well as the agony of the crucifixion, Mary may be said to have borne two crosses. And to revert to the lower level, she was cheated of her good name, as the medieval carolists did not hesitate to record, for being found with child before she knew Joseph. All these might be termed sweet cheats since all take as gospel the given story. But the interpreter eager to prove Thomas's non-Christian position might argue that the double-cross consisted in Mary's having borne a man instead of a Messiah, all later propaganda to the contrary notwithstanding. We suffered all in Jesus' fall from upper case to lower case.

In an early version of the poem, Thomas had four lines immediately preceding this final stanza:

A virgin was my sadfaced dam.
My sire was of wind and water.
Get thee behind me, my blood's tempter,
I cried out when the blood was dumb.

But these lines seem to me not to clarify Thomas's intention. To the contrary, they multiply the questions. For example, he seems to adopt a Christian attitude toward the virgin birth; but to refer to the Holy Ghost as "wind and water" is scarcely Christian. In the second sentence, the blood's tempter must be the force that causes it to flow. If this force is to be conceived as Him, a devilish Him, why should pity be called for in the next stanza?

No, this poem, which reads so easily and seems so lucid, is as difficult as anything Thomas wrote.

The questions pile up the higher the more one digs for answers. And on the top of the pile is the ultimate question: did Thomas intend lucidity and miss it, or did he intend and achieve the existent mystification?

# *This Bread I Break*

This is another of the poems that seem at first glance straightforward but on reflection turn out Delphic. It is not a juggling with tones, as in "Before I Knocked," that poses the problem but with pronouns. Three times the *I* of the poem says to some *you* that bread and wine were once oat and grape. This is both true and, as Thomas phrases it, poetical. But is it important? The answer to that question depends upon who speaks to whom.

The generalizing tendency of the first two stanzas—the first stanza moving swiftly from the dinner table to the rural scene and from *I* to *Man* in the abstract, the second stanza avoiding the personal and the indoor setting altogether—suggests that the speaker is Thomas. But the last stanza, and particularly the last line ("My wine you drink, my bread you snap") returns with a crashing specificity to first person and dinner table, and that table the particular one of the Last Supper. This stanza, too, introduces the second-person pronoun, changing the poem from general comment to direct address—unless the *you* is the equivalent of *Man*.

The several possibilities are these: Thomas speaks to someone in particular; Thomas speaks to Everyman; Christ speaks to his apostles; or Christ speaks to Everyman.

Stanford has chosen the first:

> The poet tells his mistress that in their union she drinks his wine and eats his bread (as this is an out-going energy it leaves a "desolation in the vein"). And this vital force bequeathed in sexual love is "Born of the sensual root and sap". . . . So the act of sacrifice (seeming in part an act of destruction) has involved both nature and man. . . . (Pp. 74-5.)

The transfer of vital energy from earth, air, and water to the growing plant, thence to Thomas, next to the mistress, and finally to the conceived child, each transfer involving a sacrifice, defines a sort of pantheistic eucharist.

But suppose that the speaker is Christ. And suppose further that this is the kind of Christ described in Lawrence's *The Man Who Died,* that Christ who came to realize that

> "I asked them all to serve me with the corpse of their love. And in the end I offered only the corpse of my love. This is my body—take and eat—my corpse—"
>
> A vivid shame went through him. "After all," he thought. "I wanted them to love with dead bodies. If I had kissed Judas with live love, perhaps he would never have kissed me with death. Perhaps he loved me in the flesh, and I willed that he should love me body-lessly, with the corpse of love—"
>
> There dawned on him the reality of the soft warm love which is in touch, and which is full of delight. (Pp. 204-5.)

The emphasis in Thomas's poem is upon the joy of natural, sensual growing things: the grape had joy; the oat was "merry in the wind." There is no emphasis upon *man's* joy in eating and drinking. Man is seen here only as the destroyer of joy; he lays the crops low, breaks the sun, pulls down the wind. He is not seen as having pleasure in oat or grape.

In the Lawrence story Christ, too, has neither given nor received joy. He failed because, though He maintained Himself to be "the true vine," He denied His being "Born of the sensual root and sap." And millions of Christians have negated earthiness, naturalness, sensuality, or have affirmed them only with guilt. They have taken the bread and wine of the communion not as a blood-enriching food but as a life-denying symbol. (This is Lawrence speaking.)

The speaker of Thomas's poem, then, may be understood as Christ—but not the pale Galilean; the audience as all Christians, and particularly those who have been persuaded to negativism by official negativists; the lesson as the reality of the soft warm love full of delight for all who affirm their sensual root and sap.

Marshall Stearns finds quite another meaning in the poem, arguing that Thomas "twists the traditional symbolism of communion into far different channels, saying that man destroys himself by utilizing the grape and the oat to make them wine and bread." Nothing in the poem supports this interpretation except the phrase "Make desolation in the vein," and Stearns makes no effort to identify the *I* or the *you*. Without their being identified, the phrase is meaningless.

It is not a poem of destruction merely, but of a change in one mode of existence immediately followed by another. Root and sap produce the grape; the grape produces wine; the wine produces a change in the drinker. Each of these changes is a miracle; yet each occurs in nature. Thomas carries the changes no further and I think wishes them carried no further. Yet nothing in the poem stops the Christian reader from taking the next step if he desires. I think, however, that Thomas, who permits his reader this further step, will not choose to take it with him.

## And Death Shall Have No Dominion

Although Thomas insisted, against Watkins' persuasions, upon including "Now, Say Nay" and "How Soon the Servant Sun" in *Twenty-five Poems,* he was tempted to omit this now-famous poem. He did, however, include it, perhaps to his later dismay, a dismay not unlike that of Rachmaninoff toward the popularity of his Prelude in C# Minor. Thomas wrote Watkins in 1938:

This morning the secretary of the London Verse-Speaking Choir—I think it was called—rang me up & asked me whether I could attend the final rehearsal before making an H.M.V. record, of their speaking of my "And Death Shall Have No D". I said I couldn't, so there & then the Choir recited it to me down the telephone. Oh dear. Picked voices picking the rhythm to bits, chosen elocutionists choosing their own meanings, ten virgins weeping slowly over a quick line, matrons mooing the refrain, a conductor with all his vowels planed to the last e.

Thomas may very well have been surprised by the popularity achieved by the poem, and irked by the way it was manhandled by other rendition-ists. But it was one which he himself loved to belt out (this seems the most appropriate description) and it was one suited to his methods of delivery.

Its popularity has not been due solely to its declamatory qualities. Published in a time when notes of affirmation—philosophical, political, or otherwise—did not resound among intelligent liberal humanists, it answered an emotional need in readers jaded by the anxieties of youthful Gerontions or suspicious of the doctrinaire optimism of the partisans. It affirmed without sentimentalizing; it expressed a faith without theologizing. For the liberal humanists, caught between the Communists, Fascists, and Christian converts on the one hand and the latterday Samuel Smileses on the other, it brought good tidings indeed.

There is neither ambiguity of tone nor of syntax in the poem, but just the question of whether Thomas has been content to borrow a phrase from St. Paul (*Romans,* VI, 9) or has acceded to the doctrine as well. In the preceding chapter, Paul has made this declaration: ". . . where sin abound-ed, grace did much more abound." But realizing that the casuist might impute a false causal relation, he devotes Chapter VI to answering the question, "Shall we continue in sin, that grace may abound?" The answer is "God forbid." And the reason is that, having been baptized into Christ's death, we are dead to sin, "For he that is dead is freed from sin." Further, being dead with Christ, "we believe that we shall also live with him: Knowing that Christ being raised from the dead dieth no more: death hath no more dominion over him." In sum, ". . . the wages of sin is death; but the gift of God is eternal life through Jesus Christ our Lord."

None of this is expressed or implied in Thomas's poem. Thomas Connolly has speculated that Thomas depicts heaven in the first stanza and hell in the second, and then shifts violently to versify the principle of conservation of energy in the third. The evidence that Heaven and Hell as such are in Thomas's purview is not compelling. Connolly, I think, salts the line "Though they sink through the sea they shall rise again" in order to find it "thoroughly Christian in considering the resurrection of the glorified and perfected bodies of those in heaven." The given words fit the pagan concept of death and rebirth by water rather more precisely. Assurance that Thomas is postulating a Christian Heaven and Hell is diminished by his references to the child's-play man in the moon and to the evils mythic as unicorns punished after the inquisitorial fashion.

But supposing that he is, the poem still seems to say no more than this: that however you regard it—in terms of myth, religion, philosophy, or science—death is not an end of living but a metamorphosis. The force that through the green fuse drives the flower does not cease when the flower no more lifts its head to the blows of the rain.

No personal God is mentioned, no redemptive Son of God; the question of whether spirit alone or spirit and body are reborn is not raised. The poem affirms a faith, but it is more nearly Lucretian than Pauline, and, indeed, says less of God or of gods than Lucretius does. In Lucretius, the atoms are assimilated into the gods' bodies; here they add fuel to the sun.

I have a feeling, but no evidence, that Thomas had been reading Swinburne and that this poem is a rejection of the total-annihilation theory presented by Swinburne in "The Forgotten Garden" and "The Garden of Proserpine."

In the latter poem, since in death there is "only the sleep eternal/In an eternal night," Swinburne maintains that "dead men rise up never." But the "Dead men naked" in Thomas's poem ascend to moon and stars. In "The Forgotten Garden," when the lovers die, "Love deep as the sea as a rose must wither," but in Thomas, "Though lovers be lost love shall not." And for Swinburne the dead are beyond change, whatever the perturbations of the universe:

Here death may deal not again for ever;
    Here change may come not till all change end.
From the graves they have made they shall rise up never,
    Who have left naught living to ravage and rend.
Earth, stones, and thorns of the wild ground growing,
    While the sun and the rain live, these shall be;
Till a last wind's breath, upon all these blowing,
    Roll the sea.

Till the slow sea rise, and the sheer cliff crumble,
    Till terrace and meadow the deep gulfs drink
Till the strength of the waves of the high tides humble
    The fields that lessen, the rocks that shrink,
Here now in this triumph where all things falter,
    Stretched out on the spoils that his own hand spread,

> As a god self-slain on his own strange altar,
> Death lies dead.

But in Thomas the dead are not only not beyond change, they are the changers:

> Heads of the characters hammer through daisies:
> Break in the sun till the sun breaks down,
> And death shall have no dominion.

They are not quiet, they are not even gently turning to compost in the grave, they are beating their way out hammer and tongs.

## *Then Was My Neophyte*

After the affirmation of "And Death Shall Have No Dominion," the despair of this poem comes as a shock. Death has dominion here — "I saw time murder me." One might think Thomas a person divided against himself, today finding certainties through Newman's "illative" sense, tomorrow observing the universe through scientific — that is, abstracting — eyes and arriving at disbelief. There is certainty in "Dominion," the certainty that consists in the certitude of the contemplating mind. But in "Neophyte," such certitude has become a myth one falls for and which is to be shelved in favor of the assumptions of science.

Science and religion confront one another in the poem and religion comes off badly. The earth is seen as an object sailing through space, its interior burning and sometimes erupting to pock-mark its surface. A man's foetal development on this precarious surface is compared to the race history of the snail. There is neither irony nor skepticism in these passages. But there is irony in his choice of the word "neophyte" to characterize his protagonist, for it has religious connotations that do not apply. So, too, with "twelve disciple seas" in which "disciple" means no more than "time-controlled." And skepticism is revealed in the fact that the doctrine of Love does not evidence itself in nature but in paintings of nature and in doctored motion pictures. (In "washing" a photograph, an opaque border is used to cover unwanted parts.)

It could be, of course, that in juxtaposing these two poems Thomas is dramatizing the dilemma of the post-Darwinian intellectual; and that, in the "Altarwise" sonnets which follow, he is intimating a means of solving it by what might be called a non-prescriptive grammar of assent. But this is speculation.

The poem itself seems to progress somewhat after this fashion:

1. At a given time, my beginning self was impelled to leave its foetal position in the womb and to emerge into Time (or Man had his beginning in the quaternary period of the Cenozoic Era) — that time which, to its Regulator, appears so brief that a year (or a geologic age) seems a day. This self took its place in the burning world sailing through time and space, itself burning with the compulsions (instilled by the Regulator) to stand erect (horrible fr. *horrere,* to bristle or stand erect) and propagate its kind.

In this, the human self acts like a snail — a mollusk living on land or in water. Coilèd in its shell, having white blood, often hermaphroditic, the snail, which existed 480,000,000 years ago with the beginnings of invertebrate marine life, has engaged in the process that will transform it into a land-existing creature (some forms have already made the transition), a shift from the green day and night of the sea to the vegetated, sunlit rock of land.

2. Every being that (like Theseus following the golden thread out of the Labryinth to gain his ship) leaves sea for land (the snail) or womb ("moon-blown shell" — a side-glance at Artemis's function as goddess of childbirth) for life, must be compelled by a hope for a better state.

If we consider the history of man (or snail), we will find teary grief on land and sea ("salt"); but also the soothing unction of the Regulator's love, encompassing whale and man in the quaternary and tertiary periods; thus the young child or Man (or snail, geologically young) may visualize Time as the means of achieving the objective to which, through the geologic ages and evolutionary transformation and ontogenetic recapitulation, he has been struggling.

3. At least, the *child* may be made to believe in this. But for the grown, science-trained man, such a picture (photograph, landscape, or oil) is a delusive myth—a vain hope. A motion-picture of reality taken on location with angled lighting shows inarticulate aliens and orphans and a truncated boy (related to certain spiral shells lacking the apex?) with no more knowledge of the goal than a snail in his shell.

He, who makes time run, wound the film containing the unfathomable story of life as though spinning a globe (or perhaps starting the purplish-red heart — "lake" as pigment) and then projected the delusive, heart-breaking image of love. (The "tide-hoisted screen" reminds one of the beach at ebb-tide, with its stranded helpless sea-creatures out of their element—severed, so to speak, from their homes and parks.) The fate of the mollusk is not governed by love but by the motion of the sea; if it does enable the snail to become acclimated to a terrestrial existence, the latter encounters only "the landscape grief." The tragedy of man is identical.

4. Who ends my story? The time-confined series is broken — comes to a "most lame and impotent conclusion": the rowboat excursion ends when the boat hits a rock; the hedge-row is cut down. (Perhaps, even, the gastropod foot is lamed.)

Who, asks the Regulator, could destroy the negative, soon to be made positive, of your life; could remove the immaterial foot-print made by the heel of your future-journeying, revelation-guided spirit?

Time can. (As the high tide washes the beach clean.)

The Regulator denies this. Time will not kill; the hope-filled circle will not be broken; the spirit cannot be destroyed (after all, noughts have their meaning in their interplay with crosses); the sacred heart within or behind the physical heart cannot be hacked out; you are as yet untried, a virgin, neither really alive nor really dead, but a Thel existing betwixt and between.

But the poet saw time murder him.


# The Altarwise Sonnets

It was a character in a *New Yorker* story who tossed sleeplessly in his bed because the words "Altarwise by owl-light in the half-way house" teased with their multiple possibilities of meaning. Beyond question others have suffered similarly and still others will do so, because the sonnets of which this is the opening line both bemuse the intellect and haunt the imagination. Empson was exact when he described Thomas's best lines as "ragingly good."

Evaluation of the sequence has, quite naturally, touched extremes: Daiches, who thinks the opening lines "almost a self-parody," finds the poem "congested with its metaphors" and the reader "left with a feeling of oppression"; Olson, on the other hand, places it among the great poems of our century. But there has been no division of opinion as to its difficulty. And this remains true despite the full-dress explications provided by Olson, Tindall, Kleinman, and others, and will remain true despite later contenders.

One of the difficulties attending explication consists in determining how difficult the sonnets are. One should not forget the dialogue between Thomas and Brewster Ghiselin:

> Thomas: . . . . Those sonnets are only the writings of a boily boy
> in love with shapes and shadows on his pillow.

214 ·

Ghiselin: I've wondered about the sonnets. I could never see anything very deep in them. It's good to know I need search no further.

Thomas: Well, they would be of interest to another boily boy. Or a boily girl. (Long pause). Boily-girly.

But Thomas was never, in private, merely a "boily" boy, nor are the sonnets merely steam from the singing teapot. Yet it is true that for their reader the temptations toward dedicated ingenuity are so great that every recourse to resistance must be adopted.

Thomas made understanding of the poem hard enough; Elder Olson has not made it easier. The elaborate structure that he has contrived is so wonderfully articulated, and he is so trustworthy an analyst of Thomas's poems in general, that any other analyst's strength is sapped before he begins. He cannot but feel the necessity of refuting Olson's interpretation before beginning his own. But this is climbing an Alp to get to the Alp he really wants to climb.

I am not myself going to attempt a refutation; this can best be left to dissertation-writers. I shall merely register dubiety, on the following grounds:

1. Nowhere in the rest of his work does Thomas reveal the intense interest in or thorough knowledge of astronomy and astrology that were required to write the poem as Olson conceives it.

2. In no other poem does he attempt so elaborate and pedantic a point-for-point allegory.

3. Nowhere, not even in his explanation of the "jaw for news" passage, does he himself allude to the possibility of such interpretation. He did not commonly explain his poems, but he was not averse to pointing out his ingenuity — as in the rhyme scheme of "Author's Prologue" and the seventy-two variations on the letter "I" in "I, in my Intricate Image." Could any clever young man have maintained silence about such a masterpiece of cleverness?

4. None of his close friends — not even Watkins, with whom he discussed his poems and to whom he read aloud the sonnets — seems to have been aware of their astronomical underpinning.

5. Thomas uses symbols and images and literary allusions here that he has used without such ulterior meanings in earlier poems and will again in later, and without any indication that here and here alone they take on Olson's added significance.

6. There are parallel passages in his short stories. Are they to be read there as Olson reads them in the poem?

7. The language, imagery, and narrative of the poem as it appears on the page are clearly and consistently Christian and not at all clearly astrological.

In brief, Olson altogether lacks external evidence; he assumes Thomas to be doing what he does not characteristically do; he assumes Thomas not to be doing what he characteristically does. If his interpretation is to stand, it must solve the poem's problems more convincingly and leave fewer problems unsolved than any rival interpretation. Let us glance briefly at his analysis of the first three sonnets.

> Altarwise by owl-light in the half-way house
> The gentleman lay graveward with his furies;

The time, says Olson, is 22 September, the night of the autumnal equinox. The gentleman is the constellation Hercules, which is declining to the west. The gentleman also represents the sun, which is moving south toward the constellation Ara, the Altar.

Questions: 1. Does the concept of a "gentleman" readily evoke the idea of a constellation?

2. Does not the still supineness of "lying graveward" war with the idea of stellar motion?

3. Is an initial weakness not evidenced by the necessity of bifurcating the personification? We have, so to speak, the Red Cross Knight pricking simultaneously west and south across the plain.

4. Is there an "owl-light" for the sun?

5. If the gentleman is Hercules, is he also Apollo — or merely the sun? The question here is this: do we consider the persons of the poem as things in nature or as figures in Greek mythology?

> Abaddon in the hangnail cracked from Adam,
> And, from his fork, a dog among the fairies,
> The atlas-eater with a jaw for news,
> Bit out the mandrake with to-morrow's scream.

Now the constellation and sun become an Old Testament mortal, with "destruction and perdition implicit in the flesh derived from Adam." It is, however, a character from *Greek* myth that "bites out the seed of his loins." Astronomically, what has happened is that as Canis Major, the Greater Dog, rises, the constellation Hercules and the head of Draco set, "Hercules being represented as kneeling upon one knee, with one foot on Draco."

Questions: 1. Are things not getting confused? Cerberus, which is not a constellation, must be translated into Canis Major, which is. In the Herakles myth, it was not Cerberus who wounded Herakles, but Herakles who captured and bound Cerberus, thus suggesting the conquest of Death. The dragon (Draco) which Hercules is kneeling upon is a separate entity from Hercules and has presumably been vanquished by him. That is, it is not Hercules' phallus. Therefore, when the dog bites the dragon, it is doing Hercules no harm.

2. Is Olson right when he says that Cerberus is "the only real thing, for Thomas, among the pagan myths," and this is why he is a "dog among the fairies"? The existence of death is contingent upon the existence of life. If Hercules represents life, he is not a fairy, but as real as Cerberus. The thinking seems loose here.

> Then, penny-eyed, that gentleman of wounds,
> Old cock from nowheres and the heaven's egg,
> With bones unbuttoned to the half-way winds,
> Hatched from the windy salvage on one leg,
> Scraped at my cradle in a walking word
> That night of time under the Christward shelter:
> I am the long world's gentleman, he said,
> And share my bed with Capricorn and Cancer.

It is now dawn, and Hercules, dead, appears to Thomas in Swansea as "a ghost or a dream of a ghost" whose ancestry Thomas impugns.

Questions: 1. Does the constellation Hercules disappear altogether on the 22nd of September — the time of this poem according to Olson?

2. If Hercules is down (it now being dawn), still the sun is up. Is not the identification of Hercules and sun becoming absurd?

3. Why should Thomas mock the parentage of Hercules (Zeus and Alcmene)? How indeed can one discover this pair in the line "Old cock from nowheres and the heaven's egg"?

Hercules has appeared to Thomas to tell the story of his life. But he has to postpone his narrative until the third sonnet because Thomas, immediately upon the gentleman's arrival, begins to address "the sun-symbol." First, he tells his visitor about death (though the latter, just having experienced it, is the expert) and then he tells him (who already knows) about his (the sun's) space-travels.

> You by the cavern over the black stairs
> Rung bone and blade, the verticals of Adam,
> And, manned by midnight, Jacob to the stars.

That is, the sun climbs a Jacob's ladder, the rungs of which are the vertabrae of the serpent-constellation Hydra (which is also Abaddon, the angel of the bottomless pit), and the poles of which are those imaginary lines, the longitudes of earth. Having arrived, it is addressed by a "hollow agent" (Olson describes it as "the marrowless skeleton which still acts on all life") and told that all is subject to Time.

> Questions: 1. How does the sun climb upon the Hydra's vertebrae if that snake is not in skeleton-form? But if it is a skeleton, it is dead and if it is Abaddon, then Death is dead. Is this not precisely what Thomas means in the phrase "Jacob to the stars" — which Olson fails to interpret?
>
> 2. How does the "hollow agent" fit into the allegory? Apparently Olson found no astronomical equivalent. Should this cause distrust of his other identifications? Hercules has made a special visit to speak to Thomas. Where did the hollow agent come from?

In the third sonnet, "the sun-figure" finally is permitted to break into the conversation, and he tells the story of "his adventures from the winter solstice of two years before to the autumnal equinox of the *preceding* year." (Olson's italics. Why it should be this particular span of time is not explained.)

> First there was the lamb on knocking knees
> And three dead seasons on a climbing grave
> That Adam's wether in the flock of horns,
> Butt of the tree-tailed worm that mounted Eve,
> Horned down with skullfoot and the skull of toes
> On thunderous pavements in the gardentime;

Hydra, up whose vertebrae Hercules was said to have climbed, now does some climbing of its own — as a grave, that is, Death. Which is to say that winter comes as Hydra mounts toward the zenith. Then the Ram horns down the serpent's tail, and, along with it, the constellation

Camelopardus, which, Olson says, Thomas does not see as a giraffe but as a jelly-fish or medusa. Thus spring comes.

> Questions: 1. Olson has assumed that Thomas saw a jelly-fish instead of a giraffe in Camelopardus. He has done so in order to explain the odd word "skullfoot," a translation of *cephalopod*. Has he not erred here? Jelly-fish are not *cephalopoda* but *coelenterata*. Should not "Horned down with" have the sense of "by the use of" instead of "along with"?

> 2. Has he perhaps misread the fourth line? Is it not more likely that "butt" refers to an abused person ("Adam's wether") than to a snake's tail? The idea of horning down the *tail* of a snake is absurd; the punctuation suggests an appositive; Olson's reading produces an extremely awkward inversion.

> 3. Again we have a confusion of levels: a constellation (Hydra) has mounted a non-constellation (Eve). More important, according to the traditional story, Eve had been living in eternal spring until she was seduced by the serpent. Winter and all our other woes followed that. But in Olson's reading, spring follows immediately upon a seduction that apparently occurred in mid-winter. Must tradition give way to astronomical fact?

As I said, I have no intention of refuting Olson's interpretation but only of suggesting a sufficient sense of dissatisfaction to justify doing one of my own. What Olson has done is to find a level of meaning constituting a poem in itself which Thomas may or may not have written. He has, so to speak, elaborated the anagogical without explicating the literal.

Edgar Allan Poe held that allegory succeeds only when "the suggested meaning runs through the obvious one in a *very* profound undercurrent, so as never to interfere with the upper one without our own volition, so as never to show itself unless called to the surface." Olson has called an undercurrent (which may not be there) to the surface and sunk the surface beneath the undercurrent. This is especially unfortunate with the Sonnets, since what Poe calls the "obvious" meaning is not obvious at all. The problems of establishing the characters, separating dialog from narrative proper, defining the words, distinguishing those with mere imagistic value from those with symbolic or allusive potential, working out the syntax, all this to get a consistent meaningful literal reading, are tremendous.

They are, I suspect, so great that discovering *the* meaning is out of the question. "I shall not trouble to make the meaning clear," Yeats once wrote of a poem; "a clear vivid story of a strange sort is enough. The meaning may be different with everyone." The Sonnets do not have as many possible meanings as all that, but they do lend themselves to more than one interpretation. I have seen several, each quite different from the other. And what I offer will differ from these.

A number of general questions need to be answered before getting down to line-by-line work. The first is whether the poems should be read as a continuous narrative, with a beginning, middle, and end, or as poems revolving about a single subject, like Donne's "Holy Sonnets." When Thomas read the poems to Watkins, there were only seven; later he added three, and he stated his intention of adding more. So, either he could not complete the series, or he thought it complete enough as it was.

I am going to assume a continuous narrative until I find myself bending the poem to fit my assumption. And, on the evidence of the last sonnet's tone of finality, a conclusion of sorts. That the sonnets are closely linked and cannot possibly be thought of as separate entities is evidenced by the repetitions and variations of words and phrases throughout and the appearance and re-appearance of various characters. And, though there are interruptions, a continuing action, involving at least one major character, appears to be taking place.

The next question is a double one: Who are the characters? And which are the heroes and which the villains? Answering these questions will go far toward determining the theme of the poem, which has been variously defined as follows:

1. A man's discovering from astronomical observation that "nothing is to be gained from time; he pins his faith to the cross, which he sees in the heavens, sees it as a symbol of God and Christ, as the Tree of Life." (Olson.)

2. "Incarnation represents a vicious joke played by a malicious God on Christ, Mary, and mankind." (R. M. Adams.)

3. ". . . the life-death antagonism . . . inextricably bound up with Old and New Testament mythology and sexual symbolism . . . the reconciling of the creative and destructive elements of sex." (Francis Scarfe.)

4. ". . . they announce the current of orthodox Christian feeling—feeling rather than thought — which was henceforth increasingly to dominate Thomas's work in poetry." (G. S. Fraser.)

5. ". . . another portrait of the artist as a young dog." (W. Y. Tindall.)

6. "He believed in God and Christ; the Fall and death; the end of all things and the day of eternity; while everything living carries in it its own

germ of destruction, and one can envisage life as an insane mockery, there will yet be Mercy." (Karl Shapiro.)

7. An incorporation of the poet's "view of sex in a religious context." (Stanford.)

8. "Where Milton describes the grand majesty of the Father and the infinite pity of the Son, Thomas reveals a God Who is hateful and treacherous in his tyranny and a Son Who is the unwilling victim of an unnecessary sacrifice." (H. Kleinman.)

9. "In a time of spiritual crisis the poet saw the risen Christ as the Son of God and Savior of the World." (E. H. Essig.)

To account for these varying interpretations one need only note that the "gentleman" of the second line of the first sonnet has been equated with Christ, Abaddon, Hercules, and Thomas, and in each instance with an appearance of reason. The fact is that an appeal to the words of the sonnet is not conclusive. In the end, the reader will have to make an arbitrary assumption. It ought, however, to be an assumption given direction by a knowledge of what Thomas has done in his other poems and in his prose, particularly in the recent past.

An apparently valid assumption would be one that recognizes that Thomas has interested himself in the figure of Christ, in the Eden story, in Biblical lore in general, and that he has paid little attention to Greek mythology or astronomy. It would further recognize that he has been preoccupied with time, process, and mortality but has more often concluded his poems with their defeat than with their triumph, but that this defeat has not been effected by the grace of God or the sacrifice of a Redeemer. It would still further recognize that Thomas's early evangelical training has been powerfully modified by Lawrence and Blake and that (unless he has undergone a recent conversion, of which this is the record) any Christ-figure in these sonnets will not likely be orthodox.

The Sonnets constitute the last poem of the volume called *25 Poems*. In this book, Thomas has called for integration of body and spirit, described a sensuousness-affirming Christ, denied the Resurrection but affirmed natural continuity, denied anthropomorphism, shown the life-force as leading to death but defeating it, denied certain Christian mysteries, revealed his inability to answer some significant questions, hailed the natural cycle, indicated a distrust of reason, shown fear of discarding the Christian myth, and affirmed life. He has been concerned with the relation of myth to truth, the question of death and immortality, the specific question of the truth of Christian teaching, and the possibility of a Blakean-Lawrentian re-reading. In the two poems immediately preceding the Sonnets, he has first said "Death shall have no dominion," and then, "I saw time murder me."

Given this context, the Sonnets are likely to be either negative — an outcry against Time-tainted life leading to death, or an attack upon the sentimental Christian interpretation of life; or positive — a non-Christian affirmation of life in Time, or that plus a statement of belief in some sort of post-death continuity, or an acceptance of the Christian position.

Any one of these alternatives can successfully use the Christ-figure as a major spokesman — as He was used in "Before I Knocked." If the opening sonnet presents a figure which can be recognized as having Christ's characteristics, it should be accepted as such. The first sonnet's figure is wounded and dies; he is a "gentleman"; he is dissociated from the angel of the bottomless pit but not from Adam; he has experienced an unusual ancestry; his Word lives after him; his influence is world-wide.

He would, in brief, seem to be the Christ.

Thus far, I think, I have been breaking in open doors. The next part of the hypothesis is not so easily supported. The first sonnet ends with a speech made by the assumed Christ-figure:

> I am the long world's gentleman, he said,
> And share my bed with Capricorn and Cancer.

There are no quotation-marks at the beginning or at the end of this speech. There are, indeed, no quotation marks in the Sonnets at all.

Now a major problem in the poem relates to identifying the pronouns. In the second sonnet, someone says to someone, "You rung the verticals of Adam." Who says it, and to whom? In the third, someone says, "I took my marrow-ladle"; in the fourth, "My camel's eyes will needle through the shrowd"; in the fifth, "Rose my Byzantine Adam"; in the sixth, "Till tallow I blew"; in the seventh, "Time is the tune my ladies lend their heartbreak"; in the eighth, "I unsex the skeleton"; in the ninth, "rivers of the dead around my neck"; in the tenth, "the globe I balance."

The question that arises in my mind is this: what stands in the way of considering the first twelve lines of the opening sonnet as an introduction, third-person omniscient, written by Thomas, and the rest of the sequence as a first-person exposition delivered by Christ (and therefore *really* omniscient), providing Thomas (as Michael provided Adam in *Paradise Lost*) with an eagle's-eye view of the history and meaning of Christianity? This device would make the poem an interesting sequel to "Before I Knocked" and, perhaps, "This Bread I Break"; it would give the exposition a seeming authenticity it would not otherwise have; it would add both a dramatic quality and the *frisson* of immediacy.

A quick skim of the poem at once reveals several stumbling blocks: the eleventh line of Sonnet II; the octave of IV; the seventh line of VIII;

the tenth of IX; and the conclusion of X. Can they be removed? In this instance, there can be no recourse to context; the only means of validating the hypothesis is to explicate the poem.

But perhaps before we start, an overture, some mood-music, will not be out of place. An evangelical sentence on the subject of sin: "Sin originated with Satan (Isa. 14, 12-14); entered the world through Adam (Rom. 5, 12); was, and is, universal, Christ excepted (Rom. 3, 23; 1 Pet. 2, 22); incurs the penalties of spiritual and physical death (Gen. 2, 17, 3, 19; Ezk. 18, 4, 20; Rom. 6, 23); and has no remedy but in the sacrificial death of Christ (Heb. 9, 26; Acts 4, 12) availed of by faith (Acts 13, 38, 39)."

A passage from *Paradise Lost*:

> But to the Cross he nails thy Enemies,
> The Law that is against thee, and the sins
> Of all mankind, with him there crucifi'd,
> Never to hurt them more who rightly trust,
> In this his satisfaction; so he dies,
> But soon revives . . . .

And a stanza from a sick and praying Donne:

> We thinke that *Paradise* and *Calvarie,*
> Christs Crosse, and Adams tree, stood in one place;
> Looke Lord, and find both Adams met in me;
> As the first *Adams* sweat surrounds my face,
> May the last *Adams* blood my soule embrace.

### I

A present sacrifice and the Host-to-be, Jesus, *the* gentle man, in the prime of His life as man in the world, afflicted, toward nine of the sunless hour, by the "bitter furies of complexity" (an Intricate Image above all other intricate images) approached his death.

He was wounded for our Transgressions, he was bruised for our iniquities: as, hanging from the nails, He died, the worm of death beneath Man's nail was scotched, the threat of Sheol removed from Adam-man; Him God (the reality among the myths, creator and destroyer of the world, the flesh, the devil) beholding from His prospect high, wherein past, present, future he beholds, freed from His man-animality, having not forsaken Him.

Then, body dead (the things that are Caesar's rendered unto Caesar), the crucified Christ (with maundy money to bestow), the source of life, saluter of the new day, common man among men (He who was said to be product not of sperm but heavenly inspiration, not of tainted but of immaculate egg), wounds open to the wind (or doubting Thomas's prying hand) — this Christ escaped the sepulchre of time and space (issued from the hatch of the heretofore pilotless, wind-tossed vessel; broke through the confining, finite egg), and (the crucifix-image potent, His Word collapsing 1900 years) came to me in my earliest youth as though just descended from the Cross. He said, behold these hands which span the Poles, and tune all spheres at once, pierc'd with these holes; behold that endless height which is zenith to you, and your Antipodes. (Or, My gentle influence extends from equinox to equinox, from North to South; I am the equator, the world's girdler; I have died with two thieves, I have known lust and ulcer.)

*   *   *   *   *

Note: I have used the quotes from Yeats, *Isaiah,* Milton, and Donne, because they express what I want to say, not because I think Thomas had them in mind — though he may have borrowed a thought from the Donne poem. ("Good Friday 1613, Riding Westward.")

## II

Prefatory remarks: The assumption is that Thomas is a new-born babe, desiring the sincere milk of the Word that he might grow thereby, and that Christ is at hand to instruct him. The question uppermost in his mind relates to death, and he is answered, rather riddlingly, "Death is all metaphors, shape in one history." This has been taken by some as the topic sentence of a despairing poem which proclaims the universality of death. I think this view is in error. If there were no God and death was really universal, there would be nothing with which to compare death. If Christ were God and only God, death would not be universal — could not be all metaphors. But Christ was God and man, vanquished by and vanquishing death, which vanquished and was vanquished by Christ. No conceivable metaphoric relation is impossible. And, in the single history of Christ, death has achieved its ultimate shape and meaning.

Christ now goes on to illustrate the life-death complex by describing the growth of a child in what seems to me a very ingenious passage. The pelican is used in Christian symbolism to typify the Atonement — the making "at one" of God and man through the death of Jesus. Christ has already, merely by assuming flesh, come to a literal at-one-ment with man.

I believe that Thomas has, in this passage, contrived an at-one-ment of his own, presenting two histories in a single set of words: that of the growth from infancy of Christ, and that of any child.* This extends through

---

*The first sonnet can be read as describing the Incarnation as well as the Crucifixion.

line six, at which point the speaker shifts from narrative to direct address.

\* \* \* \* \*

Death, as it must, comes to all men, as necessary to life as the metaphoric principle to poetry; implicit in the beginning, inducing recognition in the middle, it shapes the whole in the inevitable end that the unsearchable dispose of highest wisdom brings about. The child, however long he stays at the breast, inevitably grows (a plant rising to the sun, a rocket rising to extinction); the life-force removes him from infancy's dependence on the mother, giving from its store the vital stuff to "blood," make potent, the sexual stripling. It is not long before this product of the quick ejaculation in the womb himself grows to manhood and, on his way to the grave, sets another cradle rocking.

My case (we can imagine Christ saying) though analogous is different. Death's coming to Me was necessary to *your* life; My death gave all history unity, since I was born to die that God and sinner should be reconciled. I (like charity suffering long) increased slowly in wisdom and strength, but My time came to put away childish things, to say "Woman, what have I to do with thee?" and be about My Father's business. And very soon the Heavenly Father (The First Mover, whose perfect motions are all circular) like the pelican shedding His blood in Mine, brought His only begotten Son to the full manhood of "Eloi sabbachtani." I, who made Mary's womb a strange heaven and was evangelist of a brief mission in a remote province, soon lit such a candle as shall never be put out, shed a light to lighten the Gentiles, for I am the "true Light, which lighteth every man that cometh into the world"—even though My mortal life was short as Meleager's stick.

Thus it is that you, brought out of the darkness of the womb into the darkness of the World and headed for the darkness of the tomb (suffering perhaps the Dark Night of the Soul), climb your ladder of Flesh and Devil and out of darkness come to light: through faith in Me and/or the propagation of your kind.

Then (Thomas says) the wounded man—not really a man but a word, but an *active* word—went on to say (after a dramatic pause for emphasis): The numbered hairs of your head, the whole fleshly body, will decay; as Hosea said, "nettles shall possess them." They will feed the nettle's roots and those of feathering weeds that thrust their way out of the darkness of the earth into the world of seasons, the hemlock of death implicit in them as they burgeon like evergreens, to die in the darkness of winter, their seeds going into the darkness of earth or a sparrow's belly. Thus, "judgment springeth up as hemlock in the furrows of the field."

\* \* \* \* \*

Note: I have a fondness for the double interpretation of the first six lines. But one or the other may later have to be given up. The character of the Christ-figure has not yet been established. If later sonnets show Him to be anti-Resurrectionist and pro-sex or vice versa, alterations may need to be made. I have accordingly weaseled with my "and-or." As things stand, three forms of immortality — or vital continuity — are here proffered: that through the orthodox Christian means; that through sexual intercourse; and that through re-assimilation into the life-stuff. As Donne said, "Death and conception in mankinde is one."

The "hollow agent" is more often than not assumed to be Death or Abaddon; his remarks are thought to portend quietus. But (unless he is, after all, the "long world's gentleman") there has been no note of his arrival at this meeting. The phrase "hollow agent" fits him pretty well—as the angel of the bottomless pit. But it fits Christ as the Holy Spirit equally well. And what he says breathes more of hope than of despair. That verb "thrusting" is a powerful word. Besides he speaks (in "hairs of your head") only of the fate of the "skeleton in the flesh doublet" (as Beddoes puts it), not of the soul or vital stuff. And finally (with "Jacob to the stars" echoing in his mind) Death, if it were he, would do well not to disparage roots, for (as Isaiah says) a man of sorrows "shall grow up before him as a tender plant, and as a root out of dry ground."

### III

Prefatory remarks: I think it not putting too much in the space between sonnets to imagine Thomas mentally reviewing what has just been promised —vital continuity through re-assimilation and through propagation—and quirking a quizzical eyebrow as who would say, all this and heaven too? The speaker nods an affirmative head and explains. It happened like this . . .

(But before He starts, it must be noted that the first six lines—like those of II—represent a collapsing of two stories into one, this time that of the Fall and that of the Redemption. And that the final eight collapse the Incarnation and Resurrection. Perhaps Thomas got an idea from Donne's "Upon the Annuntiation and Passion.")

\*     \*     \*     \*     \*

First, there was the innocent, obedient Adam-lamb in the eternal Spring of an ascendant earth (so soon to be a grave with four active seasons) that, on maturity, the ram in the lamb, moved by the sexual drive (the chief among the drives — and by no means castrated), knocked down with horny head and hoof. Which is to say that Adam, made a fool by Satan, saw Eve carnally and took her tempestuously, and not connubially in a well-made bed.

This made it necessary that I as Lamb-Ram (you have read your Donne? "O strong Ramme, which hast batter'd heaven for mee,/Mild Lambe, which with thy blood, hast mark'd the path") replay Adam's part. (You are aware, of course, that the Annunciation, Incarnation, Crucifixion, and Resurrection all took place in the sign of the Ram.) As lamb I waited through three dormant decades for My time; as ram I preached (for three years to many dead ears) My Father's word. As Paschal lamb I permitted my sacrifice (shofared from here to eternity by skull-capped Jehu's, one might say) on the hill of skulls; as ram I harrowed hell for three "dead" days and returned to make Gethsemane potential Eden.

Looking at it another way, the spiritless spiritual advisers of the mass of Jews, blinded by pride, killed the Lamb of God—He having been taken in Gethsemane, judged (*John* 19, 13) "in a place that is called the Pavement," crucified on Golgotha, at which time "the earth did quake." But the dead lamb turned to live ram.

To accomplish the things I have mentioned, I, begotten in vaulted heaven, had to descend to earth and put on bone (as deathly as Socrates' heart-ascending hemlock). I, the harbinger of Spring, was born in mid-winter—winter, the dark time, the shoved-aside season, an old black Othello-ram of a season tupping the world's white ewe of fair weather. Winter and I ran our course—"took our shifting path through a series of changes"—winter from pole to pole and I from birth to death. But My death, of course, was a second birth; there were for Me, as for the globe, two springs.

As for this second birth: in the sepulchre I regained from impotence-producing death the conveyer of the molten living stuff, renewed My potency and left the Rip-Van-Winkle cave. My resurrection signalized (and signalizes) seasonal and spiritual spring from pole to pole. The spiritual winter, which had frozen the hearts of men since Adam's Fall, now departed earth with Me on My Jacob's-ladder ascension.

*　*　*　*　*

Note: The attentive reader will have observed that in my first reading of the opening lines "Adam's wether" is not but in the second he is castrated. This is justifiable, since the wether is a mature but not necessarily castrated male sheep, and since, instead of two-level allegory requiring coincidence, we have only typological similaritv.

## IV

Prefatory remarks: It must be remembered that the situation is this: Thomas, who had been reared a Christian, came at some point or other to disbelieve in significant tenets of the faith, but his indoctrination had been such that he was not able to abandon his belief altogether. In these Sonnets he is re-examining the Christian story with a view of coming to an interpretation that satisfies him. He is confronting and being confronted by the Word. To dramatize this, he has (according to my hypothesis) the Word assume the figure of Christ and speak to him.

Since Thomas was born into a Christian home, and heard Christian talk as soon as he could hear, it may be said that Christ scraped at his cradle—as was said in Sonnet I. Thomas is no longer physically in a cradle, but he is undergoing a spiritual re-birth. So Christ scrapes at his cradle a second time. But this time He meets a sceptic. And sceptics ask embarrassing questions.

Now—to maintain the sequence as a monolog, I need only presume the Christ-figure to be repeating the questions that Thomas has (between sonnets) asked, and read the line "My shape of age nagging the wounded whisper" as, for example, "What the sects have shaped Me into over the centuries provokes these painful questions."

For consistency's sake perhaps I should. But I think it only fair (and a good deal more dramatic) to permit Thomas a few words if only to ensure that both figures in this confrontation be made visible. In this sonnet, then, Thomas is characterized. He lives up to his name: he cannot believe what he has just heard. This doubt is perhaps due to the scepticism natural to the young and precocious. It is more significantly due to the influences of an euhemeristic age. The similarity of his "shade without shape? the shape of Pharaoh's echo?" to Eliot's "shape without form, shade without colour" suggests an eye upon *The Hollow Men.* For the men in Eliot, hollow as bamboo, whose whispers together are quiet and meaningless as "rats' feet over broken glass," the church ritual has dwindled to children's game. For Thomas, the history of the Incarnation, like the story of Eden, has dwindled to a chapter in Frazer. So a "thousand small deliberations" become the tenants of Thomas's house, and he asks his, as he thinks, unanswerable questions. But the Christ-figure supplies the answer.

\* \* \* \* \*

I (Thomas), immature, sceptical, born in a time when the multifoliate rose has withered, asked my wounded interlocutor some embarrassing questions. These, indicative of pride and lack of faith, may be thought evidences of a deformity of mind and spirit, yet they derived from a certain anguish. The implications of the questions were these: You have been glib with your paradoxes of God in man and life in death — is it not just as absurd to imagine reconciliation of such incompatibles as to imagine a rhythmically organized dictionary, a measurable beginning, gender in the spasm, definable shades in a color which is all-pervasive and undissociated, or the shape of the echo of a dead man's voice?

These were, of course, double-barreled questions, not quite as foolish as they sounded, since they hinted at such problems as these: Can the Logos be quantitatively analyzed? Can the Holy Spirit have a physical capability? Is God male or female? How can the unexperiencable infinite be comprehended? Can we be sure that what You taught has not been distorted or modified in the transmission?

I did not pause for an answer but pressed the attack with an ambiguous question about blown-out "burning gentry." Since I failed to identify the latter, the onus was upon Him to justify several cases of God's cruelty. (What I was getting at, of course, was the question of whether God is simultaneously benevolent and omnipotent.) The burning gentry could be the Sodomites, toward whom God was more vindictive than Abraham; or Lucifer and his angels; or the dying stars in Mr. Eliot's hollow valley; or the apostles upon whom at Pentecost the "cloven tongues like as of fire" descended and who later suffered therefor.

Then I made my question a personal one: Is there a place for a hollow man, not one of the lost violent souls, in God's acre? And what hope is there that the bamboo will sprout in that place of bones? Will you keep from holy ground the crooked boy? Will you supply the crooked boy with the means of achieving a similitude of straightness?

And all the questions were answered in the one word Love. What He said was this: You may, if you will, be a stuffed man, breast-piece filled with glass; you may (as you will) become bones scattered and shining. Nevertheless (as I said after the rich young man's questioning, "with God all things are possible"), I will pierce you in your death-in-life or in your death, through your shrewdness and your shroud. You do not seem to realize the difference between being and becoming. The dictionary is not a poem, but it is the stuff of which Love makes the poem. A beginning is measured by its end (the measure of a cell is the Lincoln it becomes). Though the life-stuff may initially be genderless, it is not a thing but a process, and will come to its sexual definition. You say the finite cannot contain the infinite? I see the world in a grain of sand. In brief, though God *is,* from your point of view God is what He *does,* His doing is loving, and loving is the never-ending creating of life.

The needling eye is sharp in both senses. Consider *Genesis* 6 and 7. Man, the image of God, but fleshly, his time on earth limited to a hundred and twenty years, multiplied like the mushroom. He became, really, a poisonous toadstool: "every imagination of the thoughts of his heart was only evil continually." Let us change the figure. Man, the star of the greatest story ever told on the screen, once capable of sustaining the camera's close-up, stills of whom (even shots taken on location in the fertile fields so soon to become stony) therefore graced the walls of the Producer's office, this Man, when his beauty decayed and was shown up under the klieg lights, suffered the humiliation of seeing his scenes discarded on the cutting room floor.

In plain words, God said, "I will destroy man whom I have created from the face of the earth." But, before you cry out despairingly, "A God, a God their severance ruled!" think "How fresh, O lord, how sweet and clean/Are thy returns!" For you will observe, please, imbedded in that metaphor (almost as unnoticeable as, on the waters of the flood, was Noah's ark) the Mercy that balances the Justice. An arc, as you know, is "a sustained luminous glow, sometimes having the appearance of a bow." And God did set His bow in the cloud as a token of His covenant.

*　　*　　*　　*　　*

Note: The syntax of the final quatrain is difficult. On first publication, the 11th line read "Love's *a* reflection," but the article was dropped and has never been restored. So, whether the subject is *Love* or *reflection* and whether we have a sentence or a fragment remains a puzzle. Since Olson's reading discovers none of the hope that I have suggested to be in the passage, it needs to be quoted, as a majority or minority report:

> Once the whole heaven was "a bread-sided field" of manna. Once it was near and familiar, near and friendly as any "wall of pictures" of friends and relatives in one's home.
>
> Now it is remote as if the images on the films were thrown by powerful arc lamps upon a distant screen. The screen is "the cutting flood" of space; and the aspect of the stars, now seen in their motions, not stills but moving pictures, is no longer familiar and smiling but menacing and mad.

If Olson is right, then of course all my imagined answers to the questions join the film on the cutting-room floor. Such answers are implicit in the questions, but they can be made only if Love does prevail. I think it does, working on the assumption that Thomas meant it when he said, two poems earlier, "Though lovers be lost love shall not."

V

Prefatory remarks: Significant differences separate this sonnet from its predecessors. (1) The Christ-figure does not now act but is acted upon, compelled to undergo the most strenuous vicissitudes. (2) Because of this and because He is gulled by an absurdly-caparisoned character, He now has none of the dignity with which, despite Thomas's familiar address and punning allusions, He has been invested. (3) The action, instead of being localized, takes place over vast areas of space and time. (4) The images, constituting a series, and not revolving about a specific point of reference, do not easily coalesce. (5) In themselves, the images tend to imply severances. (The final image is of a uniting, but it appears to be a most uneasy one.) (6) Obscurer and more action-packed, the sonnet does not, as the others have done, provide a subject, or instill a mood, for meditation.

The reason for their differences is that Thomas, a latter-day Baptist, is in this and the following sonnet preparing the way for his statement of a faith valid for such a one as himself — a faith which can be expressed in the familiar and archetypal images of the Christian story and which is not divorced from the essential Christian ethic as he sees it but which is sharply differentiated from the misteachings of the post-Christ interpreters. Thomas, like Blake and Lawrence, is a newfangled puritan — but, like them, with a red nose rather than a blue. But since the earlier sonnets could very easily be interpreted in orthodox Christian terms, it is necessary to shock the reader to a recognition that an unorthodoxy is about to be perpetrated. Therefore the distinct shift in point of view and tone.

As I see it, the function of this sonnet is to show how, after the death of Christ, told and re-told in I, II, and III, the true good tidings came to be misappropriated, misconstrued, misrepresented, and misapplied. It follows with a particular logic the questions of the preceding sonnet with their implied criticism of the abstrusely paradoxical nature of the Christian metaphysic and of the bleak concept of the sinner in the hand of an angry God.

The Christ-figure has answered the questions with the one word Love. But He sees words like Inquisition and Reformation forming in the questioner's mind. He is perfectly aware that officials in the churches founded in His name might deem His answer heretical. So He takes up His narrative where He had left off in order to explain how this came to be. Again there is a collapsing of stories, the tribulations of Old Testament men paralleling those of the disseminated Word.

\*     \*     \*     \*     \*

After My death, the responsibility of teaching and enforcing the New Law fell upon the Apostles. You may visualize them as sheriffs in a desert town, or each as a Gabriel announcing a birth and sounding the trump of doom. Perhaps, if you have an antipathy toward Paulinism, you will take some pleasure in seeing, in "two-gunned Gabriel," two-named Paul. Or Gabriel as the new church, with its two big guns of doctrine, Petrine and Pauline, or its spiritual and temporal powers; or as Catholicism and Protestantism. (Or, even, Gabriel, annunciator of the birth of Christ and transmitter of the Koran to Mohammed.)

In any case, they (the apostles) slipped, out of the sleeve of My seamless garment, a card which I had not put there. They fabricated a Holy Trinity and separated Mary from all other women by equivocatingly making her divine. They turned God into a hellfire-and-damnation Puritan fanatic, warring with an imaginary, ulcer-tongued Satan, they themselves having become as men "full of new wine," when that sound from heaven brought the "cloven tongues like as of fire" upon them.

In short, My Word fell upon hard times. What they taught was this: an Adam soiled with original sin; an Eve with a heart mixed up and cut from God; a God black-visaged and drunk with power; a Cain and Abel, one of them at least an armor-plated destroyer. That is, in addition to supernaturalizing the natural Me, a man, they mythified Man, a species in nature.

As the Old Testament Jews, governed by their concept of God, had their various ups and downs, My teaching now experienced march and counter-march. I, a natural man, became a thing as if in a concocted philosophy by a Yeats. Greek Orthodox and Roman Catholic quibbled over My nature. Severed from Abraham's bosom (so to speak), My Word was cast under one of the shrubs in the wilderness (Call Me Ishmael). Near dead of thirst, it revived at the milky breast (close to nature—at the "earth's sweet flowing breast") to be nearly drowned in Orientalism, or in, as Donne says, "Heresie, thy second deluge." Saved from drowning as if by Jonah's whale, it suffered its dark ages; or, like Tashtego, fell into the sperm whale's head (*Moby Dick,* Chap. 78), to be rescued by Queequeg "boldly striking out with one hand, and with the other clutching the long hair of the Indian." ("How many," as Melville says of unluckier ones, "have likewise fallen into Plato's honey head, and sweetly perished there?") Then it (the living, savorful Word) was petrified—and paulified —firmly attached (as I had been to the Cross) to the chilling monastic concept of Poverty, Obedience, and Chastity (a destroying three-headed concept, like Dante's Satan enclosed in ice). The white whale (not the right whale) destroyed Pequod-Europe; icy dogma whelped Ursinuses and Ursulas—catechisms and continence. The falsified Word turned human Virgil into prophetic White Magician; had Dante, under Virgil's tutelage (see *Inferno,* IX) teaching: "A bad conscience (the Furies) and stern obduracy which turns the heart to stone (Medusa) are impediments that obstruct the path of every sinner intent on salvation. Reason (Virgil) may do much to obviate these evil influences; But Divine aid is necessary to dissipate them altogether"—a Life-rejecting doctrine. Half-women (who covered their sex with feathers) exalted the barren straw of virginity and were beatified for luring the living to their destruction. (Or, briefly, Adam was enchained by myth.)

\* \* \* \* \*

Note: To ensure that his Furies-Medusa passage in Canto IX would be rightly read, Dante exclaimed editorially: "O ye, who have sane intellects, mark the doctrine, which conceals itself beneath the veil of the strange verses." Did he, one wonders, consider the possibility that the sane intellect caught in the enveloping folds of that veil might not escape still sane?

And the Thomas, its images more phantasmagorically fluid, is worse. It is often impossible to equate an image with a concept. Assuming such an equation, however, interpretation is still only being initiated. For the image-concept is not static and single but dynamic, reaching forward and back, like Proteus changing form in your grip. What one tries to do, then, is to let one's mind (that sane intellect) float with Thomas's from a concrete image outward to associated images. For example: man drowning in sea to Jonah to whale to White Whale to drowning Tashtego; from whaling to ice-caught whaler to Satan in ice to Medusa's freezing glance; from salt sea to Lot's wife to salt with savor; from Jonah to Christ in the sepulchre; from white whale to white, iced whaler to polar bear to *Ursus* to Ursula and Ursinus; from ice-cubed Satan in the Inferno to Dante and Virgil; from barren waste to barren vegetative matter. And so on. Hoping to float side by side with Thomas, one picks up his literary allusions and reads what he seems to have been reading or recollecting, wondering whether in addition to an image an enlightening generalization that might have been to Thomas's taste will appear.

The quotation from Melville about Plato, which concludes the chapter describing Tashtego's submersion in the sperm-whale's head, seems to fit the bill. It comes out of something Thomas had probably been reading (there are a half dozen other possible allusions to *Moby Dick* in the Sonnets); it squares with Thomas's characteristic thinking; it provides a reasonable interpretation without the reader's being compelled to force a meaning in or fly far out to find it.

But, supposing that this reasoning about the concluding lines is plausible, there is left a very juicy bone of contention. The interpretation of the sonnet as a whole hinges upon the identification of Gabriel with the Apostles. How far out have I flown to arrive at this?

In the Bible, Gabriel interpreted Daniel's apocalyptic dreams and brought good tidings to Zacharias and Mary. In Milton, he is a warrior-angel second in power only to Michael, and he guards the east gate of Eden against attempted entry. Interpreter, and spreader of the Gospel, representative of the Church Militant, defender of the gate against entry into an *earthly* paradise: does this not describe the Apostles? Now, suppose that you think that Christ's teachings were misinterpreted—that, particularly, He did not stress asceticism and otherworldliness to the degree that His followers did. Does the image of a card-sharping, Mosaic-law-enforcing, gun-slinging wind-bag suggest your distaste? Very patly.

Nevertheless, the fact that Gabriel ought in a poem about Christ to be announcing the latter's birth cannot be blinked. I have no alternative but to admit that my reading is merely conjectural, my hinge has a screw loose.

Kleinman assumes an Annunciation. Since his interpretation of the Sonnets (in a Master's Thesis) has not been widely circulated, a summary will not be out of place. As Kleinman sees it, Gabriel, propelled by the west wind (the wind of fertility and death, according to Freudian psychoanalysts), tells Mary's fortune with a pack of cards which he pulls from Jesus's sleeve (Jesus is a witness of the Annunciation). The king of spots and the jacks are the male genitalia, the queen represents the female genitalia. The deck is clearly stacked against Jesus, because the king is Death, and it is the trump card. On this level of interpretation, the "sheathed-deck jacks" are the womb-enclosed babies, Jack Baptist and Jack Christ, and the queen is Mary, whose sacred heart will be pierced by her son's agony. These two jacks merge to become the Byzantine Adam who (as John) retires to the wilderness, black-tongued and God-intoxicated, to seek salvation, and (as Jesus) becomes the one of whom it was said (*Matthew,* 11, 19), "Behold a man gluttonous, and a wine-bibber . . ." This Byzantine Adam now describes his night journey by water, the symbolic quest for rebirth. From the 8th line on, the development of the foetus is narrated in geographical terms. And two sexual acts are balanced: first, God with Mary, Gabriel acting as go-between; second, Adam with a black medusa, Satan (the frozen angel) acting as go between. In the first the Redemption; in the second, the Fall.

Kleinman takes the "climbing sea" as the amniotic fluid; the mushrooms as (1) Mary's breasts, and (2) *amanita muscaria,* the toadstool known as "the destroying angel"; the white bear as brute force or elemental power; the sirens as no longer singers of their previous destructive songs but of the *Magnificat*; the "sea-straw" as our lady's bed-straw—a cross-shaped flower used as one of the cradle herbs.

One remembers that when the sperm whale was chained to the *Pequod's* starboard, the ship leaned steeply in that direction; lashing the later-caught right whale to the larboard side permitted her to regain her even keel. Has the addition of Kleinman's interpretation to mine produced a like result? One also remembers the analogy that Melville drew from the situation:

So, when on one side you hoist in Locke's head, you go over that way; but now, on the other side, hoist in Kant's, and you come back again; but in very poor plight. Thus, some minds for ever keep trimming boat. Oh, ye foolish! Throw all those thunder-heads overboard, and then you will float light and right.

## VI

Prefatory remarks: In Sonnet V, Thomas has referred to "my Byzantine Adam," and to "salt Adam." There I read the two phrases as equating with Christ's nature and with His Word. The Byzantine Adam is simultaneously the misconstrued figure of the Savior and the misconstrued teaching. The salt Adam is the true Christ and the true teaching, which, however, is again misconstrued.

But Christian man may also be referred to as Adam, and he may be—according to how he is taught—either Byzantine or salt. That is, when Christ and His Word are salt, man is (or can be) salt. Unfortunately, Sonnet V ends, like a cliffhanger, with our tripartite hero in the direst of straits. In Sonnet VI, the Christ-figure shows how salt Adam (specified as Man), with His assistance, escapes.

*    *    *    *    *

Salt Adam (vigorous, life-full man—that evolutionary development out of the sea's hollow) thus turned by the Christian conceptualizers into a caricature in broad blacks and whites (the Black Adam of him consigned to Hell's burning crater) countered this de-humanizing of him for his destruction by illuminating the darkness about him. He read and understood the book of Nature, came to an understanding of the beginnings of the earth and of himself—recreated, so to speak, the Creation, and with the fire of his words destroyed the mysteries which give rise to myth.

The book of myth said, If mine eye offend thee with its petrifying power, pluck it out; cut out the tongue that supplies myth and fable instead of truth. And I (the power of love and the hope for continuing life in Adam), having done so and thus melted out of the freezing spell, removed from honeycomb man (the salt life strong in Me) the darkening unctuousness of religiosity.

Salt Adam, Time's trick-taking card, solved with his compass card (and true understanding of Stella Maris) the mysteries of the sea (and, with this true understanding, came to terms with the sea-animal within him)— expurged their evil; the siren voices of Sargasso's sea-bottom departed with the flowing blood of the wound which the Whole Man suffered (and inflicted) in achieving his wholeness; the erstwhile nuns lost chastity, earned breasts.

*    *    *    *    *

Notes: Kleinman takes this sonnet as a re-working of *Genesis* and *John* to describe the original creation. (It will have been noted that I associate it rather more with *Isaiah, 64.*) For him, the two leading characters are Yahweh, the old volcanic deity, and Medusa, sexuality and sin *and* the principle of the eternal feminine coexistent with God. God unites with Medusa to beget Adam, and Adam unites with the "witch of cardboard" to beget demons. "Since the procreative power of God is in His eye (light) and in His tongue (the Word), the two organs of creation must be plucked and lopped to create a third substance—man."

Thus, creation implies destruction from the first moment of genesis.

Since the eternal feminine is part of every living species and is destructive of all, Thomas, says Kleinman, sees in sexuality "death and evil, not in any moral or theological sense, but in a psychological sense."

Olson, having found in V that "Life is no more than a nightmare dream of death," now finds in VI that both man and sun are like burning candles: "Man is wounded with the birth-wound; time will see that he bleeds to death of that wound." (P. 84.)

The best defense of my more sanguine, less sanguinary interpretation is to be found in the succeeding sonnet. The destructiveness of Time will be described there, but that destructiveness is neither bloody nor a cause for despair.

Further, where a new understanding of the Lord's Prayer follows logically from the rebirth which occurs in my reading of VI, it does not appear to me to follow logically or chronologically from Kleinman's, though I must confess that Olson makes it follow astrologically from his. But Olson's reading of the present sonnet is so strained that I can put very little confidence in it.

I lack confidence in my own reading of the last two lines. First, I am not sure precisely what the "bagpipe breasted ladies" are. As sirens, they would be monsters—half-bird, half-woman—who lure mariners to destruction. As Gorgons, they would be snake-haired monsters with petrifying power. In losing their "sea-eye," they are like the Gorgons' sisters the Graiae, from whom Perseus stole their single eye, enabling him to surprise the Gorgons. At all events, they are destructive monsters—or they were, at least, until the eye and tongue were plucked and lopped. Are they, after that operation, no longer dangerous? Is that why from now on the emphasis is placed upon their musical breasts instead of upon their deadly singing and stinging? (In the next sonnet, allusions to them are not unsympathetic; they are described as "my ladies with the teats of music" who "lend their heartbreak.")

Beyond that, there is the question of identifying the wound from which the "blood gauze" is blown out. The Christ-figure, of course, is a "gentleman of wounds"; but, the erstwhile monsters, having lost eye and tongue, have not escaped unscathed.

Further, "blood gauze" may mean either *film of blood* or *bloody bandage;* and "blew out" either *departed from* or *puffed away.* In my phrase "the Whole Man suffered (and inflicted) in achieving his Wholeness," I have had it both ways. Jesus, suffering His wound, had destroyed the monsters. In the subsequent false reinterpretation of His Word, they had been revived. Now Adam, with the Word's assistance, re-discovers the Truth and destroys, or deprives of their monstrous power, the monsters again. Thomas's attitude toward monstrosity is best expressed in "Unluckily for a Death"; and there monstrosity is closely related to asceticism. It seems probable that the ladies have lost their maidenheads along with their eye and tongue and have thus become "Whole Women."

## VII

Prefatory remarks: To inscribe the Lord's Prayer on the head of a pin is merely absurd. To stamp it on that which is, even more than wheat, the staff of life, has interesting connotations: the grain of rice, like the grain of mustard seed in *Luke,* 13, 19, will grow to provide sustenance. Rice works better for Thomas here than wheat, since it is only a botanical step from the grain to the rice-paper tree. (Paper is made of the straw of rice and from the pith of the rice-paper tree.) Given the tree, we can associate it with the wood upon which the Cymry wrote. For them, the three original letters—O I U—were in the form of rays of light. Thus the "oyster vowels" of VI are tied to the "one light's language" of VII. When Salt Adam "read and understood the book of Nature," he was enabled to destroy the unnatural (and supernatural) natural history of a past tradition. But after destruction, construction. The required next step was to bring to the human being in his natural surroundings that teaching which would most humanize and least de-naturalize him. That teaching is the Lord's Prayer.

\* \* \* \* \*

Cultivate, disseminate (the Christ-figure says to Thomas) the Lord's Prayer, which is the staff of life. Find in all the varying doctrines their essential truth: all can be comprehended in this brief doctrine from the Bible's pages. Here in this tree (tree as natural plant, or tree taken as Lord's Prayer) are the three vowels (or Alpha and Omega—beginning and end); the earth-fast genesis of life (a salvational revelation); the Word that affrights the carrion crow; the single illuminating truth.

The denier at a wind-turned statement is a denier of the Word's embodiment—that is, of spirit breathed into body (Incarnation); of the embodied spirit's turning and refreshing in wind, sun, rain; and of the body's transformation (body deprived of spirit, as leaf of sap and tree of leaf) on the rood tree of death. Such a denier denies the full natural cycle. Doom on such.

This cycle is like the tune of a song: "a rhythmical, melodious, symmetrical series of tones." Mothers fix the tune—the tune of time—in those naked parasites, their babies. The baby (who sucketh long) sucks himself out of infancy's magically irresponsible (paradisal) state, out of milk (is weaned on an artery), and eventually out of Time itself (he Jacobs to the stars). So it has always been. (These Marjorie Daw mothers are maintainers of the globe's balance (the hand that . . .); fish-producers;

harmony-makers; human beings — stripped of their scales; ascended (mounted) by lovers or husbands; and measured—perhaps by their fecundity.)

These ladies give the heart-beat that will eventually break the heart—that is, they give life in time—to children who may (as I did Mary's) break their hearts. From heaven ("the pavilion of heaven is bare"—Shelley) to earth (even to Bethlehem—the house of bread), Time pursues and shapes the history of man and cloud (bread-eater and heaven-floater), runs rose and icicle through their series of changes, plants on everything his encircling hand.

*　*　*　*　*

Notes: This sonnet is interesting in three respects. First, in its rather peculiar construction; second, in its emphasis, for the first time in the sequence, upon motherhood; third, in its being—in the octave—a re-statement of the theme of Sonnet II.

The odd thing about its construction is that its affirmation—or, rather, its negation of negaters—should appear in the sixth line, to be followed by eight lines describing the apparent omnipotence of Time. The point is, however, that that omnipotence is only apparent. Time puts an end to a given entity, but it cannot break the continuity of the cycle. The cloud goes through its Shelleyan changes; the icicle turns to water, evaporates, is sucked up, is precipitated, is solidified again; the bush supplies a rose where blooms *that* rose no more; a song, in brief, is ended, but the celestial melody lingers on. The last line, then, so different in its tone from, say, "Death lays his icy hand on kings," is very far from being negative, from being an outcry against the horror of a Time-chained life. Life itself is a "wind-turned statement," and it is to be affirmed. This is why Thomas has emphasized reproductivity, that is, motherhood, and why he has recalled Stanza II with its thesis sentence "You . . . Jacob to the stars."

Interesting, too, is the development which will lead ultimately (in VIII) to God's Mary, "the long wound's woman."

In V we encountered "sirens singing from our lady's sea-straw," whom I interpreted as reproduction-deniers. In VI, love "plucked out the stinging siren's eye" and the touch-me-not's tongue, and we find them next as "bagpipe-breasted ladies" in the throes of childbirth. In VII they have become mothers to be compassionated; in VIII, all mothers are epitomized in Mary, in that, in giving their children life they are starting them on the road to death.

If one were morbid, one would think this a development from a bad to a worse state. And Thomas seems to have attracted morbid commentators. I do not think Thomas was himself morbid. Nor was he on the other hand sentimental. The development above delineated seems to me to have been intended as an exaltation of motherhood, but one which does not deny that the process of becoming a mother is a bloody, messy business. And so with the life that the process produces. The manwax burns at both ends; it also sheds a lovely light.

Salt Adam has now been given a means of maintaining right relations with his Creator. But he must, beyond this, be taught the true meaning of the crucifixion and the resurrection, a meaning cleansed of mythological accretions. The three concluding sonnets undertake this teaching.

## VIII

Prefatory remarks: I said at the beginning of this Christian voyage that Sonnet VIII might prove a stumbling-stone to interpreting the sequence as a monologue spoken by Christ. Two problems present themselves: the phrase in the third line, "the bright thorns I wept"; and the direct address in the seventh—"This was the sky, Jack Christ . . . ."

Assuming Thomas to be careful in detail, he must have known that Christ is not reported to have wept during the Crucifixion, though the women who followed him to the Cross "bewailed and lamented him." As for the direct address, there seems no good reason for Him unexpectedly and this one time to speak to Himself. The speech is out of character.

Both objections can be gotten around. As Kleinman notes, Thomas may have had in mind Crashaw's witty couplet about weeping, in "Sancta Maria Dolorum":

While, with a faithful, mutual flood,
Her eyes bleed tears, His wounds weep blood.

And the term of direct address, "Jack Christ," might be taken as referring to Thomas. The latter might have found the following illustrative quotation from Shakespeare in the unabridged dictionary—

Since every Jack became a gentleman
There's many a gentle person made a Jack —

and revised to something like this:

Every Jack's become a gentleman
Since I, the gentle man, became a Jack.

Another possibility is to consider "Jack Christ" as being in apposition with "sky." Though this may seem a desperate conjectural effort, Thomas was later to write in "Unluckily for a Death,"

Nor walk in the cool of your mortal garden
With immortality at my side like Christ the sky.

The possibility exists.

In short, with only a modicum of ingenuity, the poem can be made to fit into the general framework of a monologue spoken by Christ. That, however, the problem should arise opens avenues of exploration into the possibilities of Thomas's ingenuity. Earlier sonnets have successfully borne the burden of simultaneous double narrative. Is it not likely that Thomas would load this sonnet, dealing, as it does, with the transcendent event of Christian history, with all the traffic will bear? Such an event should be seen from more than a single point of view. And to compress more than one into the allotted fourteen lines would be an artistic triumph.

I believe that the poem can be read successfully in each of the following ways:

1. I, Christ, was crucified.
2. I, Thomas, learned from the story of the crucifixion the meaning of love.
3. It was I, Mary, who in the Nativity was crucified.
4. I, Mary, discovered the Crucifixion to be implicit in the Nativity.

Of these, only the third is particularly bizarre. Yet who can argue that a poet who conceives the idea of devoting the greater part of a poem to a foetus-Christ ("Before I Knocked") is incapable of conceiving a crucified Mary? (In the earlier poem, it will be remembered, her womb was "double-crossed.") The underlying idea would be this: It is women who, out of love, undergo intense agony, and even death, to ensure the continuity of life. It is they too who, though they suffer, say suffer the little children to come unto me, who give them their daily bread, keep them from temptation, forgive them their trespasses, and all too often have to exclaim, Father, why hast thou forsaken me.

Such a poem could be read like this:

This was the suffering of the pregnant body—in the area of the mount of Venus, a mount of Piety; the mother (the transmitter of life into time) turning the wine to vinegar; the anguish of birthing the child as great as that of watching Him die. That which breaks my flesh and gives me pain is the new world I have created; Mary in her travail is creative God; in giving birth I have the heavy responsibility of giving life, the knowledge of good and evil, and ultimate death; it is so with any woman, but I in particular, Mother of the Christ, bent with this responsibility (from my teats wood-notes—not a bagpipe drone—emanating), am the woman who knows how extended the pain of motherhood can be. Nature's dynamism (the force from the green fuse) collected from the four imagined corners of the earth to drive into Your body finger-nail and "hang nail" till, the time having come, the magic having worked, milk was in my breast and You were there imbibing, preparing to bring Your "God's in His heaven" to a slowly-awakening world. My womb was the ark of the covenant. I, crouched in pain, butt of the three-tailed worm, producing the manwax that is to gutter out in the tree between the thieves, I, the healer of a broken glory, by bringing life into the world make Death a eunuch, attest the virtue of the sun by the fact of a son, and, my heartbeat ensuring Yours, maintain the continuity of life world without end.

\* \* \* \* \*

Since I do not consider this *the* interpretation of the sonnet, I have permitted myself some latitude. And yet, in exploiting the potential of the words, I have not in any instance departed from the material available to Thomas in a good dictionary. (See Webster's *Unabridged* for *mountain, vinegar,* and *thief.*) Nevertheless, I believe that the top-level reading must take the poem as a description by Christ of the Crucifixion. On this level, the poem reads as follows:

These things occurred at the crucifixion on Golgotha: the bitter sacrifice weakened the sinew of Time, gave it a palatable flavor, and preserved its *virtú;* my tears of love and forgiveness revealed the new law of non-vengefulness; the cross, in fact black with my dried blood, came to be the blood-red emblem of this new law. Vulnerable in the flesh, I was wounded by the devilish world; Mary, creator of that to be destroyed, as grief-stricken (and rebellious?) as Eve and Miriam, a woman (like the other two Marys bent by life, knowledge, and sacrifice) sorrowing because mothers' sons must die, drawing sustenance from the earth and sky and giving it to the new life sheltered in her arms ("Oh mother turtle dove Soft source of love"—Crashaw)—she it was who brought into the world and saw out of it My time-wounded, time-wounding life.

You under the Christward shelter, note this: the sky above you is the heaven that was united with Me (associated with My name?) by the God-willed (historically necessitated?) crucifixion nails (John saw—*Revelation,* 7—"four angels standing on the four corners of the earth, holding the four winds of the earth, that the wind should not blow on the earth, nor on the sea, nor on any tree"—but it did) so that, arcing from My breast and circling the spiritually slothful earth as a covenant, sprang the red, green, and white bow of faith, hope, and love.

I, showing charity to a sinner, I, surgeon and healer and manifestation of the divine, I, in this historic moment, deprive Cadaver (Time-compelled man-animal) of his potency, exalt sex to love, temper justice with mercy; simultaneously by this testimony of the natural process over artificial code,

I give sustenance through My life and death to a close-to-nature, childlike faith.

* * * * *

There is no need to interpret the poem in terms of the other two possibilities. And it seems best to focus attention upon these two, bringing the pain of birth and the pain of death into one context. And in addition to that, and even more important, giving the woman (as woman or as White Goddess) a responsibility for the salvation of mankind equivalent to that of the man. The result promised by scripture is everlasting life, but the promise is made totally in terms of a Him. Thomas, as it seems to me, has worked carefully through V, VI, and VII, to a culminating VIII to ensure that so one-sided an idea should come under question. If V was, as was suggested, a sonnet of severances, VIII is a sonnet of conjunctions: male and female, mountain and sky, birth and death, sun and son, spirit and flesh, past and future, and so on. In sum, "December's thorn (is) screwed in a brow of holly."

With its thorns and wounds, blood, tears, nipples, and heartbeats, this is a painfully physical poem. The emphasis throughout is placed upon the body. Granting that the poem is as much about a birth as about a death, and that birth implies sex, is it possible to infer that Thomas is here doing his own version in his own way of Lawrence's *The Man Who Died?* Is his point of view that of Lady Chatterley, who saw the resurrection in this wise?

> The human body is only just coming to real life. With the Greeks it gave a lovely flicker, then Plato and Aristotle killed it, and Jesus finished it off. But now the body is coming really to life, it is really rising from the tomb. And it will be a lovely, lovely life in the lovely universe, the life of the human body.

Whether such a point of view can be said to underlie and be the cause of VIII's emphasis upon the physical and account for the collapsing (if I have made a case) of Nativity and Crucifixion will depend upon the next sonnet, which purports to deal with the (or *a*) resurrection. If the resurrection turns out to be the traditional Christian one, then, of course, Sonnett VIII will need to be re-interpreted. What, then, was the "resurrection in the desert"?

## IX

Prefatory remarks: Olson finds in this sonnet a Christless, pagan world: "The circuits of the stars are meaningless; there is no resurrection, and no escape from death and time." (P. 81.) Kleinman discovers a resurrection, but of Osiris rather than of Jesus:

Since Thomas observes an archetypal pattern rather than a chronological one, he describes Osiris' burial instead of Christ's deposition from the Cross. To him the god is always the same, only the name is different. With the ninth sonnet the narrative of the Nativity and passion ends, and with the tenth, a prophecy begins.

Hornick, thinking Kleinman errs in making "an exclusively Christian interpretation of the work," argues that "the pagan analogy is introduced to universalize the death-resurrection theme, and to direct our attention to that eclectic network of correspondence and analogy which the Christian imagery partially obscures." (P. 25.)

The single point of agreement among the three is that the world of this sonnet is pagan and that the previous Christian theme, if it persists, is undergoing de-emphasis. This is the point with which I least agree. It is true that the imagery of this sonnet is Egyptian—perhaps borrowed from E. A. W. Budge's *The Mummy;* that the resurrection referred to is Egyptian; that the resurrectional idea was Egyptian long before it was Christian, and that other religious groups had had analogous ideas; and, finally, that, where in every preceding sonnet there has been some clear allusion to the Christian story, in this there is none save in the use of the word "resurrection."

The ninth sonnet is unique among the ten. It is the only one to exploit Egyptian source-material, and the only one to avoid the Christian. Yet it is not detachable from the sequence because it is tightly laced to its predecessors in three ways: its theme, that of burial and resurrection, follows logically the crucifixion theme of VIII; its leading character is that of the earlier sonnets, the gentleman of wounds; its minor characters —king, queen, priest, prophet—are, under light disguise, the playing-card characters of V.

Granting the integration of this sonnet in the sequence, how is the sudden shift in locale and imagery to be accounted for? Very simply. With Christ dead (or apparently dead) and ensepultured, both He, in one sense, and the frightened Apostles, in another, are undergoing what can quite reasonably be called an Egyptian captivity. Christ is in the power of Time, which Thomas has elsewhere imaged as "the quiet gentleman Whose beard wags in Egyptian wind"; and the Apostles, distraught and leaderless, like the children of Israel, have nothing to look forward to but "lives bitter with hard bondage."

That is to say, instead of describing the deposition and entombment, Thomas has realized it by analogy. Any Christian (and Christ Himself) could with feeling have said during those three dark days, "My world is pyramid."

But the cardinal fact of the situation was not the burial but the resurrection. Again, Thomas could have described this, as he had described the crucifixion. Again, he found the Egyptian references pertinent without being trite. And I think that he is making an important point. Far from universalizing the death-resurrection theme (he is not re-writing *The Golden Bough*), he is showing that, though the idea had been current for thousands of years, it had not really been of historical moment until Christ and His followers made it so. By showing the "fibre-king" and the "queen in splints" as only playing-card figures in books, Thomas puts their attempts to achieve immortality on the level of child's play. The resurrection in the desert is as meaningless and historically unimportant as the works of Ozymandias. The pharaohs were as deluded as the characters of Sonnet V.

Now this question arises: is Thomas, in showing the Egyptian resurrection to be a fake, by implication denying the Christian? Perhaps the explication will give an answer.

\* \* \* \* \*

It is through ancient documents in storage-vaults that we know them: the prophets and kings reduced to paper and ink; the midnight-oil-burning copyist (not poet) who reduced them; the broken, bandaged queen. We have their names and their bodies (only the skin and bones, the flesh having been steeped and dissolved in natron); their lives collapsed, their emptied bodies are like empty gloves, and are confined, like hands in gloves, in hieroglyphic-inscribed mummy-cloth (as their names are mummified in print), their only halo made of hair-dye, their glory the golden death-mask.

It is the death-mask of scholarship that bombastically declaims: "This was the resurrection—death must be inferred from the bandage." And the mortuary spirit of scientific scholarship draws its analogy and kills Me as dead as the ineffectually Osiris-emulating Egyptians; buries that mortal wound, My mortal body, in the infertile, pyramided desert; weights it down with the pyramid's stones (those hopeful stepping-stones to heaven); and necklaces it not with the lively arms of the bride in the wedding bed but with all the dead bones of all the mortals of all time past, who had failed to cross that last of rivers.

\* \* \* \* \*

Note: My interpretation of this sonnet as an ironic thrust aimed at anthropologists and others who reduce Christ to simply another hanged god and Christianity to a Jewish version of a fertility-rite is ultimately based upon Thomas's having chosen the verb "rants," with its negative connotations. If the "mask of scholars" *rants,* what is said must be held to be suspect. The parallel of the mask is the "linen spirit." It seems only logical to give it a parallel meaning and to regard its actions with a parallel distrust.

A syntactical crux occurs with the verb "bed." This may be taken as imperative. For my purposes it serves better as the plural verb governed by "mask" and "spirit," a "they" understood.

The inferences to be drawn from this reading are these: that the Egyptian effort toward immortality was a delusion; that the scientific denigration of the Christian concept was in error. Does the further inference remain— that the Christian concept is true? This sonnet does not answer the question. We must go to the succeeding poem.

## X

Prefatory remarks: The three possibilities left at the end of Sonnet IX are these: that the resurrection of Christ, by scientists falsely diminished to the level of Egyptian myth, did actually take place as the New Testament said; or it did not take place and the dangerous delusion needs to be analyzed out of our minds; or it did not as a matter of historic fact take place but the idea of it assumes a necessary and inevitable place in the felt thought of man. That is, it is not a matter of *belief*, since belief, as someone has said, is "a mental persuasion subject to change," but a *certainty* —a whole-man sensation. Of the resurrection it may be said as Thomas said of heaven: "Heaven that never was/Nor will be ever is always true."

It is, I believe, the third of these that Thomas expresses in the tenth and final sonnet. The Christian virtues of faith, hope, and love have their validity because the universe is purposive. The most persuasive, certainty-producing symbolization of that purposiveness is the story of Christ. What the Christ-figure in the Gospels taught in this respect along with what He suggested in the way of human behavior in the light of that teaching remains the fundamental truth for a man to cling to. One need only imagine Thomas re-reading the Gospels and being so forcibly struck by the present pertinence to him of Christ's teaching that he could as if it were true postulate Christ as speaking to him in person. He would not need to put any credence in divine birth, miraculous powers, or unique death and resurrection. The single miracle was that the teaching, crucified and re-crucified over the centuries, never failed to escape the linen wrappings and the stone-barred sepulchre to give the lie to despair. It possessed this capability because its author was a man whom God had entered and imbued "with his strength and glory and might and honour and beauty and wisdom."

These last words comprise Lawrence's description (to be found in his review of Eric Gill's *Art Nonsense, and Other Essays*) of the god he worshipped. He went on to say:

This is a god we are eager to worship. And this is the god of the craftsman who makes things well, so that the presence of the god enters into the thing made. The workman making a pair of shoes

· 245

with happy absorption in skill is imbued with the god of strength and honour and beauty, undeniable. Happy, intense absorption in any work, which is to be brought as near to perfection as possible, this is a state of being with God, and the men who have not known it have missed life itself.

I should think this a very accurate description of the Christ-figure of the sonnets, the figure whose teaching (whatever the poet may have thought of its contemporary dissemination) came to have such compulsion upon Thomas. If, as Pound says, literature is news that stays news, the gospel of this god-filled craftsman is for Thomas good news that stays good news, regardless of Freuds, Darwins, Marxes, and Frazers—or Aquinas, Calvin, and Luther.

Nevertheless, if the teaching has its essential truth, its efficacy has been diminished by the accretion of myth and misinterpretation hardened into dogma. In drawing attention to the absurdity of the fabulous elements, the muckrakers have served a useful purpose. The danger is that their attack may destroy the truth along with the fable.

What Thomas is doing, then, in these sonnets is to take his stand between the reductionist and the dogmatist to defend against both what he conceives to be that irreducible truth which can permit a believer to be "at cloud quaking peace." Sonnet X stipulates the stance to be taken.

\* \* \* \* \*

Since Mine was not a fabulous Osiris-journey but the real life-story of a real man (whose glittering eye has held you during its retelling) and, archetypally, the story of Man, let My teaching, which relates to the process of time rather than to the stasis of eternity, be removed from the church-ship's sick bay, where it has been stretched, contorted, and perverted (there are few to say with Thomas Fuller, "Grant that I may never *rack* a Scripture simile beyond the true intent thereof"); let it be held by such as have their feet firmly planted on the earth (and globes of their heads supported by the atlas vertebra), the earth for which I am from pole to pole the axis; let it be held half-way between the turbulent sea and the fictitious heaven-haven. Thus shall the aspiring beings (those cocks of the rock) in the life-full harbors see as with eagle eyes the wind-turned state-ment; these aspiring but *sea-bound* beings (I Myself typify the sea, the source of life and place of death—the natural cycle; and of My teaching it may be said: "For the earth shall be filled with the knowledge of the glory of the Lord as the waters cover the sea," *Habakkuk*, 2, 14) shall descry an end implicit in every beginning and a beginning in every end—death as natural to life as the thorn to the evergreen, winter-berrying holly.

Let that fisherman of fish and of men, that key man and first holder of the keys, "witness of the sufferings of Christ," and "partaker of the glory that shall be revealed" (I *Peter,* 5), that down-to-earth and down-to-the-seas lover and denier of the truth (a non-composer of such books as *Revelations*), let him (safe on the railed landing-place of the New Covenant) ask the fish that came to walk like a man (namely, you who, after nine months in the womb's sea, came to light under the Christward shelter) what purging "hidden man of the heart" (I *Peter,* 3, 4)—the gender's strip stripped to this tree and wed to dusts and furies, but still needling through the shroud—has made the fish-man a Man-fish of whom it may be asked, "And who is he that will harm you, if ye be followers of that which is good?" (I *Peter,* 3, 13.)

(This hidden man is, of course, Myself—no eunuch though a unique man. But I have been so misrepresented that I cannot object if the above words are interpreted in the following way: Let the fisherman Peter, part of the natural process of things, ask the pontiff Peter, removed from altarless but altarwise Galilee to the altar-dominated palace on the Tiber, what bitter man born of Aphrodite-woman has altered Aphrodite into Virgin Mary and put the Garden of Venus in cloud-cuckoo-land.)

But to proceed. Let the new concept of Paradise be of an earthly paradise—of a whole life here and now on this earth: let the twin trees of growing life and growing knowledge sink their roots into the worm-fertilized earth and ascend to sun and sky till that time when the canker worm (Fear not, thou worm Jacob, the worm) builds for you a resting place (the mortal element in the sperm having made its final assertion; the written woods stripped to this tree of so-called death) on a cross the image of Mine. At which time you may ask, as a young Welsh poet has asked, ". . . which is my genesis; the granite fountain world, or the bonfire maned like a lion in the threshold of the last vault?" And you will be answered, All's one: *"One* voice then in that evening travelled the light and water waves, *one* lineament took on the sliding moods, from where the gold green sea cantharis dyes the trail of the octopus *one* venom crawled through foam, and from the four map corners *one* cherub in an island shape puffed the clouds to sea."

*　　*　　*　　*　　*

Note: I have taken the liberty of adding to the sonnet proper the concluding lines of "In the Direction of the Beginning," an effusion in *Adventures in the Skin Trade* which has much in common with the sonnets and must be read in connection with them. I have done so because the passage stresses the oneness, the reconciliation of opposites, which this final sonnet arrives at.

There are other passages in Thomas's prose which are apposite to this sonnet. Particularly these two:

> Multiply, multiply, he had said to the worms disturbed in their channelling, and had cut the brown worms in half so that the halves might breed and spread their life over the garden and go out, contaminating, into the fields and the bellies of the cattle. ("The Enemies.")

> Where the serpent sets the tree alight, and the apple falls like a spark out of its skin, a tree leaps up; a scarecrow shines on the crossboughs, and, by one in the sun, the new trees arise, making an orchard round the crucifix. ("The Orchards.")

\*     \*     \*     \*     \*

I was not sure when I started that it could be done—that is, that the entire sequence (excluding the 12-line introduction in I and the octave of IV) could be read as a monologue without bending the poems to fit the pattern. Having done it, I should not care to insist that this is the way Thomas intended the sonnets to be read, but only that this is as good a way of reading them as has thus far been suggested. It does not claim for the poet an esoteric scholarship for which there is no evidence, yet it does not diminish his achievement in the poem; it does not require him to depart from earlier practice; it does not discover him contradicting his fundamental opinions as expressed in earlier and later poems; it does not avoid the very real syntactical difficulties nor egregiously throw out the letter when it seems uncrackable and supply a melting symbol in its place; and it provides a poem with a beginning, a middle, and an end, having the virtues of unity, coherence, and emphasis.

In short, it is not indefensible. Harder to defend, of course, is the reading of each sonnet, and of individual sentences within them. The situation is simply this: there can be no final reading of the sonnets; there can be only successive explorations. The only judgment of any interpretation must be that it has blazed a few trails in the right direction without defacing blazes already made.

## *We Lying by Seasand*

The consensus is that it is two lovers lying there, one another's best. Edith Sitwell, who thinks the poem "of the greatest beauty, both visually and aurally," in this at least agrees with Henry Gibson, who finds it confusing, trite, and thoughtlessly dull.

However, nothing save the opening words "We lying" suggest any aspect of love, nor does the pronoun specify the number or the sex of the prone or supine characters. For all we are told, they may be dead: the use of the word "grave" five times, and the phrases "For in this yellow grave" and "Bound by a sovereign strip" admit the possibility. Now, what the poem says will differ according to whether we assume the characters to be alive and loving, alive but lying *as if* dead, or dead and meditating (to limit the possibilities to three). Is there any evidence that one of these is the preferred alternative? Only the most tenuous —that of verbal echoes, of odd little coincidences that one notes as he skims Eliot. For example:

Eliot — Red river, red river
Thomas — the red rivers

Eliot — the Hollow Men
Thomas — hollow/Alcove of words

Eliot — If there were the sound of water only
                    Not the cicada
Thomas — out of cicada shade

Eliot — Prophesy to the wind
Thomas — calls with the wind

Eliot — in the cool of the day, with the blessing of sand
Thomas — we lying by seasand

Eliot — the vacant interstellar spaces
Thomas — the lunar silences

Eliot — This music crept by me upon the waters
Thomas — The heavenly music over the sand

Eliot — dull canal
Thomas — still canals

Eliot — some dead master
Thomas — dry tide-master

Eliot — The houses are all gone under the sea
Thomas — Hiding the golden mountains and mansions

Eliot — shadow under this red rock
Thomas — and drown red rock

Eliot — Enter the ROCK
Thomas — rock arrival

There are a few others, but these should suffice to indicate why an inference may be drawn that at the time of writing Thomas was saturated with Eliot. Granting the inference, is it of any value in determining the direction of the poem? I think that it may be.

The significant desire of the poem's speaker is to "drown red rock," to "fend off rock arrival." This proves impossible. Nothing can be done save to lie "watching yellow until the golden weather/Breaks. . . ." What does this all mean? Assuming an Eliot-full Thomas, perhaps something like this:

We, not dead but deadened, inhabitants of a life which may be described as death's dream kingdom, lying as if in a grave, are imitating the real dead in the nearby cemetery who, from their bones, which are already dry, mock (chirping) those who are moved by the blood's flow. We lie between sea and cemetery, between womb-tomb and tomb-womb. In our half-deadness a desire for a richly-colored, many-splendored life is as useless as prophesying to the wind.

Consideration of the night sky, of the moon, dead but exerting its gravitational pull upon the tides, of a beached hulk (shall these ribs live?) should calm the turbulence of our desire; we are made aware of the oneness of things and of the inevitability and universality of endings by the music of dead heavenly spheres and the sound of wind-shifted sand which will bury fertile hill and inhabited home, terminating torment of desire satisfied or unsatisfied. In our quasi-grave (yellow-gold in color, ultimate ruler, and remedy for life's ills), we wish for past and present ("strata"), memory and desire, to disappear and the bloody future to be submerged. But the morrow (showing fear in a handful of dust) will dawn. We can only lie, half in love with easeful death, till the sun rises like that "dove descending" which "breaks the air/With flame of incandescent terror" so that one might wish to say to the mountains "Fall on us; and to the hills, Cover us."

A pretty interpretation, Mr. Pope. But is it Thomas? It is at least not out of line, either in its assumption of Thomas's imitating an earlier poet's voice or in its predication of a tragic theme, with G. S. Fraser's general comment:

Asked who was the author of the following [the last] stanza . . . an intelligent reader might well name Mr. C. Day Lewis or Mr. W. H. Auden. The turn and the mood of the last two lines in particular, suggests that preoccupation of most of the poets of the 1930's with harsh historical necessity, which Dylan Thomas on the whole did not share. (*Casebook,* 46.)

E. Glyn Lewis agrees with Fraser (Tedlock, 180), citing this poem as showing that "Occasionally, [Thomas] feels the inevitability of forces beyond the power of man, and his verse is imbued with a sense of tragic contemplation."

On the other hand, Edith Sitwell (Tedlock, 150) finds that for the young lovers "Time is no longer terrible to them in their silence of love." And David Aivaz (*Ibid.,* 209), stating the theme of the poem as "the transformation of process by vision," like Sitwell sees a happy ending:

The lovers 'lie watching' (three times repeated) until yellow becomes gold, night becomes day. Process is already the 'sovereign' (golden) strip, joining the water and rock, in line thirteen. The transformation is effected only when, in the last two lines, vision sees it as such.

Neither Sitwell nor Aivaz comments on the fact that the characters' wishes are not granted — which seems to me the poem's crux — nor appears to be much disturbed by the dawn's breaking "like a heart." And, of course, both have assumed hopeful young lovers as characters.

According to Pascal, there are three kinds of people:

. . . those who serve God, having found Him; those who are busy seeking Him, not having found Him; and the rest who live without seeking Him or having found Him. The first are intelligent and happy; the last are foolish and miserable; those between are unhappy and intelligent.

As it seems to me, Thomas is reflecting a frame of mind not uncommon to those who, as Pascal says, lie "between."

## Conversation of Prayer

Almost the first question to occur to a reader of this poem concerns the possibility of its relation to *Ash Wednesday.* In each poem the question of the efficacy of prayer engrosses attention; in each, *turn* is an operative word; in each, there is a climbing of stairs.

In his ascent toward the higher love, the speaker of Eliot's poem makes (in Part III) three turns on the stairway, each turn representing a stage in his spiritual development involving a defeat of a temptation. The last of these temptations is a sensuous pastoralism which, though in Eliot it does not characterize a child's world, recalls the kind of environment in which the young Thomas ran his heedless ways, his wishes racing through the "house high hay."

The turn or reversal which is to occur in Thomas's poem is imagized in the circular movement of the first sentence, in which the first becomes last and the last first. In line 2, we read

. . . the child going to bed and the man on the stairs,

but in 1.8 the order reverses:

. . . the man on the stairs and the child by his bed.

The child, his prayer devoid of love, sympathy, or fear (for other safety than his own) recites a jingle, makes a sound arise, but does not truly pray. The man's love, fear, grief, knowledge of death wring from him passionate entreaty in the behalf of someone else, someone whose precarious (prayer-needing) situation takes him out of himself. The reversal that occurs is this: the child's prayer is unanswered, and he is brought face to face with the terror of his own death; the man's prayer is answered, and he finds "no dying but alive and warm In the fire of his care his love in the high room." Apparently the grown-up man shall lead them.

Why does this ironic twist occur? There are several possible answers. First, prayer is inefficacious; assumed results are mere coincidences. Second, only unselfish, loving prayer is efficacious. Third, prayer is efficacious, but, by a sort of law of compensation, every favor granted demands the denial of some other. Fourth, the efficacy of prayer is not in question here: the two kinds of prayer are objective correlatives for two states of the soul, the one unphilosophical, incapable of meeting fear, and therefore death-distressed, the other inured to both bad dreams and the reality of evil and therefore death-defeating. That is, the child and the man may be Thomas young and Thomas mature, his maturing having been an ascension out of that pastoral narrowness described in *Ash Wednesday*. And fifth, G. S. Fraser's thought that the "idea of the reversibility of grace" is being expounded here:

. . . the idea that all prayers and all good acts co-operate for the benefit of all men, and that God, in His inscrutable mercy, can give the innocent the privilege of suffering some of the tribulations which have been incurred by redeemable sinners . . . . The prayers, as it were, cross in the air, the man is granted his wish, for one night at least the sick woman is happy and well again, but the sleeping boy has to endure all the man's nightmare of climbing up the stairs to discover the loved one dead. (*Casebook,* 53.)

This is an interesting theory, and though it seems quite uncharacteristic of Thomas, who never reveals such intellectualism in his religious poems, deserves to be considered. Fraser's declaration, however, that "Only this idea makes sense of the poem" may be thought to verge on the dogmatic. Oddly so, since he himself notes that it is an idea almost forgotten in Protestant countries (like Wales); that Thomas was "never interested in abstruse notions"; and that the drift of Thomas's immediately succeeding poem ("A Refusal to Mourn") can be summed up as "pantheistic pessimism." In short, everything stands against his interpretation, but, since no other will explain the poem, it must be accepted. But any of the four alternatives which I have listed "will make sense of" the poem, though with varying degrees of satisfactoriness.

The first, an expression of cynicism, belies the pervading tone of the poem; most readers will agree with Stanford that it is not possible "to read it as an anti-religious poem (or as a poem which mocks at the purpose of prayer," (Stanford, p. 92.) In an effective phrase, Stanford describes the poem's tone: he terms it "a religious poem in a minor key; a poem in which faith is not silenced but sounds, so to speak, with the soft pedal on."

The second is free of the taint of cynicism but seems unreasonably harsh on children, making, as it does, the effectiveness of prayer contingent upon a sympathetic understanding which only maturity can confer. And it runs counter to Christ's blessing of the little children. One might, of course, argue that precisely here is the point of the poem; but this runs counter to Thomas's general attitude toward children and therefore seems a doubtful reading.

The third assumes a prayer-answer with a peculiarly automatic and statistical way of balancing things; neither Justice nor Mercy, only mathematical considerations operate. Whatever kind of God Thomas believed in, it was certainly not this.

The fourth works out better than any of these three. The child, whether he mutters his "Now I lay me" or goes to bed prayerless, is by the nature of things going to encounter, in dreams and out, death and fear of death with the usual result of at least temporary morbidity. The man, if he has matured, has become able to generalize, objectify, and contextualize, will have learned to care and not to care, to find "strength beyond hope and despair/Climbing the third stair." That is, what the poem describes is the mortal child made shockingly aware of mortality and left unaware of any recourse; and the mortal man still aware of mortality but assured of the triumph of love over death. In each instance, the same grief is, as Thomas says, "flying"; one is assuaged and the other not.

The questions of whether the child and the man are or are not one

and the same, whether or not they (or he) actually pray, and whether
an actual woman or an abstract Love is near death—all these become as
irrelevant as the question of what, specifically, was Thomas's attitude
toward prayer. What we have left is a poem psychologically sound, vividly
imaged, subtly and ingeniously rhymed and rhythmed — perhaps the
least-marred expression in Thomas of the felt thought.

# Vision and Prayer

The vision that is vouchsafed Thomas is horrific rather than beatific.
That is the reason for the prayer which follows, in which Thomas begs
that the potent figure within the vision give up or be deprived of his
power. (I say "within the vision." But final interpretation of the poem
will depend upon whether the figure is construed as having an objective
as well as a subjective reality.)

The major persons of the drama are the speaker — presumably
Thomas; the mother; the child; and the sun. The mother, who appears
only in the vision and serves only to produce the child, is described as
a "splashed mothering maiden." The sun has only a walk-on role in the
vision, but in the prayer plays a crucial part. It is referred to as "the
finding one," and is described as spinning, crimson, sudden, and loud.

The child (also referred to as "the finding one") is wild and turbulent;
has a torrid crown; dispels dark from his loin; has a dawn-furying stream;
dazzles heaven; has a bonfire in his mouth; kisses boilingly; is winged;
is wounded; has a blazing breast; puts his flame in every grain of dust;
is spoken of as "the adored infant light" and "the dazzling prison,"
and has briared hands.

Thomas is a lost soul.

The action is as follows. Thomas silently listens as the mother gives
birth to the child. He says that when the dawn breaks after the child's
birth, he (Thomas) will run, vainly crying, from the previously-darkened
room into the sun. He will do so because he was lost. His effort to
escape from the child will not, however, be successful, since the latter
is winged; Thomas's cries are stilled when he sees the child's wound, and
he falls asleep against the child's breast. Then he awakens to see a vision
of the Judgment Day and of the whole panorama of the world's development. Having witnessed the total pain of universal history, he dies.
(In what sense is not explained.)

Next he delivers three prayers. The first, made in the name of believers
in total annihilation (with whose belief, he says, he is only partially in

accord) requests that the child be returned to the womb before he learns to speak. The second, made in the name of all pagans, requests that the child refuse the dead an awakening, however much they desire it, since death is comfortingly understandable and homely. The third, made in the name of the unbegotten, requests that the sun make the child's martyrdom a natural, not a mysterious one. At this point, the sun that he has been praying to takes drastic action.

> I turn the corner of prayer and burn
> In a blessing of the sudden
> Sun. In the name of the damned
> I would turn back and run
> To the hidden land
> But the loud sun
> Christens down
> The sky.
> I
> Am found.

This is the crucial point and most ambiguous event in the poem. The question which arises is this: Does the sun act on its own and affirmatively answer the prayer? Or is it the child's surrogate and act to deny the prayer?

The ambiguous pronominal reference of the concluding lines militates against a certain answer:

> O let him
> Scald me and drown
> Me in his world's wound.
> His lightning answers my
> Cry. My voice burns in his hand.
> Now I am lost in the blinding
> One. The sun roars at the prayer's end.

Has Thomas been saved from the agony of being the child's man and become a sun worshiper? Or does the sun bow to the child's greater authority and deliver Thomas to the latter's charge? Proponents of the first theory will argue that, since the child is not mentioned in the final stanza, the pronouns must refer to the sun. Proponents of the second will answer that throughout the poem *him* and *his* have regularly referred to the child and not to the sun and that therefore no ambiguity exists.

The proponents of the first theory may be said to define Thomas's position as a kind of pantheism, the proponents of the second as a kind of transcendentalism. And the latter group may be divided into those who see Thomas as a Christian and those who do not. Opinion here turns initially upon the interpretation of Thomas's second prayer:

> That he let the dead lie though they moan
> For his briared hands to hoist them
> To the shrine of his world's wound;

and, next, upon what answer is thought to be made to the third prayer:

> May the crimson
> Sun spin a grave grey
> And the colour of clay
> Stream upon his martyrdom
> In the interpreted evening
> And the known dark of the earth amen.

The pro-Christian faction will argue that only Christ can hoist the dead to his shrine, and that the sun denies the following prayer. The anti-Christian contingent will argue that the dead who are to be hoisted are not actually dead but only dead-to-love, that to be hoisted means only to learn to love; and that the sun's affirming reduction of the Crucifixion to a natural event does not deny a transcendent spiritual principle.

Briefly, these are the main alternatives:

1. The poem dramatizes Thomas's discovery of the self-sufficient divinity of the cosmos.
2. It dramatizes Christ's being reborn to Thomas and Thomas's "dying" and being reborn in Christ.
3. It dramatizes Thomas's submission to the Life Force, which may be called "God," and to the concept of Love through sacrifice—which may *not* be called Christ.

In the first and third, the figure of the child is mere personification; in the second, he has both subjective and objective reality.

I do not think that a final case may be made for any one of the alternatives. Only the desire of the reader will find the divine figure of this poem wholly immanent, or wholly transcendent, or simultaneously transcendent and immanent, or not substantially but only metaphorically present at all.

\* \* \* \* \*

The reader who has not been found, or does not want to be, or has been but thinks it bad taste to discuss the matter publicly, may very

256 ·

well suffer a discomfort or embarrassment or even a cynicism comparable to that of an Augustan toward the effusion of a seventeenth-century enthusiast. Hazlitt catches the tone in his criticism of Crashaw:

> Crashaw . . . whose imagination was rendered inflammable by the fervors of fanaticism, and who, having been converted from Protestantism to Popery (a weakness to which the "seething brains" of the poets of this period were prone) by some visionary appearance of the Virgin Mary, poured out his devout raptures and zealous enthusiasm in a torrent of poetical hyperboles.

Such a reaction as Hazlitt's has some of its source in a disingenuous partisanship. The modern reader approaching Thomas's poem, or one of Crashaw's, for that matter, easily escapes such parochialism. But he will certainly find himself questioning the integrity of Thomas's emotion. If he has in the past not criticized Crashaw on Hazlitt's grounds, he has still never been able to reconcile the poet's assumed sincerity with his ingenuity in conceit. He does not feel that wit and passion are fused but that wit employs the exclamatory mood to simulate such fusion: the self-consciousness of the poet as craftsman belies his *furor poeticus*. He is reminded of Donne's prayer:

> When wee are mov'd to seeme religious
> Only to vent wit, Lord deliver us.

He may be convinced that Vaughan saw eternity the other night but not that Crashaw saw Mary Magdalen's tears as the cream of the milky way. And Crashaw's quatrain

> Suppose he had been tabled at thy Teats,
> Thy hunger feels not what he eats:
> He'll have his teat ere long (a bloody one)
> The mother then must suck the son

will seem to him as carefully calculated as a Jesuitical argument, as unimpelled by imagination as Wordsworth's "To a Daisy," and as exemplary of that bad taste which produces obscene jokes as T. E. Brown's stanza is of that bad taste into which prudery sometimes confusedly lapses:

> When love meets love, breast urged to breast,
>   God interposes
> An unacknowledged guest,
>   And leaves a little child among our roses.

Equal uncertainty attaches to the Thomas poem. Granting that the cause of the poem is sufficient to produce the effect, do the language and imagery, with their potential of burst, and the compressing effect of the shaped stanzas combine to produce a controlled explosion of greatest possible impact? Or are the constituents so meagerly explosive that in the midst of sound and fury the earth remains unshaken? To put it less fancifully, did Thomas really have the vision he describes, or make one up to fit the occasion? Is the experience of being found uniquely and urgently his, or is it his but not so urgently as he would like it to be (for poetical purposes), therefore requiring the assistance of Francis Thompson and others? It is one thing to borrow the words to describe an indescribable emotional experience; it is another to borrow the emotion itself to piece out your own.

Still, despite the dissatisfaction one may feel with this poem, it cannot be gainsaid that the poet has undergone a shattering experience. He may have tried to make more of it than was there. ("This ambition of surprising a reader, is the true natural cause of all fustian, or bombast in poetry," said Pope of Crashaw.) Or he may have been unable to communicate what really was there and resorted to desperate poetical measures. Regardless, the poem remains as Thomas's most open avowal of his submission to—to what? to, let us say, dear, fabulous God.

# *A Winter's Tale*

It is a simple story Thomas has to tell: by the fire in his cottage on a wintry night, a lonely man close to death prays for death to come, and it does. By personifying death and the man's desire, however, and externalizing the man's emotional experience, Thomas has produced an illusion of physical activity and turned what might have been a psychological study into a narrative poem.

What he has done here he had already done in prose, in the short story "The Visitor." There, Peter, at the point of death, lies bed-ridden, attended by his wife, Rhianon. Death, under the name of Callaghan, comes to take him for a naked piggy-back ride across the Welsh landscape during which Peter sees the natural succession in nature of life, life's cessation, and its resurgence:

> Peter, in his ghost, cried out with joy. There was life in the naked valley, life in his nakedness. He saw the streams and the beating water, how the flowers shot out of the dead, and the blades and roots were doubled in their power under the stride of the spilt blood.
>
> And the streams stopped. Dust of the dead blew over the spring,

and the mouth was choked. Dust lay over the waters like a dark ice. Light, that had been all-eyed and moving, froze in the beams of the moon.

Life in this nakedness, mocked Callaghan at his side, and Peter knew that he was pointing, with the ghost of a finger, down on the dead streams. But as he spoke, and the shape that Peter's heart had taken in the time of tangible flesh was aware of the knocks of terror, a life burst out of the pebbles like the thousand lives, wrapped in a boy's body, out of the womb. The streams again went on their way, and the light of the moon, in a new splendour, shone on the valley and magnified the shadows of the valley and pulled the moles and the badgers out of their winter into the deathless midnight season of the world.

He has, of course, died in his bed, but of this he is unaware. The whole story is built toward the surprise ending:

Rhianon, with a sweet, naked throat, stepped into the room.
Rhianon, he said, hold my hand, Rhianon.
She did not hear him, but stood over his bed and fixed him with an unbreakable sorrow.
Hold my hand, he said. And then: Why are you putting the sheet over my face?

The story is therefore the poem's best commentary, at least on its most elementary level. But the greater compression of the poem; its more ambiguous allusiveness; its non-contemporary setting; its deletion of the non-mythic figure of Rhianon, which helps the reader of the story keep his bearings; the substitution of an exotic she-bird for the comparatively domesticated Callaghan; and the completely undomestic conclusion — all these give the poem a dimension and a breadth of possibilities that the story does not possess. It has, as a result, been interpreted as an allegory of sacred love, a wish-fulfillment phantasy (the she-bird equalling love instead of death), a myth of the regeneration of the tribal hero, and as a reworking of a legend decayed from a "mid-winter ceremony of the re-birth of the year (of the earth, of man)."

Of these, the last seems to fit best. Sacred love, at least in the usual sense of the phrase, is alien to Thomas's scheme of things; the poem's conclusion is too powerful to represent a man's dream world, and the analogy of the poem with the story renders doubtful the she-bird's symbolizing anything less than death; the man is too clearly any man to be regarded as a tribal hero. As I see it, Thomas is describing the suffering and the delusions of a dying man, the cessation of his life in its human manifestation, the continuing function of his dynamic stuff in the material universe. His death is a sleep and a begetting. At one with the process, he has pervasive effect from the earth's center to the far side of heaven's crystalline periphery—in "The heavens, the heaven, the grave, the burning font," lying in but hammering out of

> the whirl-
> Pool at the wanting centre, in the folds
> Of paradise, in the spun bud of the world.

Echoes of Keats's "Eve of St. Agnes" are sufficiently numerous in Thomas's narrative to suggest his recent reading. For example:

Keats:　　The *owl,* for all his feathers, was a-*cold* . . .

　　　　　And silent was the *flock* in wooly *fold*:
　　　　　Numb were the beadsman's fingers while he *told*
　　　　　. . . . . . . . . . . . . . . . . . . his frosty *breath*

Thomas:　The pale *breath* . . . . . . . . . . . . . . . . . . . . . . . . .
　　　　　And the stars falling *cold*
　　　　　　　. . . and the far *owl*
　　　　　Warning among the *folds,* and the frozen hold
　　　　　*Flocked* with the sheep white smoke of the farm house cowl
　　　　　In the river wended vales where the tale was *told*

There are others, of course, as well as non-verbal similarities: burning Porphyro sinks into Madeline's pillow; Madeline compares herself to a bird; the beadsman sits in ashes, and Thomas's man by the spit and black pot, each kneeling, praying, doing harsh penance.

The question which must arise is: does a comparison of the "Eve" and the "Tale" reveal a debt beyond the merely verbal and imagistic? I think it not improbable, though at first glance the poems may seem more different than alike. Both, of course, are laid in the past, but beyond that, they do not ostensibly compare. Keats's poem is a love-legend of the Romeo-Juliet-Lochinvar persuasion; the characters, though romantic are real; the hero and heroine are young, beautiful, and aristocratic; the background is social; the major scene takes place in a bedroom amid a wealth of sensuous detail; the result of the poem's action is to relieve the anguish of adolescent love in defiance of the strictures of filial piety. Neither Porphyro nor Madeline wins high marks for moral behavior; each accedes to the demands of the flesh; neither (though Madeline is at least superstitious) evidences any depth of religious feeling — the beadsman sitting in his ashes takes care of their souls.

Thomas's poem rises above legend to myth; the lineaments of the hero are vague, but he seems anything but young, beautiful, and aristocratic, and of the she-bird it may be said, bird thou never wert; the hero lives alone away from society; the climactic scene occurs in a snowy exterior; the result of the poem's action is a *liebestod* following upon penance and prayer. The hero, in his recognition of his sin, his repentance, his payment of his debt, dies neither alone nor unhouseled, his spiritual agony is as profound as a saint's.

In all these respects the poems differ. Yet the possibility of the "Eve" serving as Thomas's point of departure is not obviated. As Tennyson's "Saint Agnes's Eve" shows a dissatisfaction with Keats's poem, his nun praying

> Deep on the convent-roof the snows
> Are sparkling to the moon;
> My breath to heaven like vapor goes;
> May my soul follow soon,

so Thomas's "Tale" reacts against mere romantic sensuosity. (Assuming —without evidence—Thomas's familiarity with Tennyson's poem, his reaction against the asceticism there portrayed is no less vigorous.)

What Thomas has done in effect is to inspire a character in certain respects not unlike the Beadsman—alone, apart, unnoted, of low degree, of whom it might be said

> The joys of all his life were said and sung;
> His was harsh penance on St. Agnes' Eve —

to a prayer which, though not Christian, is of a kind with that of Tennyson's nun:

> Break up the heavens, O Lord! and far,
> Thro' all yon starlight keen,
> Draw me, thy bride, a glittering star,
> In raiment white and clean.

In brief, like Tennyson's and unlike Keats's, Thomas's is a religious poem; but, like Keats's and unlike Tennyson's, it is deeply, personally felt; as Keats was Porphyro, Thomas is the man. As was said before, it is a deeply, personally felt religious poem shot through with Christian imagery, but it is not a Christian poem.

The Christian images are everywhere: the valley is like a chalice; the snow-flakes like napkins or altar cloths; the smoke the color of the Lamb; snow is the bread of life; Peter's cock crows; the chimney pot is like a cowl; scrolls of fire recall both Moses and the day of judgment; the spit and black pot suggest the lance and the grail; the she-bird and her fire have pentecostal affinities. The story itself, set in a time when "the world turned old/On a star of faith," concerns an agony in a wintry garden. (It is worthwhile to read *Matthew*, 26, in connection with this poem.)

But none of this Christianizes either the poet or the poem; rather, it finds natural process sacred, but without discovering a deity immanent to it, and a man in an anguish of spiritual need finding his relief, yet not in Christ but in the dynamism of death's decay.

The poem was written in the winter of 1944-45, when Thomas lived in constant fear of the rockets. Terror, anguish, loneliness, guilt, death were naturally his mental traveling companions. Further, as he wrote to Watkins in the letter enclosing this poem, he was concerned with his father's health. That the man in the poem bears a resemblance to his father as well as to himself seems undeniable.

In the letter, Thomas comments:

I'm sending you some new poems. The long one doesn't, I think, come off, but I like it all in spite of that. It isn't really one piece though, God, I tried to make it one and have been working on it for months.

It is not quite "one piece" because of the twenty-six stanzas there are six the functional significance of which is not made fully clear. The poem may be outlined as follows:

Stanzas   1 - 2 - Description of the locale

Stanzas   3 - 6 - Introduction of the man

Stanzas   7-11 - His prayers

Stanzas  12-13 - A miraculous natural awakening

Stanza      14 - The arrival of the she-bird

Stanzas  15-16 - Continuation of the miraculous awakening

Stanzas  17-21 - The man's death

Stanzas  23-24 - The miraculous awakening ended

Stanzas  25-26 - The assimilation of man into bird

The difficulty lies in stanzas 12-13, 15-16, and 23-24, those dealing with the miracle.

Listen. The minstrels sing
In the departed villages. The nightingale,
Dust in the buried wood, flies on the grains of her wings
And spells on the winds of the dead his winter's tale.
The voice of the dust of water from the withered spring

Is telling. The wizened
Stream with bells and baying water bounds. The dew rings
On the gristed leaves and the long gone glistening
Parish of snow. The carved mouths in the rock are wind swept strings.
Time sings through the intricately dead snow drop. Listen.

.    .    .    .    .

Look. And the dancers move
On the departed, snow bushed green, wanton in moon light
As a dust of pigeons. Exulting, the grave hooved
Horses, centaur dead, turn and tread the drenched white
Paddocks in the farms of birds. The dead oak walks for love.

The carved limbs in the rock
Leap, as to trumpets. Calligraphy of the old
Leaves is dancing. Lines of age on the stones weave in a flock.
And the harp shaped voice of the water's dust plucks in a fold
Of fields. For love, the long ago she bird rises. Look.

.    .    .    .    .

The dancing perishes
On the white, no longer growing green, and, minstrel dead,
The singing breaks in the snow shoed villages of wishes
That once cut the figures of birds on the deep bread
And over the glazed lakes skated the shapes of fishes

Flying. The rite is shorn
Of nightingale and centaur dead horse. The springs wither
Back. Lines of age sleep on the stones till trumpeting dawn.
Exultation lies down. Time buries the spring weather
That belled and bounded with the fossil and the dew reborn.

In his description of the man praying, Thomas has wrought his poem
to a very high pitch—perhaps too high. There is somewhat too much of
howling, burning, rushing, hurling, engulfing: it is the melodrama of
Blake, not the drama of *Lear*. How, then, to bring the she-bird on stage
without a sense of anti-climax? Thomas's solution of his problem is
clever. A direct call to the reader, a swift directing of his attention from
the kneeling individual in agony to a general ascendancy of life in

varied forms, and then a focus again upon a gradually revealed individual figure of amazing appearance; spotlight, dissolve and general illumination, dimming, and expanding spotlight upon a new figure. Technically, it works; thematically, it produces questions.

Are the dead really (if only temporarily) resurrected? Does the man have a vision or is Thomas merely evoking in his readers a sharper power of historical imagination? That is, did the miracle occur, did it occur only in the man's mind, is it supposed to occur only in the reader's mind?

The last can be ruled out at once. The "rite is shorn," Thomas says, because of what occurs in the final stanzas:

> For the bird lay bedded
> In a choir of wings, as though she slept or died,
> And the wings glided wide and he was hymned and wedded,
> And through the thighs of the engulfing bride,
> The woman breasted and the heaven headed
>
> Bird, he was brought low,
> Burning in the bride bed of love, in the whirl-
> Pool at the wanting centre, in the folds
> Of paradise, in the spun bud of the world.
> And she rose with him flowering in her melting snow.

Then, *do* minstrels sing and dancers move, horses tread, oaks walk, and fossils come to life? And, having come to life, why do they perish again? Why, above all, do these things *exult* at our hero's plight?

What occurs in the four stanzas is both visionary and real because it is a vision of reality. Like Peter in Thomas's story, the man, death upon him, rises to a higher level of perception and sees the natural process at work in its minutest particulars and in its fullest scope — as if watching a flower unfold in a slow-motion film. He has the armed vision. But, whereas what Peter saw is presented naturalistically — with real sheep, flies, rats, weasels, fleas, worms, beetles, moles dying, sucking, growing, decaying — what is seen in the poem is turned into myth — centaur-dead horses, Philomela-like Keatsian nightingales, druidical oaks, maypole dancers. The experience is the same; the order of its telling has been raised to a higher power. The miracle is visionary; when the man dies, it ends — "The rite is shorn/Of nightingale and centaur dead horse." The vision ends; the wedding rite between man and death is concluded, and the reality of the marriage state — attritional but fecundating decomposition — succeeds. The earth exults to receive its honored guest as the man had exulted (projecting his emotion into the figures of his vision) in the answer to his prayer.

The contraries in the poem — fire and snow, hot and cold, light and dark — are epitomized in the she-bird, who is described as a burning bride with a breast of snow. She is earth and sun. As earth, she engulfs; as sun, she rises "flowering in her melting snow." As earth, she is woman-breasted; as sun, heaven-headed. W. S. Merwin refers to her as "love-in-death"; this, I think, humanizes and Christianizes the symbol too much. She is process, and neither moral nor purposive, but holy in the Blakean sense.

6

The Intricate Image

# The Force That Through the Green Fuse

This is the poem that started Thomas on his way. As Empson says, "What hit the town of London was the child Dylan publishing *The force that through the green fuse* as a prize poem in the *Sunday Referee*, and from that day he was a famous poet; I think the incident does some credit to the town, making it look less clumsy than you would think." (*Casebook,* 113.)

One of Thomas's least obscure poems, it could not have cost its earliest readers much effort to come to an understanding of its general meaning. G. S. Fraser (*Ibid.,* 40) has expressed it as well as any: "The forces, he is saying, that control the growth and decay, the beauty and terror of human life are not merely similar to, but are the very same forces as we see at work in outer nature." W. S. Merwin (*Ibid.,* 60) stresses Thomas's outgoing emotion: ". . . the doom within life is described again, but described because of emotion for things mortal, and the compassion makes the poet at once wish to be able to communicate with all other things that are doomed, to tell them he understands their plight because his own is similar, and makes him feel the depth to which he is inarticulate and painfully unable to do so."

Elizabeth Drew has been utterly defeated by the lines

> And I am dumb to tell a weather's wind
> How time has ticked a heaven round the stars.

"Is he," she asks, "describing love as a *seeming* absolute, 'A heaven round the stars,' and telling lovers that time and the seasons really control it too? It, too, is nothing but *process*?" (*Poetry: A Modern Guide to its Understanding and Enjoyment,* p. 183.) But when the poem was published, the lines read

> And I am dumb to tell the timeless clouds
> That time is all.

The earliest readers were not confronted by a time-ticked heaven and did not suffer Professor Drew's uncertainty.

However, supposing the general idea of the poem to have been immediately comprehensible, would those earliest readers have been stymied by particular lines? Or if not stymied, perhaps irritated by what might seem to them metaphorical irresponsibility? Imagine a conversation with a determined rationalist — such a one as wonders why Burns so emphasizes the redness of his "luv," who thinks of insecticide when he reads "There is a garden in her face," and who considers leaving a kiss within a cup both absurd and unhygienic.

The opening image will provoke his scorn. The flower, he will say, is the explosion. Agreed? And the stem is the fuse, and the force is the combustible in the fuse that produces the explosion. Now—according to the poem, the force is greater than the flower, and it is supposed to continue its operations after the destruction of the flower. But (and he gestures emphatically) the combustible in the fuse is never as powerful as the explosive charge it ignites. That is, the force is less than the rose. And both the combustible and the fuse are destroyed *before* the explosion occurs. Is this the case with Thomas's force and stem? It is not. Ergo, the metaphor is absurd.

Nor will he stop there. A condescending tolerance will move him to pass the imprecision of the metaphor. But he will transfer his scorn to the second of the poem's basic themes. To the first he has no objection: that that (whatever it is) which creates life and compels its maturation, ultimately destroys it. Well and good. A platitude, of course; but after all, is there anything whereof it may be said, see, this is new? But why should Thomas want to go about discussing the matter with roses, arteries, and the winds? If people who talk to themselves are suspect, what about those who talk to their blood vessels? Who would not think them "dumb" in the vulgar sense of the word?

If, thrown off balance by this attack, you mutter something about powerful emotion, expressed in vivid images and given compulsive power by dynamic verbs, and tightly packed into paralleling stanzas structured to offer statement, counter-statement, and refrain—he will catch you up short.

Emotion? he will query gently, and, musingly, Integrity of emotion? And, decisively, No. No poet who plays with words as Thomas does feels intensely. He is too busy thinking all the time, too much engaged with his dictionary. Consider, and he opens the book, the triple play on "mouth" in the second stanza. The triple-entendre is puerile — and it has an ugly sound. He is more clever when, life waning, he has the blood wax, but cleverness cancels passion out.

But that third stanza: carrying the sucking mouth of the second stanza through whirlpool and quicksand and lime-pit to the leeching lips of the fourth; playing the live sand that suffocates against the dead clay that burns; concatenating whirl — lasso — shroud — rope; obliquely relating sails to the lime that whitens them, as it whitens the bones of the man who had sailed, windless, through space; relating the shroud sail both to the leech (the edge of a sail) and to the last stanza's sheet. This man is not merely three sheets but three shrouds and three leeches to the wind.

And he shifts attack to the fourth stanza. With a quiet reasonableness. There has been, he will start, no indication that the force in this poem

270 ·

is time. If you were philosophical you might think of it as a generalized *élan vital;* if you were religious, it would be God. (Here, though he is a professed free-thinker, he shows off by quoting some possible parallel passages from Books 10, 12, 14, 23, 24, and 28 of *Job.*) But, he resumes, notice that Time in leeching to the fountain head is the equivalent of the mouth that sucks the mountain stream. However, Time is not a force; it is that within which the force works, merely the period during which a process continues. No one ever says that God is Time — though Yeats was thinking as muddily as Thomas when he wrote

> The stallion Eternity
> Mounted the mare of Time
> 'Gat the foal of the world.

But a great many people do say that God is Love. Yet here what do we find? that Love is blood, blood collected in a pool, as in a black eye, the pressure of which is eased by the suction of Time. This blood is, of course, at the "fountain head," which must be the heart. But if it is there, and not under a contusion, can it be said to drip and gather? And how can blood fallen from the heart "calm her sores"? Except in death. But to this point, death has been the destroyer; now in relieving the pain of love it becomes the healer. There's an inconsistency here.

And then *Hirudo medicinalis* becomes an arachnid (order *Acardida*) — the blood-sucking tick — and then a clock, with a heart-like audible beat. Now how about that heaven that gets ticked around the stars? Are we considering "man's small place in the well-integrated, clockwork universe?" Or "the ecstasy of love 'ticking a heaven round the stars'"? The poet says Time does the ticking. Common sense says that man, hating time, has imagined the idea of eternity, thus in a way ticking off time. And perhaps this is what Thomas meant; but in his cleverness he didn't say so.

But you know, he says, relenting, Thomas *is* clever. You remember your muttering about statement and counter-statement. Do you realize that the whole poem is the counter-statement to its counter-statement? It's like this: In each of the first three stanzas the statement is that "the force" generates life; the counter-statement is that the same force destroys. Now since the refrain refers always to a helplessness, increasing the effect of the negative counter-statement, the pervasive tone of the poem is negative. And the conclusion scarcely seems a happy one:

> And I am dumb to tell the lover's tomb
> How at my sheet goes the same crooked worm.

But it really is, because this particular crooked worm at the sheet bears Time-defeating sperm. We have been subtly led from compassion (for the hanging Christ-figure), to love, to that good joke on Time that, because of Death man has created an anti-Time (heart-beat quelling clock-tick), and finally to the idea of the infinite continuation of life-cycles. The poem itself is a perfect circle, *crooked* in the last line linking with *crooked* in the first. And as for the poet's being dumb — the poem is his own refutation. A really beautiful job!

And one is dumb to tell the determined rationalist, now reading the poem aloud á la Thomas, that in poetry absurdities don't matter when the words fall right.


# *A Process In The Weather Of The Heart*

There is a tendency among Thomas's commentators to exaggerate his fearful awareness of death. The physiological vividness of his imagery leads, I think, to over-vivid critical writing, to such phrases as "death lurks just the other side of appearance eating away the heart of life"; "incipient ruin spread through the whole universe"; "Birth is an event tinged with horror because it places a new creature squarely in the corrupting and fatal stream of time." (Mills, *Accent,* p. 119.)

This writer, quoting from the present poem the opening lines of the last stanza,

> A process in the weather of the world
> Turns ghost to ghost; each mothered child
> Sits in their double shade

comments, dramatically, "The act of procreation molds a victim to be hurled out to his death." (*Ibid.,* p. 120.) This is no a correct explication of the sense of these lines, but even if it were that, it would still, in its falsification of the tone, misrepresent the passage.

Not that Thomas is not preoccupied with death. He is. But not at all to the exclusion of a vigorous awareness of life. He is not morbid but realistic. The trouble is that as one remembers Hell and forgets Heaven in *Paradise Lost,* one remembers the images of death and decay in Thomas and forgets their contraries. But they are there. Though "Man in his maggot's barren," "the poles are kissing as they cross"; though "bags of blood let out their flies," "worlds hang on the trees."

Thomas maintains his balance better than his critics, and perhaps never better than in this completely non-morbid poem, a poem preserving balance in emotion, and balance in style.

272 ·

Of the eight sentences which compose the poem, seven begin similarly: A process; a weather; a process; a darkness; a weather; a process; a process. Only one ("The seed that") breaks the pattern. In each of the 6-line stanzas, the first sentence pauses at a semicolon after the second iamb of the second line, and the sentence reaches full stop at the end of the third. There is like parallelism between the two 3-line stanzas. The rhythm throughout is regular, save for an added (retarding) iamb in the penultimate line of the last stanza. And the short stanzas, rhyming (roughly) c b a, link with the long stanzas, which rhyme a a b c c b. In syntax and prosody, then, there is tight control.

The pairing of antitheses compounds the effect of syntax and prosody: damp - dry; golden shot - freezing tomb; night - day; life-blood - death-worm; seeing eye - blind bone; darkness - light; known sea - unknown land; harvested seed - windfall-seed; quick - dead; moon - sun; external skin - internal heart.

One would think it unlikely that, in a poem so carefully crafted, sensibility would be permitted to riot. It is not. The poem says, in effect, The heart has its seasons, of which the seasons know nothing; the world has its seasons, which the heart knows very well. And, confirming Blake, Without contraries there is no progression. If there is summer, there is winter; if there is darkness, there is light; if there is life, there is death. And, as light without darkness is undifferentiated, unshaped — which is to say that, without darkness, light is characterless— life without the fact of death and an awareness of the fact is, if not inconceivable, an immensely diminished thing.

Thomas is not an infant puling in the night. He is defining, without self-pity or melodrama, the human condition, which is not a being but a becoming. It is not of man (nor of nature) that the apostle spoke when he used the words, "with whom is no variableness, neither shadow of turning."

I do not think that the first stanza presents a consistent metaphor — heart equaling world or sun or whatnot. But what the stanza says is clear enough. In man, as in the external world, a sun, a dynamic source of energy, dries, unfreezes, illuminates. The mood is not that of "April is the cruelest month," but of "Aprille with his showres sote."

Except for the stanza's final and double-barreled word, *worm*. Taken as phallus, the word brings to a climax the stanza's affirmation. Taken as grave-yard worm, it modifies the affirmation. But an unadulterated affirmation is sheer sentimentality. (As "April is the cruelest month," in an inverted way, is.) No question—the word gives pause, but only the pause given by Chaucer's hairy mole. The spring that Thomas is describing so goldenly was, after all, preceded by and will be followed by a winter.

And in the second stanza, brought to it by that single word, we are reminded that living is a draining of the reservoir of life.

The third and fourth stanzas quite serenely accept the situation. Light, as I have said, without darkness is undefinable; the totally known may become the totally dull; every farmer knows that some seeds fail to germinate; every orchardist expects and makes allowances for windfalls. Life and death are not opponents but a team, as are sun and rain.

Life and death are, like lovers, inseparable. And it is only in the intercourse between them that further life (or death) can succeed. And though the poem ends with a death, it does so not despairingly but logically. The poem had begun with an unfreezing of a tomb; it is only a step from the death of the last stanza to the new life of the first.

The last stanza makes a characteristic Thomasian jump from the individual to the universal. The process of the heart accords with the process of the world. The annihilation of the moon is only quantitatively different from the death of a man. And every time a man dies, the moon and the sun are, from his point of view, destroyed.

There is something of Gaskell in the conceit, "A process . . ./Pulls down the shabby curtains of the skin." At least three pictorial images spring to mind: closing the curtains in the front parlor where the corpse is laid out; closing the eyelids of the dead; skinning a dead rabbit. It is the first, I think, which prevails, and it has a not unpleasant savor of Victorian domesticity and the Victorian sense of the rightness of things. Taken in conjunction with "the heart gives up its dead," it recalls the widows such as those in *Cranford* who, heartbroken and impoverished, nevertheless toughly live on.

I do not think that the poem ends, any more than it began, on a morbid, or death-obsessed, or despairing note. Nor does it leap to the other extreme. It merely states, with equability, the fact of life's ambitendency.

## Light Breaks Where No Sun Shines

Where does light break without a sun and "heart-water" move without a sea? In the third and second verses of *Genesis:* "And the Spirit of God moved upon the face of the waters"; "And God said, Let there be light: and there was light." At the time (strictly, non-time), "the earth was without form, and void"; neither sun nor sea had been created.

Under what circumstances in a man's life does an analogous situation obtain: that is, when is he without form, and void, but possessed of light and touched by the spirit? In the womb and in the tomb. What this poem proclaims is the continuous efficacy of the life-spirit whether planted at conception in flesh, or disunited from flesh at death. In the beginning is the smile of light; at the end (which is not an end, but a change), the blood forks to a sun.

In my opinion, the poem is so structured as to provide two parallel developments. The first half of each stanza (sometimes two, sometimes three lines) describes a stage in a man's development, from conception to death. The second half describes an analogous stage (although the changes are not so pronounced) in the physical processes which occur after death. The two developments can be diagramed as follows:

1.
   A. Life (Conception)
   B. Death (the body begins to decay)
2.
   A. Life (Puberty)
   B. Death (the life-stuff ascends into the atmosphere)
3.
   A. Life (Maturity)
   B. Death (the life-stuff descends as rain)
4.
   A. Life (Old Age)
   B. Death (the rain ends winter)
5.
   A. Life (Death)
   B. Death (Life: the spring plants, nourished from above and below, sprout; the sun gives to and takes from the plants)

This outline will surprise some Thomas-students because the most widely circulated explication of the poem (Marshall Stearns's) limits the poem to a "description of the state of existence: the theme is the process of living." So, in the first stanza, where

> . . . broken ghosts with glow-worms in their heads,
> The things of light
> File through the flesh where no flesh decks the bones,

he discovers a description of "those intimations of consciousness or foreknowledge as they present themselves to the child in the womb." (Tedlock, p. 127.) Bernard Krieger (*Explicator,* 15) thinks that Stearns goes wrong in this crucial passage and therefore fails to present "a unified reading of the poem." Krieger gives two readings, assuming in the first that "where no flesh decks the bones" refers to the eyes, and, in the second, to the vagina. The poem is either "about the acquisition of knowledge and its effect," or a description of sexual intercourse.

Hornick assumes a cadaver in the first stanza; a projection of human and sexual qualities upon the cosmos in the second; and, in the third and fourth, an image of the Cosmic Man: "These two stanzas present us with an image of the universe in the form of man. Dawn breaks from his eyes, the sea is his blood (windy because fertile), the rod and gushers of the sky are his sexual organs . . . , and the alternation of day and night is involved in the processes of his body." (Hornick, p. 94.)

Ralph Mills (*Accent,* XX, 123) does not explicate; but he too apparently reads the stanzas as being undivided. As he sees it, the poem "ties the physiology of man to an external, material reality":

Domination by time, by biological necessity, and an inherited alliance with the unswerving course of nature make the inner life of a person the reflection of a process . . . . The body is a microcosm; all its parts obey the same dictates, display the same behavior as the elements of the external world in which it is located. In a very real sense, the body *is* nature, for the two are inseparable. Only consciousness, spirit, the mind—call it what you will—hangs above the operations of matter, meditating on resurgence and decay.

According to my bifurcated-stanza theory, the poem reads as follows:

1. Dynamic consciousness, the same life-energy that informs the sun, has its inception in the darkness of the womb; the ebb and flow of blood has its outer counterpart in the tidal movements of the sea.

At death (when boneless worms, like miners, tunnel through the cadaver, and when the flesh falls off the bones) that life-energy breaks away from, escapes from ("files through") the body and is transferred to earth or feeds the earth-aerating worms.

2. At puberty, the possibility of a triumph over mortality through procreation is made evident (the flower of the seed of age is death; of the seed of sex is life).

From the sexless tomb, the life-energy ascends to the sun; one might consider it a gathering of figs from thistles, and a setting of two baskets of them before the temple as a gesture of contempt for death; though the mortal body burns away, its wick of energy remains, and capillarity continues as before.

3. Behold, in his maturity, the man of wisdom and strength; he is a microcosm of the world, but only metaphorically.

Behold now no differentiation of man from nature—no fencing off. In nature's unimpeded cycle, the clouds, miraculously brought to a rich fullness by the absorptive powers of the sun (the sun's smile of light like Aaron discovering—divining—and metamorphosing—making divine—the subterranean liquescence of the lamented corpse), loose the life-giving rain.

4. The light-full eyes darken in old age; shades of the evening close upon the aging man; skin is transparent over the bone.

In the grave (for the dead there is neither cold nor hot), melting snow and the seepage of April rain skin off the old, wring out the new: the color-film of spring depends upon decaying eye-lids and the like; spring feeds like a pathological growth on the rotting eye (the wild cataract leaps in glory, so to speak).

5. The light of life extinguished by the grave (fractured on secret lots), the light of death dawns: not the observer's understanding of the rain-wet lilac, but the understanding of the participator in the lilac's growth.

After death, the thinking reed becomes a reedy thought; the eye is not aloof from but a part of the miracle of growth; the blood's dynamism contributes to the sun's; over the allotted dump-heaps the dawn stands to greet the breaking dawn.

# Do You Not Father Me

W. S. Merwin has summed up the meaning of this not particularly exciting nor ingratiating poem as follows:

Such a poem as "Do You Not Father Me" carries both the subject of the individual's continuing creation, which Dylan Thomas had first developed in "Before I Knocked," and the subject of "The Force that through the Green Fuse," a stage further by identifying man the creator-creature with all other mortal creatures. (Tedlock, pp. 241-2.)

I doubt that any particular advance in Thomas's thinking is reflected in this poem, but its relation to the other two poems is definite. Such matters as the affiliation of creating love and destroying death, the sea-origin of man, the legitimacy of the concept of sin in the natural man, the oneness of biological life are explicit or implicit in all three. Indeed, the present poem might be described as a dialogue between the speaker of "Before I Knocked" (but with Christian connotations removed) and the force that drives the flower and blasts the tree.

The unifying metaphor represents the physical body as being simultaneously the seat of a tower and of a house. Each building has its distinctive features: the tower is masculine in character, a place from which armed troops issue to attack; the house is feminine, domestic, a place in which to give the long suck, a place of adorable windows. The tower bespeaks death, the house, love. But (and this is a major point of the poem) when the warriors from the tower attack the house, it is the tower that falls, and the warriors in the house contribute to life, not death.

The most irritating ambiguity of the poem is in the conjunction "nor" in the first stanza. Assuming that Everyman is questioning the Force, what is the purport of his question?

Do you not father me, nor the erected arm
For my tall tower's sake cast in her stone?

The sentence is open to two interpretations:

Do you, Force, not father me, and *do you not* embody my portion of your vital essence in nature's physical stuff?
Do you not father me, and *yet not* embody . . . .

There is still a third possibility if we take *not father* as a hyphenated construction (*not-father*), in which case the sense would run, "Do you fail to father and fail to cast . . . ." But the last alternative is absurd, and the second only tenable if a special definition of "erected arm" is supplied. Perhaps something like this:

Do you not father me, and yet fail to supply the masculine vigor, the erectile tissue necessary for my maturation?

The rest of the poem, however, does not develop such a thesis. I prefer to consider "erected arm" as a synecdoche for the physical body as a whole. These perplexities cleared away, the poem reads like this:

1

Do you not urge phallus to vagina; do you not supply life to the vigorous sperm, towards making me mortal flesh of my mother's flesh?

Do you not compel surrender to the invading phallus; do you not supply life to the egg that meets the foreign sperm; and, when sperm and egg have met to produce the new entity, Me, do you not participate with me in the urge to grow towards procreativeness?

Do you not, working within me in your persona (on the upper plane of consciousness) as affectionate sister and as Christian Sister, redefine lust leading to death as love leading to life, by sublimation easing my burden of guilt?

Do you not, as with me you increase and intellectualize your vigor, focus attention upon the full scene of summer life, ignoring or concealing the wintry death to come?

## 2

Am I not microcosm to your macrocosm, lusty, precocious, mothered, libidinous, perceptive? Do I not take responsibility for my sin and find my own salvation? Am I not one with bird and shell and with all life on the shore subject to the governance that rules the sea?

## 3

You are all these, said the life-love-death-sex complex. And all the forms of life (numberless as the sands of the shore, devoted to me, indulgent and roughly cutting) said they were mine. I am, my Babel-tower's story ended (its death-bell tolled), cut down by death (itself not subject to death); but the wrecker who raised and razed my tower fades to ineffectual ghost, because from the midst of the sea-stuff wreckage, from the land-dwelling, embodied sea-spirit, rise like ghastly spectres the new begetters. (This is a poem of homogenization; there are no well-defined dichotomies. I am you, and you are I; spirit is flesh, and flesh is spirit; sex is death, and sex is life. There appear to be few bounding lines.)

## 4

Do you not, primal ooze, beget me on—or compel me to—the earth that will destroy me (I, one of those numberless as the sands, coming to be numbered among them)? Yes, says sea-bottom obliquely: you are the father of your sisters, you are the mother, and all the little dears who, forgetful of their sea-origins, decorously play gentleman and lady. Can I, Everyman inquires, despite those whiteners of sepulchres, the winds of change, or despite the busy, preachy plasterers and whitewashers, despite propriety's turning all things contrariwise (widder-shins), can I still be the house of love? Father, mother, sister, brother, and all the rest chorus the answer: Both love and death are heedless of and beyond the control of human myth: that sin-eater, that beggar who, for a fee and a drink, at a funeral symbolically devours the sins of the deceased, affects neither love nor death.

A weird poem (or, if the poem is not, my explication is). But it is weird in its concreteness. Put abstractly—the life-force compels all life to death, and out of death educes life; living things have in common only this compulsion of the life-force; there are no categorical imperatives even for the "higher" forms of life—it is down to Darwinian earth enough.

Nothing, I think, particularly distinguishes the poem. It lacks the vividness, the inevitability of statement of "The Force," the gusto of "How Shall My Animal," the initial shock-effect and succeeding capability of arousing compassion of "Before I Knocked." It has nothing in particular to recommend it: no intricacy of rhyme or rhythm, no memorable figures of speech, no titillating compressions. It was not, one might infer, so much fathered as contrived.

It may, however, be read as an ingenious *tour de force,* and if it is so read perhaps will rise in the reader's estimation. Points of similarity suggest that Thomas is re-writing the second in Donne's sequence of sonnets known as *La Corona,* the one entitled "Annunciation":

> Salvation to all that will is nigh;
> That All, which alwayes, is All every where,
> Which cannot sinne, and yet all sinnes must beare,
> Which cannot die, yet cannot chuse but die,
> Loe, faithfull Virgin, yeelds himselfe to lye
> In prison, in thy wombe; and though he there
> Can take no sinne, nor thou give, yet he'will weare
> Taken from thence, flesh, which deaths force may trie.
> Ere by the spheares time was created, thou
> Wast in his minde, who is thy Sonne, and Brother;
> Whom thou conceiv'st, conceiv'd; yea thou art now
> Thy Makers maker, and thy Fathers mother;
> Thou'hast light in darke; and shutst in little roome,
> Immensity cloysterd in thy deare wombe.

Taking the poem as an address by Christ to his sire and dam gives it another dimension and perhaps enhances its value.

## *Where Once The Waters Of Your Face*

Poe's imp of the perverse seems to have found a local habitation in Thomas's brain. In describing a dry river-bed he humanizes it enough to make it a poem about a girl. Does he intend a river-bed like a girl, or a girl like a river-bed? It reads perfectly well either way. Elder Olson apparently reads it as the former. It seems to me a more interesting poem and the successful solution of a more difficult artistic problem if the river-bed is seen simultaneously as a feminine counterpart of a boy of summer. The point is that, out of simple language and an apparently simple subject, Thomas has achieved an unexpected complexity, in this particular poem a controlled complexity in which heterogeneities are effectively yoked.

It is illuminating to contrast Thomas's poem with Frost's sonnet, "The Silken Tent."

She is as in a field a silken tent
At midday when a sunny summer breeze
Has dried the dew and all its ropes relent,
So that in guys it gently sways at ease,
And its supporting central cedar pole,
That is its pinnacle to heavenward
And signifies the sureness of the soul,
Seems to owe naught to any single cord,
But strictly held by none, is loosely bound
By countless silken ties of love and thought
To everything on earth the compass round,
And only by one's going slightly taut
In the capriciousness of summer air
Is of the slightest bondage made aware.

Each is on the general subject of love and each makes an elaborate comparison between a girl and a non-human object, but here the similarity ends. Frost's comparison is developed like an epic simile, there being no question that the tent is a tent and the girl a girl and that the real comparison is between two identical emotional responses that the poet-observer has made to two visual stimuli. In the Thomas poem, every effort is made to break down the two distinct entities and assimilate the one into the other. Thomas is able to appear to accomplish this because in each, girl and river, generation takes place in dark, liquid depths. And he so keeps attention directed to this almost literal similarity that the figurative nature of the poem is forgotten.

There is, beyond this and partly because of this, a difference in tone. Frost is working away from the tent as a physical object to the idea it embodies—the paradox of liberty in constraint. But Thomas is concerned to emphasize the river-bed and the girl as physical things, so much concerned that he does not bound from a physical surface to a concept but bores in to dredge up a surfeit of physiological data. It is not that, in his attempt for realism, he offers the potato dirty instead of scrubbed, but that he offers it analyzed into its chemical constituents.

Frost's conception of love therefore seems more exalted than Thomas's. As he has carefully distinguished the vehicle and tenor of his comparison to achieve lucidity, he has severed love almost altogether from the physical preoccupations of sex. Thomas not only does not separate girl from river or sex from love or propagation from marriage, he welds them together by his insistence upon the physical apparatuses involved.

But the fact is that Frost's conception is not more exalted than Thomas's, nor does he in this sonnet stand out as a philosophical poet as against a visceral Thomas. For Thomas's poem ultimately is not about a girl, nor about a river-bed, but about the cosmic cycle which repeats itself in river and girl. This can be missed.

In the first stanza, for example:

> Where once the waters of your face
> Spun to my screws, your dry ghost blows,
> The dead turns up its eye;
> Where once the mermen through your ice
> Pushed up their hair, the dry wind steers
> Through salt and root and roe.

The force of the two opening lines is such that attention is diverted from the oddity of finding "The dead turns up its eye" instead of the expected ". . . turn up their eyes." And "mermen" in the parallel-structured "Where once the mermen . . . ." seems merely a superficial play of fancy. But the reference to a Polyphemus-like corpse has a significance, and the allusion to mermen is not a superficiality. The two taken together lead through the middle stanzas (though "green unraveller" means literally *unraveller of your greenness,* it recalls the supernatural power of the Green Knight; the "dolphined sea" recalls Venus as well as the strange events of Yeats's *Byzantium*) to the tomb that did not stay latched upon the dead man, to covenants between man and God, to the Eden story—in short, to articles of faith that confirm the continuation of life in the despite of all natural accidents. The victory over death is neatly epitomized in the allusion to the coral: since it is the skeletons of the coral colonies that form the reefs, their death is not a loss but a construction. What Thomas is getting at is the miraculousness of natural process—of birth, of growth, of metamorphosis and rebirth through apparent death. The evidence of Christ's nature-defying miracles has been used over the centuries to strengthen Christian faith; Thomas's "sea-faith" is validated by the wonder of nature working naturally.


## Foster The Light

The immediate problem of this poem, which is either a prayer or an exhortation, is to determine whom the poet is addressing. In the third stanza it is a "High lord esquire":

> Of mortal voices to the ninnies' choir,
> High lord esquire, speak up the singing cloud,
> And pluck a mandrake music from the marrowroot.

In the fourth, the seas:

282 ·

Roll unmanly over this turning tuft,
O ring of seas, nor sorrow as I shift
From all my mortal lovers with a starboard smile;

In the fifth, it is a colorer, a shaper, a glory:

Who gave these seas their colour in a shape,
Shaped my clayfellow, and the heaven's ark
In time at flood filled with his coloured doubles;
O who is glory in the shapeless maps,
Now make the world of me as I have made
A merry manshape of your walking circle.

One possibility is that the poem constitutes a single address—to God, an anthropomorphized life-force. A satisfactory interpretation can be devised in these terms, the only difficulty arising from the specific address in the fourth stanza to the "ring of seas." The problem, however, is a minor one; the life-force can easily be conceived as a sea, within which is the world-island, which in turn contains a man-island. Phineas Fletcher did as much in *The Purple Island*.

Or the poem can be read as three addresses: the poet to himself, in the first three stanzas; to the sea, in the fourth; and, in conclusion, to the life-force. This too makes a satisfactory poem, and, since appeals to abstract forces interest me less than self-exhortation, a more attractive one.

Fundamentally, one interpretation very nearly equates with the other because the poem seems to be written on the basis of the 17th-century's microcosm-macrocosm theory, according to which man is both an epitome of the earth and a copy of God:*

For what had all this All, which Man in one
Did not unite; the earth, aire, water, fire,
Life, sense, and spirit, nay, the powrefull throne
Of the divinest Essence, did retire,
And his owne Image into clay inspire:
So that this Creature well might called be
Of the great world, the small epitome,
Of the dead world, the live, and quick anatomie.

In either case the dominant figure of the poem is the circle of perfection, and its burden an exhortation that that circle not be broken. I shall read the poem in the second of the two ways indicated above.

*I shall borrow freely from Marjorie Nicolson's *The Breaking of the Circle* in the following paragraphs.

The person being exhorted is to foster both the bright light of day and the pale, reflected light of the moon (an orb like a man's head that, like a man's senses, says Donne, undergoes "Eclypses, sodaine obfuscations, and darknings"), perhaps in recognition of what Thomas Browne noted, that "Light that makes all things seen, makes some things invisible. The greatest mystery of religion is expressed by adumbration." An experiential understanding of the way in which inner and outer world interpenetrate is advised. No part of experience, however dark and shadowy, is to be ignored, and experience is not to be dispassionately rationalized and abstracted into cold and useful formulae instead of welcomed in its lively leafiness.

Rather, a man is to become wise in the ways of vegetable growth and careful to observe that there is a time to plant and a time to pluck up that which is planted. One with organic nature, he will welcome spring and new life (whether natural or miraculous); he will not endeavor to retard a season, nor alienate himself from any of the four; in winter, he will prepare for summer, and in autumn for winter; he will rejoice in his youth and in the morning sow his seed, remembering the days of darkness, for they shall be many.

The specific allusions of the third stanza escape me, but from desperate conjectures based on echoes I can offer a general reading that accords with the sense of the preceding stanzas. "And pluck a mandrake music from the marrowroot" recalls Donne, which recalls Eliot's dictum that Donne was a whole man (an unbroken circle of a poet) as neither Milton nor Dryden was, which recalls Yeats's condemnation of intelligent men as having brains that suck up the blood from their hearts, all of which, mixed well, leads to this: The exhorted person is to be all-fathering, making no distinctions between lower and higher—loins, heart, head; or among hell (which is a circle within the earth), earth, and heaven. He is, encompassing all experience, to protect the heart from the brain's imperialistic ingressions. And from this isthmus of a middle state (the mortal circle of the earth), he is to serve as intermediary between earth and heaven, effecting the reconciliation in realistic terms of life and death, being one "Who knoweth the spirit of man that goeth upward, and the spirit of the beast that goeth downward to the earth." This he is peculiarly equipped to do, for, as Thomas Browne said:

For first we are a rude mass, and in the rank of creatures which only are, and have a dull kind of being, not yet privileged with life, or preferred to sense or reason; next we live the life of Plants, the life of Animals, the life of Men, and at last the life of Spirits, running on in one mysterious nature those five kinds of existences, which comprehend the creatures, not onely of the World, but of the Universe.

Having in general terms placed himself organically in the context of the cosmic process, and having stated the folly of an attempted escape either in life or death, Thomas now brings himself specifically into the poem. He addresses the sea, itself a microcosm of the total process and, like it, objective and amoral. The sea, he says, is unlike mortal man (unmanly), does not die (is not cock robin), does not change (is not weathercock-wise), and does not love (is not cock-wise). It will feel no emotion, it will not change the set of its currents, regardless of what (as it seems to him) earth-shattering event occurs to Thomas. The ambiguities here permit of several alternative events: Thomas's death; his conversion from mortal to "right" (starboard) love; his immersion in physical love; his immersion in an undifferentiated love—that of cross-boned-Christ-cum-sparrowed-Venus; an end of his love; the death of his lover. In any of these cases, the sea (not a devil or the contrary) just goes rolling along.

The love mentioned in the fourth stanza cannot be singled out. It may be supernatural, natural, or human. Though this may be a matter of irrelevance to the sea, it is of some moment to the manly explicator, and he looks to the final stanza. Only to find the ambiguities compounded.

First, one notes that the opening three lines may be read as statement of fact, the direct address beginning with "O who is glory . . . ." This syntactical arrangement offers the possibility of this interpretation: the creating force which made the sea also made my consort and fixed in us the desire to couple; O you, my consort, who with your love have given color and meaning to all life, as I have made for you a man, make of me your world. (It was Thomas Browne who spoke of "That truest microcosm, the womb of our Mother.")

This is possible, but implausible. Such a conclusion has not been prepared for, and (or so it seems to me) it brings the poem to a diminished conclusion—it hath a dying fall. Nevertheless, it can be justified on the grounds that human love, however narrow its scope and brief its duration, is greater than all ocean.

Still, to read "walking circle" as a sexual allusion is to convict Thomas of having no sense of proportion. How much more satisfactory to see the phrase as either an imagizing of the definition of God as a circle whose circumference is nowhere, whose center is everywhere, or of the circuit of the sun. Now the stanza has a more general application: That which made the seas also made man, and filled all space with life and light and color and hope and love; O You who glorify infinity, I ask that, as I have jovially humanized you, you universalize me.

To be universalized in life would mean to become like Herbert's Man:

Man is all symmetrie,
Full of proportions, one limbe to another,
And all to all the world besides:
Each part may call the furthest, brother:
For head with foot hath private amitie,
    And both with moons and tides.

To be universalized in death would be to enter the natural cycle.

The last stanza does not need to be read as statement followed by direct address. The address can be assumed to begin with the first line and to be repeated at the fourth, after a deep breath at the semi-colon for the final forward surge. Since Thomas speaks of "his coloured doubles" rather than of "you," he probably did not intend such a reading. But it has its virtue.

Less immediately comprehensible, less quickly emotion-stirring than "The Force that Through the Green Fuse," this poem has not had the latter's success with the anthologists. It seems to me in its variety to have a "largesse" that the other lacks, within at least equivalent control. Thomas, ringing his changes on his circle figure (sun, moon, bone, egg, fig, planet, heart, ring of seas, world, man, God, *et al.*) has made his poem as God, according to Donne, made the world, "In such a concinnity of parts as that it was an instrument, perfectly in tune."

# The Seed-At-Zero

How seriously to regard a poem so consciously contrived, so clever in its incremental repetition, so bouncy in its rhythm (with overtones of "The Raven" and of "Hiawatha") is a question. Thomas clearly had the fun in composing it that, say, Swinburne had in composing a roundel, and it may be that he intended no more than that the heart of the hearer might smile, since to pleasure his ear the poem was wrought. Still, as a green inch may bear the hero-seed, *vers de societé* may have its significant thought. The poem has been subject to interpretation.

Unfortunately, the two interpretations which I have seen are widely divergent, and, as so often is the case, they are because there is disagreement over the identity of the poem's title-character. For Stanford the seed-at-zero represents "man with his vital forces spent; man, in other words, in a condition of death." (Stanford, p. 68.) Therefore "man's goal is not, ultimately, the womb of woman but the womb of the universe." Elder Olson, on the other hand, sees the military imagery of the first two stanzas as "a metaphor for conception (the seed storming the womb)."

(P. 101.) The seed-at-zero is not a terminal nullity but a soldier ready at the zero hour to attack.

Both are right, since the poem does not stand still but moves forward, stating the conditions of birth, pleading for the possibility of growth, and indicating the status of man in death. Zero, at first the point of departure for an ascent, later becomes the lowest point, the point of no departure.

The poem is organized in four pairs of stanzas, the second stanza of each pair, by shifting adjectives, nouns, and verbs, changing or adding to the meaning of the first. Thus, in the first pair, "*trodden* womb" becomes "*manwaged* womb"; and where, in the first stanza, the god-in-hero stumbles "Over the *manwaging* line," in the second, he *leaps* "Over the *warbearing* line." In the first two pairs of stanzas, the variants do not greatly enchance the meaning, but in the latter two they are of significance.

I take *Seed-at-zero* to represent potential life in general, animal and vegetable, and the *trodden womb* any place where fertilization may occur —the womb specifically, the earth, and various bodies of water. (The epithet *trodden* may be a recollection of Hopkins' "Generations have trod" in "The World is Charged.") The emphasis in the first pair of stanzas is upon the human seed; in the second pair, upon vegetable; the third brings the two together—"green inch" and "village green"; and the fourth, putting the man-in-seed in the seed-at-zero, concludes with all attention focused upon the human.

The opening stanzas describe how life will *not* begin. Beginning life shall not, like an Achilles storming a city, assail either awkwardly and by chance ("stumbling") or with purpose and agility ("leaping"), the man-assaulted, man-assaulting, man-bearing, man-killing womb.

It shall, rather, like the gentle rain from heaven, be mysteriously sifted from the starry skies to nourish miraculously the heavy-sounding, quaking earth, and to impregnate the sea whose surface it breaks. Quietly, irresistibly, it will penetrate the surfaces of earth and sea and seize the stronghold of virginity for its own.

That is, the origin of life is as natural (and as mysterious) as sunlight and rain. Anthropocentric deities shall not be said to thump the clouds.

The initiating process described, Thomas turns to the ensuing dangers to growth. Microcosm (humble village, green inch) and macrocosm (humble planet, high sphere) have united to produce life. Is a non-indulgent hemisphere, continent, or village green to be permitted a denial of this life? Then let the seed escape from earth's Mrs. Grundys and seek the protection of boisterous, broad-minded life-affirmers.

There are suggestions here that the hero seed, emanating from a high sphere, born in a humble village, denied by a continent, and involved with sailors, represents the truth, the way, and the life as Thomas sees it—that is, such a Truth about life as would be taught by Blake's Jesus or Lawrence's Man Who Died: a Dionysus-Christ.

Whether Thomas intended such a meaning is conjectural. But the final pair of stanzas does not disallow such a meaning. For here we arrive at a statement of what occurs to man at the time of his death. And again, as in the first stanzas, we discover what the seed will not do.

"Man-in-seed, in seed-at-zero" seems to me a phrase capable of describing man at any time of his life: at the beginning, when he is no more than a potential; at his high-noon, when he is full of seed and zeroing in upon a location for that seed; at the end, when he has gone to seed. At no time of his life — or after — will he storm heaven, any more than in the beginning he stormed earth. This is a denial of the conventional Christian concept of resurrection (and, if Christ has actually been mentioned, of The Resurrection). To the contrary, he will go violently into the earth, whence he will not re-ascend in human form.

That is, though both heaven's height and earth's depth have contributed to making man human, each becomes, for this in-between dweller, a foreign place. Home for the human being is the earth's surface. After he has died — lost his human-ness — he is done, as a man, with all three. The laws of human life (the canons of his kingdom) do not prevail in the grave.


# Now

Since in this poem every Nay opposes a negative or defeatist point of view, it states unqualifiedly though gaily Thomas's Everlasting Yea. In its background are Hamlet's meditations on self-slaughter; Donne's "And new philosophy calls all in doubt" and "The sun is lost, and the earth . . ."; and Yeats's "Things fall apart; the centre cannot hold"; none of which are mottoes for sundials. Donne has at some length discoursed on "how dry a cinder this world is," and accordingly man upon it. But Thomas refuses to cry woe and has his say about those who do. Hydroptique man, he thinks, can quench his thirst, can rediscover the ceremony of innocence, if he but lower his sights from systematized views of life and redeem his time by transmuting *me and thee* to *us*. *We* is the operative word of the poem.

Vernon Watkins tried to persuade Thomas to leave this poem (and "How Soon the Servant Sun") out of *Twenty Five Poems* as presenting "a face of unwarrantable obscurity." And he says that Thomas himself "remarked of one of them that so far as he knew it had no meaning at all." (P. 16.) So the risk here is not merely of finding the wrong meaning but of finding one that doesn't exist.

Henry Treece, rebutting some critic's charge that verse like this is "counterfeit," describes it as, "A pattern of sounds, a musical exercise, verbal 'doodling', perhaps; maybe not worth recording, or if worth recording, not worth printing, but a swindle, no! A piece of poetic high-spirits, yes!" William Empson does not like the poem and therefore does not bother about it; but, he goes on, "I assume on principle that there is something there which I feel and can't see, but could see." (*Casebook,* 106 and 112.)

I think that I have seen something; I hope that it is not a swindle.

*   *   *   *   *

1. If, the dupe of the golden-mean concept, man is tempted to moderate his anger at the fact of death and go gentle into that dry dust, he, though dry of love, should destroy Aristotle's basic premise (more dead-lock than bedrock) and cut the anchor which, however adorned, promises not hope of stability but stasis.

2. Though the Stoic see fit to leave children parentless and a sister to bear the fardels (an allusion to Cato of Utica, a side-glance at Brutus, an echo of Hamlet?), we should negate the welcome to death, the welcomer, and death itself.

3. Though it is true that the dead stir, it is not true, and we must negate the idea, that these are crow-black hell-bent sinners and phoenix-rising saints: the condition of death and of the dead is other than this.

The following—the fourth—is a stanza to throw any rider. Do the first two *so's* mean *so that* or *suppose that?* And it could read: Suppose that the stars fall and the earth goes dead; still say nay to negativism—instead of faltering, unriddle the Eleusinian mysteries of the sun. But this makes little sense because, if the "ball" fails, man will not be saying either Yea or Nay. He will, perhaps, have become part of the sun and, having been dissolved into it, may be said to have come to its solution. But I prefer another alternative. Since I have discovered in or imposed upon the poem Aristotelianism, Stoicism, and Christianity, three influential systems of thought with distinct attitudes toward death, I'll conjecture a fourth: scientism.

4. Suppose that the touch of cold philosophy unweaves a rainbow—that scientists, as Donne said, "rein the stars" and "freely . . . confess that this world's spent," and "have impaled . . ./The free-born sun," have solved the mystery of that which, traveling through the postulated ether, arrives at and leaps ·on flowers and vitalizes them while flying off. As we have said Nay to other attitudes toward death (and by inference, life), we must say Nay to that organized system of analysis which murders to dissect—invents an instrument to measure spring with—but constructs no theory of death at all.

5. Finally, we will contemptuously deny such presumed mysteries as the Dies Irae, transmigration, or metamorphosis (or any theories as to the condition of life after death). In our loving union, I am as mysterious as the life-sustaining air, the doubly-corpuscled blood, the seed-blessed phallus, and the Shelleyan cloud.


# *How Soon The Servant Sun*

Geoffrey Grigson, not the least vehement of Thomas's detractors, says, and then quotes a stanza of this poem ". . . his poetry as near as may be is the poetry of a child, volcanic, and unreasoning, who has seldom read, and little cared for, the poets of his own language, and allowed them little power over his own manipulation—or rather automatism." (*Casebook,* 121.)

Mr. Grigson is, of course, as wrong as may be on every count. No child could put this poem together; it did not erupt, it was carpentered like a piece of furniture; its obscurities did not occur, but were reasoned into it; and they were reasoned into it because poets whom Thomas read and cared for (Blake, Yeats, Empson, for example) followed such a course.

Yet, a session with the poem evokes more than a little sympathy with Grigson's irritation and can drive one to the simplicities of Alfred Noyes. For this is certainly one of the most difficult of Thomas's poems to interpret. It may be this instead of "Now," of which Thomas said that "so far as he knew it had no meaning at all." Recognizing this possibility, one says with Eliot, "There may be much more in a poem than the author was aware of," and plunges temerariously on.

The poem divides into three parts: in the first two stanzas, the "I" is concerned with the length of time to extend before he is born; in the third, he is born (and—perhaps—he dies); in the fourth and fifth, he wonders about his rebirth. The question of his birth is answered, that of his rebirth is apparently not. But in reality it is, the reply having been tucked away in the parentheses running concurrently with the questioning. That is, the poem has this second, vertical division: the non-parenthetical sentences spoken by the poem's "I" parallel the parenthetical sentences spoken by an omniscient observer.

The non-parenthetical sections of the first two stanzas run something like this:

> Time (of all odd things a titled male nurse, who has overseen the growth of great things vegetable and mineral) will tell the head and heart of me, as I, his servant-to-be, extravagantly feed myself, how soon the sun (also his servant) can fix the date for putting a bone (developing the foetus's skeletal structure) in Mother Hubbard's cupboard (womb), how soon the sun (as the draper) can supply the stuff to cover my nakedness so that I, so recently an egg, can assume human form and depart on my Columbus-adventure.

I do not know that "my masters" are heart and head; they are in "When, Like a Running Grave," and their being so here makes some sense. There is a strange insistence upon social hierarchy in this poem. Sir morrow has his title; the sun is his servant; "I" serve the sun; "I" also have "you and you" (heart and head, as I have read it) as masters, and the "I" is referred to as "man morrow" as opposed to "Sir morrow." Thus, in these first two stanzas, the "I" appears to be low man on the totem pole. But in the last two stanzas, the "I" has an "inward sir," who is simultaneously "mister and master." This is perhaps the spirit, which is master to the "I," and mister to Lord Morrow.

Elder Olson's interpretation of these two stanzas (he does not go on to the others) is quite different and deserves to be noticed:

> "Sir morrow" (the child of tomorrow, as yet unborn) will be waited upon by the "servant sun" which brings him to light and unfastens the cupboard of nature to furnish the naked egg of the seed with flesh, so that it may stand erect in the human form; the gristle will have a "gown" of bone; moisture as yet in the fog will turn the bones of death into living bone clothed with flesh. (P. 98.)

I do not have sufficient assurance in my own reading to quarrel with Mr. Olson. Suffice it to quote Eliot again—"A poem may appear to mean very different things to different readers, and all of these meanings may be different from what the author thought he meant"—and push on to the third stanza.

The "I" speaks: I awakening my soul and stretching every nerve to pay my devoirs to the sun, seek a means (a cat's claw) to dig out of my barrow; I build my skeletal framework ("the long-tailed stone") and adorn it with flesh and organs, regardless of how my mother-bearer ("the soil") complains (like a cat-clawed mouse) of my injuring her, and regardless of the fact that in dislodging the stone (building my separate identity) I am discovering death.

Death, it appears, is what is on the mind of the spirit within the body. Death of the body, that is, which means release, rebirth for the spirit.

The spirit in the body just skeletalized—master of this body but at the same time enslaved by being combined with it—wants to know when my soon-to-be-horizontally-placed, dead-level body will raise its spirit-lamp, climb a cloud, shift (the bubble moving in the spirit-level) from dead horizontal to live vertical, grow spirit-legs on the shrouded body, perhaps by ascending, as vital force, through the roots of trees. Blind in the womb it asks the question; and hell, deaf as time, either answers with a Gabriel-blast or merely echoes the spirit's question ("Blasts back the trumpet voice"). If it merely echoes, we have got nowhere in the poem. If it trumpets an answer, we arrive at a positive conclusion. This latter I think was intended and is expressed in the parenthetical statements. These can be put together as follows:

> Sir morrow mark:
> Fog has a bone
> He'll trumpet into meat.
>
> The wound records [that]
> Fog by his spring
> Soaks up the sewing tides.
>
> Sir morrow stamps
> Two heels of water on the floor of seed.

This poem within a poem is an abbreviated version of Shelley's "The Cloud": Consider the future. Today's fog is tomorrow's rain. The lowered water-level of the bay ("the wound") attests that yesterday's sea-water is today's fog. Yesterday's sea-water (today's fog) will tomorrow irrigate "the floor of seed."

What the spirit learns, then, is that, though incarnation is behovely, all shall be well.

# *Was There A Time*

The obscurest thing about this poem is Thomas's reason for publishing it. A slight thing from any point of view, it says nothing that Thomas has not said more engagingly, more provocatively, or more dramatically.

It thumps along, as though, like Richard Blackmore, he had composed his couplets to the rhythm of the carriage-tires on cobblestones. It lacks coherence: circuses do not lead associatively to books, books to maggots, or maggots to the sky; no image in the final lines hooks to images at the beginning. Thomas is heavy-handed, almost as absurdly pompous as Gray when he wheels those phalanxed personifications into a line (regardless of their doom) against the little victims. And since we know that uneasy in the Aeschylean buskins stands an inexperienced Welshman scarcely out of his teens, we cannot give more credence to his tragic stance than to Shelley's when he cries, "Wail for the world's wrong!" An unearned tragic pose is merely morbid.

Fearful, perhaps, of sentimentality, Thomas has squeezed his poem dry of any residue of sympathy. Hopkins in "Spring and Fall," takes the risk and teeters on the verge, but succeeds where Thomas fails. Ransome, in "Bells for John Whiteside's Daughter," through irony refines the potentially sentimental into the maturely philosophical. And Thomas's flat statements do not bring zero to the bone as dawning recognition of the little lame balloon-man's threat does in Cummings' "Just Spring."

The statements are flat; the poem lies flat. The first two lines give neither the visual image nor the "feel" of exuberant childhood—as every stanza in "Fern Hill" succeeds in doing. The imagined picture of a maggot being set on the track is grotesque. The epigrams at the end have the cellophane gloss of Wilde's less-successful inversions of cliché. The quasi-kenning "skysigns," which might have fitted another poem effectively, here is merely obtrusive.

The most interesting line is "under the arc of the sky they are unsafe." More meaning is compressed into the unstated antithesis between *arc* and *arch,* between the cold geometrical figure and the seven-hued testament of love, than in all the rest of the poem. One is reminded of Keat's plaintive lines against science:

> There was an awful rainbow once in heaven:
> We know her woof, her texture; she is given
> In the dull catalogue of common things . . . .

Keats's complaint is legitimate; Thomas's, against life, is not — or rather, is not in this poem made so. Statements so dogmatic on a subject so general do not persuade; they provoke rebuttal or derision.

# Here In This Spring

A certain cleverness distinguishes this otherwise inconsequential poem. The theme is the well-worn one to the effect that summer, autumn, and winter are implicit in spring, that living is a dying. The cleverness is recognizable in the way in which Thomas brings his opposites together.

In the first line, the affirmation of "spring" and "stars" is engulfed by the powerful last word, "void," a word not only operative here but preparing for the last words of the poem—"the world wears away." The next two lines are equally Janus-faced:

> Here in this ornamental winter
> Down pelts the naked weather.

The punning use of "down" and "pelts" permits rapid description of all the seasons: rain and wind make of this early-blossoming spring (or vivid autumn) a winter; white snow covers with downy goose-skin the bare earth, and finally, in summer, the noon of life, the spring bird dies.

The passive voice of "symbols are selected" and the failure to specify the selector give the second stanza the objective truth of a scientific generalization: All symbols relate to the passage of the seasons. Or perhaps it is philosophy rather than science which is invoked, a philosophy old in Pythagoras's time, and taking account of the magic that underlies the natural. The "slow rounding of four seasons' coasts" reminds one of the periplus—the coasting voyage of Hanno and the marvels that discoverer saw. The last line "And four birds' notes," is an obvious imitation of Keats's "And no birds sing" in *La Belle Dame Sans Merci* and a reminder of the "kisses four" which the knight gave the supernatural lady. Briefly, magic, religion, philosophy, and science are suggested as agreeing on the lesson needful to be taught.

It is a lesson that can be learned in any season. If the tree by its foliage speaks of summer, the worm predicts its end; if the cuckoo's wandering voice says Make it new, the slug images the attrition soon to come. And the observer cannot state the alternative preferred, give reasons for his choice. He must learn the double lesson.

Worm-time or slug-time, showing, as clock-time and calendar-time (which are abstractions) do not, organic decay, exemplifying the gnawing at tissue of time's tooth, is true time. Question: if, within the natural experience, the seasons' passage carries all living things to their end, can one infer that there is that beyond the natural which will make an end of seasons and of time?

The poem is a good example of the kind that moved Julian Symons to say, "What is said in Mr. Thomas's poetry is that the seasons change; that we decrease in vigour as we grow older; that life has no obvious meaning; that love dies . . . ," and to add the judgment that "His poems mean no more than that. They mean too little."

The comment is not true—Thomas had other subjects of discourse; it is beside the point—the question is whether what is said in the poetry is well-said; it is rather silly—these are subjects that lend themselves, and have done so for some millennia, to meaningful exercise of the intellect. If Thomas has not explored the relativity of time in depth in this particular poem, he has elsewhere.

On the other hand, it is also true that Thomas repeats himself and that this fondness for the sound of his own words does give an impression of narrowness of theme and paucity of invention. However, if there is not in the body of his work God's plenty, there is still enough to belie such a comment as Symons'.

## Hold Hard These Ancient Minutes

The sense may not be Lear's, but the words apply. Ripeness is all is the wisdom of this poem: spring is a steeplechase, a fox hunt; summer, the goal, the brush to be won.

The time is late April (the cuckoo's month); the place Glamorgan; the speaker unspecified—it may be Thomas, a farmer, a universal vital spirit, or God the husbandman; the adjuration, survive. The setting is pastoral (no "caul and suckle" here) and the tone positive (the "doom in the bulb" is under-stressed). Yet, if the traditional pastoral connotes an at-one-ment of figures with landscape, an idyllic easiness where love dies like a flower and no one loses a singing match, this is by no means a pastoral poem. It is active, noisy, with some of the propulsiveness of "John Gilpin's Ride" and a strong sense of the hang-on-for-dear-life anxiety of the very small rider on a very large horse.

The pleasure that one takes in the poem as an unanalyzed whole may perhaps change to irritation when close examination of the running double-metaphor is attempted. The elements of the metaphors (the steeplechase, the fox-hunt) do not click with well-machined ease into place. In the first stanza, for example, Time is likened to a horsy county squire, and he is said to drive forth "my men, my children, from the hanging south." One's first thought is of Time, the hunter, beating out the game. But the rest of the poem does not support this reading: the children are not the hunted but the hunters—growing things seeking fruition. An alternative is to take Time as the master of the hunt, an organizer of the steeplechase, who rousts the children out and compels them to the chase. Rousts them out of what? "The hanging south." But the growing things of Glamorgan are not driven from the south—hanging or otherwise; they are in Glamorgan, and there they stay. Perhaps "from the hanging south" modifies Time: Time, bringing the southern warmth which has been, through April, hanging fire, stimulates the growing things to come out of their wintry sedentariness. And they are advised to stick close to their expert rider, not to lag behind, not to deviate from the course. Another possibility is to visualize the spring growth having started on the south coast of Wales (hanging over the sea?) and gradually moving north over the ridings. Thus a geographical progression coincides with a temporal progression—the "Lank, fourth folly" (a steeplechase goal, Olson says) equaling April. And in "the green blooms ride upward," we have the double sense of the rising life in the individual plant and the tide of green rising up Glamorgan's hill.

The second stanza's address to the country-side (which may be summed up as saying "You are well out of winter; forget it and look forward") introduces contrasts: the utilitarian with the religious (water tower, and steeple); the industrial with the fabulous (crane, and woods in Lincoln green). These are summed up in the image of the leafless, birdless trees contrasting with the greenwood to which the birds are returning from the south. But an either-or statement is not being made. The seedy-looking tree has seed to disseminate; in the lush and lively greenwood, the deer fall dead. There is no time when life does not aspire, no time when death does not strike. This is a fact, not a matter for morbid meditation nor for backward-looking. The simple imperative of the stanza, as of the poem, remains unqualified: "Hold hard . . . to the summer's game."

In the third stanza it would seem to be no longer Time who drives the children to the chase but England.

> And now the horns of England, in the sound of shape,
> Summon your snowy horsemen . . . .

Since Time and England have nothing in common, one might infer that Thomas has lost his grip on his thematic conceit. But perhaps not. Supposing Time to be the master of hunts in England as well as in Wales, we can assume a conjunction of hunting parties as the chase progresses—as, to be literal, the fruit trees in Devon put forth blossoms ("snowy horsemen") and the earth heaves in the changing weather.

This third stanza is extraordinary in this: that the silent internal process of vegetable growth is depicted in terms of external sound and fury. Since the horns are forces of growth, they do not emit a hunting call but form buds from which blossoms will burst. The process, though silent, is not unlike that involved in the utterance of a word: "With his lips he rounded a little ball of sound into some shape, and spoke a word." (*Adventures in the Skin Trade*, p. 110.) The hill, likened to a stringed instrument, is harmoniously greening and blossoming, by harmonic vibrations putting its rocks in a context of life, perhaps mossing them over, perhaps splitting them. (The four strings may also be sound-making streams dashing against rocks.) And, finally, the sudden but silent destruction of plants—by being crushed, uprooted, or cut by shifting earth and rock—is imaged by the report of a rifle, the rending of steel, the crashing of fences, the fall of rocks. It is an amazingly worked-out conceit.

In the fourth we shift again to the fox-hunt, and a very complicated metaphor ensues.

> Down fall four padding weathers on the scarlet lands,
> Stalking my children's faces with a tail of blood,
> Time, in a rider rising, from the harnessed valley.

The question is: do we have a happy ending or not? I think so, but not with complete assurance.

The scarlet lands I take to be blossom-covered Wales and England: the children in their red coats everywhere. The weathers are apparently the feet of the fox—that is, of the Summer-to-come. They represent the contending hots and colds, wets and dries of spring which make Summer so elusive. Now, when the children have killed their quarry, the master of the hunt will cut off the fox's tail and daub blood on the children's faces, blooding them as evidence of their success. This is the hope that sight of the fox arouses.

But why should it be that it is the weathers that stalk the children rather than vice versa? There are two reasons. Hot, cold, wet, dry, though they may kill the plant, are also necessary to the growth and strengthening of the plant's stalk and the production of the scarlet blossom. The children's faces are literally *stalked*. Secondly, it is the increasing warmth of spring turning to summer that promotes growth; summer demands its foliage—the fox draws the hunter to its trail.

The passage denoting successful achievement has a powerfully ominous note. It increases in the final three lines. Here we may visualize the hunters breathing their horses and watching the hunter hawk fall upon the birds, birds which had themselves survived a long migration in the spring to reach the Welsh summer. What is to be learned? To make the most of a golden summer, bounded by an angry spring and a killing fall. Or in any event, not at any time to stand still.

As a companion-piece to the piano favorite "Rustle of Spring," the poem is satisfactory. There is no need to infer an application to human endeavor. But for those who find Nature devoid of the human barren, here is a passage from Shaw's *Too True to be Good* which, as a kind of parallel to Thomas's poem, is worth ruminating:

> ... I am by nature and destiny a preacher. I am the new Ecclesiastes. But I have no Bible, no creed; the war has shot both out of my hands. The war has been a fiery forcing house in which we have grown with a rush like flowers in a late spring following a terrible winter. And with what result? This: that we have outgrown our religion, outgrown our political system, outgrown our strength of mind and character. The fatal word NO has been miraculously inscribed into all our creeds . . . But what next? Is NO enough? For a boy, yes; for a man, never . . . . I must have affirmations to preach . . . . The preacher must preach the way of life—Oh, if I could only find it! (A white sea fog swirls up from the beach to his feet, rising and thickening around him.) I am ignorant; I have lost my nerve and am intimidated; all I know is that I must find the way of life, for myself and all of us, or we shall surely perish . . . .

# Over Sir John's Hill

The theme of this poem is justice, justice in the sense of conformity to natural law, not of punishment for a wrong doing. The birds in this poem, like the flounders and gulls of "Poem on his Birthday," kill and are killed without thought and without choice. No one here, save Thomas, the observer, who makes no point of it, feels that he is slaving to a "crouched, eternal end," or that "to-morrow weeps in a blind cage." No one, save Thomas, who does make a point of this, asks that justice be tempered with mercy. (When he says that the heron grieves, he is ironically commenting upon his own inescapable, analogizing homocentricity. The heron, however priest-like his appearance to human eyes, is the hawk's counterpart, a carnivorous bird.)

The poem is a comment upon the way things are in the animal kingdom. The hawk who executes the sparrows and such today has a noose about his own neck. And the heron below, his stiletto-beak poised for fish or frog, carries his headstone with him.

The poet makes two distinctions between himself and the birds he so justly describes. He prays God to have mercy upon the song-birds because of their song; he himself gives them a kind of life beyond death by writing their elegy. It is a just recognition of a difference in the outlook and the capabilities of a human being relative to a bird.

Does the poem, in Shapiro's phrase, reveal in Thomas a "fatal pessimism"? Not at all. Thomas grieves the birds' death, of course. He would not be "human" if he did not. But in associating his grief with that of the heron, he is showing himself to be no sentimentalist.

It is not the sentimentalist who will exclaim, "All praise of the hawk on fire in hawk-eyed dusk be sung." And it is in the sentence of which this line is a part that the essential meaning of the poem is expressed.

I prefer the poem as realistic comment; it lends itself, however, to Aesopian and to allegorical treatment. If the poem had come to the attention of Roger L'Estrange, St. Augustine, Origen, or Dante the Florentine, it might have been processed in their moralizing mills and have issued in these variant forms:

A Poet took notice that a Flock of *Sparrows* were so busy wrangling among themselves over *Insects* that they were an easy Prey for a *Hawk*. In a nearer View he saw a *Heron* calmly pursuing his Dinner as the Sparrows' feathers fell about the fishing Bird.

### The Moral

The Way to a *Man's* Heart is through his Stomach: it holds through the whole Scale of the Creation that the Great and the Little have need of one another and make use of one another for their Stomach's sake.

\* \* \* \* \*

In reading the revelation of St. Thomas, dearest brethren, we have taken heed and have sought, under his bountiful guidance, to explain according to analogy; for the revelation is bestowed upon our ears, that heavenly secrets may be manifest to our hearts.

*The hawk on fire . . . pulls . . . the small birds.* He did represent Christ our Lord. Understand the rays of his eyes as His truth, which doth seek us out and draw us to Him. The claws signify that His jealousy will never let us escape; the gallows, that we must die in Him and meet His justice. *The fishing holy stalking heron.* He nameth the heron the Holy Apostolic Church, Christ's representative on earth, which doth act as a fisherman of men (for the fish in the sea and the sparrows in the air both are men). His feet in the water, his head like a headstone denote the responsibility of the Church which extendeth from baptism to extreme unction. *I young Aesop fabling.* So St. Thomas nameth himself, ugly and deformed but a maker of beautiful songs in which the truths of gospel are riddlingly set forth, a slave till grace abounding won him freedom in his obedience to our Lord.

\* \* \* \* \*

Now the things of the old law signifying the things of the new is the allegorical sense: thus the hawk on fire is the pillar of fire by which God led the stiffnecked, wrangling Israelites out of Egypt; by the heron is meant the heathen who, hearing not the voice of the Lord, with unconcern followed their worldly ways, carrying their eternal death like a head stone heavy upon their necks. The *just hill* he likeneth to Mt. Sinai, where Moses received for mankind the Table of the Law. Young Aesop by the wear-willow river remindeth us of the continuing tribulations of those that turn their faces away from God. For Aesop is David, who singeth, By the rivers of Babylon, there we sat down, yea, we wept, when we remembered Zion. We hanged our harps upon the willows in the midst thereof. And he singeth now, when the Lord seemeth to hide himself in times of trouble, the wicked man in his pride lieth in wait secretly as a lion in his den: he lieth in wait to catch the poor: he doth catch the poor, when he draweth him into his net.

\* \* \* \* \*

The allegorical sense is the one which is hidden beneath the cloak of the fable, being a truth concealed under pretty fiction. By this hawk is meant Love; and thus may the figure be brought back to the truth. For Love is a fire in which the lover is immolated, a hawk which cruelly seizes the lover and destroys his self-hood. Such is the materialistic, self-seeking nature of those whom Love has not blessed that they stalk about the earth unheeding of the plight of the true lover, helpless, burning, and yet withal joyful in his nearness to his sun. But the Poet, dedicated to Venus, sings the sweetness of Love and Love's cruelty (for all a green willow is its garland), and prays for the lover (hot as a sparrow), prays For that sweet soul's sake, And for all sparrows' souls Set in our bead-rolls. And he writes for his epitaph: Flos volucrum formose, vale!

# *I Fellowed Sleep*

*Resolution and Dependence* would make an apt title for this poem. What is involved is the maturing individual's effort to be himself, to cut off from his two parents and achieve his personal vision. In the end, however, he recognizes that his very motivation toward that goal is his because he is human. He aspires as geologic ages of forebears aspired. On the other hand, he achieves a certain degree of independence from his recent forebears in that he defines that aspiration in natural rather than supernatural terms.

*     *     *     *     *

1. Sleep compassionately removed me from the quotidian; my inward eye awakened, circled, and illuminated me as the moon does the earth. So, in level winging flight, I traversed my sleeping man-shape, left it, and flew on into the outer space of my dream and vision.

2. I left my daytime self (my bones and binding flesh, and the earth I walked on), coming to a second ground, off the earth but far below the stars — that is, the tops of trees. There, the spirit of my female ancestors (the mother's-side) and I, apparently finding the locale repugnant, wept together. And (preferring heavenly illusion to tree-top truth) I flew aloft, leaving my mother behind.

3. We conversed (the mother a tough-minded realist, the "I" a sentimentalist).

> I: The land of my fathers is a holy, ascending, singing land.
>
> M (looking down): The earth, those tree-tops, were also your fathers' land.
>
> I (not looking down): But these cloud-coasts bear companies of sweetly father-faced angels.
>
> M: They are only dreamers, easily dispersed.

4. I, thus moved to independent action, sent back the heavenly speakers to the tomb; her mission accomplished, the mother-eyed (a kind of Earth-Mother to the father's Zeus: her function has been to put earth and sky, real and ideal, sensual and Platonic in dynamic polarity) leaves the "I" to continue on his own two feet. (In this she differs from the parent in Lawrence's *Fantasia,* p. 183, who "has not the greatness of soul to relinquish her own self-assertion, and believe in the man who believes in himself and in his own soul's efforts . . . .") I compelled these sleep-walkers to their beds, where they still lie, unaware of the spirit that animated them (and was subject to them).

5. Then, having rid myself of these illusions, I came to an understanding of the vital oneness of all matter. (Thomas in a letter to Pamela Johnson: "Every inch of this universe even to the earth and sea is crowded with people." Lawrence (*Fantasia,* p. 222): "The sun is materially composed of all the effluence of the dead. But the *quick* of the sun is polarized with the living, the sun's quick is polarized in dynamic relation with the quick of life in all living things, that is, with the solar plexus in mankind"; Blake (Letter to Thos. Butts, 2 Oct., 1800): "Each grain of Sand,/Every Stone on the Land . . ./Cloud, Meteor and Star,/Are Men seen Afar"). My hand in a girl's hair, I realized my vision; and I recognized, in terms of that eternal, unitive, natural vitality,

how trivial the sleep called life is, how significant the awakening called death.

6. Time is a ladder, feet in the earth, extending to the sun; each hour, whether a success (a love) or a failure, is an ascending rung. The monkey-blood of man through trial and error (the error is non-love) slowly makes its climb. My forebears in me, one monomaniacal spirit, compel me upward, even though the sun is seemingly blotted out.

W. S. Merwin (*Casebook*, 62) sees the poem in a different light: "'I fellowed sleep' is a visionary poem about uncreated ghosts, the dreams of the world which the world climbs always to create." If I understand him correctly, these "uncreated ghosts" have a virtue. I think, to the contrary, that they must be blown back to their beds, since they are grave gabbers, so that nothing out of the dead past will interfere with hearing the voice of "the living air." Of course the past cannot be escaped; it climbs with the present man. But the latter must not look back but forward and upward — to the sun. He must, however, look forward from this present; and this present ought to be enriched with an experience of love. This is why I have imported a girl into the poem in the key line, "I spelt my vision with a hand and hair." I have admittedly made her up out of whole hair. But I simply cannot see how a vision of a significant future can be arrived at with a hand and hair unless the hand is a boy's and the hair a girl's.

# *I Dreamed My Genesis*

This poem has been understood by David Aivaz as a description of "the progress of the sperm and the growth of the embryo," the birth of the child being their death; and by W. S. Merwin as a description of "man's birth through his death, his knowledge of death in his birth, and his passage into the world." That is, the protagonist, if not the speaker, exists in his pre-natal state.

I prefer to think of the speaker as the mature, or maturing, Thomas asleep and dreaming. I see the dream as being double-barreled, referring to Thomas as an individual and to Thomas as a type of Man, the late-comer in the evolutionary process. In brief, the poem is a variation on the theme of "I Fellowed Sleep."

Again Lawrence, in his chapter on sleep and dreams, has sentences that apply:

What is the exact relationship between us and the death-realm of the afterwards we shall never know. But this relation is none the less active every moment of our lives. There is a pure polarity between life and death, between the living and the dead, between each living individual and the outer cosmos. Between each living individual and the earth's center passes a never-ceasing circuit of magnetism . . . . It is this circuit which is busy in all our tissue removing or arranging the dead body of our past day. For each time we lie down to sleep we have within us a body of death which dies with the day that is spent . . . . This earth-current actually sweeping through us is really the death-activity busy in the service of life.                                                   (*Fantasia*, pp. 239-40.)

Thus, he continues, you must say when you go to sleep, "Here dies the man I am and know myself to be." And, when you rise, "Here rises an unknown quantity which is still myself." (*Ibid.*, p. 271.) And Lawrence finds in this new self "the unit for the next society."

Thomas, too, suffers a death in sleep and arises to a "vision/Of new man strength." The general outline is the same. But Thomas has complicated matters, because there is a dream of death within the little death of sleep, and because, as I have said, there is reason to believe that the protagonist is more than Thomas as Thomas.

What happens in the first stanza is not quite clear because the "rotating shell" is not identifiable. It has been conjectured as the sperm entering the egg; and as God hatched out of an egg (in this interpretation we are said to be witnessing the birth of God and of the universe as well as of a man). In both interpretations, we are asked to see the "breaking" as a part of the genesis. I prefer to see it as a factor in the dreaming, a breaking out from restricted vision—the restricted vision of Blake's Mundane Shell, for example. Lawrence has said that "The active mind-consciousness of the night is a form of retrospection" because it is the blood-consciousness, the most elemental form of consciousness, and he contrasts it with "vision. . .our highest form of dynamic upper consciousness." (P. 256, *Fantasia*.) He has described it as "the first and last knowledge of the living soul: the depths," and has argued that it "cannot operate purely until the soul has put off all its manifold degrees and forms of upper consciousness."

Now, since Thomas is concerned here with elementals — birth and death —, since he stresses blood, that elemental substance, and sweat, one scarcely less so (thus contrasting the physical quality of his sleep with the romanticized "first sweet sleep" of Shelley), I infer that Thomas is coming to an understanding that daytime reason had not granted.

The poem, then, will read somewhat as follows:

1. I, in an oppressive sleep, exploding like shrapnel out of the casing of upper consciousness (unlike Hamlet, he cannot, bounded in a nutshell, count himself a being of infinite space, except for his dreams), boring through and coming out on the other side of merely sensory apprehension, dreamed my beginning.

2. I shuffled off the mortal coil of my flesh, departed from the worm-measured (and worm-geared) limbs (that, in their continuing life-potential, had the worm's measure) and, myself mineral, marched and cut through the mineral grass (both grass and I sun-mettled), in this sweating sleep that had made me other than day-time man.

3. I, expensive product of millennia of biological experiments which have ultimately made me (and my kind) capable of love, explored my evolutionary history, making slow and arduous journey through the Darkest Africa of primitive, blood-conscious man geared to "the long, long African process of purely sensual understanding, knowledge in the mystery of dissolution." (*Women in Love.*)

4. I had died as primitive man and been reborn as Christian-Platonic-love-capable man. Now in my dream I died again (exploded shrapnel filing the heart's artery), participating in the deaths of my fellows.

(Lawrence, comparing the modern white races to the Africans described above, writes: "The white races, having the arctic north behind them, the vast abstraction of ice and snow, would fulfill a mystery of ice-destructive knowledge, snow-abstract annihilation" — that is, death through the triumph of science and technology. Elsewhere he is more specific (*Fantasia,* p. 266): "So if death has to be the goal for a great number, then let it be so. If America must invent this poison-gas, let her." That is, as primitive man had failed, so modern man has failed—failed because "We wanted first to have nothing but nice daytime selves, awfully nice and kind and refined. But it didn't work." (*Fantasia,* p. 270.) The unit for the next society will be "The self which rises naked every morning out of the dark sleep of the passionate, hoarsely-calling blood . . . . And the polarizing of the passionate blood in the individual towards life, and towards leader, this must be the dynamic of the next civilization." (*Ibid.,* p. 271.)

5. I, heir to the example of Socrates and other martyrs, lifted up mine eyes to the hills, product of immemorial vegetable and animal deaths, and saw them join my blood to the living stuff of the earlier killed, compelling my assimilation into and ascension with the sharp grass blades that sprang from them.

6. Their life infected me with life. Through my re-suffering of their

pain I achieved full manhood, a consummation like that of the resurrection of the glorified body.

7. In sweating sleep I dreamed my rebirth from sweating death (the two salt sweats of Adam: the sweat of the morally fallen trying to rise; the death-exudation of the mortally fallen); until, out of worn-out, excrementitious Old Adam, I awoke to the vision of the New Adam seeking the sun.

The weakness of this interpretation is, first, that I have made it sound as though Thomas was merely versifying Lawrence. I do not believe he did. But I think the direction of his thinking to have been the same. (The question of whether this occurred by coincidence or through Lawrence's example is beside the point.) Since Thomas, writing a poem, leaves inferential what Lawrence states explicitly, I have used the Lawrence to show how Thomas's full argument *could* go, knowing very well that in detail it would not absolutely coincide.

The second objection is that I have built a great deal upon the third stanza, especially in turning "costly/A creature in my bones" into "expensive product of millennia of biological experiments." This, the keystone of my interpretation, is likewise its most vulnerable area. The best defense I can make is that it seems to me as Thomasian as, and more meaningful than, any other full-dress interpretation I have seen.

# *My World Is Pyramid*

It is not until we arrive at the final couplet of this poem that we discover that it is a monologue spoken by a "secret child." The first section appears to be third-person exposition; the second section shifts to first-person autobiographical and remains so for three stanzas. In the fourth stanza, a relation is stated between the *I* and the strange characters earlier described; and in the fifth the *I* is identified. Not really identified; merely named as "the secret child" —

> My clay unsuckled and my salt unborn,
> The secret child, I shift about the sea
> Dry in the half-tracked thigh.

Jacob Korg thinks the child a devil, the cause of death (*Accent,* 17, 9); Lita Hornick thinks him a Savior; Elder Olson reads the poem as "a strange meditation on the physical child and the 'secret child'," which resolves "the problem of death in these terms, through the discovery that the 'secret child' survives." (P. 36.) I believe that Korg's interpretation can be safely ignored and that a coalescing of Olson and Hornick will offer the most precise identification.

Thomas may have got his concept of the child from Blake. *Europe* opens with these lines:

> The deep of winter came,
> What time the secret child
> Descended thro the orient gates of the eternal day.

It has been conjectured that Blake is imitating (or ironically parodying) Milton's *Hymn*:

> It was the Winter wilde,
> While the Heav'n-born-childe
> All meanly wrapt in the rude manger lies,

and that therefore Blake's "child" is Jesus. But only conjectured. Since the character in Blake is un-identifiable, and since Thomas may have borrowed only a phrase, not an idea, if he borrowed at all, source-hunting provides no solution to the specific problem.

Nevertheless, the poem seems to me a variation on a theme by Blake.

If the secret child in *Europe* is Jesus, it is not the Jesus, the holy Jesus, and nothing but the Jesus of Scripture, in whose name poverty, obedience, and chastity have been enjoined upon man. For eighteen hundred years, Blake thought, those who have conquered in the name of the Galilean (and wrought His pallor) have confined the infinite in the finite, have mummied man in the tomb of his body "till he sees all things thro' narrow chinks of his cavern." Those exploited by the priests and rationalists and imperialists have been murdered on land and sea, forsaken, expendable. Their Golgothas are everywhere, in the north and south, in the Atlantic, in the plains of Asia. And the reason is that instead of recognizing that the infinite and eternal are here and now and that "the loin is glory," man has cloven body from spirit, divorced heaven from hell (warmth from light), given in to the demoralizing strictures of Christian morality.

"Love! Love! Love! happy, happy Love! free as the mountain wind!" is the essence of Blake's teaching, "lovely copulation, bliss on bliss!" Bliss indeed when everything that lived was holy, before "man became an angel, Heaven a mighty circle turning, God a tyrant crown'd," and before the human race was told

> that Woman's love is Sin;
> That an eternal life awaits the worm of sixty winters,
> In an allegorical abode where existence hath never come.

In brief, in man's self-deluded self-denial is his death. Death's feather is a "stammel" feather, Thomas says. But *stammel* is an undergarment of linsey-woolsey (usually dyed red) *worn by ascetics.* Asceticism is death's agent. What color is glory? It is the red radiance of eternity, in the blood of a living man.

What shall a man do to be saved? Cleanse the doors of perception that "everything would appear . . . as it is, infinite"; integrate the cloven halves; let sprout and bloom the corpse planted last year in the dead house garden; permit the Dionysian principle fulfillment instead of partial, furtive recognition. In place of fission, fusion: the fusion described in "Man has no Body distinct from his Soul" — he does not leave the body like a genie from a bottle, for a body and soul comprise an acorn which will become an oak; the fusion where "Embraces are comminglings from the head even to the feet,/And not a pompous High Priest entering by a Secret Place"; and, finally, the fusion implied in "All deities reside in the human breast."

I need to say at once that though I have "commingled" Thomas's imagery with Blake's, I have not been explicating Thomas's poem but giving a brief resumé of themes in Blake on which Thomas has written his variation.

To get back to Thomas and *his* secret child, I take it as the life-force (what Lawrence calls "the life plasm" or the "central god in the machine of each animate corpus," ( *Fantasia,* 93) which informs the physical child, whose birth is described in the poem's first section. This force—infinite, eternal, creative—man never ceases trying to kill, but of course it never dies. What occurs in the poem, then, is this force's description of a birth; the raising of the question of what death and immortality are; and (in the second section) a characterization of the force, and an answer to the questions.

The force, in taking up residence in a human body, quite rightly says that his world is pyramid, cypress, and an English valley, and that his grave is everywhere. The base of a pyramid is rectangular; the child's base is four-fold, body and spirit of the father joined to the body and spirit of the mother. (The triangles rising from the base we shall come to later.) Since the figure *four* has over the centuries bemused prophets and psychologists, this simple idea could be elaborated. Blake's Four Zoas (reason, imagination, passion, instinct); Lawrence's four centres; Jung's collective and personal conscious and unconscious; Ezekiel's "living creatures"; Paracelsus' occult elements—any or all of these could be used in a discussion of the secret child's pyramid. So too with the triangles that aspire from the rectangular base. But since Thomas does not, one regretfully desists.

The cypress is a kind of vegetable counterpart of the pyramid:

symmetrically triangular in shape; associated with death, but, *sempervirens,* also with death's defeat; offering refuge and hope for new life (its wood was used to build the ark).

In brief, the child's world is a tomb and a place of metamorphosis; is animal, vegetable, mineral, and spiritual; is (in the given instance) specifically English, but supra-nationally human, and so on.

## 1.

As was said, the first section of the poem describes the creation and evolutionary development of such a world. The first stanza, given in present tense, may be thought to describe coitus.

The eternal ("unborn") life-stuff, of a kind with electrical energy, impels sperm to egg. From this union a human body will develop (a salt be precipitated) which will grow to be an old salt on the "sea of life," familiar with the salt sweat and tears of post-Adamic existence, the salt of its sea-origin in its veins. Past and future ("to-morrow's diver"; "horny milk"—now the sexual secretion, tomorrow the bone-strengthening issue of the cornucopia breast) meet in this explosive present. Thus, from this four-square basis rises a temporal triangle. Further, it is a triangular new world which has been created, every cell of which is simultaneously human, male, and female.

This is a stanza of fusions. Man and woman, sperm and egg, male cell and female cell, past and future unite. But heaven ("thunder's bone") and earth ("sea-sucked") are also brought together and possibly (Adam reminds of one and thunder of the other) Jehovah and Zeus; and the curious phrase "thunder's bone" recalls one of Thomas's favorite paradoxical fusions—the sound of shape, the shape of sound.

## 2.

The second stanza is put in past tense and would seem, therefore, to make a philosophical comment upon the first stanza's event.

Here are a half that eats away from its frozen source and in turn is frozen, and a half that leafs out like a shrub as it imbibes warm milk. That is, a predetermined shape (man's) and end (death) are joined with a possibility of growth (leafing out) and of the dissemination of seed. (*Ezekiel,* 19, 10 applies nicely: "Thy mother is like a vine in thy blood, planted by the waters: she was fruitful and full of branches by reason of many waters.") Thomas seems to have let the sperm (or male) equal the physical principle and the ovum (or female) the vital. (As in Jung's *animus-anima* or Blake's Albion-Jerusalem.) The reason may be that, after the ejaculation (however motivated by love it was) the father has no concern with the child-to-be, whereas the mother's love and responsibility are only then brought fully into play. On a higher level, it may be said that what is lacking here is that fullness of spirituality which Adam and Eve possessed before the Fall, which gave them, and would have given their offspring, the attributes of impassibility, integrity, and immortality. The puzzling causal phrase

> For half of love was planted in the lost,
> And the unplanted ghost

can be explained in these terms. The comma suggests that two ghosts are involved and that one-half of total love was planted in one and one-half in the other. The fifth stanza's allusion to a ghost "that stammered in the straw" and another that "hatched his havóc as he flew" supports this and suggests symbolic identities. Satan, who was lost, hatched havoc, inculcated fleshly lust, and was frozen in ice; Christ, who was "unplanted," was born in a manger, taught spiritual love, and was "the true vine." In any case, the result of the first stanza's union is an embryo instinct with life but deprived of love and of spirituality in their fullest degree.

As in the first stanza, opposites are brought together, but more clearly in an uneasy state of disequilibrium: frozen northern water and flowing southern milk; dead and killing ice and live and vivifying tree. And again the triangle: mineral body, "vegetable" life, and the potential, at least, of spirituality.

### 3.

The third stanza reverts to present tense and describes fetal growth.

The father's life-stuff and the mother's life-stuff are conjoined in a body which will be kept upright by the skeletal structure: ontogeny recapitulates phylogeny (the halves "limp" through their experience as fish); and they lay tracks (sleepers—railroad ties) to and from the heart, giving any nearby vampire cause for joy.

Or, in other terms, as the fetus develops, various cells are assigned definite functions; they are resolved into three categories: the *ectoderm,* source of the outer skin, hair, nails, lining of mouth and nose, the nervous system, and the lens of the eye; the *entoderm,* source of the lining of the canal which will make up the digestive tract and organs of speech and breathing; and the *mesoderm,* source of bones, muscles, blood, lymph, and reproductive organs.

The last two lines refer, as was said, to the circulatory system to be; with a side-glance, no doubt, at the feeding of the fetus by the mother. (The umbilical vein penetrates—like a stake—the abdominal wall, and grubstakes the fetus.) The street of sea with its bladders brings to mind the digestive tract; the pun on tongue-tied man alludes to the rudimentary state of the organs of speech. And the first two lines may be said to refer to the medulla oblongata and the spinal cord.

Here again, there is fusion—the broken halves are fellowed, and fission—the cells perform their separate functions; and fusion—they produce a single entity. The sea, origin of life, and the earthly grave, its final resting place, are brought together. And again the triangle appears: entoderm, ectoderm, and mesoderm.

## 4.

Stanza four divides between past process and present action, but what has happened and what is happening are equally obscure. It is only assumption on my part that the fetus is brought to the stage of birth. By emphasizing an antithesis—

> The patchwork halves *were* cloven . . .
> Rotating halves *are* horning —

the first four lines can be read as a repetition of Stanza 1: sperm and ovum, separate infinitesimal specks of slime moving through the dark forest of the uterine cavity, joined to form the death-poisoned life (thus "kissed on the cyanide" is a variation of "Bolt for the salt")—except that I cannot figure out why they should be thought to have had and now are losing a terrible, Gorgonian aspect. However that may be, they are now rotating in the womb, whirling like a pneumatic drill, blowing like Gabriel—that is, growing on the umbilicus-provided food; readying for an exit; heralding the new day of cut umbilicus and opened lungs; and no doubt growing the devil's horn-buds that Adam's sons are born with.

Or the lines can be read as continuing the third stanza's recapitulation of phylogeny theme. This interpretation requires a double reading of the words *cloven* and *horning*. The badly put-together halves are not cloven from one another but from other forms of life, vertebrate and invertebrate. That is to say that this child a-borning sloughs off non-human attributes (such as the "lanugo" or hair which covers the fetus, and the vermiform appendix) to become a man. (This gets rid of those adders!) But as a man, he can sin—be as cloven-footed as a pig or a devil. As devil, he, develops horns. But as a man he can also be an angel—as ardent a horn-blower as Gabriel.

Again the split—man from the animals, and, I think, in the last two lines, the child from the womb; and the fusions—of angel and devil, and of life (arterial blood) and death (cyanide) in the man. And again the triangle: subhuman, human, superhuman.

## 5.

Assuming now that the child is born and develops reason, he is faced with certain particularly significant questions, as: Given the fact of death (and, by the way, who or what, causes it?), what is the nature of life? Is it blood-red, ending when the heart stops pumping? or ever-green, assimilated into vegetative nature? or eternity-white (or halo-golden), translated into a higher sphere? Unfortunately, since the questioner's knowledge of the universe is of a pinpoint, since his sight is only that of a needle's eye peering through a pinprick in a thimble, and since what he sees is totally homocentric ("thumb-stained"), he can supply no answers. And, since the Christ-life-principle stammers and the Satan-death-principle misleads, he is left with a dusty answer. The two halves, fused in a cloud of unknowing, are separated from the great learning, seeing only as through a thimble darkly.

## II

And now the secret child, whose constant lot it is to undergo such "entwombment" as he has described, characterizes himself.

### 1.

My world is imaged by an Egyptian tomb. The mummy which has held me, a mum mummer, adds salt to the hot, dry, yellow, mineral, sharp, salt sand. As this body collapses in the shroud, I squeeze through the mummifying stuff that has superseded blood, ascending to sunny reality ("starlit bone"), to the physical source of light, that, like a rib-bone, spans the universe, and to that halo or glory ("parhelion") which shows the blood-and-bone-making sun divine.

### 2.

My world is imaged by the evergreen graveyard tree (my delicate roots finding nutriment in compressing mineral earth, I aspiring heavenward) and by a green, cold, wet un-Egyptian valley. Osiris-like I rise alive out of death: where, for example, the workers are shot down in the railroad yards of Mittel Europa; or where, in war or revolution, the sacrificed young die like Christ on Golgotha.

### 3.

I am that corpse you planted last year in your garden and have been honored as Christ and Balder and Dionysus, though, of course, I lodge in all men's bodies. Who look for me dead (headpiece filled with straw) in Asia could find me alive by the Atlantic.

### 4.

In brief, wherever those patchwork halves may live, I live; whenever they die, I leave. That is, when, killed by shellfire or (drowned) eaten by shell-fish, they are divided from life and face death, I ascend from their graves (their bodies turn from mass to energy) and reassume my unimpeded immaterial warmth and light. My world, which has been pyramid, now becomes pyre-amid.

### 5.

Who, then, thickens the blood to inanition? Since I animate the physical and the physical dies through living, the responsibility is mine. What divine manifestation does color reveal? The loin ensures the immortality of the decaying, bloodless flesh. (As *Ezekiel*, 1, 27-8 says: "And upward from what had the appearance of his loins I saw as it were gleaming bronze, like the appearance of fire enclosed round about; and downward from what had the appearance of his loins I saw as it were the appearance of fire, and there was brightness round about him. Like the appearance of the bow that is in the cloud on the day of rain, so was the appearance of the brightness round about. Such was the appearance of the likeness of the glory of the lord.") I, unphysical, occult, eternal, ever young, do my work, like Dionysus safe in Zeus's thigh and never damped by the vicissitudes of "life" (though I produce it), lending life to that which will die but will have its immortality through sex.

# I, In My Intricate Image

What kind of a piece of work is a man is the question Thomas addresses himself to in this, the most elaborately worked out poem of his early career. His answer is clear in its general terms. Created in the image of his image of God, man is himself a reasoning, image-making, comparing being, capable through analysis and analogy of answering such a question and communicating the answer to others. But, unlike the God which he has imaged and to which he compares himself, he is not of one piece and therefore, until he learns to harmonize the contraries of which he is compounded, not at peace. Spirit in flesh, death in life, human in animal, female in male, organic in inorganic, liquid in solid—it is such entanglements that make the *I* (in appearance so like the numeral 1) so perplexing and perplexed an organism. If body has been bruised to pleasure soul or if soul can misquote Shakespeare to complain,

> Most putrefied core, so fair without,
> Thy goodly armour thus hath cost [my] life;

that is, if the contraries fail to "Give over . . . the seawax struggle" to make the "great blood's iron single," then there will be no roaring and rising on heaven's hill. *Ezekiel,* 11, 19 furnishes the text: "And I will give them one heart and I will put a new spirit within you; and I will take the stony heart out of their flesh, and will give them a heart of flesh."

But if the sense of the whole poem is clear, that of the parts is not. After its opening generalizing stanzas, the poem shifts into narrative form, but a narrative in which who, when, where, how, why stand and wait, and seem not to serve. It has been said that "No concrete central focus of locale or event emerges but only the revolving of an incredibly rich accumulation of image and allusion around a central subject." (Hornick, 167.) A kind of compost pile, one might say. I am not satisfied with this. There is too clearly a narrative: the rivals sail; they climb; they live, they drown; they hear breakers and tongues; they are invoked to suffer "the slash of vision," and to "love like a mist on fire." And the "I" which created these rivals claws out a crocodile so that the images can roar and rise. I think it possible to identify the characters, place them in space and time, and to follow them from an inefficacious state of being through a change of life to a desired state.

The locale is darkest Thomas; the time is that of a significant turning point in Thomas's life, the point in his life at which, through the acquisition of the grace of four-fold vision, he effects the transition from natural man to imaginative man. The hero, *I*, is Thomas the *mage* who, in the process of growth, has created the "twin miracle" of body and (for want of a better word) soul, but whose magic has not thus far availed to bring them to a working partnership. The events of the poem occur in a circular voyage of self-discovery made by these two dissidents (the one a too-fleshly Lancelot, the other a too-Tennysonian Galahad) which brings them to amity. Thus the *I*, who at the beginning is really $ego^1$ plus $ego^2$, comes to his oneness; darkest Africa is civilized; Prospero heals Hamlet.

## I

I, microcosmic reproduction of macrocosm and geocosm, move through life one foot on the sidewalk, one in the gutter; cross streams one foot on a log-bridge, one on a sinking crocodile; I run scales prestissimo, one hand inept; my nature is not in balance. I am of two aspects: a thing reducible to chemical analysis, a thing capable of prayer and poetry. The latter, which, free, could produce monuments of enduring bronze, is impeded by its triple-bronze casing, drowned out by its demagogic fellow.

Spring, like the Parcae holding the distaff and drawing off the thread later to be cut short, allots the flowers their birth-spasm, their flowering, their doom's day (a Penelope unraveling what she has woven), the whole history implicit in the bulb; she sends the life-fluid through the tree, manures and waters it; she also out of colonic spasms produces that conspicuous phenomenon, man.

I, like Spring, fusing flower-like fragility and durable mineral (*male-mail*) strength, rootedness and flight, create this prodigious paradox of the self; it begins with the vital spirit in the bronze root forcing life *and* death —to the expendable leaves. (Thomas has reversed his imagery in this stanza. Where, in the first stanza, flesh was metal weighing down the spirit, here spirit is metal, having a durability not possessed by flesh. In the image of the harebell with its punning potential, Thomas epitomizes the whole matter. It is the bulb ("bronze root") which forces the flower into life. But to do this, it must be buried in mineral soil. It endures after the flower's death, however, to repeat the process. The concepts of fragility, motion, and mortality are reinforced by the puns on *hare* and *hair,* of durability by *bell,* which also recalls the "brassy orator.")

The fate or dower of natural man is a natural end—death. Man's body is like a steepled church, or, even, like the frame put about it by those building or repairing it. But a church is only a deteriorating building if no directed spiritual activity is going on within and it therefore does not perform its function of connecting past with future. To put it another way: the ox without spiritual faculties, the man who has not realized his, the devil who has destroyed his—all are excrementitious. (Both devil and ox are apt images here: the former, no longer a reflected image of God, reflects no mirror-image; the latter, castrated, has no coming blessed event to cast a shadow before.)

My imagination furnishes the evidence for this. I examine trees inside and out, from root to branch; along with wood-louse and nettle, hot house grape, snail, and flower, I await a wintry end.

Such would appear to be the end for man—a parallel to that of things in nature. The sickly soul, the dispirited body, made invalids through rivalry and thus not forming a valid man going timewise out of timelessness ("symboled harbour"), find no awaiting harbour to sail to. But this is not necessarily the end. The two, of an equality and of an honesty, are departing for a "coming-to" ("adventure"); though sea-blown, they are going to arrive. (I may be quite wrong here: the stanza may be completely negative in meaning. But the positive force of "on the level," and the conjectural significance of the shift from "rival" to "arrival" make credible the idea that a possible reversal of "The fortune of manhood" is being gently implied. It is not uncommon for Thomas to understate his antithesis. And there should be some early hint (since the poem ends happily) that after many a swan's death comes the summer.)

## II

Climbing "an exceeding high mountain" (seated upon a pinnacle of nature's "holy city"), the voyagers encounter apostle-winds and lambs white as the Host, and domesticate the wilderness. Seeing the things of nature as "in a moment of time," they see the squirrel stumble (as God sees the sparrow fall), the snail in swiftest motion, the seasonal change in trees. Briefly, they have an experience of the holiness of life, learn compassion, apprehend as if under the aspect of eternity.

Having gone high on land, they dive low in water; they run the gamut, no pride of place permitted them. As they dive, the dust of their mountain-journey is washed off (they are washed in the sea of the fish); the dead flesh (of the old Adam) sifts through the swimming-paths where the sea-creatures, totally "naturalized," spiritless, aspirationless, die their natural deaths.

Now in this two-stanza parenthesis, presumably spoken by Thomas,

Death, (who does so well with fish) is insulted by being referred to as a means, an agency, instead of as an end. "Death, you who are not the end of a circle but guardian of the point where the ascending spiral crosses its own line of ascent, you who think yourself so powerful (doom in the bulb), opening the child's eye to death-in-life and the man's to ultimate extinction, symbolizing severance in the reverse-spiral navel (immortal Adam and Eve had none), force-feeding the child for a fat end, your seed in the breath he breathes in—Death, assemble your forces, place a thrice-denying cock on a dunghill to tell Lazarus the lie that there is no coming forth, nothing to raise him from the dust." (Briefly, Death, be not proud.)

As *ego*[1] and *ego*[2] lose their egoism in their baptismal ducking, a harmonious running of the scales occurs (the music's burden being, he who would gain his life must lose it) and fish scales are shucked off. And, imprisoned in, fondled by, struck by the water till the non-human lower extremities are dead, ("the triton dangles"), they find revealed (*Revelation*, 4,6 and 15,2) the sea beyond this sea, and "them that had gotten the victory over the beast, and over his image . . . ."). Prosaically, the two rivals are approaching even closer to a corporate humanity.

("Death, your natural world is one of scratches and screeches, such as would emanate from a worn-out record placed on a non-perpendicular spindle and activated by a needle capable only of spasmodic amplification. This is the post-Fall world-on-a-bias. The pre-Fall world—to be regained —a perfect circle and 'on the level,' a world of Being rather than Becoming, stands still, and still standing, can be regained.")

### III

The one-time warring couple, caught in the rocks of a jutting island, suffer further loss of self-hood, nibbled at by living water and turtle, thought-blinding skull and feeling-negating flesh-cells decomposed.

And Thomas now speaks to them in the conclusion of this stanza and in the two that follow:

"You who, like Topsy, just growed naturally till ducked head over heels in the 'waters of life,' your excrescent parts turning turtle, though it seem as difficult as growing a tree on the Aran islands, let your two eyes combine into single sight.

"Be agonizingly aware of the need for oneness; let the piercing needle provide it, or a reefer; on the unifying spirit's pointed rod (ferule) be as the strengthening ring (ferrule) as it aims from Charing Cross to heaven; unite to erect the phallus that, like Jacob's, 'the seed shall be as the dust of the earth'; traverse hill and valley of exotic dreams—the heights and depths of experience; smoke out the 'mad' and sea-changed Hamlet from his father's dead bones—welcome the new and rich and strange; run singly (like the steam engine Tom Thumb) on the double rails, illuminating the track ahead.

"Be slashed by vision to escape your present vegetative (in the Blakean sense) state; let the buoyant sea halt the downward voyage (the muscle of maturity weakened) to the womb; stop, lovers, your quarrel, your mortal struggle; come to the loving, permeating oneness of a mist or fire and ascend from muck to outer air."

Now the miracle takes place. Thomas having called for a singleness of spirit and a loving unanimity, the single blood responds. I, who was in the grip of the birth-death ("sea and instrument") cycle, caught like a nicked key in the time-lock and thus cheated, my blood come to a rich fullness in the pumping heart, I, in a fiery vision (see *Acts* 2, 2-4) because at last I had become the truly successful mage, clawed out of my Adam-self the serpent.

The "manhood" of me had been merely form in context and without substance: the scales, snout, tail of the crocodile lay (his teeth picked by the crocodile bird) in the Nile's bulrushes, time convulsing the animal skull and the mind that is, rightly, time-defeating; and as for the oil of saints (applied for health of soul and body), unblessed man wept for his whited-sepulchre hollowness, his lack of saintly robes.

So-called "manhood" had merely concealed the fact of my mortality as natural man, the fact that surface scum directed my actions, that my super-natural spirit was deprived of its "super" aspect. But, the serpent scotched, out of chaos issued form, out of mortality immortality; and I, in my singleness of vision and of will, stormed Excelsior-heights.

---

What kind of a piece of work is the man, Thomas? Since he is no longer pieced-together, he is the paragon of animals, in action how like an angel, in apprehension how like a god. And man delights him—and woman too.

I have read this as a poem about Thomas the man. But the *I* need not be Thomas: it may be generalized to Everyman or exalted to a deity. Both man and god (and poet, too) need to undergo such an experience. Lawrence states it emphatically in *The Plumed Serpent:*

Man creates a God in his own image, and the gods grow old along with the men that made them. But storms sway in heaven, and the god-stuff sways high and angry over our heads. Gods die with men who have conceived them. But the god-stuff roars eternally, like the sea, with too vast a sound to be heard. Like the sea in storm, that beats against the rocks of living, stiffened men, slowly to destroy them. Or like the sea of the glimmering ethereal plasm of the world, that bathes the feet and the knees of men as earthsap bathes the roots of trees. Ye must be born again. Even the gods must be born again. We must be born again.

Assumption of this latter as the image's source might lead to the supposition that the poem is concerned with the change effected in the move from life to death rather than from a state of nature to a state of grace. It does not seem to me important which the reader chooses. In either situation a death and a rebirth occur. I have chosen to consider the poem as describing a stage in the development of the young Thomas to maturity only because I think that he was, when he wrote it, more closely concerned with life than with death, with his progress as a man and a poet than his dissolution as a dying animal.

---

# BIBLIOGRAPHICAL NOTE

Of the books dealing with Thomas and his poetry, I have made most extensive reference to the following:

Brinnin, John Malcolm, editor, *A Casebook on Dylan Thomas,* New York, Thomas Y. Crowell, 1960.

———, *Dylan Thomas in America,* Boston, Little, Brown, 1955.

Hornick, Lita, *The Intricate Image: A Study of Dylan Thomas,* Doctoral Dissertation, Columbia University, New York, 1958.

Kleinman, Hyman, *The Religious Sonnets of Dylan Thomas,* Master's Thesis, Columbia University, New York, 1950.

Olson, Elder, *The Poetry of Dylan Thomas,* Chicago, University of Chicago Press, 1954.

Rolph, J. Alexander, *Dylan Thomas: A Bibliography,* New York, New Directions, 1956.

Stanford, Derek, *Dylan Thomas,* New York, Citadel Press, 1954.

Tedlock, E. W., editor, *Dylan Thomas, the Legend and the Poet,* London, Heinemann, 1960.

Thomas, Caitlin, *Leftover Life to Kill,* Boston, Little, Brown, 1957; also New York, Grove Press, 1959.

Tindall, William York, *A Reader's Guide to Dylan Thomas,* New York, The Noonday Press, 1962.

Treece, Henry, *Dylan Thomas: "Dog Among the Fairies,"* London, Lindsay Drummond, 1949.

Watkins, Vernon, *Dylan Thomas Letters to Vernon Watkins,* London, J. M. Dent and Faber & Faber, 1957.

566117